CLB 804
First published in Great Britain 1985 by Colour Library Books Ltd.
© 1985 Illustrations and text: Colour Library Books Ltd.,
    Guildford, Surrey, England.
Display and text filmsetting by Acesetters Ltd.,
    Richmond, Surrey, England.
Produced by AGSA, in Barcelona, Spain.
Colour separations by Llovet, S.A., Barcelona, Spain.
Printed and bound in Barcelona, Spain by Rieusset and Eurobinder.
All rights reserved.
ISBN 0 86283 330 2

Text by
Lalita Ahmed
Maureen McCall
Denise Jarrett-Macauley
Beverley Piper

Photography by
Peter Barry

Designed by
Philip Clucas

Produced by
Ted Smart and Gerald Hughes

Editorial Direction
David Gibbon

THE COMPLETE COOKBOOK

COOMBE BOOKS

THE COMPLETE COOKBOOK

Contents

Introduction

As in any other style of cooking, Chinese food is a symbol of life and good health, forming a central part of family and social activity for many people. Through cooking, one demonstrates personal inventiveness and creativity, as well as one's cultural background, so cooking can always be seen as a pleasurable activity.

In Chinese cooking, the preparation is of great importance. Many dishes require very fine chopping and shredding of the various ingredients, and they are combined in a very orderly manner. Those ingredients which are not easily available in the Western world can be substituted by others in the recipes. It is not necessary to use only Chinese utensils as these dishes can easily be prepared using basic kitchen equipment.

The main cooking technique used to produce good Chinese food is stir-frying. A wok is ideal, but a deep, non-stick skillet will serve the purpose just as well. Stir-frying requires good temperature control and this is easily learnt through practice. The wok or pan should be heated, then the temperature reduced before adding oil. If the utensil is too hot the oil will burn, giving a charred, oily taste to the food, which may burn, too! The heat should be progressively raised for the addition of other ingredients. The whole process may take between five and seven minutes. Remember, never overcook, as this will not only destroy the crispness of the food, but also its flavor and goodness.

Chinese food incorporates six basic flavors, just like Indian food. They are: sweet, sour, salty, spicy, pungent and hot. Their employment and respective proportions must be well balanced. Flavoring is always supplemented by ready-prepared sauces, the most essential of which is soy sauce. Others commonly used are oyster and plum sauces.

Finally, garnishing should not be neglected, as presentation is every bit as important as preparation. After all, what appeals to the eye also appeals to the mind and thence to heart and stomach. A slice of cleverly carved carrot, a thin sliver of tomato and carefully arranged parsley or coriander, can add that all-important dash of color.

Cooking is always a pleasure, especially Chinese cooking. It is a challenge and a way to explore one's creative talents. In any case, who does not want their efforts to be rewarded by the pleasure of an exquisite meal?

Finally, let me wish you many hours of sheer enjoyment in the exciting world of Chinese cuisine and, above all, the enjoyment of these gratifying meals.

Soups, Sauces and Dips

Plum Sauce

PREPARATION TIME: 10 minutes plus soaking overnight

COOKING TIME: 20-25 minutes

MAKES: about 3 cups

1 cup dried apricots
1 cup golden plums, fresh or canned, pitted
⅓ cup raisins or sultanas
1 inch fresh root ginger, peeled and shredded
1¼ cups brown sugar
4 tblsp vinegar
2-3 dried red chilies
1 tsp salt

Soak apricots overnight in sufficient water to completely cover. Drain apricots and reserve liquid. Mix apricots, plums, sultanas, ginger and sugar and add 1 cup reserved apricot liquid. Bring to boil and lower heat to a gentle simmer. Simmer for 10-15 minutes until it is thick. Add vinegar and coarsely ground chilies to the sauce. Add salt and mix well to blend fruits. Cook for 5-10 minutes until thick and sticky. Cool and bottle.

Chili Oil Dip

PREPARATION TIME: 5-8 minutes

COOKING TIME: 5 minutes

MAKES: about ⅓ cup

¼ cup salad or olive oil
2 cloves of garlic, minced
3-4 coarsely ground dry red chilies
2 tblsp sesame oil

Heat the oil and fry garlic till dark brown. Add chilies and fry for a few seconds. Add sesame oil and remove from heat. Stir well and cool.

Ginger Dip

PREPARATION TIME: 5 minutes

MAKES: about ½ cup

½ cup wine-flavored vinegar
2 green onions, chopped
1 inch fresh root ginger, peeled and thinly sliced

Mix all the ingredients together and leave for 10-15 minutes before using.

Sweet and Sour Sauce

PREPARATION TIME: 5 minutes

COOKING TIME: 3-5 minutes

MAKES: about 2¼ cups

1 tsp fresh root ginger, minced
1 tblsp shredded leeks
¼ cup wine-flavored vinegar
¼ cup fine granulated sugar
Pinch of salt
½ tsp light soy sauce
1⅔ cups water
1 tblsp cornstarch

Mix all the ingredients together in a pan and bring to the boil gently, stirring constantly until it thickens. The sauce should be smooth and clear.

This page, picture left: Sweet and Sour Sauce (top), Soy Dip (center right) and Chili Oil Dip (bottom). Picture right: Hoi Sin Sauce (top), Chili Sauce (center left) and Ginger Dip (bottom).

Facing page: Green Chili and Ginger Dip (top), Garlic Dip (center left) and Plum Sauce (bottom right).

Hoi Sin Sauce

PREPARATION TIME: 5 minutes

COOKING TIME: 8 minutes

MAKES: about 2 cups

This can be bought ready-made; the home-made variety does not have quite the same flavor.

1 tblsp dark soy bean paste
2 cloves garlic, minced
1 tblsp fine granulated sugar
½ tsp salt
1 tsp all-purpose flour
½ tsp chili powder
1¾ cups wine-flavored vinegar

Mix all the above ingredients together in a pan and bring to the boil. Simmer gently for 5-6 minutes or until it thickens. Cool and bottle.

Chili Sauce

PREPARATION TIME: 5 minutes

COOKING TIME: 5 minutes

MAKES: about 1½ cups

¼ cup dried red chilies, coarsely ground
¼ cup dried apricots, chopped
1 cup wine-flavored vinegar
1 tsp salt
1 tsp fine granulated sugar
1 tsp cornstarch

Mix all the above ingredients together in a pan and bring to the boil. Simmer gently for 5 minutes until the sauce thickens. Cool and serve. Will keep bottled for a few weeks.

Garlic Dip

PREPARATION TIME: 5 minutes

MAKES: about ⅓ cup

⅓ cup wine-flavored vinegar
2 tblsp minced garlic
Pinch fine granulated sugar

Mix all the ingredients together and leave for 2 hours before using.

Soy Dip

PREPARATION TIME: 5 minutes

MAKES: about ⅓ cup

¼ cup light soy sauce
1 tblsp dark soy sauce
½ tsp fine granulated sugar
2-3 green chilies, chopped
2-3 slices fresh root ginger, minced

Mix the above ingredients together and allow to stand for 10-15 minutes before using. Keep in an airtight glass jar.

Green Chili and Ginger Dip

PREPARATION TIME: 5 minutes

MAKES: about ⅓ cup

4-5 green chilies, chopped
1 inch fresh root ginger, peeled and finely sliced
½ tsp salt
½ tsp sugar
⅓ cup vinegar

Mix above ingredients together and allow to stand for 2-3 hours before use.

Duck Soup

PREPARATION TIME: 10 minutes

COOKING TIME: 8 minutes

SERVES: 6 people

2 green onions, finely chopped
1 tblsp cooked oil, or salad or olive oil
1 inch fresh root ginger, peeled and finely chopped
1 cup cooked duck meat, chopped
1 large wedge winter melon, peeled and thinly sliced
6¼ cups chicken broth
Salt to taste
Pinch monosodium glutamate (optional)
1 tblsp Shao Hsing wine or dry sherry (optional)
1 tsp cornstarch blended with 1 tblsp broth
Freshly ground black pepper to taste

Fry the onions in the oil for 1 minute. Add ginger and duck meat. Stir-fry for 1 minute. Add winter melon and stir-fry for a further 1-2 minutes and then add broth and the remaining ingredients. Gently simmer for 2-3 minutes until the soup becomes clear. Serve immediately.

Wonton Soup

PREPARATION TIME: 10 minutes

COOKING TIME: 8 minutes

SERVES: 6 people

20-24 wontons
2 sprigs Chinese parsley, or watercress, finely chopped
6¼ cups chicken broth
2-3 green onions, finely chopped
1 inch fresh root ginger, peeled and finely chopped
Salt to taste
1 tblsp soy sauce
Pinch monosodium glutamate (optional)
½ tsp fine granulated sugar
Few drops sesame oil
¼ tsp ground white pepper

Boil wontons in a large saucepan of water for 2-3 minutes until they float to the surface. Remove and drain. Divide cooked wontons and parsley among 6-8 soup bowls. Bring broth to boil and add onions, ginger, salt and the remaining ingredients. Cook for 2-3 minutes, pour over the wontons and serve immediately.

Chicken and Mushroom Soup

PREPARATION TIME: 20 minutes

COOKING TIME: 6-8 minutes

SERVES: 6 people

1 cup small cap mushrooms, sliced
⅓ cup dried brown mushrooms, soaked and then sliced
⅓ cup dried black mushrooms, soaked and then sliced
1 tblsp salad or olive oil
6¼ cups chicken broth
1 cup shredded cooked chicken
3 green onions, finely chopped
¼ tsp monosodium glutamate (optional)
Salt to taste
1 tblsp light soy sauce
2 tsp Shao Hsing wine (optional)
Pinch ground white pepper
1 tsp cornstarch blended with 1 tblsp broth

Stir fry the mushrooms in the oil for 2 minutes and then remove them. Bring the broth to the boil in a large pan with the remaining ingredients, apart from the cornstarch and mushrooms, and simmer for 3-4 minutes. Add the blended cornstarch and the mushrooms, and simmer for 1-2 minutes. Serve immediately.

Egg Drop Soup

PREPARATION TIME: 10 minutes

COOKING TIME: 8 minutes

SERVES: 6 people

This soup derives its name from stirring beaten eggs into the boiling hot soup. On hitting the soup, the egg cooks and forms threads. The eggs can also be carefully dropped in whole, so that they cook without breaking in the hot soup.

6¼ cups chicken broth
3 green onions, finely chopped
½ cup frozen peas, or shelled fresh peas
1 bunch watercress, finely chopped
A few thin slices of fresh root ginger
Salt and freshly ground black pepper to taste
1 tblsp light soy sauce
Pinch of monosodium glutamate (optional)
1 tsp cornstarch blended with 1 tblsp water
4 eggs, beaten (or 6-8 whole eggs, see below)

Bring the chicken broth to the boil with the green onions, peas, watercress, ginger and salt and pepper to taste. Allow to simmer for 2-3 minutes. Add the soy sauce, monosodium glutamate and the blended cornstarch. Stir well until the soup is transparent and thick. Bring the soup back to the boil and stir in the beaten eggs. Serve immediately. Alternatively, put a whole egg into each warm soup bowl and ladle the hot soup over the top.

Duck Soup (top), Chicken and Mushroom Soup (center right) and Wonton Soup (right).

Chicken Noodle Soup

PREPARATION TIME: 10 minutes

COOKING TIME: 10-12 minutes

SERVES: 8 people

*1lb Shanghai noodles, or very thin
noodles
2 tblsp salad or olive oil
2 cups cooked chicken, cubed
2 cups Chinese white cabbage or
ordinary white cabbage, shredded
6¼ cups chicken broth*

Seasoning
*½ tsp fine granulated sugar
½ tsp salt
2 tsp Shao Hsing wine (optional)
½ tsp monosodium glutamate
2 tsp light soy sauce*

Add the noodles to a large pan of
boiling water. Stir to loosen the
bundles and boil for 4-5 minutes.
(The noodles should be just tender
but not overcooked.) Drain
noodles well. Meanwhile, heat the
oil in the wok and fry the chicken
for 1-2 minutes. Remove the
chicken and then fry the cabbage in
the same oil for 2 minutes. Add the
seasoning ingredients and stir fry
for 1 minute. Add the chicken and
cook for a further 1-2 minutes until
the cabbage is tender. Add the
broth and bring to the boil. Divide
noodles among 6-8 warm soup
bowls and add the hot soup. Serve
immediately.

Chinese Parsley and Fish Soup

PREPARATION TIME: 10 minutes

COOKING TIME: 7-8 minutes

SERVES: 6 people

*1lb white fish fillet, cut into 6 even-
sized pieces
4 cups chicken broth
½ inch fresh root ginger, peeled and
thinly sliced
Salt to taste
Freshly ground black pepper to taste
Pinch monosodium glutamate
(optional)
2 green onions, finely chopped
½ tsp cornstarch
2 sprigs Chinese parsley, finely
chopped
18-20 thin cucumber slices*

Wash fish in cold water and gently
simmer in chicken broth for 2-3
minutes. Remove the fish pieces
carefully. Add ginger, salt, pepper,

MSG and onion and simmer the
stock for 2-3 minutes. Strain.
Dissolve cornstarch in 1 tblsp of
water or cold broth and add to the
soup. Simmer for 2 minutes until
the soup thickens. Add fish pieces
and bring back to the boil. Serve in
soup bowls, sprinkled with
chopped parsley and cucumber
slices.

Crab and Watercress Soup

PREPARATION TIME: 10 minutes

COOKING TIME: 8-9 minutes

SERVES: 6 people

*6¼ cups chicken broth
⅔ cup white crab meat, shredded
2 green onions, finely chopped
2 bunches watercress, finely chopped
Salt and freshly ground black pepper
to taste
1 tsp cornstarch
1 tblsp water
2 tsp light soy sauce
A few drops sesame oil*

Bring the broth to the boil with the
crab meat, onions and watercress
and simmer for 4-5 minutes. Add

salt and pepper to taste. Mix the
cornstarch with the water and add
to the soup. Allow to simmer for a
further 2 minutes. Add soy sauce
and sesame oil, mix well and
simmer for 2 minutes. Serve
immediately.

Crab and Sweet Corn Soup

PREPARATION TIME: 8 minutes

COOKING TIME: 8 minutes

SERVES: 6 people

*3 tblsp water or broth
2 tblsp cornstarch
6¼ cups chicken broth
1½ cups canned creamed sweet corn
⅔ cup white crab meat, shredded
Salt and freshly ground black pepper
to taste
1 tsp soy sauce
Pinch monosodium glutamate
(optional)*

Blend water and cornstarch
together. Bring the broth to the
boil in a large pan. Add the sweet
corn, crab, salt and pepper to taste,
soy sauce and monosodium

glutamate. Simmer for 4-5 minutes.
Add the blended cornstarch to the
soup and stir over a gentle heat
until the soup thickens. Serve
immediately. Whisked egg whites
can be stirred into the hot soup
just before serving, if liked.

Hot and Sour Soup

PREPARATION TIME: 20 minutes

COOKING TIME: 7-8 minutes

SERVES: 6-8 people

*6¼ cups chicken broth
½ cup lean pork, shredded, or cubed
barbecued pork
½ cup peeled de-veined shrimps
1oz bamboo shoots, sliced
2 cloud ear fungus, soaked in boiling
water for 5 minutes and chopped
2-3 green onions, chopped
Salt to taste
1 tblsp fine granulated sugar
½ tsp monosodium glutamate
(optional)
1 tsp dark soy sauce
½ tsp light soy sauce
1½ tblsp vinegar
1 tsp chili oil or chili sauce
¼ tsp sesame oil
½ tsp Shao Hsing wine (optional)
1 egg, well beaten
1 tblsp cornstarch
2 tblsp water*

Mix broth with pork, shrimps, and
all the remaining ingredients except
the well beaten egg, cornstarch and
water. Simmer gently for 4-5
minutes. Remove from heat and
add the egg, stirring gently, until
the egg forms 'threads' in the soup.
Blend the cornstarch with the
water and add to the soup. Simmer
for 1 minute until the soup
thickens and serve immediately.

**This page: Egg Drop Soup
(top), Crab and Watercress
Soup (center) and Crab and
Sweet Corn Soup (bottom).**

**Facing page: Chicken Noodle
Soup (top), Hot and Sour Soup
(center left) and Chinese
Parsley and Fish Soup (bottom
right).**

Facing page: **Four Happiness Dumplings**
(top left), **Steamed Shrimp Pancakes**
(bottom left) and **Steamed Open Dumplings**
(right).

Snacks

Four Happiness Dumplings

PREPARATION TIME: 30-45 minutes for pastry; 20-30 minutes for filling

COOKING TIME: 20 minutes

MAKES: 30-35

Pastry
1¾ cups all-purpose flour
Pinch of salt
1 cup boiling water

Put the flour and salt into a bowl. Add the boiling water and mix quickly to make a dough. Cover and allow to stand for 20-30 minutes. Knead the dough for 2-3 minutes, sprinkling the work surface with a little cornstarch if needed. Divide the dough into 30-35 equal portions and roll each one to a circle 2½ inches in diameter.

Filling
1½ cups ground lean pork
2 black mushrooms, soaked and diced
½ cup finely chopped mixed vegetables (peas, carrots, celery, etc.)
½ tsp brown sugar or maple syrup
2½ tsp light soy sauce
¼ tsp freshly ground black pepper
1 egg
5-6 chives, finely chopped
Salt to taste
1 tblsp salad or olive oil
1½ tsp cornstarch
2 tblsp all-purpose flour mixed with a little cold water to a smooth paste

Mix the pork with the mushrooms, mixed vegetables, sugar, soy sauce, black pepper, egg, chives and salt to taste. Add the oil and cornstarch and mix well with a fork. Divide filling into 30 to 35 equal portions. Fill each dumpling wrapper with a portion of filling and shape into crescent-shaped dumplings. Steam them in an ordinary steamer or a Chinese bamboo steamer for about 20 minutes. Serve with a dip and chili sauce. To make the crescent shape, place a wrapper on a flat surface, put a little filling in the center, spread the edges with a little flour and water paste and pinch the edges of the wrapper together to seal. Pull one corner of the filled wanton around and over the other corner. Press to seal.

Steamed Shrimp Pancakes

PREPARATION TIME: 1 hour

COOKING TIME: 10-15 minutes

MAKES: 25-30

1½ cups all-purpose flour or high gluten flour
1½ tblsp cornstarch
¼ tsp salt
1 tblsp salad or olive oil
3 tblsp beaten egg
2 tblsp water
2 tblsp all-purpose flour mixed with cold water to a smooth paste

Filling
1½ cups peeled shrimps, finely chopped
2 green onions, bulb only, finely chopped
¼ tsp salt, or to taste
1 tsp cornstarch to bind

Sift the flour, cornstarch and salt into a bowl. Add the oil, beaten egg and water and mix to make a stiff dough. Leave for 30 minutes to rest. Knead well for 5-6 minutes and roll into 25-30 6 inch circles on greaseproof paper. To make the filling, mix all the ingredients except the cornstarch together, and then bind with the cornstarch. Place the filling in the center of each pancake and flatten. Spread flour and water paste around the edge of each pancake and fold up from one end to make a roll. Arrange the pancakes in a greased ordinary or Chinese bamboo steamer and cook over boiling water for 10-15 minutes. Serve piping hot with chili or soy sauce dip.

Alternative
To make rice pancakes, soak 4oz rice for 10 minutes. Grind with water to make a very fine paste of batter consistency. Add 1 tblsp oil and mix well. Line a steamer with fine muslin and spoon in a little batter; spread it out into a thin pancake. Steam for 5 minutes. Place a little filling on the pancake and roll up. Steam for 10 minutes and serve piping hot with a dip.

Steamed Open Dumplings

PREPARATION TIME: 1 hour

COOKING TIME: 10-15 minutes

MAKES: 24

Filling
1 cup medium size peeled shrimps, finely chopped
1½ cups ground pork or beef
2 black mushrooms, soaked and finely chopped
Salt to taste
½ tsp brown sugar

Seasoning
½ tsp monosodium glutamate (optional)
1 tblsp cornstarch
1½ tsp dark soy sauce
1 tsp light soy sauce
¼ tsp freshly ground black pepper
1 tblsp sesame oil
24 wonton wrappers

Mix the ground pork, shrimps, mushrooms, salt and sugar together. Add the seasoning ingredients and mix well. Allow to stand for 30 minutes. Take each wonton wrapper and spoon a little filling in the center. Fold up the edges around the filling but do not completely enclose it. (An open ended dumpling is produced with the sides of the wrapper gathered around the filling.) Flatten the base by pressing it slightly so that it will stand upright in a steamer. Grease an ordinary steamer or a bamboo steamer and arrange the dumplings in it. Steam for 15-20 minutes. Serve hot with a dip.

Wontons with Pork and Shrimp Filling

PREPARATION TIME: 30 minutes

COOKING TIME: 10-15 minutes

MAKES: 40-50

1½ cups lean ground pork
Salad or olive oil
1½ cups peeled small shrimps, finely chopped
3 green onions, finely chopped
½ tsp ground white pepper
1¼ tblsp soy sauce
1½ tsp rice wine or dry sherry
½ tsp salt, or to taste
1½ tsp cornstarch blended with 2 tblsp water
40-50 wonton wrappers
2 tblsp all-purpose flour, mixed with a little cold water to a smooth paste

Fry pork in 2 tblsp oil until it loses its pink color. Add shrimps and onions and fry for 3-4 minutes. Add pepper, soy sauce and wine. Season with salt and stir fry for 1-2 minutes. Add the blended cornstarch and stir over a moderate heat until thickened. Allow to cool before filling the wontons. Divide filling into 40-50 equal portions. Take a wonton wrapper, moisten the edges with the flour and water paste. Place a portion of filling in the center of the wonton and gather up the edges to make a neat round, or shape in such a way as to make a triangle or any other shape that you prefer. Once you have shaped all the wontons, deep-fry them in hot oil until crisp and golden. You will need to fry them in 3 or more batches. Drain well on absorbent paper before serving.

Fried Meat Dumplings

PREPARATION TIME: 10 minutes

COOKING TIME: about 15 minutes

MAKES: 48 dumplings

2 tblsp salad or olive oil
2 cups lean ground beef or lamb
2 green onions, chopped
2½ tblsp light soy sauce
½ tsp salt
1¾ tblsp rice wine or dry sherry
2 tsp cornstarch mixed with 2 tblsp water
Dumpling wrappers (see recipe)

2 tblsp all-purpose flour mixed to a
    paste with cold water
Oil for deep frying

Heat the 2 tblsp oil in a pan and fry the ground meat and onion for 2-3 minutes. Add the soy sauce, salt and wine. Cook gently for 2 minutes and then stir in the cornstarch and water mixture. Stir over the heat until the mixture thickens. Put the meat mixture into a dish and leave to cool. Divide into equal portions – about 48. Take a round dumpling wrapper and place a portion of filling in the center. Moisten the edges of the wrapper with a little flour and water paste, gather the edges up and over the filling and pinch together to seal. Shape neatly. Continue to make the remaining dumplings in the same way. Deep-fry the dumplings in moderately hot oil, cooking a few dumplings at a time, until they are golden brown. Drain thoroughly on absorbent paper. Serve with chili sauce dip.

Dumpling Wrappers (*Chiao Tze P'i*)

PREPARATION TIME: 50-60
                          minutes
MAKES: 40-50 wrappers

2¼ cups all-purpose flour
¾ cup cold water

Sift the flour into a bowl and add the cold water, a little at a time, and mix to a firm dough. Knead the dough on a flat surface for 4-5 minutes. Cover with a damp cloth or wrap in plastic wrap. Leave to stand at room temperature for 30-40 minutes. Roll out on a well-floured surface as thinly as possible, until almost transparent. Cut into round or square pieces to suit your requirements. Use within a few hours of making otherwise they will dry out.

Wonton Wrappers

PREPARATION TIME: 5-6 hours
(including standing time)
MAKES: 40-50 wrappers

1 cup all-purpose flour
2 tblsp beaten egg
2 tblsp cold water
Cornstarch

Sift flour and gradually add the beaten egg and water mixed together. Mix to a stiff dough. Knead firmly for 5-6 minutes and wrap in plastic wrap. Leave to stand at room temperature for 4-5 hours. Roll out into a very large square on a work surface dusted with cornstarch. The pastry should be almost transparent. Cut into 40-50 3 inch round or square wrappers. Dust each wrapper with cornstarch before stacking. Store the wrappers, wrapped securely in plastic wrap, in the refrigerator, for up to 24 hours. If they are allowed to dry out they will split during cooking.

Spring Roll Wrappers

PREPARATION TIME: 20 minutes, plus chilling time

MAKES: 12 wrappers

1 scant cup all-purpose flour
1 egg, beaten
A little cold water

Sift the flour into a bowl. Make a well in the center and add the beaten egg and a little cold water. Mix to a soft yet firm dough, adding a little extra water if necessary. Knead the dough until it is really pliable (this helps to make the gluten work). Chill, covered, for 4 hours or overnight. Allow to come back to room temperature. Roll out the dough on a well-floured surface to about ¼ inch thick. Cut into 12 equal pieces, and then roll each piece to a square about 6x6 inches – each square should be very thin.

Spring Rolls

PREPARATION TIME: 20-30 minutes

COOKING TIME: about 20 minutes

MAKES: 12

2 cups lean, raw pork or beef, finely shredded
1 cup small to medium, shelled shrimps (either uncooked or boiled)
4 green onions, finely chopped
Salad or olive oil
2 tsp fresh root ginger, peeled and shredded
1⅓ cups white cabbage, shredded
1-1¼ cups bean sprouts
1¼ tblsp soy sauce
Salt to taste
12 spring roll wrappers, each 6 inches square (see recipe)
2 tblsp all-purpose flour, mixed with a little cold water to a smooth paste

Fry the shredded pork and the shrimps with the spring onions in 1 tblsp of oil for 2-3 minutes. Add the ginger, cabbage and bean sprouts, and stir fry for 2-3 minutes. Add soy sauce, and season with a little salt if desired. Remove from the heat and allow to cool. Lay out the spring roll wrappers on a clean working surface, with one point of each wrapper facing you. Divide the

filling mixture into 12 equal portions and place one portion of filling just above the front point of each wrapper. Fold in the opposite side points, so that they overlap slightly like an envelope – secure the side points with a little flour and water paste. Starting with the point facing you, roll each wrapper up around the filling, securing the remaining point with a little flour

and water paste. Repeat in exactly the same way with the remaining spring roll wrappers. They will keep a better shape if you chill them for 1 hour before cooking. Deep fry over a medium heat until golden brown and crisp. Drain thoroughly on absorbent paper and serve hot with a selection of dips or chili sauce. The spring rolls can be frozen, uncooked.

This page: Fried Meat Dumplings (top right), Spring Rolls (center left) and Wontons with Pork and Shrimp Filling (bottom). Facing page: Spiced Beef (top), Steamed Beef Szechuan Style (bottom left) and Beef with Green Pepper and Chili (bottom right).

Meat Dishes

Spiced Beef

PREPARATION TIME: 30 minutes

COOKING TIME: 5-6 minutes

SERVES: 4 people

Marinade
1 tsp fine granulated sugar
2-3 star anise, ground
½ tsp ground fennel
1¼ tblsp dark soy sauce
¼ tsp monosodium glutamate
(optional)

1lb fillet of beef, cut into 1 inch strips
1 inch fresh root ginger, peeled and
crushed
½ tsp salt
2 tblsp salad or olive oil
4 green onions, sliced
½ tsp freshly ground black pepper
1¼ tblsp light soy sauce

Mix the marinade ingredients together. Add the beef strips, ginger and salt, and marinate for 20 minutes. Heat the oil in a wok and stir fry the onions for 1 minute. Add beef, ground pepper and soy sauce and stir fry for 4-5 minutes. Serve with a dip.

Steamed Beef Szechuan Style

PREPARATION TIME: 40 minutes

COOKING TIME: 15 minutes

SERVES: 4 people

3 slices fresh root ginger, minced
1 tsp salt
1 tsp fine granulated sugar
Freshly ground black pepper
1 tblsp salad or olive oil
2 tblsp rice wine or dry sherry
1½ tblsp chili bean paste
2½ tblsp dark soy sauce
3-4 green onions, finely chopped
1lb fillet of beef, cut into 2 inch long
strips
⅔ cup ground rice
1 large lotus leaf or several cabbage
leaves

For the marinade, mix the ginger, salt, sugar, pepper, oil, wine, bean paste, soy sauce and half of the onions. Add beef strips and mix

well. Leave to marinate for 15-20 minutes. Heat the wok and dry roast the ground rice for 2-4 minutes till rice changes color from white to light brown. Roll the marinated beef in the roasted ground rice to give a thin, even coating. Line the bamboo steamer with a well-oiled lotus leaf or a few old and tough cabbage leaves. Arrange the coated beef strips in a

neat pile on top. Steam fairly quickly for 10-15 minutes over boiling water. Garnish with the remaining chopped onions before serving. Serve hot with chili sauce.

Beef with Green Pepper and Chili

PREPARATION TIME: 30 minutes

COOKING TIME: 10-12 minutes

SERVES: 4 people

1lb fillet of beef, cut into 1 inch strips

Seasoning
2 tblsp dark soy sauce
1 tsp sesame oil
Pinch baking soda
¼ tsp ground black pepper

½ tsp salt

Oil for frying
2 green peppers, seeded and thinly
 sliced
1 onion, peeled and sliced
2 green onions, chopped
1 inch fresh root ginger, peeled and
 sliced
2 garlic cloves, peeled and chopped
3 green chilis, sliced

Sauce
2½ tblsp chicken broth
½ tsp monosodium glutamate
 (optional)
1½ tsp dark soy sauce
Salt to taste
Few drops sesame oil

Marinate beef with the seasoning
ingredients for 15 minutes. Heat 2
tblsp oil in a wok and stir fry green
peppers and onions for 2 minutes.
Remove to a plate. Reheat wok,
add 2-3 tblsp oil and fry ginger,
garlic, and green chilis for 1 minute.
Add beef and stir fry for 4-5
minutes. Add sauce ingredients,
mixed together, and the fried
peppers and onions. Stir fry for a
further 2 minutes and serve.

Diced Pork with Sweet Corn

PREPARATION TIME: 25 minutes
COOKING TIME: 15-20 minutes
SERVES: 2 people

Marinade
Pinch salt
2½ tsp dark soy sauce
¼ tsp fine granulated sugar
1 tsp rice wine
1 tblsp water

1½ cups pork loin, diced
Oil for deep frying
2 slices fresh root ginger, peeled and
 diced
1 clove garlic, peeled and chopped
1 cup chicken broth

Seasoning
¼ tsp salt
¼ tsp freshly ground black pepper
¼ tsp fine granulated sugar
1 tsp rice wine or dry sherry
Few drops sesame oil

1 tsp cornstarch mixed with 1 tblsp
 water
1 cup canned creamed sweet corn
1 egg, well beaten
4 green onions, chopped

Mix the marinade ingredients
together. Add the pork and leave
to marinate for 15 minutes. Drain
the pork and discard the liquid.
Heat the wok and pour in the oil
for deep frying. Fry the pork until
light brown. Remove the pork and
drain. Reserve the oil for future
use. Heat 1 tblsp oil in the wok and
add the ginger and pork. Stir fry for
3 minutes. Add the broth and
simmer for 3 minutes. Add the
seasoning ingredients and simmer
for 2-3 minutes. Add the blended
cornstarch and water and simmer
until the sauce thickens. Add the
sweet corn and beaten egg and
cook for 2-3 minutes. Serve
sprinkled with chopped onions.
Serve this dish with plain boiled
rice or noodles.

Pork Stuffed Mushrooms

PREPARATION TIME: 15-20
 minutes
COOKING TIME: 12 minutes
SERVES: 4 people

Filling
1 egg
2 tsp cornstarch
2 tsp rice wine or dry sherry
¼ tsp minced fresh root ginger
6 water chestnuts, finely chopped
½ cup peeled medium shrimps,
 chopped
1½ cups ground lean pork
¼ tsp salt
¼ tsp freshly ground black pepper
½ tsp fine granulated sugar
2 tsp chili sauce

16 large, open mushrooms
2½ cups chicken broth
Oil

Mix all the filling ingredients
together. Remove the mushroom
stalks. Divide the filling into 16
portions. Bring the chicken broth
to the boil. Add the mushrooms
and leave to stand off the heat for 5
minutes, covered. Drain the
mushrooms and discard the broth.
Top each mushroom with a portion
of filling. Put the stuffed
mushrooms into a well oiled
steamer. Steam for 10-12 minutes
over boiling water. Serve as a snack,
as a starter or as a side dish.
Alternatively, serve with a simple
sauce made from thickened
chicken broth. Pour the sauce over
the steamed mushrooms.

Sliced Pork in Wine Sauce

PREPARATION TIME: 30 minutes	
COOKING TIME: about 16 minutes	
SERVES: 4 people	

Seasoning

1¼ tblsp wine-flavored vinegar
1¼ tblsp light soy sauce
1 tblsp rice wine or dry sherry
2 tsp soy paste
1 tsp freshly ground black pepper
1 tsp salt
1 tsp Shao Hsing wine
1lb pork fillet, cut into 2 inch long, thin slices
1 tblsp cornstarch
4 tblsp salad or olive oil
½ inch fresh root ginger, finely chopped
3 green onions, chopped
1 green pepper, seeded and diced

Sauce

2 tsp cornstarch
4 tblsp dry white wine
½ cup chicken broth
2 tsp dark soy sauce
1 tsp fine granulated sugar
½ tsp salt

Mix the seasoning ingredients together. Add the pork slices and leave to marinate for 10-15 minutes. Drain the pork and roll in the cornstarch. Leave on one side. Discard the marinade. Heat half the oil in the wok until smoking. Add the pork, reduce the heat, and stir fry for 4-6 minutes until lightly browned. Remove the pork and keep on one side. Discard any oil

Diced Pork with Sweet Corn (far left), Sliced Pork in Wine Sauce (top left) and Pork Stuffed Mushrooms (left).

the meat balls and serve with chopped green onions and green pepper rings sprinkled on top. Serve as a snack, as a starter or as a side dish.

Pork Chop Suey

PREPARATION TIME: 35 minutes

COOKING TIME: 10 minutes

SERVES: 3-4 people

Marinade
1 tblsp water
½ tsp baking soda
2½ tsp dark soy sauce

½lb pork fillet, sliced into 2 inch
*   pieces*
3 tblsp cooked oil or cooking oil
1 onion, peeled and cut into pieces
1 clove of garlic, peeled and sliced
⅓ cup bamboo shoots, sliced
2 cups bean sprouts

Seasoning
Pinch salt
Pinch freshly ground black pepper
Pinch monosodium glutamate
*   (optional)*
3 tblsp light soy sauce
1 tsp fine granulated sugar
1 tsp cornstarch

Sauce
1 tsp cornstarch
1 tblsp water

Mix the marinade ingredients together. Add the pork and leave for 15 minutes to marinate. Drain the pork and discard the marinade. Heat the oil in the wok and stir fry pork for 2-3 minutes. Remove the pork. Add the onion, garlic and bamboo shoots to the wok and stir fry for 1-2 minutes. Add the bean sprouts and stir fry for 2 minutes. Remove onto a dish and add the mixed seasoning ingredients. Leave for 10 minutes. Return the pork and the vegetables to the wok. Add the blended sauce ingredients. Bring to the boil gently, stirring until the sauce thickens. Serve immediately.

This page: Steamed Pork with Salted Cabbage (top), Pork with Green Pepper (center right) and Pork Chop Suey (bottom). Facing page: Fried Pork with Vegetables (top left), Bean Sprouts with Chopped Pork (center right) and Deep Fried Pork Meat Balls (bottom).

left in the wok. Add the remaining oil to the wok and stir fry the onions, ginger and green pepper for 3-5 minutes. Return the fried pork to the wok and cook for a further 2-3 minutes with the vegetables. Remove onto a serving dish. Mix the cornstarch from the sauce ingredients with 2 tblsp water. Add the remaining sauce ingredients to the wok and bring to the boil. Add the blended cornstarch. Stir and simmer until the sauce thickens, simmer for 1-2 minutes. Pour over the pork and serve.

Deep Fried Pork Meat Balls

PREPARATION TIME: 25 minutes

COOKING TIME: about 12 minutes

MAKES: 16 meat balls

1lb coarsely ground lean pork
1 small onion, finely chopped
1 green chili, chopped
Salt and freshly ground black pepper
*   to taste*
½ inch fresh root ginger, peeled and
*   finely chopped*
1 egg, beaten
1 tblsp cornstarch
2 tsp dark soy sauce
2 sprigs Chinese parsley, finely

*   chopped*
1 tsp cooked oil
Oil for deep frying
2 green onions, chopped (for
*   garnishing)*
1 green pepper, seeded and cut into
*   rings (for garnishing) (optional)*

Mix the ground pork with the chopped onion, chili, salt and pepper to taste, chopped ginger, beaten egg, cornstarch, soy sauce, parsley and cooked oil. Leave to stand for 10 minutes. Mould into 16 even-sized balls. Heat the oil in the wok for deep frying and slide a few pork balls into the oil. Fry over a gentle heat for 5-6 minutes until golden brown and tender. Remove and drain on kitchen paper. Fry all

Braised Hong Kong Beef

PREPARATION TIME: 30 minutes

COOKING TIME: about 15-17 minutes

SERVES: 4 people

2 tblsp salad or olive oil

1lb fillet of beef, sliced into matchstick size strips

1 onion, peeled and sliced

1 inch fresh root ginger, peeled and cut into thin strips

3-4 fresh tomatoes, cut into thin wedges

½lb carrots, scraped and cut into 2 inch sticks

2½ tsp brown sugar

½ tsp five spice powder

2¼ tblsp light soy sauce

1 tblsp rice wine or dry sherry

2 tblsp water

Salt to taste

Heat the oil in a wok and fry the beef for 3-4 minutes. Add the onion, ginger, tomatoes and carrots. Stir fry for 2-3 minutes. Add the sugar, five spice powder, soy sauce, wine and water. Season with salt to taste and cook gently for 8-10 minutes. Serve as a side dish.

Pork with Green Pepper

PREPARATION TIME: 20 minutes

COOKING TIME: 1 hour 15 minutes

SERVES: 4 people

1lb pork fillet, cut into 2 inch strips

Seasoning

¼ tsp fine granulated sugar

¼ tsp monosodium glutamate (optional)

1¼ tsp light soy sauce

2 tsp sweet bean paste

2 tsp Shao Hsing wine or dry sherry

4 tblsp chicken broth

Oil for deep frying

2 cloves garlic, peeled and cut into thin strips

1 green pepper, seeded and sliced into strips

1 green chili, sliced into strips

1 red chili, cut in half then sliced into strips

Sauce

1 tsp cornstarch

1 tblsp water

Boil the pork in water for ¾ hour until cooked. Drain the pork and discard the water. Mix the seasoning ingredients together and stir in the pork. Leave to stand for 10 minutes. Heat the wok and add

the oil for deep frying. When oil is very hot fry the drained pork for a few minutes until golden brown. Remove and drain the pork and keep the oil for future use. Reheat the wok and add 1 tsp oil and stir fry the garlic for 1 minute. Add the pepper and chilies and stir fry for 1 minute. Add the remaining seasoning mixture and the pork. Stir fry over a gentle heat for 1-2 minutes and then add the blended sauce ingredients. Cook until the sauce thickens. Remove from the heat and serve immediately. Serve with mixed fried rice or rice noodles.

Steamed Pork with Salted Cabbage

PREPARATION TIME: 25 minutes

COOKING TIME: 2 hours

SERVES: 4 people

1lb pork fillet cut into ½ inch thick slices

Salt

2 cups cabbage, shredded (Chinese white or plain green cabbage)

Seasoning

1 tblsp fine granulated sugar

2 tblsp cooked oil

1 tsp monosodium glutamate (optional)

4 tblsp broth or water

Salt and freshly ground black pepper

1¼ tblsp dark soy sauce

Oil for deep frying

Sauce

1 tsp cornstarch

1 tblsp water

Boil the pork in 2 cups water for ¾ hour until tender. Drain the pork and discard the water. Boil 2 cups fresh water with 1 tsp salt and add the cabbage. Cook for 2 minutes. Drain, rinse in cold water and then drain again. Season the cabbage with 1 tsp of the sugar and 1 tblsp of the cooked oil. Mix well and keep on one side. Place the pork in a dish and mix with the dark soy sauce. Leave for 10 minutes. Drain. Mix all the seasoning ingredients together. Heat the oil for deep frying and fry the pork until it turns lightly golden. Drain and add to the seasoning mixture. Keep the oil for future use. Place the pork and the seasoning mixture into a deep dish and put the boiled cabbage on top. Cover and steam over boiling water for 1 hour. Drain off any excess liquid and retain. Heat the wok and add the cabbage liquid.

Add the blended sauce thickening of cornstarch and water. Stir over the heat until the sauce thickens. Pour over the cabbage and pork and serve.

Bean Sprouts with Chopped Pork

PREPARATION TIME: 15 minutes

COOKING TIME: 10 minutes

SERVES: 4 people

2 cups ground lean pork

Marinade

½ tsp salt

1¼ tblsp light soy sauce

1 egg white, beaten

1 tsp cornstarch

3 cups bean sprouts

Salad or olive oil for cooking

Seasoning

½ tsp salt

½ tsp fine granulated sugar

½ tsp monosodium glutamate (optional)

2 tsp soy sauce

1 tsp rice wine or dry sherry

1 tblsp oyster sauce

½ inch fresh root ginger, peeled and thinly sliced

2-3 green onions, chopped

½ cup chicken broth

Sauce

½ tsp cornstarch

1 tblsp water or broth

Few drops of sesame oil

Mix the pork with the marinade ingredients and keep on one side for 10 minutes. Trim the bean sprouts and chop them coarsely. Heat 2 tblsp oil in the wok. Stir fry the bean sprouts for 1 minute to evaporate excess water and moisture. Remove the bean sprouts and keep on a plate. Mix the seasoning ingredients together. Heat 3 tblsp oil in the wok until it smokes. Stir fry the pork for 2 minutes and then add the ginger, onions and bean sprouts. Stir fry for 2-3 minutes. Add the seasoning ingredients and stir fry for 1 minute. Add the chicken broth and the blended sauce ingredients. Cook until the sauce thickens. Serve immediately.

Spiced Liver (top), Sliced Beef in Oyster Sauce (center right) and Braised Hong Kong Beef (right).

Oil for frying
1 small onion, peeled and thickly
   sliced
3 green onions, chopped lengthwise
2 leeks, white part only, cut into 1½
   inch slices
1 tsp sesame oil

Mix the marinade ingredients with
the beef strips. Leave to marinate
for 20 minutes. Mix all the
seasoning ingredients together in a
small bowl. Heat 2 tblsp oil in a
wok and when it is smoking, add
the beef. Reduce the heat and stir
fry for 4-5 minutes. Remove the
meat and keep the oil for future
use. Heat the wok, add 2 tblsp
fresh oil and stir fry the onion and
leeks for 2 minutes. Add seasoning
mixture and beef and stir fry for 1-2
minutes. Sprinkle sesame oil over
the top and mix well. Serve
immediately. Use as a main dish or
a side dish.

Shredded Beef with Vegetables

PREPARATION TIME: 15 minutes

COOKING TIME: 10 minutes

SERVES: 2-3 people

8oz lean beef, cut into thin strips
Pinch salt
4 tblsp salad or olive oil
2 red and green chilies, cut in half
   then sliced into strips
1 tsp black vinegar
1 stem of celery, cut into 2 inch thin
   strips
2 carrots, cut into 2 inch thin strips
1 leek, white part only, sliced into 2
   inch thin strips
2 cloves, garlic, peeled and finely
   chopped

Seasoning
1 tsp light soy sauce
1 tsp dark soy sauce
2 tsp Shao Hsing wine
1 tsp fine granulated sugar
Pinch monosodium glutamate
   (optional)
½ tsp freshly ground black pepper

Spiced Liver

PREPARATION TIME: 10 minutes

COOKING TIME: 20 minutes

SERVES: 4 people

1lb lamb's liver, cut into 1 inch cubes
½ cup soy sauce
3-4 green onions, chopped
2¼ tblsp rice wine or dry sherry
2 tsp fine granulated sugar
1 inch fresh root ginger, peeled and
   finely chopped
½ tsp freshly ground black pepper
Pinch anise powder

Boil the liver in sufficient water to
just cover, for 3-4 minutes. Drain
well. Add soy sauce, green onions,
wine, sugar, ginger, pepper and
anise powder. Simmer gently for
10-15 minutes, covered, until the
liver is tender. Serve as a side dish.

Stir Fried Beef with Onions

PREPARATION TIME: 30 minutes

COOKING TIME: 10 minutes

SERVES: 4 people

Marinade
1 tblsp cornstarch
1 egg white
1 tblsp salad or olive oil
1 tsp baking soda

1lb beef fillet, cut into 1 inch strips

Seasoning
1 tsp Shao Hsing wine
1¼ tblsp light soy sauce
1 tsp dark soy sauce
½ tsp salt
½ tsp freshly ground black pepper
1 tsp monosodium glutamate
   (optional)

**This page: Stir Fried Beef with
Onions (top), Shredded Beef
with Vegetables (center left)
and Sesame Beef with Dates
(bottom). Facing page: Beef
with Green Beans (top), Beef
Steak with Ginger (center
right) and Sweet and Sour Beef
(bottom).**

Put the beef into a bowl and sprinkle with salt; rub salt into meat. Heat 1½ tsp oil in a wok until it begins to smoke. Reduce heat and add beef and chilies and stir fry for 4-5 minutes. Add remaining oil and stir fry beef until it turns crispy. Add vinegar and mix until it evaporates, then add celery, carrots, leeks and garlic. Stir fry for 2 minutes. Mix the seasoning ingredients and pour over the beef and cook for 2 minutes. Serve immediately.

Steamed Lamb with Mushroom Sauce

PREPARATION TIME: 20-25 minutes

COOKING TIME: 2 hours 10 minutes

SERVES: 6 people

2¼lb boned leg of lamb, cut into 1 inch cubes
2 onions, thinly sliced
Salt and freshly ground black pepper
2 tsp salad or olive oil
2 cloves of garlic, peeled and sliced
1 tsp cornstarch
Pinch monosodium glutamate (optional)
6 tblsp light soy sauce
3½ tblsp rice wine or dry sherry
1 tsp crushed black pepper
1 inch fresh root ginger, peeled and thinly sliced
Few drops sesame oil

Put the lamb into a saucepan and add sufficient water to cover. Boil for 5 minutes. Drain the lamb and retain the water. Arrange the lamb cubes in a deep dish and sprinkle the onions on top. Season with pepper and salt. Heat the oil in a wok and fry the garlic until brown. Remove the garlic and discard. Mix together the cornstarch, monosodium glutamate, soy sauce, wine, crushed pepper, ginger and 4 tblsp reserved lamb broth. Stir the cornstarch mixture into the oil in the wok and cook for 1-2 minutes. Pour over the lamb. Cover the lamb with overlapping foil and tie around the rim. Put the dish in a steamer and steam over boiling water for 2 hours. Serve with the sesame oil sprinkled over the lamb.

Lamb with Tomatoes

PREPARATION TIME: 20 minutes

COOKING TIME: about 10 minutes

SERVES: 2 people

2 tsp cornstarch
½ tsp salt
1½ tblsp light soy sauce
4½ tblsp water
3 tblsp salad or olive oil
½ inch fresh root ginger, sliced
8oz lamb fillet, cut across the grain in thin strips of ½x2 inch
2 green onions, chopped
1 onion, peeled and cut into 1 inch pieces
1 green pepper, seeded and cut into strips
1 tsp curry powder
3-4 small, firm tomatoes, cut into ½ inch pieces

Mix the cornstarch, salt, soy sauce, water and 1 tsp of the oil together. Keep on one side. Heat the remaining oil in a wok and fry the ginger and lamb for 2-3 minutes. Add the onions, green pepper and curry powder and stir fry for 3-4 minutes. Stir in the cornstarch mixture and cook for 1 minute. Add the tomatoes and cook until the sauce thickens. Serve as a side dish.

Mongolian Lamb with Onions

PREPARATION TIME: 20 minutes

COOKING TIME: 8-10 minutes

SERVES: 4 people

1lb lean, boned lamb, cut into ¼x2 inch strips
1 egg white
2 cloves of garlic, sliced
½ tsp five spice powder
½ inch fresh root ginger, peeled and thinly sliced
1 tblsp cornstarch
1¼ tblsp light soy sauce
3½ tblsp rice wine or dry sherry
2 tblsp water
3 tblsp cooked oil
6 green onions, chopped

Mix the lamb with the egg white, garlic, five spice powder, ginger root and 1 tsp cornstarch and 1 tsp soy sauce. Keep on one side. Mix the

Lamb with Tomatoes (below left), Steamed Lamb with Mushroom Sauce (right) and Mongolian Lamb with Onions (below right).

remaining cornstarch, soy sauce, wine and water together. Heat the wok and add the oil. When it begins to smoke, add the beef mixture. Reduce the heat and stir fry for 3-4 minutes until the meat browns slightly. Remove and keep on one side. Add the onions and the cornstarch, soy sauce and wine mixture to the wok. Stir until it thickens. Return the meat to the wok and simmer gently for 3-4 minutes, or until the meat is tender. Serve as a main dish.

Sweet and Sour Beef

PREPARATION TIME: 15 minutes
COOKING TIME: 15 minutes
SERVES: 4 people

Batter
A generous ½ cup all-purpose flour
1½ tsp baking powder
4 tblsp cornstarch
1 tblsp salad or olive oil

3 tblsp salad or olive oil

8oz fillet of beef, cut into 1 inch cubes
1 onion, peeled and cut into wedges
1 inch fresh root ginger, peeled and thinly sliced
1 clove garlic, peeled and thinly sliced
1 green pepper, seeded and chopped

Sweet and Sour Sauce
4 tblsp brown sugar
¼ tsp salt
4 tblsp wine-flavored vinegar
1 tsp fresh root ginger, peeled and minced

⅓ cup water
1 tblsp cornstarch
2 tsp cooked oil
Few drops food coloring
Oil for deep frying

For the batter: sift the flour, baking powder and cornstarch. Beat in the oil and add sufficient water to make a thick, smooth batter. Heat the 3 tblsp oil in a wok and stir fry the beef for 2 minutes. Remove the beef. Fry the onion, ginger, garlic and green pepper for 2-3 minutes in the same oil. Remove the wok from the heat. Mix the sauce ingredients together and add to the wok. Return the wok to the heat and bring to the boil gently. Lower the heat and simmer gently for 2-3 minutes until thick and clear. Meanwhile, dip the beef cubes into the batter and deep fry in hot oil until golden brown and crisp. Drain on absorbent paper. Arrange in a deep dish and pour the hot sauce over the beef. Serve with a chow mein dish or fried rice. Thinly sliced carrots, cucumber and zucchini may also be added along with the onion, ginger and green pepper.

Barbecued Pork
(Kan Hsiang Ch'a Shao or Char Siu)

PREPARATION TIME: 3 hours

COOKING TIME: 1 hour to 1 hour 30 minutes

SERVES: 6-8 people

4½lb loin of pork

Seasoning
1 tblsp ginger juice
Few drops red food coloring
5 tblsp brown sugar
1 cup light soy sauce
1 tsp salt
1 tblsp Mue Kwe Lo wine (or a mixture of 2 tsp dry sherry and 1 tsp apricot brandy)

8oz honey, melted

Remove the bones from the loin of pork. Cut pork into 1½ inch wide strips. With the aid of a fork scrape the surface of the pork lightly to form grooves in which the seasoning can lodge. Mix the seasoning ingredients together and rub well into the pork strips. Leave to marinate for at least 1½ hours. Thread the pork strips onto a long metal skewer and hang to dry for 1 hour. Put the pork onto a wire rack in a roasting tin. Brush with melted honey and roast in the oven at 350°F, for 1-1½ hours, basting with honey frequently. When cooked, brush the pork with any remaining honey and leave to 'dry' slightly. Serve hot or cold, sliced thinly on a serving plate.

Pork Spare Ribs

PREPARATION TIME: 25 minutes

COOKING TIME: 40-45 minutes

SERVES: 4 people

16-20 pork spare ribs
1 tsp salt
Salad or olive oil
1 tsp ginger paste

Pork Meat Balls in Sauce (left), Pork Spare Ribs (above) and Barbecued Pork (right).

1 tsp garlic paste
1 tsp onion paste
Pinch monosodium glutamate
   (optional)
1 tsp light soy sauce
1 tsp cornstarch
1 egg
½ tsp Shao Hsing wine
½ tsp chili oil

Sauce
3 tblsp brown sugar
3 tblsp black vinegar
1 tblsp ketchup
1 tsp cornstarch
1 tsp water
1 tblsp dark soy sauce
½ tsp salt
½ tsp freshly ground black pepper

Trim excess fat from spare ribs and rub with salt. Add 4 tblsp oil to the wok and fry the ginger, garlic and onion for 1-2 minutes. Add the spare ribs and stir fry for 6 minutes. Remove to a dish and add the monosodium glutamate, light soy sauce, cornstarch, egg, wine and chili oil. Marinate for 10 minutes. Prepare the sauce by mixing all the ingredients together in the wok and bringing them gently to the boil. Simmer for 2-3 minutes and add the spare ribs along with their marinade. Stir fry until the liquid is reduced to half its original quantity.

Put all the ingredients onto a baking tray and spread out evenly. Bake at 375° for 25 minutes. Baste occasionally with the liquid from the tray and oil. The spare ribs should have browned well and be well coated with seasoning. Serve hot or cold.

Pork Meat Balls in Sauce
(Sha Kwo Shih-tzu-Tou)

PREPARATION TIME: 25 minutes
COOKING TIME: 45 minutes
SERVES: 4 people

Seasoning
Pinch monosodium glutamate
   (optional)
1 tblsp Shao Hsing wine
1 inch fresh root ginger, peeled and
   ground
2 green onions, white part only,
   minced
½ tsp salt
2 tsp cornstarch

2 cups ground lean pork
¼ cup bamboo shoots, chopped
⅓ cup dried Chinese mushrooms,
   soaked, drained and sliced
1 egg, beaten

Cornstarch to roll the meat balls in
6oz Chinese white cabbage, cut into
   3 inch pieces or 8oz ordinary green
   leafy cabbage, cut into 3 inch
   pieces
1 tblsp cooked oil
Oil for deep frying
1 tblsp cornstarch
3 tblsp water
1 small onion, peeled and finely
   chopped
1 inch fresh root ginger, peeled and
   finely chopped
1¼ chicken broth

Sauce
Salt to taste
½ tsp monosodium glutamate
   (optional)
1¼ tblsp light soy sauce
1 tsp dark soy sauce
1 tblsp cooked oil
1 tsp sesame oil

Mix seasoning ingredients together. Add the pork, bamboo shoots, mushrooms and egg and mix well. Shape into 15-16 even-sized balls and roll them in cornstarch. Keep aside on a dish. Blanch cabbage for 1 minute in boiling water and the cooked oil. Drain the cabbage and discard the water. Heat the wok and add the oil for deep frying. When quite hot deep-fry the meat balls, a few at a time, for 4-5

minutes. Remove and drain. Keep warm in a large casserole dish. Keep oil for future use. Mix the 1 tblsp cornstarch with the 3 tblsp water and keep aside. Reheat the wok and add 1 tsp deep frying oil. Stir fry the onion and ginger for 2 minutes. Add the chicken broth and stir in the blended sauce ingredients. Bring to the boil and add the meat balls. Simmer gently for 30 minutes. Add the cabbage, sesame oil and the blended cornstarch mixture. Stir over the heat until the sauce thickens.

Sesame Beef with Dates

PREPARATION TIME: 20 minutes, plus 30 minutes to marinate

COOKING TIME: 12-15 minutes

SERVES: 4 people

Seasoning A
½ tsp baking soda
1¼ tblsp light soy sauce
1 tblsp salad or olive oil
1¾ tsp cornstarch

1lb beef fillet, thinly sliced into 2 inch pieces
20 dried dates (red or dark), soaked and stoned

Seasoning B
1 tsp monosodium glutamate (optional)
1½ tsp brown sugar
2 tsp bean paste
A generous ¾ cup beef broth
Salt to taste

4 tblsp cooked oil, or plain oil
1 inch fresh root ginger, peeled and thinly sliced
2 green onions, sliced

Sauce
1¼ tblsp cornstarch
2½ tblsp water or broth
2 tblsp sesame seeds

Mix the ingredients for seasoning A. Mix with the beef and marinate for 30 minutes. Drain meat and discard marinade. Drain soaked dates; slice most of them into 4 long pieces, leaving a few whole. Mix the dates with seasoning B. Heat oil in a wok and stir fry beef for 4-5 minutes. Add ginger, green onions, dates and seasoning B and gently bring to the boil. Add the blended sauce ingredients. Cover and simmer for 3-4 minutes over a gentle heat until the sauce thickens and becomes clear. Remove from the heat, place on a serving dish and keep warm. Heat a wok or

skillet and add the sesame seeds. Dry roast for 2 minutes until they begin to crackle and turn golden brown. Sprinkle over the beef and serve immediately.

Shredded Pork with Preserved Vegetables

PREPARATION TIME: 30 minutes

COOKING TIME: 6-8 minutes

SERVES: 3 people

Pinch monosodium glutamate (optional)
2 tsp cornstarch
Salt and freshly ground black pepper to taste
½lb lean pork, shredded
Oil for deep frying
1 inch fresh root ginger, peeled and shredded
½ cup shelled green peas, lightly cooked
½ tsp fine granulated sugar
2 tsp Shao Hsing wine or dry sherry
8oz mixed Shanghai preserved vegetables, in brine
1 tsp sesame oil

Mix the monosodium glutamate, cornstarch and a pinch of salt. Add the pork and let it stand for 15 minutes. Heat the oil in a wok and deep fry the pork for 3 minutes. Remove the pork and drain. Reserve oil for future use. Reheat wok and add 2 tsp deep fried oil. Stir fry the ginger and green peas for 1 minute. Add the pork and sprinkle with the sugar, wine and salt and pepper to taste. Stir fry for another minute and add the well-drained preserved vegetables. Allow to heat through and then stir gently. Sprinkle on the sesame oil and serve. Serve as a side dish or on a bed of plain fried noodles.

Beef Steak with Ginger

PREPARATION TIME: 20-25 minutes

COOKING TIME: 10-12 minutes

SERVES: 2-3 people

Seasoning
½ tsp baking soda
3 tblsp light soy sauce
2 tblsp rice wine or dry sherry
½ tsp salt
½ tsp ground black pepper

½ tsp fresh root ginger, peeled and minced
½lb beef fillet, sliced into 1 inch pieces

Sauce
1 tsp fine granulated sugar
¼ tsp monosodium glutamate (optional)
1¼ tblsp) dark soy sauce
3½ tblsp broth
Few drops sesame oil
1 tsp Shao Hsing wine

4 tblsp salad or olive oil
1 inch fresh root ginger, peeled and thinly sliced
4 green onions, chopped
½ cup bamboo shoots, thinly sliced
2 green chilies, sliced

Mix the seasoning ingredients with the minced ginger. Add the beef and marinate for 20 minutes. Drain the beef and discard the marinade. Mix the sauce ingredients together. Heat 3 tblsp oil in the wok and fry the sliced ginger and onions for 2 minutes. Add the bamboo shoots and chilies and stir fry for 1-2 minutes. Remove to a plate. Add the remaining oil to the wok and fry the beef for 2-3 minutes. Add the fried vegetables and stir fry for 2 minutes. Add the well-stirred sauce ingredients and simmer gently until the mixture thickens. Simmer for another 1-2 minutes. Remove from heat and serve.

Beef with Green Beans

PREPARATION TIME: 30 minutes

COOKING TIME: 12 minutes

SERVES: 4 people

Seasoning
½ tsp baking soda
1 tsp cornstarch
1¼ tblsp light soy sauce
2 tblsp water
1 tsp cooked oil

1lb lean beef, thinly sliced into 1 inch pieces

Sauce
¼ tsp salt
1 tsp monosodium glutamate (optional)
1½ tsp light soy sauce
1½ tsp dark soy sauce
1 tsp Shao Hsing wine (optional)
½ cup broth
2 tsp cornstarch

3 tblsp salad or olive oil
2 cloves of garlic, peeled and sliced
1 onion, peeled and cut into wedges
1 inch fresh root ginger, peeled and thinly sliced
6oz Chinese long beans, cut into 3 inch pieces (or whole tender green

beans)
Salt and freshly ground black pepper to taste

Mix seasoning ingredients together. Add the beef and marinate for 20 minutes. Drain the meat and discard the marinade. Mix the sauce ingredients together. Heat 2 tblsp oil in the wok until it smokes. Reduce the heat and add the garlic and the beef and stir fry for 3-4 minutes. Remove the meat and keep on one side. Add the remaining oil to the wok and add the onion, ginger and long beans and stir fry for 2-3 minutes. Add the fried beef. Cover and fry for a further 1 minute. Stir in the sauce ingredients and bring to the boil. Simmer gently for 2-3 minutes. Season with salt and pepper. Remove from heat and serve.

Sweet and Sour Pork

PREPARATION TIME: 20 minutes, plus 20 minutes to marinate

COOKING TIME: 15-20 minutes

SERVES: 4 people

Batter
3 tblsp all-purpose flour
1 tblsp cornstarch
1½ tsp baking soda
2 tblsp salad or olive oil

12oz lean pork, cut into 1 inch cubes

Seasoning
1 tsp fine granulated sugar
1 tsp salt
2½ tblsp light soy sauce
1½ tsp dark soy sauce
1 tblsp cooked oil
1 tblsp water

Cornstarch
Oil for deep frying
2 cloves garlic, cut into thin strips
1 large onion, peeled and cut into ½ inch pieces
1 carrot, sliced into ⅛x1x2 inch thin pieces
Pinch salt

Sweet and Sour Sauce
3 tblsp brown sugar
1 tblsp ketchup
1 cup chicken broth or water
4 tblsp wine-flavored vinegar
1½ tsp light soy sauce
Few slices fresh root ginger, peeled
1 tblsp cornstarch
Few drops of red food coloring
2 tsp cooked oil

Mix the batter ingredients together, adding sufficient water to make a

Diced Pork with Walnuts

PREPARATION TIME: 30 minutes
COOKING TIME: 16-18 minutes
SERVES: 3 people

¾ cup shelled walnuts
Oil for deep frying

Seasoning
1¾ tsp light soy sauce
Few drops sesame oil
Salt and freshly ground black pepper
  to taste
1 tblsp salad or olive oil
1 tblsp water
1 tblsp cornstarch
Pinch monosodium glutamate
  (optional)

½lb pork fillet, cut into cubes
1 carrot, thinly sliced
1 onion, peeled and cut into pieces
3 green onions, chopped
1 inch fresh root ginger, peeled and
  thinly sliced

Sauce
⅓ cup broth
1 tsp cornstarch

Cook the walnuts in boiling water for 3-4 minutes. Drain the nuts thoroughly. Deep fry the walnuts until lightly browned. Remove and drain. Use oil for cooking. Mix the seasoning ingredients together and add the pork. Leave to marinate for 15 minutes. Discard marinade. Heat 2 tblsp oil in the wok and stir fry the carrots for 2 minutes. Add the onions and root ginger and stir fry for 1 minute. Add 2 tsp of the sauce broth and remove to a plate. Add the drained pork cubes and 1 tblsp oil to the wok and stir fry for 4-5 minutes. Mix the remaining broth and the cornstarch together for the sauce. Return the walnuts and carrots to the wok, together with the blended sauce ingredients. Mix well and simmer until the sauce thickens. Remove and serve immediately. Serve with rice noodle or fried rice.

thick coating batter. Wash and drain the pork. Mix with the seasoning ingredients and marinate for 15-20 minutes. Drain the pork and discard the marinade. Roll the pork cubes in cornstarch. Heat the oil for deep frying. Dip the pork cubes in batter and fry in the hot oil until golden brown. Fry a few at a time until all the pork has been

fried. Drain well and keep warm in a low oven. Heat wok and add 2 tsp deep fried oil. Stir fry the garlic, onions and carrots for 3-4 minutes. Season with salt and fry for a further minute. Mix the sweet and sour sauce ingredients together and add to the wok. Stir the mixture until it thickens. Pour over the fried pork cubes and serve immediately.

Note: sliced green peppers can also be added along with the carrots and onions.

Sweet and Sour Pork (top right), Diced Pork with Walnuts (center) and Shredded Pork with Preserved Vegetables (bottom left).

Poultry

Roast Crispy Duck

PREPARATION TIME: 15-20 minutes plus 6-8 hours to dry

COOKING TIME: 1 hour 30 minutes

SERVES: 4-6 people

4½lb duck, prepared for cooking
1 cup water
6 large green onions cut into 2 inch lengths
5 tblsp maple syrup
½ tsp red food coloring
2½ tblsp ketchup

Wash the duck and pat it dry on a clean cloth. Ease the fingers between the skin and flesh of the duck, starting at the neck end and working the length of the bird. Put a stick or large skewer through the neck and the cavity of the duck to wedge it securely. This will make the duck easier to handle. Hold the duck over the sink and pour boiling water all over it. Pat the duck dry. Melt half the maple syrup and dissolve in the water. Stand the duck on a rack over a deep tray. Slowly pour the dissolved syrup over the duck. Pour the syrup liquid over the duck 3 or 4 times. Leave the duck in a cool place for 6-8 hours, or overnight, until the skin is dry. Remove the stick. Stand the duck on a rack in a roasting tin. Preheat the oven to 400°F, and cook for 30 minutes. Turn over and cook the underside for a further 30 minutes. Melt the remaining maple syrup with the ketchup and add the food coloring. Spread over the duck and cook for a further 30 minutes. (The duck should have a crisp, red skin.) Remove the duck skin in squares. Slice the duck flesh and serve with the skin on the top. Serve the following dip as an accompaniment.

Duck Dip
4oz brown sugar
5 tblsp sweet bean paste
2½ tblsp sesame oil
½ cup water

Heat the wok and add the mixed ingredients. Cook for 3-4 minutes until the sugar has dissolved and the dip is smooth. Serve in individual cups.

Sliced Duck with Bamboo Shoots

PREPARATION TIME: 30 minutes

COOKING TIME: 10 minutes

SERVES: 2-3 people

2¼lb small duck
1 tsp monosodium glutamate (optional)
3 tsp cornstarch
2½ tblsp water
4oz broccoli, chopped
3 tblsp salad or olive oil
2-3 green onions, chopped
1 inch fresh root ginger, peeled and thinly sliced
1 clove garlic, peeled and finely chopped
⅔ cup bamboo shoots sliced
½ tsp fine granulated sugar
Salt and freshly ground black pepper to taste
5 tblsp chicken broth
2 tsp rice wine or sweet sherry
Few drops sesame oil

Cut the duck flesh into bite-size

pieces, removing all the bones. Mix the MSG, with ⅔ of the cornstarch and 1 tblsp water. Stir into the duck. Marinate for 20 minutes. Cook the broccoli in boiling water for 1 minute. Drain thoroughly. Heat the wok and add the oil. Stir fry the onions, ginger, garlic and bamboo shoots for 1-2 minutes. Add the duck pieces and stir fry for 2-3 minutes. Add the sugar, salt and pepper to taste, broth rice wine and sesame oil. Stir fry for 3 minutes. Add the remaining cornstarch and water blended together. Stir over the heat until the sauce thickens. Serve immediately, as a side dish.

Duck with Ginger and Pineapple

PREPARATION TIME: 20 minutes

COOKING TIME: 2 hours to 2 hours 45 minutes

SERVES: 4-6 people

½ inch fresh root ginger, peeled and crushed
1½ tblsp soy sauce
4½lb duck, prepared for cooking
Salt and freshly ground black pepper to taste
3 tblsp salad or olive oil
4 inches fresh root ginger, peeled and thinly sliced
¾ cup bean sprouts
3 green onions, chopped
2 carrots, peeled sliced and blanched in boiling water for 2 minutes
2 tsp brown sugar
1½ tblsp wine-flavored vinegar
1½ cups canned pineapple chunks in syrup
1¼ tblsp cornstarch mixed with 2½ tblsp water

Mix together the crushed ginger, half of the soy sauce and salt and pepper to taste. Wash the duck and pat it dry. Rub the outside of the duck with salt and put on a wire rack in a roasting tin. Roast at 350°F, for 30 minutes. Brush the ginger and soy sauce mixture over the duck. Baste frequently with the sauces from the pan and roast for 2 hours, turning the bird occasionally to brown all sides. Remove and slice the duck in small pieces. Heat the oil in a wok and stir fry the sliced ginger, bean sprouts, onions and carrots for 1-2 minutes. Add the duck slices and cook for 1 minute. Then add the brown sugar, vinegar and pineapple chunks in their syrup. Bring to the boil and cook for 2-3 minutes. Add the blended cornstarch and remaining soy sauce and cook until the sauce thickens. Serve as a main dish along with noodles or rice.

This page: Stewed Chicken and Pineapple (top right), Fried Shredded Chicken on Cabbage (center left) and Chicken and Cashew Nuts (bottom right). Facing page: Sliced Duck with Bamboo Shoots (top), Duck with Ginger and Pineapple (bottom left) and Roast Crispy Duck (bottom right).

Chicken Green Chili

PREPARATION TIME: 10 minutes, plus 10 minutes to marinate
COOKING TIME: 10 minutes
SERVES: 4 people

Sauce
1 tsp light soy sauce
1 tsp dark soy sauce
Salt to taste
2 tsp cornstarch
1 tsp sesame oil
1 tsp vinegar
1 cup chicken broth

Seasoning
Salt to taste
Freshly ground black pepper to taste
Pinch monosodium glutamate (optional)
2½ tblsp) dark soy sauce
1¼ tblsp light soy sauce
1 tsp cornstarch
2 tsp rice wine or dry sherry

1lb boned chicken, cut into bite-size pieces
3 tblsp salad or olive oil
3 green onions, chopped
1 inch fresh root ginger, peeled and sliced
2 cloves of garlic, peeled and sliced
1 green pepper, seeded and chopped
2-3 green chilies, sliced lengthwise

Mix the sauce ingredients together. Mix the seasoning ingredients together and add the chicken. Marinate for 10 minutes. Drain the chicken and discard the liquid. Heat 1 tblsp oil and stir fry the onions, ginger and garlic for 2 minutes. Remove to a dish. Add the remaining oil and stir fry the chicken for 3 minutes. Add the blended green peppers and chilies and stir fry for 2 minutes. Add the onion mixture and the well blended sauce ingredients and cook for 3-4 minutes until the sauce thickens. Serve immediately.

Chicken and Mushrooms

PREPARATION TIME: 15 minutes, plus 10 minutes to marinate
COOKING TIME: 10-12 minutes
SERVES: 3-4 people

Seasoning
½ tsp salt
2½ tblsp light soy sauce
2 tsp cornstarch
1 tsp rice wine or dry sherry
Pinch monosodium glutamate (optional)

½lb chicken breast, cut into bite-size pieces

Sauce
Salt to taste
Freshly ground black pepper to taste
1¼ tblsp light soy sauce
1 cup chicken broth
2 tsp cornstarch

1 tsp oyster sauce

2 tblsp salad or olive oil
1 onion, peeled and chopped
1 clove of garlic, sliced
½ inch fresh root ginger, peeled and thinly sliced
3 dried black mushrooms, soaked and sliced
½ cup open mushrooms, sliced
½ cup buttom mushrooms, sliced

Mix the seasoning ingredients together. Marinate the chicken in the seasoning mixture for 10 minutes. Mix the sauce ingredients together. Heat the oil in a wok and fry the onion, garlic and ginger for 2-3 minutes. Remove and keep on one side. Fry the drained chicken in the remaining oil for 4 minutes. Add the mushrooms and stir fry for 1 minute. Add a little extra oil if necessary. Return the fried onion mixture to the wok and stir fry until well mixed. Pour the blended sauce ingredients into the wok and cook gently until the sauce thickens. Serve piping hot.

Chicken Fry with Sauce (below right), Chicken Green Chili (below center) and Chicken and Mushrooms (far right).

Chicken Fry with Sauce

PREPARATION TIME: 20 minutes

COOKING TIME: about 24 minutes

SERVES: 4 people

1 tblsp cooked oil
1 tsp sesame oil
2 tblsp sesame seeds

Sauce
2 cloves garlic, minced
2 green onions, finely chopped or minced
1 tsp Chinese black vinegar, or brown vinegar
3½ tblsp dark soy sauce
1 tsp light soy sauce

½ tsp monosodium glutamate (optional)
½ tsp salt
1½ tsp fine granulated sugar

8 chicken thighs, or 1lb chicken, cut into small joints

Heat the wok and add the oils. Stir fry the sesame seeds till they change color to golden brown. Remove to a dish. Mix sauce ingredients together and add the sesame seeds. Wipe the wok and add the chicken. Add sufficient water to cover, and cook for 20 minutes until the chicken is tender. De-bone the chicken and quickly cut into bite-size pieces. Arrange the chicken on a plate and spoon the sauce over the top. Serve immediately.

Stewed Chicken and Pineapple

PREPARATION TIME: 30 minutes

COOKING TIME: 15 minutes

SERVES: 4 people

Seasoning
2½ tblsp light soy sauce
1 tblsp salad or olive oil
1 tblsp cornstarch
1 tsp salt
½ tsp sesame oil
2 tblsp water

1½lb boned chicken breast, cut into cubes

Sauce
1½ tsp cornstarch
1 cup water or chicken broth
2½ tsp dark soy sauce
Salt to taste

2 tblsp salad or olive oil
1 onion, peeled and cut into chunks
2 green onions, finely chopped
1 inch fresh root ginger, peeled and thinly sliced
4-5 pineapple rings, cut into chunks

Mix the seasoning ingredients together. Add the cubed chicken and marinate for 10-12 minutes. Mix the sauce ingredients together

in a bowl. Heat the oil in a wok and fry the onions for 2 minutes until just tender. Add the drained chicken and fry for 3-4 minutes. Add the root ginger and fry for 1 minute. Add any remaining marinade and the sauce ingredients and bring to the boil. Cook, stirring, until the sauce thickens then add the pineapple chunks. Heat through. Remove from the heat and serve with fried rice.

Chicken Chop Suey

PREPARATION TIME: 30 minutes	
COOKING TIME: 15 minutes	
SERVES: 4 people	

2½ tblsp light soy sauce
1 tsp brown sugar
Salt to taste
1lb boned chicken, cut into 1 inch
    pieces
2 tblsp salad or olive oil
1 onion, cut into chunks
2½ cups bean sprouts
2 tsp sesame oil
¼ tsp monosodium glutamate
    (optional)
1 tblsp cornstarch
1 cup chicken broth

Mix the soy sauce with the sugar and salt and add the chicken pieces. Allow to marinate for 5 minutes. Drain the chicken and reserve the marinade. Heat the wok and add the oil. Fry the chicken for 2-3 minutes. Remove the chicken. Fry the onions for 2-3 minutes and add the bean sprouts. Stir fry for 4-5 minutes. Return the chicken to the pan and add the sesame oil. Dissolve the monosodium glutamate and the cornstarch in the broth and pour over the chicken mixture. Cook for 2-3 minutes, stirring, until the sauce thickens. Serve as a side-dish.

Deep Fried Crispy Chicken

PREPARATION TIME: 3 hours	
COOKING TIME: 13-14 minutes	
SERVES: 4 people	

3-3½lb chicken, prepared for cooking

Seasoning
1 tsp salt
½ tsp five spice powder
2 tblsp maple syrup
2 tblsp brown vinegar
⅔ cup wine-flavored vinegar

Oil for deep frying

Wash the chicken and hang it up by a hook to drain and dry. The skin will dry quickly. Pour boiling water over the chicken 4-5 times to partially cook the skin. This will make the skin crisp during frying. Rub salt and five spice powder well inside the chicken cavity. Dissolve the maple syrup and vinegars in a pan over a gentle heat. Pour over the chicken. Repeat several times, catching the syrup solution in a drip tray. Leave the chicken to hang and dry for 1½-2 hours, until the skin is smooth and shiny. Heat the oil for deep frying. Deep fry the chicken for 10 minutes. Ladle hot oil carefully over the chicken continually, until the chicken is deep brown in color. (The skin puffs out slightly.) Cook for a further 3-4 minutes and remove from the oil. Drain on absorbent paper. Cut into small pieces and serve with a dip.

Chicken and Cashew Nuts

PREPARATION TIME: 15 minutes	
COOKING TIME: 15 minutes	
SERVES: 4 people	

12oz chicken breast, sliced into 1 inch
    pieces
1 tblsp cornstarch

Seasoning
1 tsp salt
1 tsp sesame oil
1¼ tblsp light soy sauce
½ tsp brown sugar

Oil for deep frying and stir frying
¾ cup cashew nuts
2 green onions, chopped
1 small onion, peeled and cubed
1 inch fresh root ginger, peeled and
    sliced
2 cloves of garlic, sliced
1 cup snow peas (mange tout)
½ cup thinly sliced bamboo shoots

Sauce
2 tsp cornstarch
1 tblsp Hoi Sin sauce
1 cup chicken broth
Pinch monosodium glutamate
    (optional)

Roll the chicken pieces in cornstarch. Discard the remaining cornstarch. Mix the seasoning ingredients together and pour over chicken. Leave to stand for 10

minutes. Heat oil for deep frying in a wok and fry cashew nuts until golden brown. Remove the nuts and all but 2 tblsp of the oil; drain the nuts on kitchen paper. Heat the oil remaining in the wok and stir fry the onions, ginger and garlic for 2-3 minutes. Add snow peas and bamboo shoots and stir fry for 3 minutes. Remove the fried ingredients. Add 1 tblsp oil to the wok and fry the chicken for 3-4 minutes. Remove the chicken. Clean the wok and add a further 2 tblsp oil and return chicken, cashew nuts and fried onions etc. to the wok. Prepare the sauce by mixing the cornstarch, Hoi Sin sauce, chicken broth and monosodium glutamate together. Pour over the chicken. Mix well and cook until the sauce thickens and becomes transparent. Serve hot with a chow mein dish. Alternatively, a few chunks of pineapple will add extra zest to the dish.

Fried Shredded Chicken on Cabbage

PREPARATION TIME: 20 minutes	
COOKING TIME: 12 minutes	
SERVES: 4 people	

1lb Chinese white cabbage, cut into 1
    inch pieces
Pinch baking soda

Seasoning
1¼ tblsp light soy sauce
1 tblsp cornstarch
¼ tsp sesame oil
¼ tsp freshly ground black pepper
½ tsp fine granulated sugar
½ tsp salt
1¼ tblsp water
1 tblsp salad or olive oil
Pinch monosodium glutamate
    (optional)

2 tblsp salad or olive oil
1 onion, peeled and roughly chopped
1 inch fresh root ginger, peeled and
    thinly sliced
1lb boned chicken breasts, shredded
4-6 mushrooms, sliced

Sauce
3 tblsp chicken broth
¼ tsp sesame oil
1 tsp light soy sauce
1 tsp cornstarch
1 tsp monosodium glutamate
    (optional)

Wash cabbage and blanch in boiling water with a pinch of

baking soda for 2 minutes. Drain well. Mix the seasoning ingredients together. Heat the wok and add the oil. Fry the onions, ginger and chicken for 2-3 minutes. Add the mushrooms and fry for further 2 minutes. Add the broth and cook for 4-5 minutes. Mix the sauce ingredients together and pour over the chicken. Cook for 2 minutes. Serve immediately.

Steamed Chicken

PREPARATION TIME: 20-30 minutes	
COOKING TIME: 15-20 minutes	
SERVES: 4 people	

1½lb boned chicken

Seasoning
1¼ tblsp light soy sauce
1 tsp brown sugar
1 tsp salt
1 tblsp cornstarch
2 tblsp oil or cooked oil
½ tsp monosodium glutamate
    (optional)

4oz dried mushrooms, soaked in
    boiling water for 5 minutes and
    sliced, (or ordinary mushrooms)
½ inch fresh root ginger, peeled and
    sliced
4 green onions, finely chopped
2 tblsp broth or water, if needed

Cut the chicken into 1 inch pieces. Mix the seasoning ingredients together and mix with the chicken. Leave to marinate for 15 minutes. Place a plate in a steamer and put the chicken, mushrooms, ginger, half the onion and the broth on top. Steam over boiling water for 15-20 minutes. Serve with the remaining onions sprinkled over the chicken. The steaming can also be done on a greased lotus leaf or a banana leaf. The flavor is quite stunning.

Tangerine Peel Chicken

PREPARATION TIME: 30 minutes	
COOKING TIME: 12-15 minutes	
SERVES: 4 people	

1lb boned chicken breast, cut into 1
    inch pieces

Facing page: Chicken Chop Suey (top left), Steamed Chicken (center right) and Deep Fried Crispy Chicken (bottom left).

Seasoning

½ tsp salt
1½ tsp brown sugar
½ tsp monosodium glutamate (optional)
1 tsp dark soy sauce
2½ tsp light soy sauce
1 tsp rice wine or dry sherry
2½ tsp brown vinegar
1 tsp sesame oil
2 tsp cornstarch

Oil for deep frying
1-2 red or green chilies, chopped
½ inch fresh root ginger, peeled and finely chopped
2 inches dried tangerine peel, coarsely ground or crumbled
2 green onions, finely chopped

Sauce

½ tsp cornstarch
1-2 tblsp water or broth

Mix the chicken pieces with the seasoning ingredients and stir well. Leave to marinate for 10-15 minutes. Remove the chicken pieces and reserve the marinade. Heat wok and add the oil for deep frying. Once it starts to smoke add the chicken pieces and fry for 4-5 minutes until golden. Drain chicken on kitchen paper. Tip off the oil, leaving 1 tblsp oil in the wok, and stir fry the chilies, ginger, tangerine peel and onions for 2-3 minutes. When they begin to color add the chicken and stir fry for 1 minute. Mix the reserved marinade with the sauce ingredients and pour over the chicken. Stir and cook for 2-3 minutes until the sauce thickens and the chicken is tender. Serve immediately.

Roast Spiced Duck

PREPARATION TIME: 3-4 hours to dry, and 1 hour to glaze

COOKING TIME: 1 hour

SERVES: 4-6 people

4½lb duck, prepared for cooking
1 tsp five spice powder
1½ tsp salt
5 tblsp maple syrup
1½ tblsp wine-flavored vinegar
Salad or olive oil

Wash and dry the duck. Rub in the five spice powder and salt. Close the cavities of the duck by securing both ends with small skewers. Mix the maple syrup and vinegar together with a little water and bring to the boil. Spoon this liquid over the duck several times, collecting the liquid in a tray. Hang the duck by its neck for 3-4 hours to dry. Preheat the oven to 450°F.

Place the duck in a roasting tin. Rub oil into the skin. Roast in the oven for 1 hour, basting with any remaining maple syrup and vinegar liquid. If the duck is not quite tender, cook for a little longer. Slice the duck onto a warmed serving dish and serve immediately.

Roast Peking Duck

PREPARATION TIME: 15 minutes plus 2-3 hours to dry out the skin

COOKING TIME: 1 hour 20 minutes

SERVES: 4-6 people

4½lb duck, prepared for cooking
4½ cups boiling water
2½ tblsp maple syrup
1 cup water
2-3 seedless oranges, peeled and cut into rings
2 tblsp salad or olive oil
Salt and freshly ground black pepper

Sauce

2½ tsp cornstarch
5 tblsp water or broth
Pinch monosodiumm glutamate (optional)
2½ tsp light soy sauce
1 tsp rice wine or dry sherry

To Garnish

4 green onions, cut into 2 inch lengths

Wash and dry the duck. Put a stick or skewer through the neck and the cavity of the duck so that it is easier to handle. Hold the bird over the sink and pour the boiling water over it. Hang the duck up to dry. Melt the syrup and water together and spoon over the duck several times, catching the liquid on a drip tray each time. Leave the duck to dry for 2-3 hours in a cool place. Save any liquid that drops off. Preheat the oven to 400°F. Place the duck, breast side down, in a roasting tin and roast for 30 minutes. Lift out the duck. Put the orange rings into the tin and sit the duck on top, breast side uppermost. Baste with the oil and season with salt and pepper. Roast for a further 45-50 minutes until tender. Cut off the duck joints and slice the breast meat. Arrange with the orange slices on a serving dish and keep warm.

To Make the Sauce

Mix the sauce ingredients together and add any reserved maltose liquid. Bring to the boil gently, stirring, until the sauce thickens. Pour over the cooked duck and sprinkle with the onions.

Steamed Duck in Wine Sauce

PREPARATION TIME: 20 minutes

COOKING TIME: 30 hours 30 minutes

SERVES: 4-6 people

4½lb duck, prepared for cooking
Generous ½ cup Kao Liang wine, or mild red wine
½ tsp monosodium glutamate (optional)
1 inch fresh root ginger, peeled and thinly sliced
3 green onions, chopped
1 tsp salt

Roast Spiced Duck (top), Roast Peking Duck (above) and Steamed Duck in Wine Sauce (right).

1 tsp fine granulated sugar
1¼ tsp) cornstarch

Place the duck in a large pot. Add water to cover and boil for 5-7 minutes. Remove the duck and drain well. Mix all the remaining ingredients together apart from the cornstarch. Place the duck in a deep dish and stand over a steamer. Pour the wine mixture over the duck. Cover and steam for 2-3 hours until the duck is quite tender. Remove the duck and strain the cooking liquid. Place the duck on a serving dish, either whole or cut into slices. Blend the cooking liquid with the cornstarch.

Bring to the boil and stir until thickened. Pour over the duck. Serve immediately

Chicken Chow Mein

PREPARATION TIME: 30 minutes

COOKING TIME: 20 minutes

SERVES: 4 people

1lb egg noodles or spaghetti, broken into small pieces
1 onion, peeled and thinly sliced
½ cup mushrooms, sliced
3 green onions, chopped
2 cloves of garlic, peeled and chopped
Salt to taste
Pinch monosodium glutamate
4 tblsp salad or olive oil
1½ cups chicken meat, finely shredded
2½ tblsp light soy sauce
1 tsp fine granulated sugar
1 tblsp rice wine or dry sherry
⅓ cup chicken broth

Cook the noodles in boiling, salted water for 4-5 minutes until tender. Drain and rinse under cold water. Drain once again and add 2 tblsp oil; mix well to prevent the noodles from sticking together. Heat 2 tblsp oil in a wok and fry the onions and garlic for 2 minutes. Add chicken and stir fry for 3-4 minutes. Add mushrooms. Sprinkle over the wine, sugar, soy sauce, monosodium glutamate and salt to taste. Cook until the mixture is fairly dry. Add noodles and stir well to mix. Sprinkle over the broth and cook once again until dry. Serve with chili sauce and dark soy sauce. ½ cup sliced green beans, ⅓ cup lightly cooked peas or ⅓ cup shredded carrot may also be added, along with the chicken pieces.

Peking Duck with Pancakes

PREPARATION TIME: for duck 2-3 hours; for pancakes 6 minutes

COOKING TIME: for duck 1 hour 20 minutes; for pancakes 15 minutes

SERVES: 6-8 people

4½lb Peking duck, roasted
16-20 green onions, sliced into 3 inch pieces

Pancakes (Po Ping)
1lb all-purpose flour
Pinch salt
1¼ tblsp salad or olive oil
1 tsp sesame oil
Tepid water for kneading
Flour for rolling

To Make Pancakes
Sift the flour and salt into a mixing bowl. Make a well in the center and add the oils and water, a little at a time, and work in the flour. Make a pliable dough. Remove from the bowl and knead well for 2-3 minutes. Cover with a damp, clean

cloth and allow to rest for 10 minutes. Knead again for 1 minute and divide the dough into 16-20 even-sized balls. Roll each ball in flour and roll out into a 4-6 inch circle. Place a skillet on the heat and when moderately hot place the rolled circle of dough on it; cook for ½-1 minute. Little bubbles will appear; flip over and allow to cook for 1-1½ minutes. Pick the pancake up and check whether little brown specs have appeared on the undersides; if not, then cook for few seconds more. Use a clean tea towel to press the pancakes gently, this will circulate the steam and cook the pancakes. Prepare the rest of the pancakes in the same way and keep them stacked, wrapped in foil to keep them warm.

To Make Dip
5 tblsp brown sugar
4 tblsp bean paste (sweet)
1 tblsp sesame oil
1 tblsp olive oil or peanut oil
1 cup water

Other Dips, Ready Prepared
4 tblsp Hoi Sin sauce
4 tblsp Chinese barbecue sauce

Mix sugar, bean paste and water

together. Warm the wok, add the oil and then the sugar mixture. Bring to boil and, when the sugar has melted, remove and put in a bowl. Place the duck on a cutting board and cut thin slices from the breast area and thighs. Place a pancake on an individual plate, cover with a slice of duck and a few strips of onion, spread on a dip of your choice, roll up like a pancake and eat. To make very crisp duck, cut duck into large joints and deep fry them till crispy.

Sweet and Sour Chicken

PREPARATION TIME: 30 minutes

COOKING TIME: 20 minutes

SERVES: 3-4 people

½ tsp salt
3 tsp cornstarch
2 chicken breasts, cut into ½ inch cubes
1 onion, peeled and roughly chopped into ½ inch pieces
¼ cup sliced bamboo shoots
1 green pepper, seeded and thinly

sliced
1 inch fresh root ginger, peeled and thinly sliced
2 carrots, scraped and thinly sliced into 1 inch long pieces
1 garlic clove, peeled and chopped
2 tblsp salad or olive oil

Batter
1 cup all-purpose flour
1 tblsp cornstarch
1 small egg

Oil for deep frying

Sauce
1 tblsp brown sugar
1¼ tblsp wine-flavored vinegar
1¼ tblsp soy sauce
1 tblsp ketchup
2 cups chicken broth
Pinch monosodium glutamate (optional)
2½ tsp cornstarch

Mix salt and cornstarch and roll chicken pieces in it. Make the batter by mixing the sieved flour and cornstarch with the egg and sufficient water to make a thick batter. Beat well. Heat oil for deep frying. Dip the chicken pieces into the batter and deep-fry until golden brown and crisp. Drain on

absorbent paper and keep warm. Heat the 2 tblsp oil in a wok and stir fry the onion, ginger and garlic for 2-3 minutes. Add the carrots and fry for 2 minutes. Add the green pepper and fry for 2 minutes. Add bamboo shoots, season with salt and stir well. Mix all the sauce ingredients together. Pour over the cooked vegetables. Cook 2-3 minutes until the sauce thickens. The sauce should become transparent. Arrange fried chicken pieces on a serving dish and pour the sweet and sour sauce over them. Serve as a side dish.

This page: Peking Duck with Pancakes.

Facing page: Tangerine Peel Chicken (top), Sweet and Sour Chicken (center left) and Chicken Chow Mein (bottom).

Fish and Seafood

Prawns with Broccoli

PREPARATION TIME: 10 minutes

COOKING TIME: 8-10 minutes

SERVES: 4 people

1lb peeled medium size shrimp
Oil for deep frying

Sauce
½ cup chicken broth
2 tsp cornstarch
Freshly ground black pepper and salt to taste
Pinch monosodium glutamate (optional)
1 tsp fine granulated sugar

Seasoning
2 tblsp cooked oil, or oil from deep frying the shrimps
Pinch salt
½ tsp fine granulated sugar
Pinch monosodium glutamate (optional)
2 tsp cornstarch

8oz Chinese broccoli, or Continental broccoli, cut into 3 inch pieces
1 carrot, peeled and sliced
2 cloves garlic, peeled and chopped
½ inch fresh root ginger, peeled and chopped

Deep fry the shrimps in hot oil for 1-2 minutes. Drain the shrimp and keep on one side. Keep the oil. Mix the sauce ingredients together. Mix seasoning ingredients together in a separate bowl. Cook the broccoli in boiling water for 1 minute. Drain and add cold water to cover. Drain once again and mix the broccoli with the seasoning ingredients. Heat the wok and add 2 tblsp cooked oil. Add the carrot, garlic and ginger and stir fry for 1 minute. Add the broccoli and stir fry for 1 minute more. Add the shrimps and stir fry for ½ minute then add the blended sauce ingredients. Cook gently until the sauce thickens. Serve immediately.

Shrimps with Bean Curd

PREPARATION TIME: 10 minutes

COOKING TIME: 8 minutes

SERVES: 4 people

1lb peeled medium size shrimp

Seasoning
1 tsp light soy sauce
Pinch salt
1 tsp fine granulated sugar
1 tsp cornstarch

1 inch fresh root ginger, peeled and finely choppped
2 tblsp salad or olive oil
1 clove of garlic, peeled and chopped
1 red chili, chopped
2-3 beancurd cakes, cubed
4 tblsp chicken broth
1 tsp cornstarch
2 tblsp water

Mix the shrimps with the seasoning ingredients and half of the ginger. Heat the oil and stir fry the ginger and shrimps for 2 minutes. Add the garlic and fry for 1 minute. Add the chili, cubed beancurd and broth. Simmer for 2-3 minutes. Mix the cornstarch with the water and remaining crushed ginger and pour over the shrimp mixture. Simmer gently until the sauce thickens. Serve immediately.

Shrimp in Hot Sauce

PREPARATION TIME: 10 minutes

COOKING TIME: 6 minutes

SERVES: 4 people

12oz cooked unshelled shrimp

Seasoning
1 tsp brown vinegar
1 tsp Shao Hsing wine
Pinch salt

Sauce
1 tsp cornstarch mixed with 1 tblsp water
2 tsp ketchup
Salt and freshly ground black pepper to taste

2 tsp fine granulated sugar
½ tsp monosodium glutamate (optional)
1 tsp hot chili sauce
1 cup chicken broth
2 tblsp cooked oil

Wash shrimps and drain well. Mix the seasoning ingredients together. Mix the sauce ingredients together in a separate bowl. Heat the oil in a wok and deep fry the shrimps for 1 minute. Remove the shrimps and drain. Keep the oil. Reheat the wok and add 2 tsp oil and stir fry the onion, celery and garlic for 1 minute. Add shrimps and the blended sauce ingredients. Bring to the boil and simmer gently for 3-4 minutes. Stir in the seasoning mixture.

Fish in Wine Sauce

PREPARATION TIME: 20 minutes

COOKING TIME: 15 minutes

SERVES: 3-4 people

Marinade
¼ tsp salt
1 egg white
2 tsp cornstarch
1 tsp wine-flavored vinegar

10-12oz mullet or carp fillet, cut into 2 inch slices
Oil for deep frying

Shrimp in Hot Sauce (top right), Shrimps with Bean Curd (center right) and Prawns with Broccoli (bottom right).

1 cup chicken broth

Seasoning
Pinch monosodium glutamate
   (optional)
Pinch salt
Pinch freshly ground black pepper
1 tsp fine granulated sugar
2½ tsp cornstarch
1½ tblsp water
1 cloud ear fungus, soaked and boiled
   for 2 minutes, and then chopped
2 dried Chinese mushrooms, soaked
   and sliced

Mix the marinade ingredients
together. Marinate the fish in the
marinade for 10 minutes. Heat a

generous quantity of oil in the wok
and deep fry the drained fish
pieces, a few at a time, until the
flesh is white. Remove and drain
the fish. Keep the oil for future use.
Clean the wok. Add the chicken
stock to the wok and bring to the
boil. Simmer gently and stir in the
seasoning ingredients. Simmer for
few seconds and then add the
cornstarch blended with the water.
Add the fish and simmer until the
sauce thickens. Add the fungus
and mushrooms. Simmer for 1
minute. Serve immediately.

Fish with Chicken and Vegetables

PREPARATION TIME: 25 minutes

COOKING TIME: 15 minutes

SERVES: 4 people

1lb plaice or lemon sole fillets, cut into
   2 inch pieces
8oz boned chicken, cut into 2 inch
   slices
6 dried Chinese mushrooms, soaked
   and sliced
½ cup button mushrooms, sliced
½ cup bamboo shoots, sliced
½ cup shredded mustard green, kale,
   or broccoli or 4 asparagus tips,
   chopped
1 cup mixed diced vegetables (peas,
   carrots, bean sprouts, etc)
1 small onion, peeled and sliced
1 tsp salt
Cooked oil

Marinade
¼ tsp salt
1 tsp white pepper
½ tsp monosodium glutamate
   (optional)
2 tsp cornstarch
1 tblsp cooked oil
¼ tsp sesame oil

Sauce
1 cup chicken broth
Salt to taste
Freshly ground black pepper to taste
½ tsp monosodium glutamate
   (optional)
2 tsp cooked oil
1 tsp lemon juice

Wash the fish and drain. Mix the marinade ingredients together and marinate fish for 10-15 minutes. Blanch the mustard green, kale or broccoli in boiling, salted water for 1 minute. Drain and keep on one side. Heat the wok with 1 tblsp cooked oil and stir fry the mixed vegetables and the onions for 2 minutes. Add the mustard green and stir fry for 1 minute. Drain and remove onto a plate. Brush a deep plate with cooked oil and arrange the drained fish, mushrooms, chicken and bamboo shoots in alternate rows. Place the dish over a steamer. Cover and steam over boiling water for 7 minutes until cooked. Remove the steamer from heat and keep on one side. Heat the wok and add the sauce ingredients and fish marinade. Bring to the boil and simmer for 1 minute, until thickened. Put the steamed fish, mushrooms etc. onto a serving plate and pour the hot sauce over the top. Serve immediately.

Fish with Vegetables and Bean Curd

PREPARATION TIME: 20 minutes

COOKING TIME: 15 minutes

SERVES: 4 people

4 squares bean curd, cut into 1 inch
   squares

Sauce B
1 tblsp Shao Hsing wine
1¼ tblsp dark soy sauce
1¼ tblsp light soy sauce
2½ tsp brown sugar
Pinch salt
Pinch white pepper
3¾ cups chicken broth

8oz cod fillet, cut into 2 inch slices

Seasoning for Fish A
½ tsp salt
½ tsp Shao Hsing wine
1¾ tblsp cornstarch

3 tblsp salad or olive oil
1½ cups shredded Chinese cabbage,
   or Chinese leaves

Seasoning for Cabbage C
½ tsp brown sugar
Pinch salt

1 tsp cornstarch

1 inch fresh root ginger, peeled and
   shredded
2 green onions, chopped
1½ tblsp cornstarch mixed with 2
   tblsp water
½ cup bean sprouts
Few slices of green pepper, diced
1 small carrot, chopped
2 tblsp frozen peas (or lightly cooked
   fresh ones)

Soak the bean curd in cold water for 2 minutes. Drain well. Mix the sauce B ingredients and keep on one side. Wash the fish and drain well. Mix seasoning A ingredients and marinate fish for 10-12 minutes. Heat the wok and add half the oil. When very hot, add the cabbage and seasoning C ingredients and stir fry for about 2 minutes. Drain the cabbage well. Discard any liquid. Heat wok and add the remaining oil. Add the ginger and onions and stir fry for 1 minute. Add sauce B ingredients and bring to the boil. Add fish and boil for 1 minute. Add the bean curd and simmer over a low heat for 5-6 minutes. (The bean curd should become spongy to the touch). Add the blended

cornstarch and water. Stir and simmer until the sauce thickens. Add the cabbage and other vegetables and simmer for a further 2 minutes. Serve immediately.

Boiled Shrimp

PREPARATION TIME: 5 minutes, plus 10 minutes for the sauce

COOKING TIME: 10-15 minutes

SERVES: 6 people

Sauce
2½ tblsp dark soy sauce
3½ tblsp light soy sauce
½ inch fresh root ginger, peeled and
   shredded
2 green onions, finely chopped
1 red chili, seeded and shredded
4 tblsp cooked oil
2 tsp ketchup

2lbs medium or large uncooked
   shrimps in their shells
Salt

Mix the sauce ingredients together. Wash the shrimps and drain. Place the shrimps into a wire basket and lower into a large pan of boiling, salted water. Boil for 10-12 minutes. Drain. Serve the drained hot shrimps with small bowls of sauce for dipping.

Cantonese Prawns

PREPARATION TIME: 10 minutes

COOKING TIME: 15 minutes

SERVES: 4 people

3 tblsp salad or olive oil
2 cloves garlic, finely crushed
1lb peeled medium shrimps
2 inches root ginger, peeled and finely
   chopped
1 cup uncooked pork or bacon, finely
   chopped

Sauce
1¼ tblsp rice wine or dry sherry
1¼ tblsp light soy sauce
1 tsp fine granulated sugar
1 cup broth or water
1 tblsp cornstarch mixed with 2 tblsp
   broth or water

2-3 green onions, chopped
2 eggs, lightly beaten

Heat 1 tblsp oil in a wok. Add the garlic and fry for 1 minute. Add the shrimp and stir fry for 4-5 minutes. Remove to a dish. Keep warm. Add the remaining oil to the wok and fry the ginger and pork for 3-4 minutes until it loses its color. Add

the mixed sauce ingredients to the wok and cook for 1 minute. Add the onions and cook for 1 minute. Add the beaten eggs and cook for 1-2 minutes, without stirring, until it sets. Spoon the egg mixture over the shrimps. Alternatively, add the shrimps along with the beaten eggs. Allow the eggs to set and then mix gently. Serve at once.

Shrimp and Ginger

PREPARATION TIME: 10 minutes

COOKING TIME: 10 minutes

SERVES: 4-6 people

2 tblsp salad or olive oil
1½lb peeled medium shrimp
1 inch fresh root ginger, peeled and finely chopped
2 cloves garlic, peeled and finely chopped
2-3 green onions, chopped lengthwise into 1 inch pieces
1 leek, white part only, cut into strips.
1 cup shelled peas, lightly cooked
2 cups bean sprouts

Seasoning
2½ tblsp dark soy sauce
1 tsp fine granulated sugar
Pinch monosodium glutamate (optional)
Pinch of salt

Heat the oil in a wok and stir fry the shrimps for 2-3 minutes. Remove the shrimps to a dish. Reheat the oil and add the ginger and garlic and fry for 1 minute. Add the onions and stir fry for 1 minute. Add the leek, peas and beansprouts. Stir fry for 2-3 minutes. Sprinkle over the seasoning ingredients and return the shrimps to the wok. Cover and cook for 2 minutes. Serve immediately.

Shrimp and Cauliflower

PREPARATION TIME: 15 minutes

COOKING TIME: 14-15 minutes

SERVES: 4-6 people

3 tblsp salad or olive oil

Facing page: Fish with Vegetables and Bean Curd (top), Fish in Wine Sauce (center right), Fish with Chicken and Vegetables (bottom). This page: Shrimp and Ginger (top), Boiled Shrimp (center) and Cantonese Prawns (bottom right).

1 clove garlic, peeled and finely
   chopped
1lb medium size shrimps, peeled
10oz cauliflower florets, cut into
   smaller pieces
1 cup water or broth
Salt to taste
1½ cups shelled peas, lightly cooked

Sauce
2 tsp cornstarch
2 tblsp broth or water
Freshly ground black pepper to taste

Heat the oil in a wok and fry the
garlic for 2 minutes. Add the
shrimps and cook for 3 minutes.
Remove the shrimps. Add the
cauliflower and fry for 2-3 minutes,
stirring constantly. Add broth,
cover and simmer for five minutes.
Add salt to taste and the peas and
cook for a further 2-3 minutes.
Return the shrimps to the wok and
stir well. Add the blended sauce
ingredients and gently simmer until
it thickens. Serve immediately.

Snow Peas with Shrimp

PREPARATION TIME: 10 minutes

COOKING TIME: 6-8 minutes

SERVES: 4-6 people

1 tsp cornstarch
1 tsp fine granulated sugar
1 tsp dark soy sauce
1 tblsp water
3 tblsp salad or olive oil
1lb peeled medium size shrimps
1 cup chicken broth
½ tsp salt
1⅓ cups snow peas (mange tout)
¾ cup water chestnuts, sliced
1 small onion, peeled and cut into
   small pieces
1 stem celery, cut into ¼ inch pieces
Pinch monosodium glutamate
   (optional)

Mix together the cornstarch, sugar,
soy sauce and water. Heat the oil in
a wok. Add the shrimps and stir fry
for 2 minutes. Add the broth, salt,
snow peas, water chestnuts, onions
and celery. Cover and cook for 2
minutes. Stir in the monosodium
glutamate. Stir in the cornstarch
mixture and simmer gently until
the sauce thickens. Serve as a side
dish.

Prawns with Cashew Nuts

PREPARATION TIME: 10 minutes

COOKING TIME: 7-8 minutes

SERVES: 4 people

3 tblsp salad or olive oil
¾ cup cashew nuts
2 tsp cornstarch
1 cup chicken broth or water
1 onion, peeled and cut into small
   pieces
⅓ cup sliced green beans
⅔ cup Chinese cabbage, or white
   cabbage, shredded
½ cup bamboo shoots, sliced
1lb peeled medium shrimp
Salt and freshly ground black pepper
   to taste
4 rings pineapple, cut into chunks

Pinch monosodium glutamate
   (optional)

Heat 1 tblsp oil in a wok and stir fry
the cashew nuts until light brown.
Remove the nuts and keep on one
side. Mix the cornstarch with 2
tblsp water or broth and keep on
one side. Reheat the wok with the
remaining oil and fry the onion for
1 minute. Add the beans, cabbage
and bamboo shoots and stir fry for
2-3 minutes. Add the cashew nuts
and shrimps and then add the

remaining broth, salt and pepper,
and the pineapple. Simmer for 1
minute and then add the MSG
and cornstarch mixture and cook
until the sauce thickens. Serve
immediately.

**Shrimp and Cauliflower (top
right), Prawns with Cashew
Nuts (center left) and Snow
Peas with Shrimps (bottom).**

Vegetables

Braised Cauliflower with Chili

PREPARATION TIME: 5 minutes

COOKING TIME: 10 minutes

SERVES: 4 people

4 tblsp salad or olive oil
1 inch fresh root ginger, peeled and thinly sliced
1 small cauliflower, cut into 1 inch florets
2-3 green or red chilies, sliced into quarters and seeded
3 green onions
Salt to taste
1 tsp fine granulated sugar
1¼ cups chicken broth
1½ tsp cornstarch
1½ tblsp water

Heat the wok and add the oil. Stir fry the ginger for 1 minute. Reduce the heat and add the cauliflower and chilies. Stir fry for 3-4 minutes. Add the green onions, season with salt and sprinkle with sugar. Mix for 1 minute and then add the broth. Cover and cook for 2 minutes. Add the blended cornstarch and water and stir over the heat until the sauce has thickened.

Fried Bean Curd with Mushrooms

PREPARATION TIME: 15 minutes

COOKING TIME: 12-15 minutes

SERVES: 4 people

8oz large cap mushrooms, sliced

Seasoning
1 tblsp rice wine or dry sherry
2 tsp fine granulated sugar

4 dried Chinese mushrooms, soaked and sliced
Pinch baking soda
8oz mustard green or spinach, cut into 3 inch pieces
4 squares beancurd (tofu), cubed
Salad or olive oil
1 inch fresh root ginger, peeled and shredded
2 green onions, chopped
½ cup cooked ham, shredded

Sauce

1½ tblsp oyster sauce
1½ tsp dark soy sauce
1½ tblsp cornstarch
6 tblsp broth or water
Freshly ground black pepper

Blanch the fresh mushrooms in water for 1 minute. Drain the mushrooms and discard the water. Mix the seasoning ingredients together and marinate all the mushrooms for 5-6 minutes. Discard marinade. Bring 5 cups of water to the boil and add the baking soda and salt. Blanch the greens for 2 minutes. Drain the greens. Discard water. Sprinkle ½ tsp salt over the beancurd. Deep fry in hot oil until golden brown. Drain and remove. Heat 2 tblsp oil in the wok and stir fry the ginger, onions and ham for 2-3 minutes. Return the mushrooms to the wok and mix with the ginger and onions. Add the blended sauce ingredients and bring to boil. Add the bean curd and simmer until the sauce thickens. Arrange the greens on a dish and pour the sauce over them. Sprinkle with freshly ground black pepper.

Fried Vegetables with Ginger

PREPARATION TIME: 10 minutes

COOKING TIME: 13-15 minutes

SERVES: 6 people

2¼lb mixed Chinese green vegetables (cabbage, spinach, kale, broccoli, Chinese leaf etc.)
½ cup snow peas (mange tout)
1 tsp baking soda
2 tsp fine granulated sugar
1 tsp salt
1 tsp cooked oil
4 tblsp salad or olive oil
1 inch fresh root ginger, peeled and ○ shredded
1 green pepper, seeded and diced
1 green or red chili, sliced into strips

Sauce
2 tsp dark soy sauce
1 tsp fine granulated sugar
1 cup chicken broth
2 tsp cornstarch
1 tsp five spice powder

To Serve

½ tsp sesame oil
Freshly ground black pepper to taste

Cut the green vegetables into 3 inch pieces. Bring a large pan of water to the boil and add the seasoning ingredients. Add the snow peas and greens and cook for 4-5 minutes. Drain green vegetables and discard water. Add 1 tblsp oil to the vegetables and keep covered. Heat the remaining oil in the wok and stir fry the ginger for 1 minute. Add the green pepper and chilies and stir fry for 1-2 minutes. Add the blended sauce ingredients and stir well. Simmer gently for 3-4 minutes. Add the green vegetables and cook for 1 minute. Serve immediately, sprinkled with sesame oil and pepper.

Bamboo Shoots with Green Vegetables

PREPARATION TIME: 10 minutes

COOKING TIME: 10-12 minutes

SERVES: 4 people

Salad or olive oil for cooking
8oz spinach, or chopped broccoli

Seasoning
½ cup chicken broth or water
¼ tsp monosodium glutamate (optional)
¼ tsp salt
¼ tsp fine granulated sugar

1 cup bamboo shoots, sliced

Sauce
1½ tsp light soy sauce
Pinch monosodium glutamate
1½ tsp cornstarch
3 tsp water
1 tblsp cooked oil

Heat 2 tblsp oil in the wok. Fry the spinach for 2 minutes and add the mixed seasoning ingredients.

Fried Vegetables with Ginger (top right), Mustard Green with Crab Sauce (center left) and Fried Bean Curd with Mushrooms (bottom).

2 cups chicken, shredded (cooked or uncooked)

Seasoning
2 tblsp light soy sauce
½ tsp fine granulated sugar
1½ tblsp cornstarch
3 tblsp broth or water

Heat 4 tblsp oil in the wok and stir fry the garlic for 2 minutes. Add the eggplant, which will soak up all the oil. Stir fry for 3-4 minutes, stirring constantly to avoid burning. Add the bean paste, chili powder, and salt to taste and mix well. Add the chicken broth. Cover and cook for 4-6 minutes, simmering gently. Remove the eggplant and arrange on a dish. Save the sauce. Clean the wok and heat the remaining oil. Stir fry the ginger for 1 minute. Add the onions and chicken and stir fry for 2 minutes. Add the blended seasoning ingredients and the reserved eggplant sauce and simmer gently until it thickens. Pour over the eggplant and serve immediately.

Szechuan Eggplant

PREPARATION TIME: 15 minutes
COOKING TIME: 18-20 minutes
SERVES: 3-4 people

Salad or olive oil
1 large eggplant, cut into strips 2 inches long and ½ inch thick
3 cloves garlic, peeled and finely sliced
1 inch fresh root ginger, peeled and shredded
1 onion, peeled and finely chopped
2 green onions, chopped
1 cup cooked and shredded chicken
1 red or green chili, cut into strips

Seasoning
1 cup chicken broth
1 tsp fine granulated sugar
1½ tsp wine-flavored vinegar
½ tsp salt
½ tsp freshly ground black pepper

Sauce
1½ tsp cornstarch
1½ tblsp water
1 tsp sesame oil

Heat the wok and add 3 tblsp oil. Add the eggplant and stir fry for 4-5 minutes. The eggplant absorbs a lot of oil; keep stirring or else it will burn. Remove from wok and keep on one side. Heat the wok and add

Simmer for 1 minute and remove from the wok onto a dish. Heat the wok and add 1 tblsp oil. Add the bamboo shoots and fry for 1-2 minutes. Return the spinach mixture to the wok. Cook for 3 minutes. Mix together the ingredients for thickening the sauce. Add to the wok and cook for 1-2 minutes. Serve with roast Peking duck, or as a side dish.

Braised Eggplant and Chicken with Chili

PREPARATION TIME: 10 minutes
COOKING TIME: about 15 minutes
SERVES: 4 people

⅓ cup salad or olive oil
2 cloves of garlic, peeled and sliced

1lb eggplant, cut into 2x2½ inch pieces
1 tblsp soy bean paste (or canned red kidney beans, made into paste)
½ tsp ground dry chili or chili powder
Salt
1¾ cups chicken broth
1 inch fresh root ginger, peeled and sliced
2-3 green onions, chopped

2 tblsp oil. Add the garlic and ginger and fry for 1 minute. Add the onions and fry for 2 minutes. Add the chicken and chili. Cook for 1 minute. Return the eggplant to the wok. Add the blended seasoning ingredients and simmer for 6-7 minutes. Stir in the blended sauce ingredients and simmer until the sauce thickens. Serve with extra sesame oil if desired. This dish goes well with Yung Chow fried rice or rice supreme.

Lettuce and Bean Sprouts with Soy Sauce

PREPARATION TIME: 15 minutes

COOKING TIME: 5 minutes

SERVES: 4 people

1½ cups bean sprouts (moong or soya)
8oz lettuce
1 tblsp salad or olive oil
1 inch fresh root ginger, peeled and shredded

1 green or red chili, seeded and split in half
Salt and freshly ground black pepper

Sauce
3 tblsp light soy sauce
2 tsp dark soy sauce
1½ tblsp medium white wine or rice wine
½ tsp fine granulated sugar
Salt and freshly ground black pepper to taste
½ tsp sesame oil

Trim the bean sprouts by pinching off the grey and brown ends, as they impart a bitter taste to the dish. Pick off bean seed skin if using soya beans. Cut soya bean sprouts in 2-3 pieces. Rinse in cold water and drain. Wash and drain lettuce before shredding into 2 inch pieces. Heat the oil in the wok and stir fry the ginger and chili for 1 minute. Add the lettuce and toss for 1 minute. Drain and remove on to a plate. Place the bean sprouts in a colander and pour boiling water over them. Drain throughly and add to the lettuce. Sprinkle with salt and pepper and keep covered.

Mix the sauce ingredients together in the wok. Stir over the heat until blended. Pour this sauce over the vegetables and serve immediately.

Sweet and Sour Cabbage

PREPARATION TIME: 10 minutes

COOKING TIME: 10 minutes

SERVES: 4 people

1lb white cabbage, shredded
½ tsp baking soda
1 tsp salt
2 tsp fine granulated sugar
1 tblsp salad or olive oil

Sauce
2½ tblsp fine granulated sugar
2½ tblsp wine-flavored vinegar
1 cup chicken broth or water
Pinch salt
1¼ tblsp) cornstarch
Few drops red food coloring
1 tsp ketchup

Boil the cabbage in a large pan of water with the baking soda, salt, and sugar for 2-3 minutes. Drain the cabbage and discard the boiling water. Keep the cabbage in cold water for 5 minutes. Drain and keep on one side. Heat the wok and add the oil. Fry the cabbage until it is heated through. Remove onto a serving dish. Add the well-stirred sauce ingredients to the wok and gently bring to the boil, stirring. Stir over the heat until the sauce thickens. Pour over the cabbage and serve immediately.

Facing page: Bamboo Shoots with Green Vegetables (top right), Sweet and Sour Cabbage (center left), Szechuan Eggplant (bottom).

This page: Lettuce and Bean Sprouts with Soy Sauce (left), Braised Eggplant and Chicken with Chili (center) and Braised Cauliflower with Chili (right).

Egg Dishes and Curry

Lamb Curry

PREPARATION TIME: 15 minutes
COOKING TIME: 50 minutes
SERVES: 4 people

2 tblsp salad or olive oil
1 onion, peeled and chopped
1 inch fresh root ginger, peeled and
  chopped
2 cloves of garlic, chopped
1lb lean, boned lamb, cut into cubes
1-2 carrots, scraped and sliced
1 tsp five spice mixture
Salt to taste
2 chilies, chopped
2 tblsp ketchup
2½ tblsp cornstarch
1 green pepper, seeded and chopped

Heat the oil and fry the onion for 2 minutes. Add the ginger and garlic and fry for 1 minute. Add the lamb and carrots and stir fry for 3-4 minutes. Sprinkle over the five spice powder and add the salt, chilies and ketchup. Stir in 1¼ cups water. Cover and simmer for 30-35 minutes. Mix 2 tblsp water with the cornstarch and add to the curry. Add the green pepper and simmer for 5 minutes. Serve with rice.

Prawn Curry

PREPARATION TIME: 10 minutes
COOKING TIME: 8 minutes
SERVES: 4 people

2 tblsp salad or olive oil
1 onion, peeled and chopped
1 carrot, cut into strips
1 cup snow peas (mange-tout)
1 inch fresh root ginger, peeled and
  chopped
2 cloves garlic, chopped
1lb large shrimps, peeled and de-
  veined
2 tsp curry powder
Salt to taste
2 green chilies, sliced
2 tblsp cornstarch

Heat the oil and fry the onion for 2 minutes. Add the carrot and snow peas and fry for 2 minutes. Add the ginger, garlic and shrimp and stir fry for 1-2 minutes. Sprinkle over the curry powder and add the salt, green chilies, and 1¼ cups water. Mix the cornstarch with 1 tblsp water and add to the curry. Cook gently until the curry thickens. Serve with rice.

Chicken Curry

PREPARATION TIME: 15 minutes
COOKING TIME: 40 minutes
SERVES: 4-6 people

2 tblsp salad or olive oil
1 onion, peeled and chopped
2 cloves of garlic, peeled and chopped
1 inch fresh root ginger, peeled and
  finely chopped
3lb chicken, boned and cut into small
  pieces
3 tsp curry powder
1½ tsp chili powder
½ tsp salt
⅔ cup mixed frozen vegetables
1 green pepper, seeded and chopped
3 tsp cornstarch

Heat the oil and fry the onion for 2 minutes. Add the garlic, ginger and chicken and fry gently for 5 minutes. Add the curry powder, chili powder, salt and 1¾-2 cups of water. Cover and cook gently until the chicken is tender. Add the mixed vegetables and green pepper and cook for 3-4 minutes. Add the cornstarch, dissolved in 2 tblsp water, and simmer until the sauce thickens. Serve with plain boiled rice.

Shrimp Fu Yung

PREPARATION TIME: 10 minutes
COOKING TIME: 4 minutes for filling; 3-4 minutes for each pancake
SERVES: 6 people

Salad or olive oil
1-2 cloves of garlic, chopped
1 cup small shrimps, peeled
1 cup green beans, sliced
1 carrot, shredded
6 eggs

Sauce
Salt and freshly ground black pepper
  to taste
1 cup chicken broth
¼ tsp salt
3 tsp soy sauce
1 tsp fine granulated sugar
1 tsp vinegar
1½ tsp cornstarch

Heat 2 tblsp oil in a wok. Add the garlic and stir fry for 1 minute. Add the shrimps and stir fry for 1 minute. Add the beans and carrot and stir fry for 2 minutes. Remove and keep on one side. Beat the eggs with salt and pepper to taste, and add the cooled shrimp mixture. Clean the wok and heat 1 tsp oil. Pour in 5 tblsp of the egg mixture and cook like a pancake. When the egg is set, turn the pancake over and cook on the other side until lightly golden. Place on a warm platter and keep warm.

To Make the Sauce
Beat the broth with the other sauce ingredients and stir over a gentle heat until the sauce thickens. Serve the pancakes with this sauce.

Egg Fu Yung

PREPARATION TIME: 5 minutes
COOKING TIME: 8-10 minutes
SERVES: 3-4 people

6 eggs
1½ tblsp soy sauce
3-4 green onions, chopped
Salt and freshly ground black pepper
  to taste
3 tblsp oil
1½ cups bean sprouts

Beat the eggs and soy sauce together and add the green onions and salt and pepper to taste. Heat the oil in a skillet or wok and stir fry the bean sprouts for 2-3 minutes. Pour in the beaten egg mixture. Leave over a moderate heat to set. Broil to set and brown the top. Cut into wedges and serve immediately. Alternatively, stir the mixture while it is cooking so that it turns out like scrambled egg.

Prawns in Egg Custard

PREPARATION TIME: 5 minutes
COOKING TIME: 20 minutes
SERVES: 6 people

8 eggs
Salt and freshly ground black pepper
  to taste
Pinch monosodium glutamate
  (optional)
1 tsp Shao Hsing wine
1¼ cups chicken broth
1¼ cups water
1lb large shrimps, peeled and de-
  veined
2 tsp cooked oil

Beat the eggs in a bowl, add the seasoning, MSG and wine. Bring the broth and water to the boil and add to the eggs. Add shrimps and set the bowl over a steamer. Cover and steam over simmering water for about 15-20 minutes, until the custard has set. Serve with the cooked oil spooned over the top.

Stir Fried Eggs with Shredded Meats and Vegetables

PREPARATION TIME: 15-20 minutes
COOKING TIME: 15 minutes
SERVES: 4 people

½ cup cooked chicken, shredded
¾ cup cooked pork or beef, shredded
Salt to taste
¼ tsp soy sauce
4 tblsp salad or olive oil
4 eggs, beaten
2 green onions, chopped
⅓ cup dried mushrooms, soaked and
  sliced
⅓ button mushrooms, sliced
2 cloud ear fungus, boiled in water
  for 3 minutes and thinly sliced
2 cups Chinese white cabbage,
  broccoli or green leafy cabbage,
  shredded
1-2 green or red chilies, chopped
2 sprigs Chinese parsley, chopped
Pinch monosodium glutamate
  (optional)

Put the chicken and pork into a bowl with ¼ tsp salt and the soy sauce. Leave for 10 minutes. Heat the wok and add 2 tblsp oil. Add the beaten eggs and stir fry for 2-3 minutes until they resemble scrambled egg. Keep on one side. Reheat the wok and add the remaining oil. Fry the onions and meats for 2 minutes. Remove from the wok and keep on one side. Stir fry the cabbage and chilies in the wok for 1-2 minutes. Cover and gently cook in its own juice until tender – approx 3-4 minutes. Return the meats, mushrooms and egg to the cabbage and add the parsley and MSG. Stir fry for 1-2 minutes. Serve with extra soy sauce and Shao Hsing wine sprinkled over it, if desired.

Lamb Curry (right), Prawn Curry (below) and Chicken Curry (bottom).

Marbled Eggs

PREPARATION TIME: 10 minutes

COOKING TIME: 1 hour
10 minutes to 1 hour 15 minutes

MAKES: 6-8

These are eaten cold, dipped in a sauce, as a starter or a snack. Allow 1 egg per person.

6-8 eggs
4 tblsp tea leaves
1 inch cinnamon stick
2-3 star anise
3 tblsp dark soy sauce
2 tblsp light soy sauce

Boil the eggs for 8-10 minutes until hard boiled. Drain and cool quickly by placing in iced water. Tap each egg shell with the back of a spoon until cracks appear all over. Bring enough water to the boil to cover the eggs. Add tea leaves, cinnamon, star anise, soy sauces and stir. Add the eggs and simmer gently for at least 1 hour. Allow to cool and then shell before serving.

Egg Pancakes with Filling

PREPARATION TIME: 10 minutes

COOKING TIME: 6-7 minutes for each pancake

SERVES: 4-6 people

6 eggs
Salt and freshly ground black pepper to taste
1 cup lean pork, finely chopped or ground
½ cup small cap mushrooms, chopped
1 tsp rice wine or dry sherry
1 tsp light soy sauce
½ tsp fine granulated sugar
1 tsp fresh root ginger, minced
Oil

Beat the eggs and season with salt and pepper. Mix the pork with the mushrooms, wine, soy sauce, sugar and ginger. Add salt and pepper to taste and mix well. Heat the wok and add 1 tsp oil. Spoon in 3 tblsp of the beaten egg and spread into a 3 inch circle. Place 3 tsp filling into the center of the egg. When the underside of the egg sets but the top is still moist, fold the egg circle over to make a crescent shape; press gently to seal the edges. Cook for 4 minutes on a low heat to cook the filling. Make the remaining pancakes in the same way. Serve with a chili sauce or dip, or with stir fried vegetables as a main dish.

Noodles with Pork Fu Yung

PREPARATION TIME: 20 minutes

COOKING TIME: about 20 minutes

SERVES: 4 people

½ tsp baking soda
1 tblsp water
8oz lean pork, thinly sliced
8oz cake noodles
2 tsp cornstarch
Few drops sesame oil
Salt and freshly ground black pepper
to taste
½ tsp fine granulated sugar
Salad or olive oil
2 cloves of garlic, finely chopped
1 inch fresh root ginger, peeled and sliced
2-3 green onions, chopped
6 eggs, well beaten

Mix the baking soda and the water together. Mix in the pork and marinate for 10-12 minutes. Drain. Cook the noodles in boiling, salted water for 3-4 minutes. Drain, rinse in cold water and drain once again. Toss in 1 tblsp oil. Heat 2 tblsp oil in the wok and brown the garlic. Add 1 tsp salt and the noodles and stir fry for 3-4 minutes, until they turn light brown. Remove and keep on one side. Heat sufficient oil for deep frying in the wok and deep fry the pork for 3-4 minutes, drain and remove. Tip off the oil. Heat 1 tblsp oil in the wok. Add the ginger and onions and stir fry for 1-2 minutes. Add the pork and then pour in the beaten eggs, mixing well. Add the cornstarch, sesame oil and sugar and cook until the mixture thickens. Pour over the noodles and serve immediately.

This page: Marbled Eggs (top), Noodles with Pork Fu Yung (center right) and Stir Fried Eggs with Shredded Meats and Vegetables (bottom left).

Facing page: Prawns in Egg Custard (top left), Egg Pancakes with Filling (top right), Shrimp Fu Yung (center left) and Egg Fu Yung (bottom right).

Rice and Noodles

Rice with Ground Beef

PREPARATION TIME: 10 minutes

COOKING TIME: 25 minutes

SERVES: 6 people

2 tblsp salad or olive oil
8oz ground beef
3 green onions, chopped
½ inch fresh root ginger, peeled and
* sliced*
2 cloves garlic, peeled and sliced
1½ tblsp soy sauce
1 green pepper, seeded and chopped
1lb rice, thoroughly washed
½ tsp salt
1 tsp freshly ground black pepper, or to
* taste*

Heat the oil and fry the ground
beef, onions, ginger and garlic for 5
minutes. Add the soy sauce and
green pepper and fry for 5-6
minutes. Cook the rice with
sufficient water to come 1 inch
above the rice level, and the salt,
for 5-6 minutes or until the rice is
semi-cooked, and the water is
almost absorbed. Spread the beef
evenly over the rice. Cover and
cook for 6-8 minutes over a very
gentle heat. Remove and serve well
mixed. Season with salt and pepper
to taste.

Assorted Meat Congee

PREPARATION TIME: 20 minutes

COOKING TIME: 1 hour
                          45 minutes

SERVES: 6 people

1lb rice
9½ cups chicken broth
4oz tripe, well washed and chopped
* (optional)*
4oz pig's or lamb's liver, sliced
1 cup cooked beef, ham, lamb,
* chicken or pork, chopped*
4oz white fish fillets, thinly sliced
1 tsp sesame oil
3 green onions, chopped
1½ tsp salt, or to taste
1½ tsp freshly ground black pepper
½ inch fresh root ginger, peeled and
* sliced*

Wash the rice well and put it into a
large saucepan. Add the chicken

broth and the tripe (if used). Cook
gently for 1-1½ hours, or until the
tripe is well cooked and the rice has
become a soft pulp. In a separate
saucepan, boil the sliced liver for 5
minutes in water. Drain and add to
the rice. Add the cooked meat,
fish, sesame oil, half the onions, salt
and pepper and the slices of ginger.
Cook for further 10-15 minutes
covered. Pour into large bowls and
serve topped with the remaining
chopped onions.

Rice Supreme

PREPARATION TIME: 10 minutes

COOKING TIME: 15 minutes

SERVES: 6 people

3 tblsp salad or olive oil
1½ tblsp) light soy sauce
2 eggs, beaten
1 small onion, peeled and finely sliced
½ cup small shrimps, peeled
½ cup large shrimps, peeled

½ cup white fish, cubed
2 green onions, finely chopped
½ a small green pepper, seeded and
* cut into strips*
1lb rice, cooked and cooled
Salt to taste
1 tsp freshly ground black pepper
3 tblsp ketchup
½ cup frozen peas

Heat 1 tblsp oil in the wok and
pour in the beaten eggs. Cook to
make a thin omelette. Cut into
thin strips. Heat 1 tblsp oil in the
wok and stir fry the onion for 2
minutes. Add the shrimps and fish
and stir fry for 3-4 minutes.
Remove the fish mixture to a plate.
Heat the remaining oil in the wok.
Add half the green onions and the
green pepper and stir fry for 2
minutes. Add the rice and season
with salt and pepper. Add the
ketchup, peas, fried fish and
shrimps. Add the soy sauce and stir
fry for 3 minutes. Serve with the
egg strips arranged on top of the
rice. Sprinkle with the remaining
chopped green onions.

Vegetable Rice

PREPARATION TIME: 10 minutes

COOKING TIME: 5-8 minutes

SERVES: 6-8 people

1lb rice, cooked
2 cups Chinese cabbage, or Chinese
* leaves, shredded*
1 cup sliced green beans
¾ cup frozen peas
3 green onions, chopped
1½ tblsp light soy sauce
Salt to taste

Rinse the cooked rice in cold water
and drain. Put the moist rice into a
pan. Arrange the Chinese cabbage,
sliced beans, peas and onions on
top. Cover and cook over a gentle
heat for 4-6 minutes. Sprinkle with
soy sauce and add salt to taste. Stir
the vegetables evenly into the rice'
and raise the heat for a few
seconds. Serve immediately.

Plain Fried Rice

PREPARATION TIME: 5 minutes,
plus cooling time

COOKING TIME: 10-11 minutes

SERVES: 4-6 people

1lb Patna or long grain rice
¼ tsp monosodium glutamate
2 tblsp salad or olive oil
Salt

Wash the rice in 4-5 changes of
cold water. Drain the rice and put
into a large pan or wok. Add
sufficient cold water to come 1 inch
above the level of the rice. Bring to
the boil. Stir once and reduce the
heat to simmer. Cover and cook
gently for 5-7 minutes until the
water has been totally absorbed
and the rice is separate and fluffy,

**This page: Vegetable Rice
(top), Assorted Meat Congee
(center right) and Rice
Supreme (bottom).**

**Facing page: Yang Chow Fried
Rice (top), Plain Fried Rice
(center left) and Rice with
Ground Beef (bottom).**

with the necessary amount of stickiness to be handled by chopsticks. (If necessary cook for a little longer.) Spread the rice out on a tray and cool. Sprinkle with the monosodium glutamate. Heat the oil in a wok or large skillet and add the rice. Stir fry for 1-2 minutes. Add salt to taste and stir fry for a further 1-2 minutes.

Yang Chow Fried Rice

PREPARATION TIME: 10 minutes
COOKING TIME: 6-8 minutes
SERVES: 6 people

3 tblsp salad or olive oil
1 egg, beaten
1 cup cooked meat, chopped (pork, lamb, beef)
1 cup medium shrimps, shelled and chopped
½ cup shelled green peas, lightly cooked
2 green onions, chopped
1lb dry, cooked rice
Salt to taste
1 tsp monosodium glutamate (optional)

Heat 1 tblsp oil in a wok. Fry the beaten egg until set, and break into small lumps. Remove the egg. Add the remaining oil and fry the meat, shrimps, peas and onions for 1-2 minutes. Add the cooked rice and sprinkle with salt and monosodium glutamate. Fry for 3 minutes. Mix in the cooked egg and serve immediately.

Sizzling Rice or Singing Rice

PREPARATION TIME: 50 minutes
COOKING TIME: 2 hours, plus time for deep frying sizzling rice

4oz short grain rice

When rice is cooked, the crust that forms on the bottom of the pot can be dried and then deep fried. When it is immersed in gravy or soup it makes a sizzling noise, hence the name. Once made or collected, the rice crusts can be kept for months.

To Make a Rice Crust

Wash rice in 4-5 changes of water until the water runs clear. Drain the rice and put it into a pan with 1¼ cups of water; bring to the boil. Reduce heat to low and cook for 20 minutes, simmering gently. Turn off the heat and let the rice stand, covered, for 25-30 minutes. Take a non-stick skillet and transfer the rice to it. Spread evenly to a thickness of ½ inch. Cook on a very gentle heat for 40-50 minutes. Turn over and cook gently for another hour. The rice should be very dry. Break into 2 inch squares and store in a glass jar with a lid.

To Cook Sizzling Rice

Pour oil into a pan to a depth of 2 inches and bring to a moderately high temperature (375°F). Add the rice squares and fry until golden brown. Remove and drain on kitchen paper. Serve with soup or any stir fried dish.

Shrimp Egg Rice

PREPARATION TIME: 20 minutes
COOKING TIME: 17-18 minutes
SERVES: 4-6 people

1lb long or medium grain rice
2 eggs
½ tsp salt
4 tblsp oil
2 green onions, chopped
1 large onion, peeled and chopped
2 cloves garlic, peeled and chopped
1 cup small peeled shrimps
½ cup shelled peas, lightly cooked
2 tblsp dark soy sauce

To Cook the Rice

Wash rice in 4-5 changes of water. Add cold water to come 1 inch above the rice level and bring to the boil. Stir once and reduce the heat to simmer. Cover the pan and gently cook the rice for 5-7 minutes until the rice is dry and the liquid has been totally absorbed. Remove from the heat, add cold water to cover and drain throughly. Spread the rice on a large tray and separate the grains with a fork.

Beat the eggs in a bowl and season with a pinch of salt. Heat the wok and add 1 tblsp oil. Add the onions and stir fry for 2 minutes. Add the beaten eggs. Allow to set slightly and then stir the mixture until it scrambles. Remove onto a plate. Heat the wok and add 1 tblsp oil. Fry the garlic for 1 minute then add the shrimps and cook for 2 minutes. Add the peas, and stir fry for 1 minute. Remove onto a plate.

Heat the wok and add the remaining oil, a little salt to taste and the cooked rice. Stir fry to heat the rice through. Stir in the soy sauce, shrimp mixture and the cooked eggs, gently stirring the mixture to blend. Serve immediately.

Shrimp Egg Rice (below), Sizzling Rice or Singing Rice (bottom left) and Plain Rice (bottom right).

Plain Rice

PREPARATION TIME: 5 minutes	
COOKING TIME: 5-7 minutes	
SERVES: 4-6 people	

1lb rice
Pinch salt
2 tsp salad or olive oil

To make a bowl of plain rice, take any grade of long or medium grain rice. Wash the rice in 4-5 changes of water and then add enough cold water to come 1 inch above the rice level. Add the salt and oil and bring to the boil. Stir once. Cover and simmer gently for 5-7 minutes until the water has been totally absorbed. Remove from the heat and serve. Plain boiled rice should be fluffy, yet have enough moisture around the rice so that the grains can be picked up easily by chopsticks.

Noodles in Soup

PREPARATION TIME: 10 minutes	
COOKING TIME: 6-8 minutes	
SERVES: 4-6 people	

1lb small rounds of cake noodles
Salt
5½ cups chicken or beef broth
1 cup cooked shredded chicken
2 eggs, hard boiled and sliced
1⅓ cups Chinese napa cabbage, or
   iceberg lettuce, finely shredded
2 green onions, thinly sliced

½ cup bamboo shoots, sliced
2 sticks celery, chopped
1 leek, chopped
2 green onions, shredded
4 tblsp broth
3 tblsp soy sauce

Soak the rice noodles in warm water for 10-15 minutes. Drain thoroughly. Heat half the oil in a wok. Add the chicken, shrimps, bamboo shoots, celery, leeks and green onions and stir fry for 2-3 minutes. Add the broth and salt and pepper to taste. Simmer for 2 minutes and then drain the chicken and vegetables. Heat the remaining oil, add the rice noodles and stir over the heat for 1 minute. Add the soy sauce and stir into the chicken and vegetable mixture. Cook together for 2-3 minutes. Serve immediately.

Meat and Prawn Chow Mein

PREPARATION TIME: 20 minutes
COOKING TIME: 12-15 minutes
SERVES: 4-6 people

1lb dried Chinese noodles, or broken spaghetti
Salt to taste
4 tblsp salad or olive oil
2-3 green onions, chopped
1 cup cooked ham, shredded
1 cup large shrimps, peeled and de-veined
1 cup shredded carrots
1 cup green beans, sliced
1 tsp fine granulated sugar
1½ tblsp rice wine or dry sherry
1 cup cooked chicken, shredded
1½ cups bean sprouts
3½ tblsp soy sauce

Cook the noodles in boiling, salted water for 4-5 minutes. Rinse under cold water and drain thoroughly. Toss in 1 tblsp oil. Heat the remaining oil in a wok. Add the onions, ham, prawns, carrots and green beans and stir fry for 2-3 minutes. Add the salt, sugar, wine, chicken and bean sprouts. Cook for 2 minutes. Add the cooked noodles and soy sauce. Cook for 1-2 minutes. Serve immediately.

This page: Deep Fried Noodles (top), Stir Fried Shanghai Noodles (center), Fried Rice Noodles (bottom). Facing page: Meat and Prawn Chow Mein (top), Noodles in Soup (center), Rice Noodles Singapore Style (bottom).

Cook the noodles in boiling, salted water for 5 minutes. Drain thoroughly. Heat the broth and add salt to taste. Serve the cooked noodles in bowls, and pour over the hot broth. Garnish with chicken, sliced eggs, cabbage and green onions.

Stir Fried Shanghai Noodles

PREPARATION TIME: 10 minutes
COOKING TIME: 5-6 minutes
SERVES: 4 people

1½ cups white cabbage, shredded
½ tsp sesame oil

3 tblsp cooked oil
1 cup cooked chicken or pork, shredded
1lb thick Shanghai noodles, cooked until just tender
2½ tblsp) soy sauce
½ tsp monosodium glutamate (optional)
Freshly ground black pepper to taste

Cook the cabbage in boiling water for 1 minute. Drain thoroughly. Heat the oils in a wok. Add the meat and stir fry for 2-3 minutes. Add the cooked noodles, soy sauce, monosodium glutamate and salt and pepper to taste. Add the cabbage, heat through and serve immediately.

Deep Fried Noodles

Boil noodles for 5 minutes. Drain thoroughly on absorbent paper. Deep fry in hot oil until crisp and golden.

Fried Rice Noodles

PREPARATION TIME: 25 minutes
COOKING TIME: 10 minutes
SERVES: 4-6 people

1lb rice noodles
3 tblsp salad or olive oil
1 cup cooked chicken, shredded
½ cup small shrimps, peeled and de-veined

Rice Noodles Singapore Style

PREPARATION TIME: 15 minutes, plus soaking time for noodles

COOKING TIME: about 15 minutes

SERVES: 4-6 people

8oz rice noodles
Salad or olive oil
2 eggs, beaten
½ inch fresh root ginger, peeled and shredded
1½ cups bean sprouts
1 cup cooked ham, pork or chicken, shredded
3 tblsp chives, finely chopped
2 cloves garlic, finely chopped
Salt to taste
2 tblsp chicken broth
3 tblsp soy sauce
3 green onions, chopped

Soak the rice noodles in warm water for 10 minutes and then drain well. Heat 1 tblsp oil in a skillet or wok and fry the beaten eggs to make a thin pancake. Slide onto a plate and cut into thin strips. Heat the wok or skillet and add 1 tblsp oil. Fry the ginger and bean sprouts for 2 minutes. Slide onto a plate. Heat the wok or skillet with a further 1 tblsp oil and fry the pork or chicken and the chives for 1-2 minutes. Slide onto a plate. Heat 2 tblsp oil in the wok or skillet and brown the garlic. Add the rice noodles and stir fry for 2-3 minutes. Add salt to taste, chicken broth, bean sprouts and pork or chicken. Mix well, sprinkle with soy sauce and stir over the heat for 1 minute. Top with the strips of egg pancake and spring onions and serve immediately.

Noodles with Beef and Almonds

PREPARATION TIME: 15 minutes

COOKING TIME: 10 minutes

SERVES: 4 people

3 tblsp salad or olive oil
1 onion, chopped
4 cloves of garlic, chopped
1 inch fresh root ginger, peeled and sliced
8oz lean beef, thinly sliced
½ cup carrots, diced
½ cup sliced green beans
½ cup water chestnuts, sliced
½ cup mushrooms, sliced
2 green chilies, sliced in half

Salt
1 tsp fine granulated sugar
1 tsp monosodium glutamate (optional)
1 cup chicken broth
⅔ cup blanched almonds
1lb noodles, cooked until just tender

Heat 2 tblsp oil in a wok. Fry the onion, garlic, ginger and beef for 3 minutes. Add the carrots and green beans and fry for 2 minutes. Add the water chestnuts, mushrooms and green chilies and fry for 1 minute. Add salt, sugar, MSG and broth. Simmer for 1 minute. Remove to a dish and keep warm. Clean the wok and add the remaining oil. Fry the almonds and noodles for 1-2 minutes. Mix with the cooked vegetables and season with soy sauce. Serve immediately.

Egg Noodles with Meat Sauce

PREPARATION TIME: 15 minutes

COOKING TIME: 20-22 minutes

SERVES: 4-6 people

3 tblsp salad or olive oil
3 cloves garlic, chopped
1 inch fresh root ginger, peeled and shredded
1 onion, chopped
1 green pepper, seeded and sliced
1lb ground beef
½ tsp salt
1 tblsp ketchup
1 tblsp soy sauce
½ tsp freshly ground black pepper
½ cup chicken broth
1 tsp cornstarch
1lb egg noodles
2 green onions, chopped

Heat 2 tblsp oil in a wok. Fry the garlic and ginger for 1-2 minutes. Add the onion and fry for 2-3 minutes. Add the green pepper and the ground beef and fry for 1 minute. Add half the salt, ketchup, soy sauce and ground pepper. Fry for a further 3 minutes. Blend the broth and cornstarch and add to the wok. Cook until thickened and the meat is tender. Meanwhile, cook noodles in boiling, salted water for 3-4 minutes, and drain. Rinse in cold water and drain once again. Heat the remaining oil in a

pan. Add the noodles and toss over the heat until heated through. Arrange on a plate and top with the meat sauce. Garnish with chopped green onions.

Fried Noodles with Shredded Chicken

PREPARATION TIME: 15 minutes

COOKING TIME: about 10 minutes

SERVES: 4 people

Salad or olive oil
2 cups cooked chicken, shredded
1 clove of garlic, chopped
2-3 green onions, chopped
4oz whole green beans (or long Chinese beans, cut into 3 inch pieces)
1lb noodles, cooked until just tender
1½ tblsp cornstarch
1 cup chicken broth
2 tblsp soy sauce
2 tblsp oyster sauce
½ tsp wine
½ tsp fine granulated sugar
¼ tsp salt

Heat 2 tblsp oil in a wok and cook the chicken for 2 minutes. Remove the chicken. Add the garlic, green onions and beans and fry for 2 minutes. Remove the vegetables. Heat 2 tblsp oil in the wok and toss the pre-boiled noodles over the heat for 2 minutes. Arrange on a plate and keep warm. Return the fried chicken, onion and green beans to the wok and stir fry for 1 minute. Dissolve the cornstarch in the chicken broth and add to the wok. Add the soy sauce, oyster sauce, wine, sugar and salt and pepper to taste. Simmer until the sauce is thick. Pour over the bed of noodles and serve immediately.

This page: Noodles with Beef and Almonds (top), Egg Noodles with Meat Sauce (center) and Fried Noodles with Shredded Chicken (bottom).

Facing page: Chinese Bean Buns (top), Red Bean Filled Dim Sums (center right) and Candied Apples (bottom).

Sweets

again for 2 minutes and then divide the dough into 12-14 portions. Flatten into thick, circular shapes 4 inches in diameter. Place a chopstick on each circle of dough to mark it in half, and then in half again. Cut along the marks to within ⅓ of the center. Place one portion of filling in the center of the dough circle and fold the cut ends in to meet in the center, to form a rosette. Secure by pinching ends of dough together. Place a piece of greased foil over the pinched ends and place the buns on a greased baking tray. Brush with a little milk. Bake at 375°F for 20-25 minutes.

Red Bean Filled Dim Sums

PREPARATION TIME: 45-50 minutes

COOKING TIME: 10-12 minutes

MAKES: about 24

¼ cup fine granulated sugar
1¼ cups warm water
1¼ tblsp dry yeast
3¾ cups all-purpose flour
2 tblsp melted shortening
1 egg white, beaten

Filling
¾-1 cup sweet bean paste
Red food coloring

Dissolve the sugar in the warm water and add the yeast. Stir until dissolved. Leave in a warm place until frothy. Sift the flour into a mixing bowl and add the melted shortening and the yeast mixture. Mix together. Turn the mixture onto a floured surface and knead to a smooth and elastic dough. Roll into a long sausage and divide into 24 equal portions. Roll each portion into a 2 inch flat circle. Brush edges of dough with beaten egg white. Place 1 tblsp of filling into the center of each circle and pull the dough around it to enclose the filling. Pleat the open edges in a circular fashion, so that a small opening is left in the middle of the pleating. Place a small piece of greased foil over the pleats on each dim sum. Leave for 10-12 minutes until the dough becomes springy to

Chinese Bean Buns

PREPARATION TIME: about 2 hours, including proving time

COOKING TIME: about 30 minutes

MAKES: about 14

¼ cup milk
⅓ cup fine granulated sugar
½ tsp salt
1½ tblsp shortening
¼ cup warm water
2 tsp dry yeast
1 egg, beaten

2¼ cups all-purpose flour

Bring the milk almost to the boil. Stir in the sugar, salt and shortening. Cool slightly. Put the warm water and yeast into a bowl and stir to mix. Add the lukewarm milk mixture. Add the beaten egg and 1 cup of the flour and beat until smooth. Add the remaining flour and mix to a dough. Turn dough out on to a well-floured board and knead until smooth and elastic. Place in a greased bowl. Brush the dough with oil and

cover. Leave to rise in a warm place until doubled in size (about 1 hour).

Filling
⅓ cup sweet bean paste
2 tblsp fine granulated sugar
2 tblsp chopped walnuts
1 tblsp shortening

Heat the filling ingredients together in a wok for 5-6 minutes until smooth and shiny. Remove and cool. Divide the filling into 12-14 portions. Knead the risen dough

Below: Stuffed Lychees (left), Sweet Almond Pudding (center) and Agar-Agar Pudding (right).

the touch. Put a dab of red food coloring on each dim sum. Arrange the dim sums in a bamboo steaming basket and steam over boiling water for 10-12 minutes. The dim sums are ready when they are dry and smooth. Alternatively they can be baked at 350°F for about 20 minutes.

Agar-Agar Pudding

PREPARATION TIME: 5 minutes

COOKING TIME: 4-5 minutes

SERVES: 4 people

2½ cups milk
½ cup fine granulated sugar
2 tblsp ground almonds
4 tblsp agar-agar (also called Chinese grass)
2 tblsp blanched and chopped almonds

Mix the milk, sugar and ground almonds together in a pan and stir over the heat for 4 minutes. Add the agar-agar and stir until dissolved. Stir in the chopped almonds. Pour into a shallow dish 1 inch deep. Cool and keep in refrigerator until set. Serve chilled, cut into diamond or square shapes.

Almond Cookies

PREPARATION TIME: 20 minutes

COOKING TIME: 12-15 minutes

MAKES: 60 cookies

1 generous cup shortening
½ cup fine granulated sugar
⅓ cup brown sugar
1 egg, beaten
Few drops almond essence
2¼ cups all-purpose flour
Pinch salt
1½ tsp baking powder
½ cup blanched almonds
1 egg yolk
2 tblsp water

Cream the shortening with the sugars until light and fluffy. Add the egg and almond essence and beat until smooth. Sift the flour, salt and baking powder. Mix the dry ingredients into the creamed mixture. Shape into small balls on a lightly floured surface. Flatten slightly and press an almond into the center of each one. Place onto a greased cooky sheet. Mix the egg yolk with the water. Brush the cookies with the egg glaze. Bake at 350°F for 12-15 minutes.

Sweet Almond Pudding

PREPARATION TIME: 4-5 minutes

COOKING TIME: 6 minutes

SERVES: 4-6 people

1 cup blanched almonds
1¾ cups water
¾ cup fine granulated sugar
4 tblsp rice powder, or ground rice
⅔ cup milk

Blend the blanched almonds and water in the blender. Put into a pan and bring to the boil. Add the sugar and stir over the heat until the sugar has dissolved. Add the rice slowly to the milk and stir gradually into the simmering sugar and almond mixture. Cook gently until the mixture thickens. Remove from the heat and pour into a serving dish. Serve hot or cold.

Sweet Dumplings

PREPARATION TIME: 10 minutes

COOKING TIME: 15-20 minutes

MAKES: 10-12

Salad or olive oil
½ cup fine granulated sugar
⅓ cup plain red bean paste
⅓ cup desiccated coconut
4 egg whites
1½ tblsp all-purpose flour
4 tblsp cornstarch
Confectioner's sugar

Heat 1 tblsp oil in a wok and add the sugar, bean paste and coconut. Stir fry for 4-5 minutes until the sugar melts and the paste is smooth and shiny. Fry for a few minutes more and then allow to cool on a dish. Whip the egg whites until stiff and mix with the flour and cornstarch to a smooth batter. Beat well. Clean the wok and heat sufficient oil for deep

frying. Make 10-12 even-sized balls from the bean paste mixture. Dip each ball into the batter and then deep fry for 3-4 minutes until golden and crisp. Fry a few at a time and drain on kitchen paper. Dust with sifted confectioner's sugar before serving.

Stuffed Lychees

PREPARATION TIME: 20 minutes

SERVES: 6 people

3 cups canned lychees, stones removed
4-5 rings canned pineapple
Few drops vanilla essence or almond essence

Drain the lychees into a bowl, reserving the juice. Slice each pineapple ring into ½ inch long strips. Press one or two strips of pineapple into each lychee. Arrange the pineapple-filled lychees in a deep serving dish. Mix the pineapple and lychee liquid with a few drops of essence. Spoon over the stuffed fruits. Serve well chilled. Alternatively, stuff the lychees with maraschino cherries, mango, canned pears, oranges etc.

Facing page: Sweet Dumplings (top), Almond Cookies (center left) and Date Cake (bottom right).

Glossary

Agar-agar: this is a specially prepared, dried sea weed which is sold in the shops as Chinese grass. The white, fibrous strands require soaking and are used like gelatine. Agar-agar is also sold in ground powder form. It is used for puddings and as a setting agent. All Chinese and Oriental shops sell it.

Anise, star: this is an eight pointed clove with a strong anise smell and flavor, and is one of the spices which goes into "Chinese five spice" powder. It can be purchased in powder or whole form. It is used to flavor red-cooked poultry and many meat dishes.

Bean curd (Tau fu): this comes in soft, custard-like squares and is made from soya beans. It is highly nutritious and is one of the most important Chinese foods. It is available only from Chinese grocers and is also sold in dried form as bean curd stick, in brine, and fried.

Bean pastes: sauces made from soya beans which are sold in cans and jars. Once opened, they should be kept refrigerated. There are many varieties of bean paste:
Hot bean paste, which is made with chilies and is salty.
Soya bean paste, which is dark in color, very salty and is made with fermented soya beans.
Sweet bean paste, which is made with black soya beans, sugar, flour and spices.
Yellow bean paste, which is made with yellow soya beans and this too is quite salty in taste.

Bean sprouts: these are shoots of mung beans or soya beans. The soya beans are stronger in flavor. They are readily available from most supermarkets and Oriental shops. Fresh bean sprouts will keep for several days if refrigerated in a perforated plastic bag; discard any discolored shoots. The topped and tailed sprouts are known as 'Silver Sprouts' and are used for very special dishes.

Black bean sauce: this can be bought ready made from shops, or made with 3-4 tblsp steamed, black soya beans mixed to a paste with 2 tblsp oil and 2 tblsp sugar.

Broccoli, Chinese: a dark green, leafy vegetable which bears small white flowers; it looks very much like miniature broccoli. It is sold only in Chinese grocers and, if not available, it can be substituted by Chinese cabbage or ordinary broccoli.

Cabbage, Chinese white: there are two main varieties. One is called Pak-choy, and the other, a more tender flowering white cabbage, is called Choy-sum. Chinese leaves and Tientsin cabbage are sold in supermarkets and Oriental shops and also in many fruit and vegetable markets. Chinese leaves are tightly packed and have creamy white leaves with a thick central stalk. They are often used in salads in place of lettuce. All these cabbages can be substituted by ordinary cabbage.

Chestnuts, water: these are the bulb-like stems of the bulrush. They are slightly sweet and have a crisp texture. They are usually sold in cans; occasionally they are sold in their natural form. They are available from some supermarkets and all Oriental and Chinese shops. Canned water chestnuts will keep for 3-4 weeks after opening if refrigerated and kept in water. The water should be changed daily. Chestnuts are also ground to a flour, which is used for making batter.

Chili oil: this can be brought ready-prepared. Chili oil can also be made by infusing dried chilies in hot vegetable oil, but it will not keep for as long as the ready-prepared variety.

Chili sauce: this is a very hot, spicy and tangy sauce made from chilies and vinegar. Chili sauce can be purchased from many supermarkets and all Chinese grocers. It is used to season a wide variety of savory Chinese dishes.

Chinese wine: there are many kinds of wine made from rice. Chinese rice wine can be substituted by ordinary dry sherry in most recipes. Rice wines vary considerably in quality, but they are all very strong.

Cloud ear: this is known by many names i.e. wood ear, snow fungus, sea jelly or jelly sheet. It is actually a dried fungus which, when soaked in water, resembles a puffed ear, hence the name. It has no flavor and is used only to add texture to a dish. It will keep for a month in its dried form.

Cooked oil: many Chinese dishes require cooked oil in the recipe. It is made by heating vegetable, peanut or any other kind of oil until it smokes.

Dates: these are sold in dried form and will keep for a month. There are two varieties: black and red, and they can be purchased from most Oriental shops. They resemble dried prunes and are used in sweet, and some savory, stir fried dishes. Ordinary dried dates can easily be used in their place.

Fennel (dried): this is sold in seed form and the tiny, pale green seeds resemble caraway seeds. Fennel is sold in supermarkets, health food shops and in Chinese grocery shops and is an important ingredient in Five-spice powder.

Five-spice powder: this is a strong, coffee-colored seasoning made with equal parts of fagara (brown peppercorns), cinnamon bark, clove, fennel and star anise. All the spices are ground to a fine powder and it is used sparingly.

Flour: many varieties of flour are used in Chinese cookery, the main one being the ordinary unleavened flour, which is usually a finely ground wheat flour. It is used to make most steamed breads and some pastries.

High gluten flour: this is used to make wonton wrappers. It is a strong flour with a high gluten content and can therefore be rolled very thinly.

Tang flour: this is made from a low-gluten wheat. The flour is used for making clear wrappers for 'dim sum'; when cooked, this flour becomes transparent.

Ginger: fresh root ginger is a vital ingredient in Chinese cooking; nearly all the traditional meat and fish dishes use root ginger. Sprouting ginger is the best and it is used for preserving foods in vinegar and for pickling. The tough, older roots are strong in flavor. The texture may be fibrous but if you chop the ginger finely with a sharp knife it will release its full flavor. Ginger not only gives a distinct taste to a dish but it helps the digestion as well. Fresh ginger cannot be substituted by ground or preserved ginger. It is widely available.

Glutinous rice: this is also known as 'sticky' rice. It is a special variety of Chinese rice which has opaque grains, and when cooked turns transparent and very sticky. It is used for making both puddings and savory dishes.

Hoi Sin sauce: this is a sweet, brownish-red sauce made from soya beans, salt, sugar, chili, garlic, vinegar and flour. It has a sweet, tangy flavor and can be bought from Chinese shops or large supermarkets. It is used in cooking as well as being served as a dip for meats etc. It is also known as seafood sauce or barbecue sauce.

Long beans: these are one of the many typical Chinese vegetables. As the name suggests, they are longer than the ordinary beans. They are obtainable from most Chinese shops and from Oriental grocers and can be substituted by lobia beans or ordinary green beans (string beans).

Melon, winter: this is a very large, green-skinned melon with a soft, white flesh and a delicate taste. It is sold fresh in Chinese shops or Oriental grocers but can also be purchased cubed in cans. Peeled and seeded marrow or cucumber can be used as a substitute.

Monosodium glutamate: this is a white, crystalline substance commonly known as MSG. It is used extensively in Chinese cookery for tenderising meat and for enhancing the flavor of dishes. It is sometimes sold under the names of Aji No Moto and Vi Tsin and is also called 'taste powder'. It should be used sparingly, as too much will spoil the dish, and can be totally omitted from recipes if preferred.

Mooli: mooli or muli is a crisp, white variety of radish. It grows to about 10 inches in length and 4 inches in diameter. It has a stronger taste than ordinary red radish and is eaten in salads and as a vegetable. It has a sharp, crunchy texture and flavor.

Mushrooms: there are many varieties of dried mushrooms which are used in Chinese cooking. Follow the recipe to see the type suggested. To prepare dried mushrooms for cooking, soak in hot water for ½ hour. Drain and season with ½ tblsp wine and a little sugar. (See also Chinese mushrooms and cloud ear).

Mustard green: this is also known as leaf mustard. It has a slightly bitter taste and is crunchy in texture. It is used in soups and stir fried dishes. It is only sold in Oriental and Chinese grocery shops. Use broccoli as the nearest substitute.

Noodles: there are many different kinds of noodles. Some are made from wheat flour, some from rice flour and some from bean flour. All these varieties of noodles are obtainable from Chinese and Oriental grocers, and many are sold in supermarkets and other food shops. Noodles can be substituted by spaghetti, though the flavor will not be the same.

Bean thread noodles: thin, white, transparent noodles made from moong bean flour. They should be soaked before use.

Cake noodles: these are bound together in tight balls.

Rice sheet noodles: these are made from rice and come in wide, flat sheets. They are also sold in dried form.

Rice stick noodles: sometimes called rice vermicelli these are very thin noodles made from rice, and they are soaked in hot water for 10-12 minutes before use. If deep fried they become very light and crisp, like wafers.

Shanghai noodles, thin: these are mostly used in soups and are thin and pale in color. The basic noodles are made from wheat flour.

Shanghai noodles, thick: these are yellowish in color and are made from wheat flour enriched with egg. Commonly sold in dried form, in the shape of small and large cakes, they are also sold fresh in Chinese shops; these fresh noodles can be kept in plastic bags in the refrigerator for up to 1 week.

Oyster sauce: this is a special sauce produced from soya sauce and oysters which have been fermented together. It is used as a flavoring and as a coloring and also as a condiment. Once opened it will keep in the bottle for several months.

Parsley (Chinese): otherwise known as fresh coriander, this is a herb of Indian origin, which is used as a flavoring and a garnish. The flat leaves have a strong flavor and can not be substituted by Western parsley.

Preserved Chinese vegetables: these are specially prepared dried vegetables, which retain their original flavor. Preserved vegetables are also sold in cans and jars, packed in a brine solution.

Rice: there are many different varieties of rice. Long grained rice is the variety usually used for making simple rice dishes, but a special, glutinous, medium-grain rice is used for making puddings and savory dishes.

Sesame oil: an aromatic oil produced from sesame seeds. This has a special flavor and is used both as a seasoning and as a vital ingredient in some sauces. Sold in bottles, it is available from most general grocery, chemist and health food shops.

Sesame paste: a paste made from ground sesame seeds. It is sold ready-made in cans and jars. Always buy it with a layer of oil floating on top; the oil should be mixed in before use. This is the oil which comes from grinding sesame seeds. Sesame paste is also known by the name of Tahin or Tahina. It can be substituted by unsalted peanut butter.

Sesame seeds: there are two varieties of these tiny seeds, one white and the other black. Both are used for garnishes, as well as for making pastes, sweets and fillings and can be purchased from Oriental and Chinese grocers.

Snow peas (mange tout): these are delicate, flat pea pods and the whole vegetable is eaten. They are either eaten raw or lightly cooked and they add character and color to many dishes. Will keep for a few days if kept in perforated plastic bags in the refrigerator.

Soya sauce: there are two kinds of soya sauce; one is dark and the other is light. Both are used for flavoring soups, stir fried dishes and for seasoning nearly all Chinese foods. They are extracts made from fermented soya beans. The dark soya sauce is thicker, and stronger in flavor while the lighter varieties are the weaker infusions of the fermented beans. The first extract is the strongest and the best. Soya sauces are sometimes flavored with mushrooms, oysters and shrimp roe.

Broths: Chinese cooking needs broth of one sort or another in almost all dishes. There are two main kinds of broth that are used. It is very useful to make home made broth and keep it refrigerated for 5-7 days.

Chicken broth: 2lbs chicken trimmings (bones, neck, skin, wings, claws etc), 3½ pints water, 1 inch fresh root ginger, peeled and minced, 1 medium onion, peeled and thinly sliced, salt, freshly ground black pepper. Put chicken trimmings and water into a pan. Bring to the boil and simmer for 10 minutes. Skim and add ginger, onions and seasoning; simmer for

1-1½ hours. Strain and use.

Superior broth or strong broth: 1 boiling chicken, 4oz loin of pork, cubed, 1oz Yunnan ham, cubed, 3½ pints water, ½ inch fresh root ginger, peeled and thinly sliced, 2 green onions, chopped, salt, freshly ground black pepper. Place chicken, pork and ham into a pan with the water and bring to the boil. Cook for 10 minutes and skim. Add ginger, green onions and season with salt and pepper. Simmer for 1½ hours. The fat should not be skimmed off completely as this gives the stock its characteristic flavor.

Tangerine peel, dried: the best sun-dried peels are several years old. Peel is used as a seasoning for stews and other dishes. It is a little expensive, however, and can be ommitted from the recipe, or substituted by home-dried peels.

Vinegar: Chinese vinegars are made from fermented rice, by the process of distillation, and there are four main varieties:

Black vinegar: this is similar to malt vinegar, but not quite so strong. It has a stronger flavor than other Chinese varieties and is used as a flavoring and as a condiment.

Red vinegar: this is distinctly red in color as the name suggests, and is used particularly with seafood dishes and as a condiment.

Sweet vinegar: this is almost like port in flavor, very sweet and rich black in color. It is used mainly for braised and stewed dishes and has a sharp taste.

White vinegar: this is not as strong as European white vinegar; it is more tangy, yet milder. When substituting one vinegar for another taste carefully.

Yunnan ham: this is a special kind of Chinese smoked ham which is produced by a salting and smoking process. Substitute: good cuts of European smoked ham, smoked gammon or lean rashers of smoked bacon.

Index

INDIAN
COOKING

Contents

Omelette (far left), Khageea (center) and Egg Curry (right).

Introduction

India is a vast country with a greatly varied climate and terrain. Each of its many regions boasts its own special style and flavor of cooking, just as each has its own, quite different, language and customs. For example, the same simple vegetable dish may be made in 1,000 different ways by the various castes and regions of India. In Kashmir, which lies in the north, it will be mild and saffron will feature in the preparation. In Uttar Pradesh, which includes the foothills of the Himalayas, it will be simple, with a subtle taste. In Delhi-Haryana it will be made in the exotic Mogul style; rich and creamy. In the south of India, in Tamil Nadu, the same dish will become spicy and pungent, for this is the major spice-growing area. Incidentally, the curry which we know today derives from the Keres, a dish characteristic of this southern area. Similarly, the coastal regions of India show a preference for fish and seafood. I have tried to include recipes in this book from all the regions of India.

Indian cooking has developed from a purely vegetarian variety to today's mixed style, artistically absorbing the culinary styles of all the subcontinent's past invaders: Persians, Greeks, Romans, Mongols, French, Portuguese and British, in the process.

Curry, as we know it today, was introduced to Europe, especially to Great Britain, by army officers returning from India. They asked their cooks, or *khansamas*, to make a mixture of spices which could be taken home to Europe and used to make the dish for which they had developed a taste while in India. This mixture of spices was named curry powder. Curry quickly became a dish associated with life in India. The demand increased rapidly and some companies set themselves up to export this mixture to Europe. Some ardent curry lovers even went so far as to bring their cooks back from India with them.

After the independence, and partition, of India there was a mass exodus of people to Great Britain, Africa and other parts of the world. They took with them their eating habits and spices, and soon Africa was cultivating those same spices. The mass migration of Asians in the 1960s and 1970s, from East Africa and the Indian subcontinent to Great Britain and other parts of Europe, brought Indian food to the notice of everyone. Suddenly it became as much a part of the British way of life as a cup of 'tea'.

It is no longer strange to find curry included on the average family menu. Although it is sometimes thought that curry, with all its spices, is bad for your health, nothing could be further from the truth. The combination of various spices is there not only to complement the flavor and enhance the taste, but also to help digestion. They act as a kind of catalyst, helping the natural enzymes to digest the food. The only spice which is included in a dish purely to add pungency is chili. Even so, every recipe can be modified according to your own taste by decreasing, increasing or even totally omitting a spice altogether. Similarly, the quantity of cooking oil, ghee or fat can be varied according to one's liking.

There is one factor which, above all, makes Indian cooking stand out in the success charts. No matter how inexperienced the cook, or whether the recipe has been correctly followed or not, the ultimate result will always be at least edible. The skill is in making the dish a masterpiece, and that is where individual artistry and imagination play their part. No other style of cooking, except perhaps Chinese, allows such enormous room for flexibility. You can increase or reduce the spices to suit your own palate and it is possible to produce an excellent dish even if one or more spices are not available. Therefore, it is not surprising that, given the same ingredients, four different cooks could produce four different tasting curries. It is the blending of the spices which plays the most important role. This great flexibility has allowed me to take into account the vegetables most readily available in the European and American markets.

Indian food is always colorful, but its beauty is enhanced by the garnishing. Chopped chili, coriander leaves and artistically cut vegetables – like carrots, cucumbers and radishes – are used freely.

Eating is always an occasion in an Indian household, and so it should be. Sharing a table and food symbolises harmony, love and togetherness, so Indian meals are particularly geared for sharing. If a meal is cooked with four to six people in mind, it could easily stretch to eight or ten people if friends happen to drop by unexpectedly.

Indian meals are not served in different courses, like European meals. All the dishes are served at the same time, with the exception of the sweets. The meals are traditionally served either by the most senior lady in the house or by the mistress of the house. These days, however, it is increasingly the fashion to help yourself.

The dishes will take you from Kashmir in the north to the southernmost tip of India. I hope this book will not only help to guide you in the pleasures of Indian cooking, but also to give you a better understanding of spices and their many and varied uses. Happy cooking!

Rasgullas (top left), Paneer Ki Kheer (left) and Jallebi (right).

Sherbets and Snacks

Lassi
(YOGURT SHERBET)

PREPARATION TIME: 5-7 minutes

SERVES: 6 people

1¼ cups natural yogurt
¼ cup fine granulated sugar
Pinch of salt
4 cups water
Pinch of saffron
2 tsp lemon juice
Ice cubes

In a mixing bowl beat yogurt well; add sugar and salt, beat again and add water. Dissolve sugar by stirring well. Add saffron and lemon juice and serve with ice cubes.

Tandi Masala Chaaey
(SPICED ICE TEA)

PREPARATION TIME: 10 minutes

SERVES: 4 people

2½ cups water
1 teabag or
2 tsp orange peko tea leaves
Sugar to taste
4 cloves
1 inch cinnamon stick
4 small cardamoms, seeds removed
   and ground
Crushed ice
Fresh lemon juice

Boil ⅔ cup of water. Put tea, sugar, cloves, cinnamon stick and crushed cardamom seeds into a tea pot. Pour on boiling water and allow to stand for 2-4 minutes. Stir well, strain, and mix with remaining cold water. Allow to cool. Mix and serve in tall glasses with crushed ice and lemon juice to taste.

This page: Lassi (left), Mint Barley (center) and Tandi Masala Chaaey (right).

Facing page: Badam Ka Sherbet (left), Lemon Sherbet (center) and Spiced Grape Sherbet (right).

(Normally served before the meal)

Green Mango Sherbet

PREPARATION TIME: 10-12 minutes

SERVES: 6 people

2 green, unripened mangoes
4 cups water
Pinch of salt
Sugar to taste
Crushed ice

Boil mangoes for 10 minutes. Remove from water and cool. Remove skins gently. Scrape all the pulp from around the stone and skin. Dissolve pulp in water. Add salt and sugar. Stir well to mix. Serve on crushed ice.

Mint Barley

PREPARATION TIME: 15 minutes

SERVES: 4 people

2½-3 cups water
⅓ cup broken barley
6-8 mint leaves, finely chopped
Pinch of salt
Sugar to taste
Fresh lemon juice

Boil 1¼ cups water and add barley; simmer for 5 minutes. Strain and discard barley. Add remaining water and finely chopped mint leaves. Add salt and sugar to taste. Chill and serve on ice with lemon juice.

Lemon Sherbet

PREPARATION TIME: 5 minutes

SERVES: 6 people

Sugar to taste
Pinch salt
5 cups water
Juice of 2 lemons
1 tsp grated lemon rind
Few mint leaves, bruised
Ice cubes

Dissolve sugar and salt in water. Add lemon juice and lemon rind. Add mint leaves and stir well. Serve in tall glasses with ice. ½ cup of gin or vodka may be added.

Spiced Grape Sherbet

PREPARATION TIME: 10 minutes

SERVES: 6 people

8oz white seedless grapes
4oz black grapes, seeded
2 cloves
4 cups water
Pinch of salt
6 small cardamoms, seeds removed
    and crushed
Sugar to taste
2 tsp lemon juice
Pinch of freshly ground pepper
Pinch of ground cinnamon
Crushed ice

Wash grapes and liquidize with cloves; strain through a sieve to collect juice. Add 1 cup water to grapes and strain once again to collect the juice. Mix grape juice with remaining water; add salt, crushed cardamom seeds and sugar. Add lemon juice, pepper and cinnamon. Mix well. Serve on crushed ice.

Passion Fruit Sherbet

PREPARATION TIME: 10 minutes

SERVES: 4-6 people

8-10 passion fruit
3 cups water
Sugar
Pinch of salt
1-2 drops of red food coloring
    (optional)
Ice cubes

Cut passion fruits in half. Remove the pulp and blend with the water. Strain and dissolve sugar; add salt. Add red food coloring, if desired, as this will make the sherbet pink. Serve with ice cubes.

Blackcurrant Sherbet

PREPARATION TIME: 10 minutes

SERVES: 1 cup

1 cup fresh or frozen blackcurrants
3 cups water
⅓ cup fine granulated sugar
Pinch of salt
1 tblsp lemon juice
Ice cubes

Mash blackcurrants in a bowl or blend them in a liquidizer. Add water and mix well, then strain. Dissolve sugar and salt in blackcurrant liquid and add lemon juice. Serve with ice cubes.

Badam Ka Sherbet
(ALMOND SHERBET)

PREPARATION TIME: 10 minutes

SERVES: 4 people

1¾ cups milk
⅔ cup water
⅓ cup fine granulated sugar
1½ tblsp blanched almonds, soaked
    in water
1½ tblsp pistachio nuts, soaked and
    skin removed
Pinch of saffron
6 small cardamoms, seeds removed
    and crushed
3-4 drops rosewater
Ice cubes

Mix milk and water and dissolve sugar. Liquidize almonds and pistachio nuts with a little diluted milk. Dissolve saffron, add crushed seeds of cardamom and add rose essence. Serve with ice cubes, or well chilled.

Dahi - Wada
(DAAL DUMPLINGS IN YOGURT)

PREPARATION TIME: 5 minutes
and 1 hour for soaking

COOKING TIME: 30 minutes

SERVES: 4 people

1 cup urid daal, washed and soaked
    for 1 hour
½ cup moong daal, washed and
soaked for 1 hour
½ tsp salt
1 inch root ginger, peeled and finely
    chopped
¼ tsp chili powder or
2 green chilies, finely chopped
4 tblsp mixed sultanas and raisins
Salad or olive oil for deep frying

For Yogurt Sauce:
2 cups natural yogurt
¼ tsp salt
½ tsp cumin seed
2 sprigs fresh green coriander,
    chopped for garnish

Blend drained urid daal and moong daal with sufficient water in a liquidizer to make a very thick purée. Put liquidized urid and moong daal into a mixing bowl; add salt, ginger, chilies and mixed fruits. Mix well. Add small spoonfuls of the mixture to the hot oil to make small dumplings. (To make more uniform wadas, dampen your hands in water, and form a little mixture into a flat, round shape before lowering the mixture gently into the oil.) Fry both sides for 3-4 minutes, or until golden brown. Drain on kitchen paper. Make all the wadas in this way.
To make the sauce, mix yogurt and salt together. Soak fried wadas in water for 2-3 minutes. Gently squeeze out any excess water and arrange on a flat serving dish. Pour the yogurt evenly over them. Dry roast the cumin and coriander

seeds for 1-2 minutes in a skillet. Place the roasted spices in folded kitchen paper and crush with a rolling pin to give a coarse powder. Sprinkle ground spice mixture over the yogurt. Garnish with chopped fresh green coriander. Alternatively, sprinkle with a pinch of paprika powder.

Pakoras or Bhajias
(DEEP FRIED CHICK PEA FLOUR FRITTERS)

PREPARATION TIME: 15 minutes

COOKING TIME: 10 minutes

SERVES: 4 people

1 cup baisen flour
Pinch of salt
½ tsp chili powder
½ tsp baking soda
Salad or olive oil for deep frying

Vegetables and Fruits
1 small potato, peeled and sliced into
    ⅛ inch thick wafers
1 small eggplant, cut into thin slices
1 small onion, sliced
1 green pepper, seeded and sliced into
    rings
3-4 flowerets of cauliflower, separated
    into smaller pieces

Mix baisen flour, salt, chili powder and soda; add sufficient water to make a coating batter. Mix well and allow to stand for 3-4 minutes. Dip the prepared vegetables, one by one, into the batter; fry them, a few at a time, for 4-5 minutes in hot oil, until golden brown on both sides. Drain well. Serve hot or cold with chutney.

Other suggestions
Pineapple rings, apples, tomatoes, spinach leaves, green chilies, bread slices cut into quarters, semi-ripe bananas, sweet potatoes, swede, parsnips, chicken and fish pieces.

This page: Blackcurrant Sherbet (center) and Passion Fruit Sherbet (right).

Facing page: Pakoras (top), Ghoogni (center left) and Dahi Wada (bottom).

Crispy Rolls or Curry Patties

PREPARATION TIME: 1 hour
COOKING TIME: 30 minutes
MAKES: about 16-20

2 cups all-purpose flour
Salt
1 tblsp cornstarch
¼ tsp baking soda
1½ tblsp butter or margarine
Chosen filling (see below)
2 tsp flour and a little water to make
   a thick paste.
Salad or olive oil for deep frying

Crispy rolls can be made with either a vegetable or meat filling. The rolls themselves are made in the same way for either filling. Sift flour, salt, cornstarch and soda. Rub in butter. Make dough with water. Knead well and leave to stand for 10 minutes. Knead once again and divide into 4-6 portions. Roll each portion as thinly as possible on a lightly-floured surface, then cut into 4 inch squares. Heat skillet and cook on both sides for ½ minute each. Make the rest similarly. Take a square wrapper and place a little filling slightly above one corner and fold corner over the filling. Bring the two side corners over as if to make the folds of an envelope. Secure with a little flour and water paste and press to seal. Roll over the folded edge to make a neat roll. Seal the flap with flour and water paste. Make all the rolls. Heat oil, and deep fry a few at a time until golden brown. Drain on kitchen paper and serve hot with either chutney or ketchup.

Vegetable Filling

1 onion
2 tblsp salad or olive oil
1lb potatoes, peeled and cubed
⅔ cup shelled or frozen peas
Salt
1 tsp ground black pepper
Salad or olive oil for deep frying

Fry onion in the 2 tblsp salad or olive oil for 3-4 minutes. Add cubed boiled potatoes and peas and sprinkle with salt and pepper. Mix well and cook for 3-4 minutes. Cover and allow to cool.

Meat Filling

1 tblsp salad or olive oil
1 onion, peeled and thinly sliced
⅓ cup grated cabbage
⅓ cup grated carrots
⅓ cup sliced green beans
⅓ cup frozen peas
Salt
½ tsp ground black pepper
⅓ cup sprouted beans
1⅓ cups shredded cooked meat
2-3 tsp lemon juice

Heat oil and fry onions for 2 minutes. Add cabbage and carrots and fry for 3 minutes. Add green beans and peas and sprinkle with salt and black pepper. Cover and cook for 4-5 minutes. Add sprouted beans and stir fry for 2 minutes. Add shredded meat. Mix well, add lemon juice and stir the mixture. Cook for 2-3 minutes. Remove from heat, cool and use for filling.

Aloo-Bonda
(POTATO BALLS IN BATTER)

PREPARATION TIME: 20 minutes
COOKING TIME: 15 minutes
SERVES: 6 people

Batter
1 scant cup baisen flour
Salt
Pinch baking powder
¼ tsp chili powder
⅔ cup water
Oil for deep frying

Filling
1lb potatoes, peeled, boiled and
   cubed
1 onion, peeled and chopped
2 sprigs fresh green coriander,
   chopped
1 inch root ginger, peeled and finely
   chopped
1-2 green chilies, chopped
1 tblsp lemon juice
Freshly ground black pepper to taste
Salt
2 tsp dry mango powder

Sift flour and salt together with baking powder and chili powder. Add water and mix well to make a smooth batter. If the batter is too thick add a little extra water; if too thin, add a little extra sifted baisen flour. Put aside to rest. Put the cubed potatoes into a bowl with the chopped onions, coriander, ginger, chilies and lemon juice; mix well and sprinkle with pepper, salt and mango powder. Shape into small balls about the size of a golf ball. Dip the potato bonda into the baisen batter and slide them into the hot oil. Fry a few at a time until the bonda are golden brown. Drain on kitchen paper and serve hot with chutney. Aloo-bondas can be eaten cold, but they do not freeze well.

Dokhala

PREPARATION TIME: overnight for soaking and 10-12 hours for fermenting
COOKING TIME: 30-40 minutes
SERVES: 6 people

2 cups channa daal (split chick pea),
   washed
1-2 green chilies
1 inch root ginger, peeled and sliced
Salt to taste
Pinch of asafoetida
1 tsp baking soda
4 tblsp salad or olive oil
6-8 curry leaves
½ tsp mustard seed
3 tblsp grated fresh coconut
2 sprigs coriander leaves, chopped

Soak channa daal overnight. Drain and grind with the green chilies, ginger and a little water into a coarse paste. Beat with a circular motion to incorporate air; leave to

ferment for 10-12 hours (use a warm place like an airing cupboard, and cover the pan). After it has fermented, add salt, asafoetida, soda and half the oil. If too thick, add 2 tblsp water. Beat again. Grease a flat, 2-2½-inch-deep pie dish with oil and spread the mixture evenly into it. Steam over

a large saucepan for 15-20 minutes. Allow to cool slightly. Heat the remaining oil; add curry leaves and mustard seeds and pour over dokhala evenly. Serve garnished with grated coconut and chopped coriander leaves. Cut dokhala into 1 inch square pieces. Dokhala can be frozen for future use.

Khari Sevian
(SAVOURY MINCE VERMICELLI)

PREPARATION TIME: 10 minutes
COOKING TIME: 20 minutes for mince and 10 minutes for sevian
SERVES: 4 people

1 onion, peeled and finely chopped
1½ tblsp salad or olive oil
½ tsp ginger paste
¼ tsp garlic paste
8 oz ground lean lamb or beef

Salt
1 tsp ground black pepper
¼ cup butter
2 cups broken vermicelli
Juice of 1 lemon

Fry onion in oil for 3-4 minutes.
Add ginger, garlic, ground meat and
salt. Fry for 6-7 minutes. Add
ground black pepper. Mix well.
Cover and cook until meat is dry.
Remove from heat and put aside.
Heat the butter in a non-stick pan
and fry vermicelli for 1-2 minutes.
Add cooked meat and stir fry for 1
minute. Add 1¼ cups water. Cook
until dry. Sprinkle with lemon juice
and serve hot.

Khari Sevian (far left), Aloo Bonda (below), Crispy Rolls (center) and Dokhala (bottom).

Ghoogni
(GREEN PEA FRY OR SPICED GREEN PEAS)

PREPARATION TIME: 5 minutes

COOKING TIME: 10 minutes

SERVES: 4 people

1 onion, peeled and chopped
1 tblsp salad or olive oil
2 green chilies, cut in half
1 inch root ginger, peeled and chopped
3 cups shelled or frozen peas
¼ tsp ground black pepper
2 sprigs fresh green coriander, chopped
¼ tsp salt
Juice of 1 lemon

Fry onion in oil until tender (2-3 minutes); add green chilies and ginger. Fry for 1 minute and add green peas. Stir and cook for 5-6 minutes. Add black pepper, chopped coriander and salt. Cook for a further 2 minutes. Pour into a serving dish and sprinkle with lemon juice. Serve hot with tea.

Samosa
(DEEP FRIED STUFFED SAVORY PASTRIES)

PREPARATION TIME: 30 minutes

COOKING TIME: 15 minutes

MAKES: 32-40

1 cup all-purpose flour
Pinch of salt
½ tsp baking powder
1½ tblsp salad or olive oil

Flour paste
1 tblsp all-purpose flour, mixed with a little water to form a thick paste
Oil for deep frying

Samosas may be made with either a vegetable or meat filling (they are made in the same way for either filling). Sift flour and salt and add baking powder. Mix in oil and add the water, a little at a time, to form a dough. Knead well and set aside. When the filling has been made: knead dough again and make 16-20 even-sized balls. On a lightly floured surface roll each ball into a thin circle, 5 inches in diameter. Cut across the center and apply the flour paste along the straight edge and bring the two corners together, overlapping slightly to make a cone. Secure by pressing the pasted edges together. Fill the

cone with the filling, apply paste to te open mouth and seal the edge. Prepare the rest of the samosas in the same way. Fry the samosas, a few at a time, in hot oil until golden brown. Drain on kitchen paper and serve hot or cold with a sweet chutney or ketchup.

For Vegetable Filling
1 tblsp oil
1 onion, peeled and chopped
2 tsp garam masala powder
½ tsp salt
½ tsp chili powder
1 lb potatoes, peeled, cubed and boiled for 4 to 5 minutes
4 tblsp frozen or shelled peas
2 tsp dry mango powder

To make the filling: heat the oil and fry onion until just tender. Sprinkle with garam masala, salt and chili powder. Fry for one minute and add drained potatoes and peas. Mix well and fry for 2-3 minutes until potatoes are tender. Sprinkle with mango powder or lemon juice. Allow to cool.

Meat Filling
1 onion, peeled and chopped
2 tblsp salad or olive oil
1 lb ground lamb or beef
1 tsp ginger paste
1 tsp garlic paste
2 tsp ground black pepper
½ tsp salt

Fry onion in oil until golden brown. Add the ground meat, ginger and garlic paste, black ground pepper and salt. Fry the mixture for 8-10 minutes until dry. Remove from pan and allow to cool. Samosas made with ground meat can be frozen either half fried, or unfried. Fry straight from the freezer when required. They can also be thawed before frying without any damage or alteration to taste.

Tikias
(POTATO-MINCE PATTIES)

PREPARATION TIME: 20 minutes

COOKING TIME: 20-30 minutes

MAKES: 20-25

1 onion, peeled and chopped
1½ tblsp ghee or
1 tblsp salad or olive oil
8 oz ground lamb or beef
1 cup frozen or shelled peas
2 sprigs fresh green coriander leaves, chopped

2-3 small green chilies, chopped (optional)
1 tsp ground black pepper
1 lb boiled potatoes, peeled and mashed
1-2 tsp salt
1-2 eggs, beaten
Salad or olive oil for frying

Fry onion in ghee or oil until just tender (2-3 minutes). Add ground meat, peas, coriander leaves, chilies and black pepper. Fry for 4-5 minutes. Cool and mix with mashed potatoes and salt. Make 20-25 small, flat burger shapes. Heat the oil in a skillet and dip tikias in beaten egg to coat. Shallow fry in hot oil. Fry on each side for 2-3 minutes. Serve hot or cold with chutney.

Khageea
(SPICED SCRAMBLED EGG)

PREPARATION TIME: 6 minutes

COOKING TIME: 10 minutes

SERVES: 2-3 people

1 onion, peeled and chopped
2 tblsp salad or olive oil
½ tsp chili powder
¼ tsp ground turmeric
1 green chili, chopped
2 sprigs fresh coriander leaves, chopped
2 tomatoes, chopped
Salt to taste
1 tblsp water
4 eggs, well beaten

Fry onion in oil for 2 minutes. Add spices, green chili and coriander leaves; stir fry for 1 minute. Add chopped fresh tomatoes. Season with salt and sprinkle in the water. Add beaten eggs. Cover and cook on gentle heat for 6-7 minutes. Stir and mix egg over gentle heat. (Khageea should look like spiced scrambled eggs.) Serve with parathas for any meal, including a hearty breakfast.

Wada
(DAAL FRITTERS)

PREPARATION TIME: 2-3 hours

COOKING TIME: 20 minutes

SERVES: 6 people

½ cup urid daal, washed and soaked for 2-3 hours
½ cup yellow, de-husked moong

daal, washed and soaked for 2-3 hours
1 onion, peeled and finely chopped
1-2 tsp salt
2-3 sprigs fresh green coriander leaves, chopped
1 small green chili finely chopped, or
½ tsp chili powder
1 inch root ginger, peeled and finely chopped
¼ tsp baking soda
Salad or olive oil for deep frying

Grind drained urid and moong daal with a little water to a coarse thick paste. Pour into a mixing bowl and add onion, salt, coriander leaves, chili powder or green chilies, ginger and soda. Mix well and set aside for 4-5 minutes. Fry small spoonfuls of the mixture in hot oil, a few at a time, for 3-4 minutes until golden brown. Drain and serve hot with chutney.

Omelette

PREPARATION TIME: 5 minutes

COOKING TIME: 5 minutes

SERVES: 1 person

2 eggs, separated
1 small onion, finely chopped
1 tomato, thinly sliced
1 green chili, finely chopped
1 sprig coriander leaves, finely chopped
1 tsp water
Salt to taste
1 tblsp salad or olive oil

Beat egg white until stiff. Add egg yolk and beat well. Mix in chopped onion, tomato, chili, coriander and water. Grease a skillet well with oil. Heat the skillet and pour the egg mixture into it. Sprinkle with salt to taste. Cover and cook the omelette for 2-3 minutes until the sides leave the pan. With a flat spoon or spatula, ease up the base of the omelette, and turn it over to cook the other side. Cover and cook for another 2-3 minutes. Serve hot with ketchup or chutney, along with rotis or parathas.

Facing page: Tikias (top left), Samosa (top right) and Wada (bottom).

Ganthia
(BAISEN STICKS)

PREPARATION TIME: 10 minutes
COOKING TIME: 10-15 minutes
MAKES: about 30

Scant 2 cups baisen flour
¼-½ tsp salt
½ tsp baking soda
½ tsp omum (ajowan)
20 whole peppercorns, crushed
Pinch asafoetida
3 tblsp olive oil
Salad oil for frying

Sift flour, salt, soda and omum together. Add crushed peppercorns, asafoetida and 2 tblsp warm olive oil. Rub in well and knead with sufficient water to make a stiff dough. Take 1 tsp olive oil, rub over dough and knead. Repeat twice more until dough is quite smooth. Pass lumps of dough through a sev mould or spaghetti machine with a large hole setting. Fry the shaped baisen sticks in hot oil, over a low heat, until golden brown and crisp. Drain on kitchen paper and store in airtight containers. Serve with tea or drinks.

Egg Curry

PREPARATION TIME: 10 minutes
COOKING TIME: 20 minutes
SERVES: 3 people

1 large onion, peeled and chopped
1½ tblsp ghee or
1 tblsp salad or olive oil
1 inch cinnamon stick
1 bay leaf
4 small cardamoms
6 cloves
1 tsp garlic paste
1 tsp ginger paste
1 tsp ground coriander
1 tsp ground cumin
¼ tsp ground turmeric
1 tsp garam masala powder
1 tsp chili powder
1⅓ cups canned tomatoes, crushed
Salt to taste
¾ cup water
6 eggs, hard boiled and shelled
2 sprigs fresh green coriander leaves,
  chopped
2 green chilies, chopped

Fry onion in oil for 2-3 minutes. Add cinnamon, bay leaf, cardamoms and cloves. Fry for 1 minute. Add ginger and garlic pastes. Stir the mixture; add coriander, cumin, turmeric, garam masala and chili powder. Add canned tomatoes and salt to taste. Cook the spices for 5 minutes. Add water, cover and bring to the boil. Add eggs and cook for 10-12 minutes. Garnish with green chilies and fresh coriander leaves. The gravy can be increased or reduced as required. Serve with plain boiled rice.

Nimki and Papadi

PREPARATION TIME: 10 minutes
COOKING TIME: 15-20 minutes
MAKES: about 48

Scant 2 cups all-purpose flour
¼ tsp salt
½ tsp baking soda
1 tsp onion seed (kalongi)
½ tsp omum
Pinch of asafoetida
3 tblsp olive oil
Salad oil for deep frying

Sift flour, salt, and soda; add onion seed and omum. Add asafoetida and rub-in olive oil. Knead with sufficient water to make a stiff dough. Knead for 3-4 minutes until smooth. Make 2 equal portions. Roll out each portion as thinly as possible, to about ⅛ inch thick. Then cut the first piece of dough diagonally into strips both ways to make small bite-size diamond shapes and prick with a fork. Roll out the other dough to a similar thickness and cut neat round shapes with a clean, sharp jar lid or a biscuit cutter. Heat the salad oil and fry the shapes until golden brown and crisp. Drain on kitchen paper and allow to cool before storing them in jars or tins. These can be stored for up to 2 months. Serve with tea or drinks. The diamond shapes are called Nimki and the round shapes are called Papadi.

Ganthia (top) and Nimki and Papadi (bottom).

Meat, Poultry and Fish

Bhoona Gosht

PREPARATION TIME: 15 minutes

COOKING TIME: 1 hour

SERVES: 4 people

1 onion, peeled and chopped
3 tblsp salad or olive oil, or
2 tblsp ghee
1 inch cinnamon stick
6 small cardamoms
1 bay leaf
6 cloves
3 large cardamoms
1 tsp ginger paste
1 tsp garlic paste
1lb braising steak, lamb or beef,
    cubed
2 tsp ground coriander
2 tsp ground cumin
1 tsp chili powder
¼ tsp ground turmeric
4 large tomatoes or
⅔ cup canned tomatoes
1 cup water
Salt to taste
2 green chilies, chopped
2 sprigs fresh coriander, chopped

Fry onion in oil or ghee until light brown. Add cinnamon, cardamoms, cloves, bay leaf. Fry for one minute. Add ginger and garlic pastes and fry for further one minute. Add meat and sprinkle with coriander, cumin, chili and turmeric. Mix well and fry for 10 minutes. Add chopped fresh or canned tomatoes. Season with salt and add water. Cover and cook for 40-45 minutes on low heat, until meat is tender. Add chopped chilies and coriander.

Kofta Curry

PREPARATION TIME: 15 minutes

COOKING TIME: 30 minutes

SERVES: 4 people

1lb lean ground meat
½ tsp ginger paste
1 tsp garlic paste
1 egg
1 tsp ground garam masala
½ tsp chili powder

For sauce
1 onion, peeled and finely chopped
about 1½oz ghee or

2-3 tblsp salad or olive oil
6 small cardamoms
1 inch cinnamon stick
6 cloves
1 bay leaf
1 tsp garlic paste
1 tsp ginger paste
1 tsp ground cumin
½ tsp chili powder
¼ tsp ground turmeric
2 tsp ground coriander
Salt to taste
⅔ cup natural yogurt
2 tblsp ketchup
2½ cups water

To garnish
2 green chilies, chopped
2 sprigs fresh coriander, finely
    chopped

Mix ground meat with ginger, garlic paste and egg. Add garam masala and chili powder. Mix well and make 16-20 even-sized balls. Keep in a cool place.

Sauce
Fry onion in oil or ghee for 4 minutes until light golden brown. Add cardamom, cinnamon, cloves and bay leaf. Stir fry for one minute. Add garlic and ginger pastes and fry for another minute. Sprinkle with cumin, chili, turmeric and coriander. Stir well and add yogurt and ketchup. Add water, cover and bring to boil. Add salt. Slide meat balls one at a time into the saucepan. Shake the saucepan to settle the meat balls; do not stir otherwise the balls will break. Cover and simmer gently for 20 minutes. Garnish with chopped chilies and coriander leaves. Serve with rice or chapatis.

Keema Methi

PREPARATION TIME: 30 minutes

COOKING TIME: 30 minutes

SERVES: 4 people

1 onion, peeled and chopped
1½ tblsp ghee or
2 tblsp olive oil or salad
4 small green cardamoms
1 inch cinnamon stick

1 bay leaf
6 cloves
1 tsp ginger paste
1 tsp garlic paste
1lb ground lamb or beef
1 tsp chili powder
2 tsp ground coriander
2 tsp ground cumin
¼ tsp ground turmeric
⅔ cup natural yogurt
Salt to taste
1 bunch fresh methi leaves, stemmed
    and chopped, or
1 tblsp dry kasuri methi leaves

Fry onion in oil till just tender. Add cardamoms, cinnamon stick, bay leaf, cloves and fry for one minute. Add ginger and garlic pastes and cook for one minute. Add ground meat. Stir the mixture and sprinkle with chili, coriander, cumin and turmeric. Mix well and cook for 5 minutes. Add well-stirred yogurt and fresh methi leaves or dry methi. Cover and cook till liquid is absorbed. Season with salt. Serve with chapati or rice.

Dam Ke Kebab
(BAKED KEBAB)

PREPARATION TIME: 30 minutes

COOKING TIME: 1 hour

SERVES: 4 people

1lb lean ground beef
1 tsp ginger paste
1 tsp garlic paste
2 green chilies, ground or finely
    chopped
2 tsp garam masala
⅔ cup natural yogurt
¼ tsp meat tenderizer
2 sprigs fresh coriander leaves, finely
    chopped
1 tsp chili powder
2 eggs, beaten
1 onion, peeled, thinly sliced, and
    fried until crisp
Salt to taste
2 green chilies, chopped
Juice of 1 lemon
Salad or olive oil

Mix together the ground beef, ginger and garlic pastes, ground chili, garam masala, yogurt, meat tenderizer, half the finely chopped

coriander, chili powder, eggs and crisply fried onions. Mix well and season with salt. Spread the meat mixture to ½ inch thick in a well-greased baking tray. Brush with oil and bake in a preheated oven, 350°F for 20 minutes. Reduce temperature to 300°F for a further 20-30 minutes, or until liquid has evaporated. Cut into 2 inch squares. Garnish with chopped chihies and remaining fresh coriander leaves. Sprinkle with lemon juice before serving.

Boti-Kebab

PREPARATION TIME: 6 minutes
plus 3-4 hours to marinate

COOKING TIME: 30 minutes

SERVES: 4 people

1lb shoulder or leg of lamb, cut into
    bite size pieces
1 tsp ginger paste
1 tsp garlic paste
1 tsp chili powder
¼ tsp salt
2 tblsp brown vinegar
Juice of ½ a lemon
Salad or olive oil for basting
1 green pepper, seeded and cut into 1
    inch pieces
1 large onion, cut into 1 inch pieces
3-4 tomatoes, quartered

Mix meat with ginger, garlic, chili powder, salt and vinegar and leave to marinate for 3-4 hours. Sprinkle with lemon juice and rub spices well into meat; keep aside. Heat broiler. Thread pieces of meat onto skewers, alternating them with tomato, green pepper and onion. Brush with oil and broil for 3-4 minutes. Turn kebabs and continue cooking until meat is tender. Sprinkle with lemon juice and serve with mixed salad.

Facing page: Bhoona Gosht (top left), Kofta Curry (center right) and Keema Methi (bottom).

Dum Ke Kebab (left), Sheikh Kebab and Boti Kebab, skewered, (center) and Shami Kebab (right).

Rogan Josh (below).

Rogan Josh
(RICH LAMB WITH NUTS)

PREPARATION TIME: 20 minutes

COOKING TIME: 1 hour

SERVES: 4 people

1 onion, peeled and sliced
2½ tblsp ghee or
4 tblsp salad or olive oil
6 green cardamoms
4 large cardamoms
6 cloves
2 bay leaves
1 inch cinnamon stick
1 inch root ginger, crushed
3 cloves garlic, crushed
1lb boned lean lamb or beef, cut into cubes
1 tsp ground cumin
1 tsp chili powder
2 tsp paprika
1 tsp ground coriander
⅔ cup natural yogurt
1 tsp salt
2 tblsp chopped, blanched almonds
1 tblsp ground poppyseeds
1½ cups water
1 pinch saffron

Fry onion in ghee or oil until lightly browned. Stir fry cardamoms, cloves, bay leaf and cinnamon for 1 minute. Add ginger and garlic pastes, stir and add the meat. Sprinkle on, one at a time, the cumin, chili, paprika and coriander. Fry the mixture for 2 minutes. Add yogurt and salt; cover and cook for 5-7 minutes until dry, and oil separates. Add almonds and poppyseeds. Stir fry for 1-2 minutes and add water. Cover and cook for 40-50 minutes, simmering gently until meat is tender and the mixture is fairly dry. Sprinkle with saffron. Cover and cook gently for another 5-10 minutes, taking care not to burn the meat. Stir the mixture a few times to mix saffron. Rogan josh is a dry dish, with moist spices around the meat. Serve with pulao, nan or parathas.

Shami Kebab

PREPARATION TIME: 40 minutes

COOKING TIME: about 30 minutes

SERVES: 4 people

1lb leg of lamb, or beef, cubed
1¼ cups water
1 small onion, peeled and thickly sliced
1 inch root ginger, peeled and sliced
3 cloves of garlic, peeled and chopped
1 tblsp channa daal, washed, and presoaked in water for 10 minutes
1 inch cinnamon stick
1 bay leaf, finely crushed
1-2 eggs
Salt
6 cloves, ground
6 small cardamoms, ground
10 whole peppercorns, ground
1 tsp whole black cumin, ground
Salad or olive oil for frying

For filling
1 small onion, peeled and thinly sliced
2 tsp natural yogurt
Pinch of salt
1 sprig fresh coriander leaves, chopped

Pressure-cook meat with water, onion, ginger, garlic, channa daal, cinnamon and bay leaf for 15-20 minutes. Remove lid and evaporate remaining liquid. Remove cinnamon stick. Use an electric blender to mix the mixture to a sausage meat consistency. Add egg, season with salt, and sprinkle with ground spices. Mix well. Make 10-12 even portions. Mix onions, yogurt and coriander. Take a portion of meat, make a depression in the center, put a little of the onion yogurt filling in the center and pat the meat paste into a round, flat shape, to enclose the filling (about 2 inches in diameter). Continue to make the rest of the shamis in the same way. Heat oil in a skillet and fry the shamis light brown, for 2-3 minutes on each side. Serve with lemon wedges, onion salad and pitta bread.

Sheikh Kebab

PREPARATION TIME: 30 minutes

COOKING TIME: 20 minutes

SERVES: 4 people

1lb lean ground beef or lamb
1 onion, finely minced
1 green chili, ground to a paste
2 tsp kasuri methi
½ tsp chili powder
2 tsp garam masala powder
¼ tsp salt
2 sprigs fresh coriander leaves, chopped
1 tsp ginger paste
1 tsp garlic paste
2 eggs, beaten
Salad or olive oil
Lemon quarters

Picture below: Dum Ka Ran (top) and Masala Chops (bottom).

during cooking, add a little water or stock.

Masala Chops

PREPARATION TIME: 15 minutes

COOKING TIME: 20-30 minutes

SERVES: 4 people

4 lamb steaks
⅔ pint natural yogurt
1 tsp garlic paste
1 tsp ginger paste
1 tsp chili powder
1 tsp ground black pepper
1 tsp ground cumin
1 tsp salt
Salad or olive oil for basting

To garnish
Lemon wedges

Place lamb steaks in a bowl and add yogurt, garlic and ginger pastes, spices and salt. Mix spice mixture well into the lamb. Keep aside for 5-6 minutes. Pour on 2 tblsp oil and mix well. Spread aluminium baking foil over broiler tray. Arrange lamb steaks on top and broil for 5-6 minutes each side. Baste with oil if required. Alternatively, arrange lamb steaks on a baking tray and cook them in preheated oven, 350°F, for 30-35 minutes, turning them once. Serve hot with mixed salad and garnished with lemon wedges.

Dum Ka Ran

PREPARATION TIME: 24 hours
to marinate

COOKING TIME: 2 hours

SERVES: 8 people

5-6lb whole leg of lamb
2 cups natural yogurt
3 tblsp brown vinegar
1 tsp salt
Juice of 2 lemons
2 tsp chili powder
¼ tsp red food coloring
2 tsp garlic paste
2 tsp ginger paste
¼ tsp fine granulated sugar
Salad or olive oil for basting
Aluminium foil

Put meat in a large container and make 3-4 half-inch-deep cuts. Mix yogurt, vinegar, salt, lemon juice, chili powder, food coloring, garlic paste, ginger paste and sugar. Mix well and pour over the meat. Press

Mix the ground meat in a bowl with the onion, green chili, methi, chili powder, garam masala, salt, coriander, and ginger and garlic pastes; mix well. Add the beaten eggs and mix well. Let mixture stand for 10 minutes. Rub a skewer with a little oil. Take some of the mixture and spread it round the skewer to approximately 4 inches in length. Make the remaining sheikh kebabs. Cook them under the broiler, brushed with oil, for 3-4 minutes, turning frequently to cook all sides evenly. Serve piping hot with lemon quarters, tamarind pulp, or yogurt and mint chutney. A side salad of onions and plain roti goes well with sheikh kebab.

Tali-Kaleji/Gurda/Dil

PREPARATION TIME: 15 minutes

COOKING TIME: 40-45 minutes

SERVES: 4 people

½lb pig's liver, cut into half-inch cubes
4 lambs' kidneys, halved and cored
2 hearts, cored and cut into 1 inch pieces
1 tsp chili powder
2 tsp ground coriander
¼ tsp ground turmeric
2-3 cloves of garlic, or
1 tsp garlic paste
1 piece of root ginger or
1½ tsp ginger paste

2 tblsp ghee or
3 tblsp salad or olive oil
Salt to taste
Juice of 1 lemon

Rinse all the meats in lightly salted water and remove visible fats and sinew. Drain well and toss in chili powder, coriander, turmeric, ginger and garlic and set aside for 5 minutes. In a large saucepan, melt the oil or ghee and add the meat mixture. Cook gently for 40-45 minutes, stirring occasionally. Add salt to taste. The color will change to dark brown. When the mixture is dry and the oil separates, remove from heat and sprinkle with lemon juice. If the meats become too dry

well into the cuts and cover the container; refrigerate overnight to marinate. Turn once. Next day remove meat and discard marinade. Wrap in baking foil. Cook in a preheated oven at 375°F for 1-1¼ hours. Baste occasionally with oil and turn the meat to brown evenly. Reduce heat to 325°F, and cook for another 45 minutes. Serve with daal and pulao.

Karai Gosht

PREPARATION TIME: 15 minutes

COOKING TIME: 40-60 minutes

SERVES: 4 people

1lb lean beef, pork or lamb, cut into 1 inch pieces
1 tsp chili powder
1 tsp ground cumin
1 tsp ground coriander

1 tblsp aniseed powder
2 tsp kasuri dry methi leaves
⅔ cup natural yogurt
3 tblsp ghee or
4 tblsp salad or olive oil
1 large onion, peeled and sliced
2 bay leaves
2 inch cinnamon stick
6 cloves
6 small cardamoms
2 inch root ginger, peeled and crushed
4 cloves of garlic, peeled and crushed
¾ cup water
Salt to taste

In a bowl mix the meat with chili, cumin, coriander, aniseed powder, methi leaves and yogurt. Keep aside. Fry onion in oil until tender (4-5 minutes). Add bay leaves, cinnamon, cloves, small cardamoms, ginger and garlic and fry for 2 minutes. Add marinated meat, water and salt to taste. Cover the pan and cook for 30 minutes. Transfer the meat to a wok or large

skillet and stir fry until the liquid has almost evaporated. Add extra water gradually, if needed, and keep stir frying until meat is tender. The oil should separate. This is a dry dish.

Meat Do Piaza

PREPARATION TIME: 15 minutes

COOKING TIME: 50-60 minutes

SERVES: 4 people

1 small onion, peeled and chopped
2½ tblsp ghee or
3 tblsp salad or olive oil
1lb shoulder or leg of lamb, cubed
1 tsp ginger paste
1 tsp garlic paste
1 inch cinnamon stick
6 cloves
6 small cardamoms
1 tsp chili powder

1 tsp ground coriander
2 tsp ground cumin
⅔ cup water
Salt to taste
2 large onions, peeled and cut into thin rings
Juice of 1 lemon
2 sprigs green fresh coriander leaves, chopped
1-2 green chilies
Extra oil if needed

Fry chopped onion in oil or ghee until just tender. Add meat, ginger, garlic, cinnamon, cloves, cardamoms, chili powder, coriander

This page: Tali Kaleji/Gurda/Dil (left), Meat Palak (center right) and Meat Madras (bottom right). Facing page: Meat Do Piaza (top), Korma (center right) and Karai Gosht (bottom).

and cumin. Fry for 5-6 minutes. Add water and salt to taste. Cook covered for 30-40 minutes on low heat until meat is cooked and liquid has evaporated. Add onion rings – they can be fried in a little extra oil if desired. Stir the meat; cover and cook for a further 10-15 minutes. The onions should be tender. Sprinkle with lemon juice and add green chilies and coriander. This is a dry dish. Serve with pulaos or puri.

Meat Palak

PREPARATION TIME: 30-45 minutes

COOKING TIME: 1 hour

SERVES: 4 people

4 tblsp ghee or
4 tblsp salad or olive oil
1 medium onion, peeled and chopped
1 bay leaf
1 inch cinnamon stick
4 small cardamoms
6 cloves
1 inch root ginger, crushed
3-4 cloves of garlic, crushed
1lb lean lamb or beef, cubed
2/3 cup natural yogurt
1 tsp chili powder
1/2 tsp ground turmeric
2 tsp ground coriander
2 green chilies, chopped
2 sprigs of fresh green coriander, chopped
1lb leaf spinach, boiled and puréed (or canned or frozen spinach purée)
Salt to taste

Heat the oil and fry the onion until light golden brown. Add bay leaf, cinnamon, cardamoms and cloves. Fry for one minute. Add ginger and garlic paste and fry for a further minute. Add meat and yogurt and sprinkle with chili, turmeric and coriander. Season with salt and cook with the lid on until moisture evaporates (30-40 minutes). Add puréed or canned spinach, mix well and cook for a further 15-20 minutes on a low heat until oil rises to the top. Garnish with chopped chili and coriander.

Chicken Masala

PREPARATION TIME: 10 minutes and marinate overnight

COOKING TIME: 40-50 minutes plus 10 minutes

SERVES: 8-10 people

3lb chicken, cut into 8-10 pieces
2 tblsp salad or olive oil
2/3 cup natural yogurt
1 tsp ground ginger
1 tsp garlic paste
2 tsp ground cumin
2 tsp garam masala
1 tsp salt
Juice of 1 lemon
2 tsp ground black pepper
2 tsp ground mango
1 tsp kasuri methi
1 tsp dry mint powder

Marinate chicken pieces overnight in a well-mixed marinade made from the oil, yogurt, ginger, garlic, cumin, garam masala, salt and lemon juice. Roast chicken with marinade, wrapped in baking foil, in a preheated oven 375°F, for 40-50 minutes. Save the liquid and mix with the black pepper, mango, methi and mint powder. Mix well and keep aside. Cool chicken slightly and cut into bite size pieces. Pour in the liquid mixture and mix well. Transfer onto baking tray and bake for further 10-15 minutes until the chicken pieces are dry. Serve as a snack, or with cocktails.

Meat Madras

PREPARATION TIME: 10 minutes

COOKING TIME: 1 hour

SERVES: 4 people

1 onion, peeled and chopped
2 tblsp ghee or
3 tblsp salad or olive oil
3/4 inch cinnamon stick
4 small cardamoms
2 bay leaves
6 fresh curry leaves
6 cloves
1 tblsp grated fresh coconut, or shredded coconut
1/4 tsp fenugreek seeds, crushed
3 cloves garlic, peeled and chopped
1 inch root ginger, peeled and sliced
1lb braising steak or lamb, cut into cubes
Salt to taste
1 tsp chili powder
2 tsp ground coriander
2 tsp ground cumin
1/4 tsp ground turmeric
4 tomatoes, quartered
1 cup water
2 green chilies, quartered (optional)
2 sprigs fresh green coriander, chopped
Juice of 1 lemon

Fry onion in ghee or oil until just tender (2-3 minutes). Add cinnamon, cardamoms, bay leaves, curry leaves, cloves, coconut, fenugreek seeds, garlic and ginger and fry for 1-2 minutes. Add meat and fry for 3 minutes. Sprinkle with chili, coriander, cumin, and turmeric. Stir well and add water. Cover and cook for 20 minutes. Add salt, and cook for a further 15-20 minutes until liquid has evaporated. Add tomatoes, chili and coriander leaves. Cover and cook for 10 minutes on a low heat. Sprinkle with lemon juice. Serve with parathas.

Chicken Tomato

PREPARATION TIME: 30 minutes

COOKING TIME: 40-50 minutes

SERVES: 4-6 people

1 onion, peeled and chopped
3 tblsp salad or olive oil or
2 tblsp ghee
1 inch cinnamon stick
1 bay leaf
6 cloves
6 green cardamoms
1 inch root ginger, peeled and sliced
4 cloves garlic, peeled and chopped
3lb roasting chicken, cut into 8-10 pieces
1 tsp chili powder
1 tsp ground cumin
1 tsp ground coriander
2 cups canned tomatoes, crushed
1 tsp salt
2 sprigs fresh green coriander leaves, chopped
2 green chilies, halved

Fry onion for 2 minutes in oil or ghee. Add the cinnamon, bay leaf, cloves, and cardamoms; fry for 1 minute then add ginger and garlic. Fry for half a minute. Add chicken pieces. Sprinkle with chili powder, cumin, coriander. Fry for 2-3 minutes and add crushed tomatoes. Season with salt and add chopped green coriander and chilies. Stir chicken to mix well. Cover and cook for 40-45 minutes until chicken is tender.

Chicken Tandoori

Although the true taste of tandoori (clay oven) is not achieved, a very good result is obtained by baking in a conventional oven.

PREPARATION TIME: 10 minutes and marinate overnight

COOKING TIME: 30-40 minutes

SERVES: 4-6 people

3lb chicken, cut into 8-10 pieces
1 tsp garlic paste
1 tsp ginger paste
1 tsp ground black pepper
1 tsp paprika
1/4 tsp red food coloring
1 tsp salt
3 tblsp brown vinegar
Juice of 1 lemon
2/3 cup natural yogurt
1 tsp dry mint powder
Salad or olive oil
1 lemon, cut into wedges

Mix all the ingredients together, apart from the lemon wedges and oil. Marinate chicken overnight. Arrange chicken pieces on baking tray. Brush with oil and bake in preheated oven 375°F for 40 minutes, turning them over so that they bake evenly. Bake until dry and well browned. Serve with lemon wedges.

Korma

PREPARATION TIME: 15 minutes

COOKING TIME: 40-50 minutes

SERVES: 4 people

2 tblsp ghee or
3 tblsp salad or olive oil
1 medium onion, peeled and thinly sliced
1 inch cinnamon stick
6 cloves
6 small cardamoms
1 bay leaf
1 tsp small whole black cumin seeds
2 tsp ginger paste
1 tsp garlic paste
1lb shoulder of lamb, cubed
1 tsp chili powder
1 tsp ground coriander
2 tsp ground cumin
1/4 tsp ground turmeric
2/3 cup natural yogurt
3/4 cup water
Salt to taste
2 sprigs fresh coriander, chopped
2 green chilies, halved
1 tblsp ground almonds

Facing page: Chicken Tandoori (top), Chicken Tomato (center right) and Chicken Masala (bottom).

Fry onion in oil or ghee until golden brown. Add cinnamon, cloves, cardamoms, bay leaf and black cumin. Fry for 1 minute and add ginger and garlic paste. Stir for half a minute. Add meat and sprinkle with chili, coriander, cumin and turmeric. Mix well and add yogurt. Cover and cook for 10-15 minutes, stirring the mixture occasionally. Add water, salt to taste and cover. Cook on low temperature for 30-40 minutes, or until meat is tender. Korma should have a medium-thick gravy. Add ground almonds, green chilies and coriander leaves, and a little hot water if necessary. Serve with rice or chapatis.

Pork Vindaloo

PREPARATION TIME: 15 minutes

COOKING TIME: 1-1¼ hours

SERVES: 4 people

1 large onion, peeled and chopped
3 tblsp ghee or
3 tblsp salad or olive oil
1 inch cinnamon stick
6 cloves
6 green cardamoms
1 tsp ginger paste
1 tsp garlic paste
1lb lean pork, cut into cubes

3 tblsp brown vinegar
1 tsp chili powder
1 tsp ground cumin
2 tsp ground coriander
2 tblsp tamarind pulp concentrate
2 tsp ketchup
2 tsp brown sugar
Water
2 sprigs fresh green coriander leaves, chopped
1-2 green chilies, chopped
Salt to taste
1 tblsp salad or olive oil, for tempering
6-8 curry leaves

Fry onion in ghee or oil until light brown. Add cinnamon stick, cloves and cardamoms. Fry for half a minute. Add ginger and garlic pastes and pork and fry for 5 minutes, or until liquid from the pork has evaporated. Add vinegar, chili, cumin, coriander, tamarind pulp, ketchup and sugar. Cover and cook for 10-15 minutes. Add a little water if the mixture is too dry. Sprinkle with coriander leaves and chopped chili. Cook on a low heat for 30-40 minutes or until the pork is tender. The dish should have a rich gravy. Heat tempering oil and add the curry leaves. When leaves turn crisp and dark, pour the flavored oil and leaves over the curry. Mix well before serving. Serve with boiled rice.

Chicken Dhansak

PREPARATION TIME: 20 minutes

COOKING TIME: 40-50 minutes

SERVES: 6 people

3 tblsp ghee or
3 tblsp salad or olive oil
1 onion, peeled and chopped
4 cloves garlic, chopped
1 inch ginger paste
¼ tsp ground turmeric
1 tsp chili powder
2 tsp ground cumin
2 tsp ground coriander
4 green cardamoms, ground
8 peppercorns, ground
1 inch cinnamon stick, finely crumbled
2 tomatoes, quartered
3lb chicken cut into 10-12 pieces (ribcage discarded)
2½oz toor daal (yellow lentils), washed in a few changes of water
2½oz moong daal, washed in a few changes of water
2½oz masoor daal (red lentils) washed in a few changes of water
1 medium eggplant cut into ½ inch cubes
4oz red pumpkin, peeled and cut into 1 inch cubes
4 sprigs fresh methi leaves, chopped, or
4oz spinach leaves, chopped
2 sprigs fresh green coriander leaves,

chopped
3¾ cups water
Salt to taste
1 tblsp brown sugar (or grated jaggery)
2 tblsp tamarind pulp concentrate
1 onion, sliced and fried until brown
1 lemon, sliced

Heat the ghee or oil in a deep skillet and fry chopped onion until light brown. Add garlic, ginger, turmeric, chili, cumin, coriander, ground cardamom, peppercorns and cinnamon stick; stir fry for 1 minute. Add tomatoes and cook for 2-3 minutes. Add chicken and cook until the juices have evaporated (10-15 minutes). Add the daals, eggplant, pumpkin, methi

This page: Chicken Makhani (left), Dum Ka Murgh (center) and Chicken Dhansak (right).

Facing page: Goan Curry (top) and Pork Vindaloo (bottom).

fry for 1-2 minutes. Add pork and fry for 5-7 minutes or until liquid from pork has evaporated. Add tamarind pulp, yogurt, turmeric, black pepper, cumin, coriander, sugar, coconut and salt to taste. Mix well; cover and cook for 20-30 minutes. Add a little water if the mixture is too dry. Add green coriander and chili. Cover and cook for 20-25 minutes or until pork is tender. The dish should have a smooth gravy. Serve with plain boiled rice.

Dum Ka Murgh
(WHOLE CHICKEN OR CHICKEN JOINTS)
The recipe can be used for both jointed and whole chicken.

PREPARATION TIME: 30 minutes
COOKING TIME: 1 hour
SERVES: 4-6 people

1 onion, finely minced
2 tsp ground coriander
1 tsp chili powder
¼ tsp ground turmeric
1 tblsp ketchup
1 tsp ginger paste
1 tsp garlic paste
½ tsp salt
⅔ cup natural yogurt
3lb chicken, cut into 8-10 pieces
Salad or olive oil

Mix onion, coriander, chili, turmeric, ketchup, ginger, garlic and salt with yogurt. Rub the mixture onto the chicken pieces. Brush with oil and bake in an oven at 375°F for 50 minutes to 1 hour, brushing frequently with oil until the liquid has evaporated and the chicken is cooked. For a whole chicken, bake with the above spices, wrapped in baking foil, for 1½ to 1¾ hours, then evaporate the liquid.

Chicken Makhani
(BUTTER CHICKEN)

PREPARATION TIME: 20 minutes
COOKING TIME: 1 hour
SERVES: 4-6 people

⅔ cup natural yogurt
1 tsp ginger paste
1 tsp salt
¼ tsp red or orange food coloring
3lb chicken, cut into 8-10 pieces, with skin removed
Salad or olive oil
¼ cup butter

leaves and fresh coriander. Mix well and add the water. Add salt. Cover and cook on low heat until chicken is tender (20-30 minutes). Remove from heat and take chicken pieces out. Mash daal with the aid of a masher, or beat with an egg whisk, until the daal blends with the water to form a smooth, greenish gravy. Return chicken to skillet and sprinkle with sugar or jaggery and tamarind pulp. Cover and cook for 10 minutes. Before serving, a little extra water may be used to thin down the gravy if it is too thick. Garnish dhansak with onion rings and lemon slices and serve with rice.

Goan Curry

PREPARATION TIME: 20 minutes
COOKING TIME: 1 hour
SERVES: 4 people

3 tblsp ghee or
3 tblsp salad or olive oil
1 large onion, peeled and chopped
1 bay leaf
1 inch cinnamon stick
5 green cardamoms
6 cloves
1½ tsp garlic paste
1 tsp ginger paste
8 curry leaves
1lb lean pork, cut into cubes

1 tblsp tamarind pulp concentrate
⅔ cup natural yogurt
¼ tsp ground turmeric
1 tsp ground black pepper
1 tsp ground cumin
1 tsp ground coriander
½ tsp brown sugar
1 tblsp shredded coconut
Salt to taste
⅔ cup water
2 sprigs fresh green coriander leaves, chopped
2 green chilies, chopped

Heat oil or ghee and fry onion until golden brown. Add bay leaf, cinnamon, cardamoms, cloves, garlic, ginger and curry leaves and

1 inch cinnamon stick
6 cloves
6 green cardamoms
1 bay leaf
⅔ cup sour cream
¼ tsp saffron, crushed
⅔ cup pouring cream
Salt to taste
2 tsp ground almonds
¼ tsp cornstarch
1 tblsp water

Mix yogurt, ginger paste, salt and red coloring and rub into chicken. Let it marinate overnight. Place in an ovenproof dish and brush with oil. Bake in oven, 375°F, for 40-50 minutes. Save the liquid, if any. In a saucepan, melt butter and fry cinnamon, cloves, cardamoms and bay leaf for 1 minute. Add sour cream and chicken liquid. Add crushed saffron and pouring cream. Cover and simmer gently for 5-6 minutes. Add chicken pieces and adjust seasoning. Add ground almonds. Dissolve cornstarch in water and add to the chicken. Let it thicken. Cover and simmer for 3-4 minutes. Remove from heat. Serve with nan.

Malabari Chicken

PREPARATION TIME: 20 minutes

COOKING TIME: 40-50 minutes

SERVES: 6 people

1 large onion, peeled and chopped
3 tblsp ghee or
3 tblsp salad or olive oil
1 inch cinnamon stick
6 green cardamoms
6 cloves
1 bay leaf
1 tsp ginger paste
1 tsp garlic paste
3lb chicken, cut into 10-12 pieces
1 tsp chili powder
1 tsp ground cumin
1 tsp ground coriander
⅔ cup natural yogurt
1 tsp salt
1 tblsp coconut cream
1 tblsp flaked almonds
1 tblsp raisins
½ cup water
2 tblsp evaporated milk
2 sprigs fresh green coriander leaves, chopped (optional)
2 green chilies, chopped (optional)
1 cup canned pineapple chunks

Fry onion in ghee or oil until tender (3-4 minutes). Add cinnamon, cardamoms, cloves and bay leaf and fry for one minute. Then add ginger and garlic paste.

Stir fry for half a minute. Add chicken. Stir and cook for 2-3 minutes. Sprinkle with chili, cumin and coriander. Stir and mix well. Add yogurt and salt. Cover and cook for 10 minutes or until yogurt is dry and oil separates. Add coconut cream, almonds, raisins and water. Cover and cook for 20-30 minutes. Add evaporated milk and cook for 5 minutes. Add coriander leaves, green chilies and pineapple chunks. Mix gently and cook for another 5 minutes. Malabari chicken is a moist curry with a thick, rich sauce. It is served with pulao rice.

Chicken Tikka

PREPARATION TIME: 10 minutes

COOKING TIME: 30 minutes

SERVES: 6 people

⅔ cup natural yogurt
1 tsp chili powder
2 tsp ginger paste
2 tsp garlic paste
2 tsp garam masala powder
½ tsp salt
¼ tsp red food coloring
3lb chicken, cut into 2½ inch pieces
Juice of 1 lemon
Salad or olive oil

1 lemon, cut into wedges

Mix yogurt with chili powder, ginger and garlic, garam masala, salt and red food coloring. Pour over chicken pieces and mix well. Sprinkle with lemon juice. Mix well. Line the broiler pan with baking foil. Arrange chicken pieces on top. Brush with oil and broil them for 4-5 minutes on each side. Brush with oil occasionally and continue cooking until chicken is tender. Serve with wedges of lemon and a crisp lettuce salad.

Maach Bhaja
(MACKEREL FRY)

PREPARATION TIME: 10 minutes

COOKING TIME: 15 minutes

SERVES: 4 people

2 large mackerel, gutted and cut into 1 inch thick slices
1 tsp chili powder
1 tsp ground turmeric
1 tsp salt
Salad or olive oil for frying
Lemon juice

Wash fish thoroughly. Drain and dry well. Sprinkle with chili powder, turmeric and salt. Rub in well. Heat oil and fry fish, a few

pieces at a time, for 3-4 minutes on each side. Drain on kitchen paper. Serve with lemon juice sprinkled over fish.

Sprat Fry

PREPARATION TIME: 10 minutes

COOKING TIME: 15-20 minutes

SERVES: 2-3 people

8oz cleaned sprats, washed and dried
¼ tsp ground turmeric
1 tsp chili powder
1 tsp salt
Salad or olive oil for deep frying
Lemon juice

Rub sprats well with turmeric, chili powder and salt. Gently heat oil and fry fish, a few at a time, for 6-8 minutes, until crisp. Drain on kitchen paper. Sprinkle with lemon juice and serve.

Masala Fish
(WHOLE FRIED FISH)

PREPARATION TIME: 10 minutes

COOKING TIME: 15 minutes

SERVES: 6 people

1 tsp ginger paste
1 tsp garlic paste
1 tsp salt
3 sprigs fresh green coriander leaves, crushed
2 green chilies, crushed
1 tsp ground black pepper
¼ tsp ground turmeric
1 tblsp water
6 herring or rainbow trout, gutted, washed and dried
Salad or olive oil
Lemon slices

Make 3 diagonal slits on each fish. Mix together the ginger, garlic, salt, coriander, chili, ground pepper and turmeric. Add the water. Rub spices over fish, and inside the cuts. Broil for 10-15 minutes, brushing with oil and turning the fish occasionally, until cooked. Garnish with lemon slices.

This page: Malabari Chicken (top) and Chicken Tikka (bottom).

Facing page: Main dish – top to bottom – Masala Fish, Maach Bhaja, Sprat Fry and Cod Roe Fry.

Cod Curry

PREPARATION TIME: 15 minutes
COOKING TIME: 20 minutes
SERVES: 3-4 people

3 tblsp ghee or
3 tblsp salad or olive oil
1 large onion, peeled and chopped
1 inch cinnamon stick
1 bay leaf
1 tsp ginger paste
1 tsp garlic paste
1 tsp chili powder
1 tsp ground cumin
1 tsp ground coriander
¼ tsp ground turmeric
⅔ cup natural yogurt
1-2 green chilies, chopped
2 sprigs fresh green coriander leaves,
  chopped

1 tsp salt
1lb cod fillet, cut into 2 inch pieces

Melt ghee or oil and fry onion until golden brown. Add cinnamon, bay leaf, ginger and garlic pastes. Fry for 1 minute. Add chili, cumin, coriander and turmeric. Fry for 1 minute. Add yogurt, chopped green chilies and fresh coriander leaves. Add salt and cover. Simmer for 2-3 minutes. Add ⅔ cup water. Bring to boil. Add cod. Cover and cook gently for 15-18 minutes. Serve with rice.

Prawn Curry

PREPARATION TIME: 15 minutes
COOKING TIME: 20 minutes
SERVES: 4 people

1 large onion, peeled and chopped
3 tblsp ghee or
3 tblsp salad or olive oil
1 inch cinnamon stick
6 green cardamoms
6 cloves
1 bay leaf

1 tsp ginger paste
1 tsp garlic paste
1 tsp chili powder
1 tsp ground cumin
1 tsp ground coriander
½ tsp salt
1 green pepper, chopped into ½ inch
  pieces
1½ cups canned tomatoes, crushed
1lb large shrimps, peeled
2 green chilies, chopped
2 sprigs fresh green coriander leaves,
  chopped

Prawn Curry (left), Cod Curry (center), and Fish Kebab (right).

Fry onion in oil or ghee until just tender (3-4 minutes). Add cinnamon, cardamoms, cloves and bay leaf. Fry for 1 minute and then add ginger and garlic pastes. Add chili, cumin, coriander and salt. Fry for half a minute. Add chopped green pepper and tomatoes, then bring to the boil. Add prawns, cover and bring to boil. Cook for 10-15 minutes. Add chopped green coriander leaves and chopped chilies. Serve with plain boiled rice.

Cod Roe Fry

PREPARATION TIME: 5 minutes

COOKING TIME: 15 minutes

SERVES: 2-3 people

½lb soft cod roes
¼ tsp ground turmeric
1 tsp chili powder
½ tsp salt
1 tblsp all-purpose flour

For batter
1 cup baisen flour, sifted
¼ tsp salt
1 egg, beaten
Water
Salad or olive oil for deep frying

Put cod roes in a mixing bowl. Sprinkle with spices, one at a time, and add salt. Rub well so as to coat the roes thoroughly, then roll them in flour and keep aside. For the batter: mix the baisen flour, salt, egg and sufficient water to make a smooth coating batter. Heat oil gently. Fry the roes, a few at a time, well coated in batter, until crisp and golden. Drain on kitchen paper and serve hot.

Fish Kebab

PREPARATION TIME: 20 minutes

COOKING TIME: 15 minutes

SERVES: 3 people

10oz whiting or coley fillet (or other white fish)
1 onion, peeled and chopped
1 inch root ginger, peeled and finely chopped
1 green chili, finely chopped
2 sprigs fresh green coriander leaves, finely chopped
1 egg, beaten
2 tsp garam masala powder
Salt to taste
1 tsp ground black pepper
Juice of 1 lemon
Salad or olive oil

Boil fish in water for 8-10 minutes. Cool and drain. Remove skin and bones and mash fish flesh. Add choped onion, ginger, chili, coriander leaves, egg, garam masala, salt, black pepper and lemon juice. Beat or grind into a smooth paste. Devide into 10-12 equal-sized portions, and pat each portion into a flat burger shape. Heat oil in a skillet and shallow fry on each side for 3-4 minutes. Serve with onion salad.

Vegetables, Pulses and Chutney

Narangi Piyaz Salad (ONION AND ORANGE SALAD)

PREPARATION TIME: 15 minutes

SERVES: 2-3 people

2 large seedless oranges
6 green onions, finely chopped
Salt
2 tsp lemon juice
¼ tsp ground black pepper
½ tsp brown sugar
2 tsp salad or olive oil

Peel oranges and separate into segments. Cut each segment in half. Add onions, salt, lemon juice, pepper, sugar and oil. Gently toss to mix. Serve as a side salad.

Channa (CHICKPEA)

PREPARATION TIME: soaking overnight

COOKING TIME: 20-30 minutes

SERVES: 4 people

8oz chickpeas
1 tsp baking soda
3 tblsp ghee or
3 tblsp salad or olive oil
1 onion, peeled and chopped
1 bay leaf
1 inch cinnamon stick
4 black cardamoms
1 tsp ginger paste
1 tsp garlic paste
1 tsp ground coriander
1 tsp chili powder
¼ tsp ground turmeric
5 tomatoes, chopped or
1-2 green chilies, cut in half
Salt to taste
2 sprigs fresh green coriander leaves, chopped

Soak chickpeas overnight in 3 cups water with the baking soda. Drain chickpeas and boil in 2½ cups of water for 10-12 minutes in a pressure cooker. Strain and save the liquid. Heat ghee or oil and add onion, bay leaf, cinnamon and cardamoms. Fry for 1-2 minutes. Add ginger and garlic pastes. Fry for 1 minute. Sprinkle with

coriander, chili and turmeric. Mix well and fry for half a minute. Add tomatoes, green chilies and chickpeas. Mix well and add 1 cup chickpea cooking liquid. Cover and simmer gently for 10-15 minutes. Add salt and green coriander. The chickpeas should disintegrate when pressed between thumb and index finger. If not fully tender, add extra water and continue cooking. Channa is a thick, moist dish. Serve with kulcha or nan.

Kassi Mooli (GRATED MOOLI)

PREPARATION TIME: 10 minutes

SERVES: 4 people

8oz mooli
Salt to taste
Juice of 1 lemon
1 green chili, finely chopped
1 sprig fresh green coriander leaves, chopped

Wash and scrape mooli. Wash again and grate. Drain in a sieve and let some of the liquid run through. Press and squeeze gently. Put the drained grated mooli in a dish. Sprinkle with salt and lemon juice and mix in green chili and fresh coriander leaves. Serve with daal and roti. Note: mooli has a very strong smell; always store well wrapped in cling film, in the refrigerator.

Red Cabbage and Carrot Salad

PREPARATION TIME: 10 minutes

SERVES: 4 people

½ small red cabbage, finely chopped
2-3 carrots, peeled and grated
3 tblsp raisins
1 tsp brown sugar
¼ tsp salt, or to taste
⅔ cup sour cream
2 tsp lemon juice

Mix cabbage, carrots and raisins.

Sprinkle with sugar and salt and pour over the well-stirred sour cream. Sprinkle with lemon juice and mix well. Serve with any meal as a side salad. A thin mayonnaise may be used in place of sour cream.

Lobia Curry (BLACK EYED LOBIA BEAN CURRY)

PREPARATION TIME: soak overnight and 10 minutes

COOKING TIME: 30-40 minutes

SERVES: 4 people

8oz lobia beans, washed and soaked overnight in water
1 onion, peeled and chopped
3 tblsp ghee or
3 tblsp salad or olive oil
1 bay leaf
1 inch cinnamon stick
1 tsp ginger paste
1 tsp garlic paste
¼ tsp ground turmeric
1 tsp ground coriander
1 tsp chili powder
4 tomatoes, chopped
Salt to taste
2 green chilies, halved and chopped
2 sprigs fresh green coriander leaves, chopped

Boil drained lobia beans in 2½ cups water for 20 minutes. Cool. Fry onion in ghee or oil for 3-4 minutes. Add bay leaf, cinnamon, ginger and garlic pastes and fry for 2 minutes. Add turmeric, ground coriander, chili powder and stir the mixture well. Add drained boiled lobia beans and tomatoes. Add salt, chopped chili and fresh coriander leaves. Cover and cook for 10-15 minutes on gentle heat. The gravy should be thick. Serve with rice or rotis.

This page: Narangi Piyaz Salad (top) and Red Cabbage and Carrot Salad (bottom) with Kassi Mooli.

Facing page: Lobia Curry (top), Razma (center right) and Channa (bottom).

Aloo Methi
(POTATO AND FRESH FENUGREEK LEAVES)

PREPARATION TIME: 10 minutes

COOKING TIME: 10 minutes

SERVES: 3 people

3 tblsp ghee or
3 tblsp salad or olive oil
1 tsp cumin seed
1 pinch asafoetida (hing)
3 medium potatoes, peeled and cut
　into chunks
1 bunch fresh methi leaves, chopped
1 tsp chili powder
1 tsp ground coriander
Salt
¼ tsp ground turmeric
Juice of 1 lemon

Heat ghee or oil and add cumin seed and hing. When seeds begin to crackle, add potatoes. Fry and cook potatoes for 3-4 minutes then add methi leaves. Mix well and sprinkle with chili powder, coriander, salt and turmeric. Stir the mixture to distribute spices evenly. Cover and cook on low heat for 6-8 minutes. Add lemon juice before serving.

Kachhoomar
(SHREDDED ONION SALAD)

PREPARATION TIME: 20-25 minutes

SERVES: 4 people

1 large Spanish onion, finely sliced
　into rings
¼ tsp salt
¼ tsp chili powder
1 sprig fresh green coriander leaves,
　chopped

Aloo Gajjar (left), Toorai Tarkari (center) and Aloo Methi (right).

1 green chili, chopped
1 tblsp lemon juice
2 tomatoes, chopped (optional)

Put the onion slices into a dish with the salt, chili powder, fresh coriander, green chili and lemon juice. Mix well so as to release onion juice. Add tomatoes and mix well. Serve with meat or with kebabs.

Aloo Gajjar

PREPARATION TIME: 10 minutes

COOKING TIME: 10-15 minutes

SERVES: 2-3 people

3 tblsp ghee or
2 tblsp salad or olive oil
1 tsp cumin seeds
2 medium potatoes, peeled and cut into ½ inch cubes
3 medium carrots, scraped and cubed
1 tsp chili powder

1 tsp ground coriander
¼ tsp ground turmeric
Salt to taste
Juice of half a lemon

Heat ghee or oil and add cumin seeds. When they begin to crackle, add potatoes. Fry for 3-4 minutes then add carrots. Stir the mixture and sprinkle with chili, coriander, turmeric and salt. Stir fry the mixture for 1-2 minutes then cover and cook on low heat for 8-10 minutes. Sprinkle with a little water to help cook carrots. Sprinkle with lemon juice before serving.

Razma
(RED KIDNEY BEAN CURRY)

PREPARATION TIME: razma to be soaked overnight

COOKING TIME: 40-50 minutes

SERVES: 4 people

8oz red kidney beans, washed
1 tsp baking soda
3 tblsp ghee or
3 tblsp salad or olive oil
1 onion, peeled and chopped
1 inch cinnamon stick
1 bay leaf

3 black cardamoms
1 tsp ginger paste
1 tsp garlic paste
1 tsp chili powder
1 tsp ground coriander
1 tsp garam masala powder
¼ tsp ground turmeric
1 cup canned tomatoes, crushed
Salt to taste
2 green chilies, halved
2 sprigs fresh green coriander leaves, chopped

Soak kidney beans in 2½ cups water with baking soda overnight. Next day, pressure-cook the kidney beans in 2½ cups fresh water for 5-8 minutes. Cool and drain the beans, retaining the liquid. Heat ghee or oil and fry onion for 2-3

minutes. Add cinnamon, bay leaf, cardamoms, ginger and garlic pastes. Cook for 1 minute. Add chili powder, ground coriander, garam masala and turmeric. Stir the spices well. Add tomatoes and salt. Add kidney beans and cook the mixture for 2-3 minutes. Add 1 cup bean cooking liquid. Sprinkle with green chili and fresh coriander leaves. Simmer for 15-20 minutes. Add extra liquid if gravy is too thick. Remove from heat and serve.

Saag Bhaji
(BRUSSELS SPROUT BHAJI)

PREPARATION TIME: 6 minutes

COOKING TIME: 10 minutes

SERVES: 4 people

3 tblsp ghee or
3 tblsp salad or olive oil
1 tsp five spice mixture (panch-
   phoran)
1 bay leaf
1 inch cinnamon stick
1lb Brussels sprouts, cut in half
1 tsp chili powder
1½ tsp ground coriander
¼ tsp ground turmeric
Salt
1 tsp brown sugar
4 cloves, ground
Juice of 1 lemon

Heat ghee or oil and add five spice
mixture. Add bay leaf and
cinnamon stick and fry for half a
minute. Add Brussels sprouts. Mix
well and sprinkle with chili powder,
coriander and turmeric. Add salt to
taste and stir well to blend all the
spices. Cover and cook on gentle
heat for 8-10 minutes, stirring the
mixture occasionally. Sprinkle with
sugar and ground cloves. Mix well.
Cover and cook for another 2-3
minutes. Sprinkle with lemon juice
before serving.

Toorai Tarkari
(ZUCCHINI CURRY)

PREPARATION TIME: 10 minutes

COOKING TIME: 15 minutes

SERVES: 3 people

1½ tblsp salad or olive oil
1 tsp cumin seeds
½lb zucchini, peeled and sliced into
   ¼ inch thick rounds
½ tsp chili powder
1 tsp ground coriander
¼ tsp ground turmeric
3-4 tomatoes, chopped
Salt to taste
1 green chili, halved
1 sprig fresh green coriander leaves,
   chopped

Heat oil and add cumin seeds.
When they crackle add zucchini
slices. Stir and sprinkle with chili
powder, coriander and turmeric.
Mix well and add chopped
tomatoes. Sprinkle with salt, green
chili and fresh coriander. Cover
and cook for 10-12 minutes.

Phalon-Ka-Chaat
(SWEET AND SOUR FRUIT SALAD)

PREPARATION TIME: 20-25
minutes

SERVES: 6 people

2 bananas, peeled and sliced
1 large guava, chopped
1 pear, peeled and chopped
2 ripe peaches, skinned, stoned and
   sliced
2 slices fresh pineapple, peeled and
   chopped
1 small fresh pawpaw, peeled, seeded
   and cut into chunks
A few grapes, seeded
1 apple, peeled, cored and chopped
2 tsp lemon juice
Salt
¼ tsp ground black pepper
¼ tsp chili powder
Pinch of black rock salt (kala namak)

Put all the fruits into a large bowl.
Sprinkle with lemon juice, salt,
pepper and chili. Mix well. Add
pinch of ground black rock salt
(kala namak). Mix and serve as a
starter, side salad or snack. Note:
many other fruits may be added i.e.
mango, kiwi, plum, lychees, melons.

**Pochari Kosambri (top left),
Kachhoomar (top right) and
Phalon-Ka-Chaat (bottom).**

Baigan Dahivaley
(EGGPLANT SLICES IN YOGURT)

PREPARATION TIME: 10 minutes

COOKING TIME: 10-15 minutes

SERVES: 3 people

1 tsp chili powder
¼ tsp ground turmeric
1 large eggplant, cut into ¼ inch
   thick round slices
Salad or olive oil for deep frying
1¼ cups natural yogurt
1 tsp garam masala powder
¼ tsp salt
1 green chili, chopped
1 sprig fresh green coriander leaves,
   chopped

Rub chili and turmeric into
eggplant slices. Deep fry eggplant
slices, a few at a time, in oil for 2-3
minutes, and drain on kitchen

paper. Beat yogurt and add garam
masala powder, salt, green chili and
fresh coriander. Mix well. Arrange
eggplant slices on a flat serving
plate or dish. Pour yogurt over
evenly. Serve as a side dish.

Pachari Kosambri
(VEGETABLE, NUT AND COCONUT SALAD)

PREPARATION TIME: 20-25
minutes

SERVES: 4 people

4oz grated white cabbage
1 small onion, peeled and finely
   chopped
1 small apple, grated
1 firm mango, peeled and grated
Juice of 1 lemon
¼ tsp salt
2oz grated fresh coconut
1 green chili, chopped
2 sprigs fresh green coriander leaves,
   chopped
¾ cup bean sprouts
½ cucumber, grated
3 tblsp skinned unsalted peanuts,
   lightly roasted and coarsely ground

Put grated cabbage, onion, apple
and mango into a bowl. Mix well,
squeeze and discard excess juice.
Drain well. Sprinkle with lemon
juice, salt, coconut, green chili and
fresh coriander. Add bean sprouts
and cucumber and mix gently. Add
lightly roasted and coarsely ground
peanuts. Mix and serve. Note:
other nuts, like cashews, chiroli,
pecan, walnut and hazelnuts may
be used. Grated carrots may also
be included if desired.

Green Bean Bhaji

PREPARATION TIME: 10 minutes

COOKING TIME: 10-12 minutes

SERVES: 3-4 people

3 tblsp oil or melted ghee
1 tsp urid daal
2-3 green chilies
6-8 fresh curry leaves
12oz frozen sliced green beans,
   unthawed
Salt to taste
1 tblsp shredded coconut

Heat oil or ghee and add urid daal,
green chilies and curry leaves. Stir
fry for half a minute. Add beans
and sprinkle with salt. Cover and
cook for 6-8 minutes. Sprinkle with
coconut and mix well. Cover and
cook for 3-4 minutes. Serve with
chapatis.

1 medium green pepper, seeded and
   cubed
½lb mixed frozen vegetables
Salt to taste
1 tsp ground turmeric
1 tsp ground coriander
1 tsp chili powder
3-4 tomatoes, chopped
2 sprigs fresh green coriander leaves,
   chopped
1-2 green chilies, chopped

Heat ghee or oil and fry onion and
cumin seeds for 2-3 minutes. Add
potatoes and stir fry for 4-5
minutes. Add cauliflower, eggplant
and green pepper and cook for 4
minutes. Add mixed vegetables.
Stir to mix well. Sprinkle with salt,
turmeric, coriander and chili
powder. Add chopped tomatoes.
Stir and cover. Cook on low heat
for 5-6 minutes. Add fresh
coriander and chopped chili. Mix
and serve. To make a moist curry
add ⅔ cup water after tomatoes
are added.

Dum Aloo
(SPICED POTATO CURRY)

PREPARATION TIME: 10 minutes

COOKING TIME: 15 minutes

SERVES: 4 people

3 tbls ghee or
3 tblsp salad or olive oil
1 bay leaf
1 onion, minced finely
½ tsp ginger paste
½ tsp garlic paste
½ tsp whole mustard seed
½ tsp cumin seed
1lb small potatoes, with skins on,
   washed and dried
¼ tsp ground turmeric
2 tsp ground coriander
1½ tsp chili powder
⅔ cup natural yogurt
¼ tsp salt

Mushroom Aloo Bhaji
(POTATO AND MUSHROOM BHAJI)

PREPARATION TIME: 5-6 minutes

COOKING TIME: 10-12 minutes

SERVES: 4 people

3 tblsp ghee or
3 tblsp salad or olive oil
1 onion, peeled and chopped
1lb potatoes, peeled and cubed
½ tsp salt
2 tblsp garam masala powder
½lb button mushrooms, sliced
Lemon juice

**Mattar Paneer (top left), Saag
Bhaji (top right) and Baigan
Dahivaley (bottom).**

Heat ghee or oil and fry onion until
tender (2-3 minutes). Add
potatoes and fry for 5-6 minutes.
Sprinkle with salt and garam
masala. Mix well and cover. Cook
for 4-5 minutes until potatoes are
tender. Add mushrooms. Stir well.
Cover and cook for 2-3 minutes.
Sprinkle with lemon juice to taste.
Remove from heat and serve.

Mili-Juli Sabzi
(MIXED VEGETABLE BHAJI)

PREPARATION TIME: 15 minutes

COOKING TIME: 10-15 minutes

SERVES: 4 people

3 tblsp ghee or
3 tblsp salad or olive oil
1 onion, peeled and chopped
1 tsp cumin seeds
1 medium potato, peeled and
   chopped
3 cauliflower florets, cut into small
   pieces
1 small eggplant, cubed

Heat ghee or oil and add bay leaf
and onion. Fry for 3-4 minutes.
Add ginger and garlic and fry for 1
minute. Add mustard and cumin
seed. Add potatoes, mix well and
cook for 4-5 minutes, stirring
continuously to avoid burning.
Sprinkle with turmeric, coriander
and chili powder. Add yogurt and
salt to taste. Mix gently; cover and
cook for 8-10 minutes until
potatoes are tender and most of
the liquid has evaporated. Sprinkle
with a little water if potatoes are
not quite tender. Dum aloo is a dry
dish, with the potatoes coated with
spices. Serve with puri.

Khata-Meetha Kaddu (SWEET AND SOUR PUMPKIN)

PREPARATION TIME: 10 minutes

COOKING TIME: 15-20 minutes

SERVES: 4 people

3 tblsp ghee or
3 tblsp salad or olive oil
1 bay leaf
1 inch cinnamon stick
6 green cardamoms
6 cloves
1 tsp five spice mixture (panch-phoran)
2 medium potatoes, peeled and cut into chunks
1lb pumpkin, peeled and cut into chunks
1 tsp chili powder
1½ tsp ground coriander
¼ tsp ground turmeric
½ tsp salt
2 tsp brown sugar
1 tblsp tamarind pulp concentrate
3 tblsp water

Heat oil and add bay leaf, cinnamon, cardamom, cloves and five spice mixture and fry for half a minute. Add potatoes and fry for 4 minutes. Add pumpkin. Stir vegetables and cook for 3 minutes. Sprinkle with chili powder, coriander, turmeric, salt and sugar. Stir the mixture to blend the spices. Add tamarind pulp and water. Cover and cook on gentle heat for 8-10 minutes until potatoes are tender. This is a moist curry, without gravy. Serve with paratha or puri.

Palak Paneer (PANEER AND SPINACH)

PREPARATION TIME: 20 minutes and overnight for paneer. Follow paneer making recipe.

COOKING TIME: 10 minutes

SERVES: 3-4 people

1lb fresh leaf spinach
3 tblsp ghee or
3 tblsp salad or olive oil
8oz paneer, cut into cubes
1 onion, peeled and finely chopped
1 inch root ginger, peeled and finely chopped
4 tomatoes, chopped
1 tsp chili powder
1 tblsp lemon juice
1 tsp ground coriander
1½ tblsp unsalted butter
¼ tsp ground turmeric
¼ tsp salt

Boil fresh spinach in 2½ cups water for 5 minutes. Drain and save water. Mash or purée spinach and keep aside. Heat ghee or oil and fry paneer cubes until light brown. Remove. In the same oil fry onion and ginger for 3-4 minutes. Add tomatoes and sprinkle with chili, coriander, turmeric and salt to taste. Cover and cook for 2-3 minutes. Add paneer, puréed spinach and lemon juice. If too dry, use 2-3 tblsp spinach water to moisten the curry. Remove from heat and serve with knobs of butter on top. This is a thick, moist curry.

Daal Pulses

PREPARATION TIME: 5 minutes

COOKING TIME: 10 minutes

SERVES: 4 people

8oz split or dehusked moong daal, washed in 2-3 changes of water
2½ cups water
¼ tsp ground turmeric
1 tsp ground coriander
Salt to taste
1 small onion, peeled and chopped
3 tblsp unsalted butter, or clarified butter
1 green chili, chopped
2 cloves garlic, peeled and chopped

To garnish
1 sprig fresh green coriander leaves, chopped

Boil moong daal in water until tender and soft. Drain. Mash the daal with a potato masher or egg beater. Add turmeric, ground coriander and salt to taste. Simmer

This page: Khata-Meetha Kaddu (top), Palak Paneer (right), Dum Aloo (bottom).

Facing page: Green Bean Bhaji (top), Mili-Juli Sabzi (right) and Mushroom Aloo Bhaji (bottom).

until volume is reduced by ⅓rd. Fry onion in butter until golden brown and add chili and garlic. Fry until garlic is browned. Pour over daal. Garnish with chopped fresh coriander. Serve with rice or chapatis.

Khari Urid Daal
(DRY URID DAAL)

PREPARATION TIME: 5 minutes

COOKING TIME: 10-15 minutes

SERVES: 4 people

8oz white dehusked urid daal, washed in 3-4 changes of water
Salt to taste
¾ cup water

For garnish
1 onion, peeled and sliced
3 tblsp unsalted butter
1 green chili, chopped
1 inch root ginger, peeled and sliced
1 sprig fresh green coriander leaves, chopped

Cook drained urid daal covered with salted water, on a low heat, until the water has evaporated. Fry onion in butter until golden brown. Add chopped chili and ginger and fry for 2-3 minutes. Pour over dry daal. Garnish with chopped coriander. Serve with roti or paratha.

Masoor Daal
(RED LENTIL)

PREPARATION TIME: 6 minutes

COOKING TIME: 20-25 minutes

SERVES: 4 people

8oz red lentils
1 tsp chili powder
2 tsp ground coriander
¼ tsp ground turmeric
¼ tsp salt
1 sprig fresh green coriander leaves, chopped
4 tomatoes, chopped
1 onion, peeled and chopped
3 tblsp butter
1 green chili, halved and chopped

Wash lentils in 4-5 changes of water, until water is clear. Drain. Add 2½ cups water; cover and simmer gently, without stirring, for 10-15 minutes until lentils are thoroughly cooked. Blend with a masher or beat with an egg beater. Add chili powder, ground coriander, turmeric, salt, fresh coriander and tomatoes. Cover

Below: Sambhar (top), Masoor Daal (center) and Arhar Toor Daal (bottom).

and simmer for 6-8 minutes. Remove from heat. Fry onion in butter, until brown; pour over daal. Garnish with chopped chili. Serve with rice or chapati.

Arhar Toor Daal
(YELLOW LENTIL)

PREPARATION TIME: 5-6 minutes

COOKING TIME: 20-25 minutes

SERVES: 4 people

8oz toor daal
¼ tsp ground turmeric
1 tsp ground coriander
¼ tsp salt
6 curry leaves
1 green chili, split in half
1 tblsp grated fresh coconut or shredded coconut
1 sprig fresh green coriander leaves, chopped
1 tsp mustard seed
3 tblsp butter

Wash toor daal in 4-5 changes of water. Drain. Add 2½ cups water, turmeric, salt and coriander. Cover and simmer gently for 10-15 minutes until daal is well cooked

and soft. Blend with the aid of a masher or an egg beater. Add curry leaves, coconut, chili and coriander leaves. Cover and cook for further 8-10 minutes. Heat butter and fry mustard seed for half a minute. Pour over daal. Serve with rice or rotis. Toor daal should have a smooth, thick consistency.

Sabut Masoor
(WHOLE LENTIL)

PREPARATION TIME: 5 minutes

COOKING TIME: 20-25 minutes

SERVES: 4 people

3 tblsp butter
1 onion, peeled and chopped
1 bay leaf
1 inch cinnamon stick
1 tsp ginger paste
1 tsp garlic paste
8oz daal, washed in 3-4 changes of water
Water
1 tsp ground coriander
½ tsp chili powder
¼ tsp ground turmeric
3 tomatoes, chopped
1 green chili, chopped
1 sprig fresh green coriander leaves, chopped

Salt to taste

Heat butter and fry onion until golden brown. Add bay leaf, cinnamon stick, ginger and garlic pastes and fry for 1 minute. Add drained daal and water. Cover and simmer gently for 12-15 minutes. The daal should be well cooked. Beat with a potato masher or egg beater to blend. Sprinkle with coriander, chili and turmeric. Add tomatoes, green chili and fresh coriander leaves. Season with salt. Mix well; cover and cook gently for 7-10 minutes. Remove from heat and serve with rice or chapatis. The daal should have gravy of medium consistency. If too dry, add a little water and boil for 2-3 minutes.

Sambhar
(DAAL AND VEGETABLE)

PREPARATION TIME: 10 minutes

COOKING TIME: 20-30 minutes

SERVES: 4 people

8oz toor daal
1 carrot, peeled and sliced
1 potato, peeled and cubed
6-8 okra (bhindi), topped and tailed and cut into 1 inch pieces
1 small zucchini, sliced
1 small eggplant, halved and sliced

The following spices should be dry roasted and ground into a powder:
1 tsp coriander seed
1 tsp cumin seed
2 whole dry red chilies
2 tsp channa daal
¼ tsp fenugreek seed (methi)
6 curry leaves
2 tblsp tamarind pulp concentrate
1 green chili, slit in half
Salt to taste
1 sprig fesh green coriander leaves
1 tblsp salad or olive oil, for tempering
½ tsp mustard seed
¼ tsp asafoetida (hing)

Wash toor daal in 4-5 changes of water until water is clear. Drain. Add 1¼ cups water; cover and simmer gently for 6-10 minutes. Remove any froth that forms. When daal is soft, beat with a potato masher or whisk. In a separate pan, boil all the vegetables with the ground, roasted spice mixture and the 1¼ cups water, for 4-5 minutes. Mix daal and vegetables along with liquid and stir gently to give a smooth

Sabut Masoor (top), Khari Urid Daal (right) and Lal Mireh Aur Moong Phali (bottom).

mixture. Add curry leaves, tamarind pulp, salt, chopped chili and fresh coriander. Simmer for 10-15 minutes. Remove to a serving dish. For tempering, heat oil and fry mustard seed and asafoetida for half a minute and pour over sambhar. Serve with boiled rice.

Butter Beans and Green Capsicum

PREPARATION TIME:	10 minutes
COOKING TIME:	10 minutes
SERVES:	3 people

1 tblsp salad or olive oil
1 onion, peeled and chopped
8oz butter beans, soaked and partly cooked (or broad beans)
1 large green pepper, seeded and chopped
¼ tsp ground turmeric
½ tsp chili powder
1 tsp ground coriander
Salt to taste
4-5 tomatoes, chopped
1 green chili, chopped
1 sprig fresh green coriander leaves, chopped

Heat oil and fry onion for 3-4 minutes. Add beans and green pepper. Cook for 4-5 minutes. Sprinkle with turmeric, chili and ground coriander. Add salt and tomatoes. Mix well. Cover and cook for 5-6 minutes on low heat. Add green chili and fresh coriander. Cook covered for 2-3 minutes. If too dry, add 2 tblsp water. This is a dry dish.

Stuffed Peppers

PREPARATION TIME:	20 minutes
COOKING TIME:	30-35 minutes
SERVES:	4 people

3 tblsp ghee or
3 tblsp salad or olive oil
1 onion, peeled and finely chopped
1 potato, peeled and diced
8oz mixed frozen vegetables
1 tsp garam masala powder
½ tsp chili powder
2 tsp dried mango powder
Salt to taste
8 quite small green peppers
Salad or olive oil for frying peppers

Heat ghee or oil and fry onion until tender (3-4 minutes). Add potatoes and cook for 4-5 minutes. Add mixed vegetables, and sprinkle with garam masala, chili powder, mango powder and salt to taste. Cover and cook gently until potatoes are tender. Remove from heat and cool. Wash and dry the green peppers. Remove top by slicing across to form a lid. Remove center pith and seeds. Heat about 3 tblsp oil and fry peppers laid sideways, for 1-2 minutes; cook on all sides. Drain well. Fill each pepper with vegetable filling and arrange them on a baking tray. Bake in preheated oven, at 325°F for 20 minutes. Serve.

Aloo Gobi

PREPARATION TIME:	10 minutes
COOKING TIME:	10-12 minutes
SERVES:	3-4 people

1 large onion, peeled and chopped
4 tblsp ghee or
4 tblsp salad or olive oil
2 medium potatoes, peeled and cut into chunks
1 medium cauliflower, cut into small florets
2-3 green chilies, chopped
2 sprigs fresh green coriander leaves, chopped
1½ inch root ginger, peeled and finely chopped
Salt to taste
Juice of 1 lemon
2 tsp garam masala

Fry onion in ghee or oil until just tender (about 2-3 minutes). Add potatoes and fry for 2-3 minutes. Add cauliflower and stir fry for 4-5 minutes. Add green chilies, coriander, ginger and salt. Mix well. Cover and cook for 5-6 minutes on low heat, or until potatoes are tender. Sprinkle with lemon juice and garam masala before serving. Serve with parathas.

Nau-Rattan Chutney
(NINE JEWELED CHUTNEY)

PREPARATION TIME: 20 minutes

COOKING TIME: 20-30 minutes

MAKES: about 2½ cups

1 banana, peeled and sliced
1 apple, cored and chopped
1 large mango, peeled stoned and
    sliced
3 rings of canned pineapple, chopped
1 cup canned peach slices, chopped
4oz dates, pitted and sliced
2oz ginger root, peeled and chopped
3 tblsp raisins
1 cup soft brown sugar (or jaggery)
2-3 dry red chilies
¾ cup brown vinegar
1 tsp salt
½ tsp cumin seed
½ tsp coriander seed
½ tsp onion seed
½ tsp aniseed seed
4 tblsp chopped blanched almonds

Put all the fruits into a saucepan
with the dates, ginger, raisins, sugar,
chilies and vinegar. Add salt and
simmer gently for 10-15 minutes.
Roast and grind the cumin,
coriander, onion seed, aniseed and
almonds. Mix into the fruit
mixture and cook for 5-6 minutes.
Cool and bottle. Chutney should
be thick and sticky.

Lal Mireh Aur Moong Phali Chutney
(RED-HOT CHUTNEY)

PREPARATION TIME: 5 minutes

MAKES: about 1 cup

1 large red pepper
3-4 whole dry red chilies
3 tblsp unsalted peanuts
½ inch root ginger, peeled and sliced
Juice of 3 lemons
Salt

Halve red pepper, remove pith and
seeds. Blend red pepper, chilies,
peanuts and ginger in the liquidizer.
A few spoons of lemon juice may
be needed to blend the mixture.
Pour into a bowl. Add salt and the
lemon juice. Mix well and serve.
(Red-hot chutney can be frozen.
Freeze in small tubs in small
quantities.) Can be kept
refrigerated in sealed bottles for up
to 2 months.

Dahi-Podina Chutney
(YOGURT AND MINT CHUTNEY)

PREPARATION TIME: 5-6 minutes

MAKES: ⅔ cup

⅔ cup natural yogurt
4 tsp fine granulated sugar
2-3 sprigs mint leaves, chopped
Salt

Put yogurt, sugar and mint into a
blender; liquidize for 1-2 minutes.
Add salt and mix. Serve with
kebabs, samosa and pakoras. Ready
made concentrated mint sauce may
be used in place of fresh mint
leaves.

Inset illustration, far left: Meethi Tomatar Chutney (top), Tmali Ki Chutney (right) and Dahi-Podina Chutney (bottom).

Main illustration: Chutneys. Adrak Khajoor Ki Khati Mithi (top), Nau-Rattan (right), Coriander, Green Chili and Coconut (bottom), Coconut and Urid Daal (left) and Red Pepper and Peanut (center).

Tmali Ki Chutney (TAMARIND CHUTNEY)

PREPARATION TIME: 6 minutes

COOKING TIME: 10-12 minutes

MAKES: about ½lb

½lb dry tamarind pods
¾ cup fine granulated sugar or jaggery
¼ tsp salt
1 tsp chili powder
1 tsp cumin seed, roasted and lightly ground
1 tsp coriander seed, roasted and lightly ground

Soak tamarind pods in ⅔ cup of boiling water for 5 minutes. Squeeze pods to remove soft pulp. Strain through sieve or squeeze by hand. Add a little fresh warm water to the pulp and repeat, taking 3 extracts. The first one is the thickest and subsequent ones will be lower in strength. Take 1 cup thick tamarind extract. Discard the pods. Add the sugar, salt, chili powder and ground, roasted cumin and coriander seeds to the tamarind extract. Mix well. Adjust sugar and salt if necessary. Serve with kebabs. Tamarind chutney can be kept refrigerated for up to 1 month.

Adrak Khajoor Ki Khati Mithi Chutney (DATE AND GINGER CHUTNEY)

PREPARATION TIME: 20-30 minutes

MAKES: about 2 cups

4oz fresh dates, halved, stoned and sliced
2oz fresh root ginger, peeled and cut into matchstick-size strips
Flesh of 1 small, unripe mango, peeled and thinly sliced
3 tblsp raisins and currants mixed
2 tblsp chopped blanched almonds
¾ cup water
¾ cup fine granulated sugar (or grated jaggery)
¼ tsp salt
1 tsp red chili powder

Put dates, ginger, mango, raisins and currants, and almonds into a saucepan. Add water. Keep aside for 6-8 minutes. Add sugar (or grated jaggery), salt and chili powder and simmer gently. Cook for 15-20 minutes until chutney is thick and sticky. Remove, cool and serve. The chutney can be bottled and kept in or out of the refrigerator for up to 3 months.

Meethi Tomatar Chutney (SWEET TOMATO CHUTNEY)

PREPARATION TIME: 5-6 minutes

COOKING TIME: 10-15 minutes

MAKES: 1¼lbs

1½ tblsp ghee or
1 tblsp salad or olive oil
1 inch cinnamon stick
1 bay leaf
6 cloves
1 tsp mustard seed
1 tsp chili powder
¼ tsp turmeric powder
¼ cup fine granulated sugar
1lb tomatoes, chopped
3 tblsp raisins
½ tsp salt

Heat ghee or oil and fry cinnamon, bay leaf and cloves for 1 minute. Add mustard seed. When they begin to crackle, add chili, turmeric and sugar. Mix well and add tomatoes. Mix well and add raisins and salt. Cover and simmer for 8-10 minutes. Add a little water if liquid thickens too much. Tomato chutney should have a medium thick consistency. Serve hot or cold. Once cooked it can be kept in refrigerator for 4-6 weeks.

Aloo-Mattar and Mirchi Bhaji
(POTATO, PEA AND GREEN PEPPER CURRY)

PREPARATION TIME: 15 minutes

COOKING TIME: 10 minutes

SERVES: 3-4 people

1 onion, peeled and chopped
3 tblsp ghee or
2 tblsp salad or olive oil
2 medium potatoes, peeled and cut into chunks
1 tsp ground coriander
1 tsp chili powder
¼ tsp ground turmeric
8oz frozen green peas
1 green pepper, seeded and cut into chunks
1⅓ cups canned tomatoes, crushed
Salt to taste
2 green chilies, cut into quarters
2 sprigs fresh green coriander leaves, chopped
½ cup water

Fry onion in ghee or oil until just tender (about 2-3 minutes). Add potatoes and fry for 5-6 minutes. Sprinkle with ground coriander, chili powder and turmeric. Mix well and add peas and green pepper. Stir and add tomatoes; season with salt. Add chopped green chilies and fresh coriander. Add water, cover and cook for 5-6 minutes until potatoes are tender. The dish should have a thick gravy.

Bharey Bhindi
(WHOLE STUFFED OKRA)

PREPARATION TIME: 20-30 minutes

COOKING TIME: 15-20 minutes

SERVES: 3 people

½lb bhindi (okra), washed, dried, topped and tailed
1 large onion, peeled and thickly sliced
4 tblsp ghee or
4 tblsp salad or olive oil
2 tsp ground coriander
2 tsp ground cumin
1 tsp ground turmeric
1 tsp chili powder
Salt to taste
1 tblsp dry mango powder
1 tblsp aniseed (sauf) powder

Split okra or bhindi halfway down. Fry onion for half a minute in 1 tablespoon of oil or ghee and remove. Mix coriander, cumin, turmeric and chili powder, and put a little of this spice mixture into each split okras. Heat the remaining oil in a skillet or wok. Add stuffed okras. Sprinkle with salt and stir well. Cover and cook on low heat for 5-6 minutes. Add fried onions, then sprinkle with mango and aniseed powder. Cover and cook for 3-4 minutes. Serve with roti.

Tendli Bhaji with Cashew Nuts

Tendli is an Asian vegetable that looks like a gooseberry and tastes like zucchini.

PREPARATION TIME: 10 minutes

COOKING TIME: 12-15 minutes

SERVES: 3 people

2 tblsp salad or olive oil
3 tblsp cashew nuts
3-4 cloves of garlic, peeled and crushed
½ tsp mustard seed
6-8 curry leaves
2-3 dry red chilies (or fresh green chilies)
½lb tendli, washed, dried and cut in half lengthways
Salt to taste
2 tsp shredded coconut
¼ tsp ground turmeric

Heat oil and fry cashew nuts until light brown. Remove the nuts and then fry the garlic until light brown. Add mustard seed, curry leaves and red or green chilies. Fry for half a minute. Add tendli, sprinkle with salt and stir the mixture. Sprinkle with shredded coconut, turmeric and fried cashew nuts. Cover and cook on low heat for 10-12 minutes, or until tendli is tender.

This page: Aloo-Mattar and Mirchi Bhaji (left), Bharey Bhindi (center) and Tendli Bhaji with Cashew Nuts (right).

Facing page: Butter Beans and Green Capsicum (top), Aloo Gobi (left) and Stuffed Peppers (bottom).

Bread and Rice

Ubley Chawal
(BOILED RICE) 1

This method of cooking rice in a large quantity of water is very safe, and is ideal for all grades of rice, especially for starchy short and medium grades. It is also good for cooking large quantities, as the fluffiness can be controlled. Use a few drops of lemon juice to whiten the rice.

COOKING TIME: 10-15 minutes

2 cups Basmati rice
Pinch salt
Few drops lemon juice

Wash rice in 4-5 changes of water until water is clear. Drain rice and put into a large pan. Fill pan with cold or tepid water, to come 2-4 inch above the rice level. Add pinch of salt and bring to boil gradually. When boiling, add drops of lemon juice to bleach the rice and cut the starch formation. Boil for 7-10 minutes, covered, or until the rice is almost cooked and has a hard core in the center. Test by pressing a few grains of rice between thumb and forefinger. Drain well and cover the top of the pan with a clean cloth or foil and put the lid on lightly. Replace on a very low heat. The moisture around the rice is enough to form steam and cook the core of each rice grain in 2-4 minutes. Serve with or without butter/ghee, with daal or curry.

Ubley Chawal
(BOILED RICE) 2

PREPARATION TIME: 5 minutes
COOKING TIME: 15 minutes

This method is only suitable for cooking long grain types of rice such as Basmati, American, Deradun or Pahari. In cooking, the rice absorbs twice its dry measure of liquid; bearing this in mind always measure rice with a cup and then measure twice the amount of water.

2 cups Basmati rice
Pinch salt
Lemon juice

Wash rice in 4-5 changes of water until water is clear. Drain rice and put into a large pan. Fill the pan with measured quantity of water and let the rice soak for 10-15 minutes. The longer it stands the better the result. Add salt and lemon juice and gently bring to boil. Stir once or twice when boiling and simmer, covered, until rice is almost cooked with a hard center, about 7-10 minutes. The water should be totally absorbed. Do not stir rice during cooking. Keep on a low heat for a further 1-2 minutes to evaporate any remaining moisture and complete the cooking of the rice. Serve.

Sada Pulao (left), Meat Pulao (below, far left) and Ubley Chawal (below left).

Sada Pulao
(CUMIN FRIED RICE)

PREPARATION TIME: 5 minutes, plus 15 minutes to soak the rice.

COOKING TIME: 15 minutes

SERVES: 6 people

2 cups Basmati or American long
   grain rice
4 tblsp butter or ghee
1 tsp cumin seed
¼ tsp ground turmeric
1 tsp salt

Wash rice in 4-5 changes of water. Drain well and add 4 cups of water. Cover and set aside for 10-15 minutes. Heat ghee or butter and add cumin seed. Fry for a few seconds; do not allow to burn. Add the strained rice, retaining the water. Add turmeric and salt. Mix well and add the strained water. Bring to the boil, cover, and lower the temperature. Do not stir rice. Cook for 10-12 minutes, until water is absorbed and the rice is tender. Serve with any curry.

Meat Pulao

PREPARATION TIME: 15 minutes

COOKING TIME: 1 hour

SERVES: 6 people

1 small onion, peeled and sliced
4 tblsp ghee or butter
1 inch cinnamon stick
6 green cardamoms
3 large cardamoms
6 cloves
1 bay leaf
1 tsp whole black cumin seeds
1 tsp ginger paste
1 tsp garlic paste
8oz lean pork or lamb, cut into cubes
1 tsp ground coriander
1 tsp ground cumin
⅔ cup natural yogurt
1 tsp salt
2 cups Basmati rice

Fry onion in butter until golden brown. Add cinnamon, cardamoms, cloves, bay leaf and cumin seed. Fry for 1 minute. Add ginger and garlic pastes and fry for ½ minute. Add meat and sprinkle with ground coriander and cumin. Stir and add yogurt and salt. Mix well; cover and cook for 10-12 minutes until yogurt is dry and oil separates. Add 1¼ cups of water and cook until meat is tender (20-25 minutes). Remove from heat.

Strain meat from its liquid. Take a large saucepan and add the measured, washed rice. Add the gravy from the meat, making it up to 4 cups with water. Add the meat and the spices. Adjust seasoning. Bring to the boil and then lower the heat; give a stir, cover, and cook on low heat without stirring for 10-15 minutes, until water is totally absorbed and the rice is tender. Serve with a curry.

Biryani

There are two methods of making biryani: one with uncooked meat and the other with cooked meat. Both styles give equally good results but have slightly different flavors.

Method 1

In this method meat is marinated and cooked with semi-cooked rice.

PREPARATION TIME: 15-20 minutes, and at least 1 hour for meat to marinate.

COOKING TIME: 60-70 minutes

SERVES: 6 people

10oz lean lamb, cut into cubes
²/₃ cup natural yogurt
1 tsp salt
1 tsp ground coriander
1 tsp ground cumin
1 tsp chili powder
½ tsp ground turmeric
1 tsp ginger paste
1 tsp garlic paste
2 onions, peeled and sliced
Salad or olive oil for frying
3-4 green chilies, chopped
2 sprigs fresh green coriander leaves, chopped
2 cups Basmati rice
1 inch cinnamon stick
6 small cardamoms
6 cloves
2 bay leaves
1 tsp black cumin seed
2 tsp salt
3 tblsp ghee or butter, melted
1-2 tsp saffron dissolved in 6 tblsp milk

In a small bowl, mix the meat, yogurt, salt, coriander, cumin, chili turmeric, ginger and garlic pastes. Cover and set aside to marinate for at least 1 hour. (For best results marinate overnight.)

For boiling rice
Fry onions in plenty of oil, until brown and crisp. Drain on kitchen paper. Put the meat and marinade into a large saucepan. Add half of the fried onions, half of the chopped chilies and the coriander. Mix well. Put the washed rice into a separate saucepan with plenty of water to cover; add the cinnamon, cardamoms, cloves, bay leaf, black cumin and salt. Bring to the boil. Cook for 3-4 minutes until rice is half cooked. Drain well and put the steaming rice over the meat. Sprinkle with the remaining fried onions, chilies and coriander leaves. Make 5-6 holes in the rice

with the handle of a wooden spoon, for the steam to escape, and pour saffron milk all over the rice. Sprinkle with lemon juice and melted butter or ghee. Cover with the lid and place the pan over a moderate heat. As soon as steam is visible, lower the temperature. Cook for 45-50, minutes rotating the pan, so that all areas receive even heat. The rice will cook with the steam formed by the milk and yogurt, and moisture from the meat. Lower heat to minimum and cook for another 10 minutes. Serve biryani from one end of the saucepan, mixing meat with rice with the aid of a spoon. Serve with a mixed vegetable raita.

Method No 2

This method is the layering method. It involves two stages.

Stage 1
Cooking the meat

Stage 2
Layering the meat with rice

1 onion, peeled and chopped
5 tblsp ghee or
5 tblsp salad or olive oil
1 tsp ginger paste
1 tsp garlic paste
10oz lean lamb, cut into cubes
1 tsp ground coriander
1 tsp chili powder
¼ tsp ground turmeric
1 tsp ground cumin
²/₃ cup natural yogurt
1 tsp salt
½ tsp saffron
1 tblsp milk
1 onion, peeled and thinly sliced
Salad or olive oil for deep frying
2 cups Basmati rice
1 inch cinnamon stick
6 cloves
1 tsp black cumin seed
1 bay leaf
6 small cardamoms
2 tsp salt
2 sprigs fresh green coriander leaves, chopped
2-3 green chilies, chopped
Juice of 1 lemon

Fry chopped onion in ghee or oil, in a large pan, until light brown. Add ginger and garlic pastes and fry for another ½ minute. Add meat and coriander, chili, turmeric and cumin powder. Add yogurt and salt. Mix well and cook with lid on for 10-15 minutes until dry. Add 1½ cups water. Cover and cook for 8-10 minutes, on low heat, until meat is tender and there is about ½ cup gravy left.

For rice
Dissolve saffron in milk. Deep fry sliced onion in oil until crisp and brown, and drain on kitchen paper. Wash rice in 4-5 changes of water. Drain and put into a pan. Add plenty of water and the cinnamon, cloves, black cumin, bay leaf and cardamoms. Add salt and bring to boil. Cook until rice is nearly done. (The rice should increase in size but still have a hard center.) Drain well, leaving whole spices in the rice; divide rice in two. Line the saucepan base with half the rice, and top with the drained cooked meat, saving the sauce. Sprinkle with half the fried onion, half the fresh coriander and chili. Cover with the remaining rice. Sprinkle top with the remaining fried onion, chili and coriander. Sprinkle with lemon juice and saffron milk. Pour the meat gravy all round. Make a few holes in the rice with the handle of a spoon for steam to rise. Cover and cook on gentle heat for 4-5 minutes. Mix before serving. Serve with mixed vegetable raita.

Tahiri

PREPARATION TIME: 10 minutes

COOKING TIME: 20 minutes

SERVES: 6 people

1 onion, peeled and sliced
4 tblsp ghee or butter
1 inch cinnamon stick
6 cloves
6 cardamoms
1 tsp black cumin seed
1 tsp whole black pepper
1-2 bay leaves
¾ cup shelled or frozen peas
2 cups Basmati rice, washed in 4-5 changes of water
3-4 tsp salt

Fry onion in ghee or butter until light brown. Add cinnamon, cloves, cardamom, black cumin, pepper and bay leaf. Fry for ½ minute. Add peas and cook for 2 minutes. Add rice and 4 cups water and salt. Bring to boil. Cover and lower heat to simmer. Cook for 10-12 minutes until rice is cooked and water is absorbed. Serve with vegetable or meat curry.

Vegetable Pulao

PREPARATION TIME: 15 minutes

COOKING TIME: 15 minutes

SERVES: 6 people

2 cups Basmati or any long grain rice
4 tblsp ghee or butter
1 onion, peeled and chopped
1 inch cinnamon stick
1-2 bay leaves
6 small cardamoms
4 large cardamoms
6 cloves
1 tsp salt
8oz peeled and sliced mixed vegetables (see below)
1 tsp ground coriander
1 tsp garam masala powder
1 tsp ground turmeric
1 tsp chili powder
Salt to taste

Wash rice in 4-5 changes of water – drain well. Heat butter or ghee and fry onion until light brown. Add cinnamon, bay leaf, cardamoms, and cloves. Fry for 1 minute. Add mixed vegetables and fry for 4-5 minutes. Add drained rice and sprinkle with coriander, garam masala, turmeric and chili powder. Mix well. Add 4 cups of water. Add salt to taste. Bring to boil. Reduce heat; cover and cook gently for 12-15 minutes, without stirring, until water is completely absorbed. Serve by itself, with a raita or with a curry.
Recommended vegetables:- Can be used in any combination. No leafy vegetables or pithy vegetables like marrow, zucchini, gourd etc. are advisable as they will make the pulao soggy.

1-2 eggplant, cut into ½ inch chunks
1-2 potatoes, peeled and diced
1-2oz shelled or frozen peas
1-2 carrots, peeled and diced
2oz sliced green beans
1-2oz corn kernels
2-3 cauliflower flowerets, cut into smaller pieces
1-2oz broad beans, frozen or shelled

Facing page: Vegetable Pulao (top), Khichri (left) and Shahi Pulao (bottom).

Khichri
(KEDGEREE)

PREPARATION TIME: 6 minutes

COOKING TIME: 10-15 minutes

SERVES: 6 people

1 cup Basmati rice
1 cup red lentils
¾ tsp salt
½ tsp ground turmeric
1 tsp ground coriander
4 tblsp butter
1 large onion, peeled and chopped
1-2 green chilies, chopped

Mix rice and lentils. Wash in 4-5 changes of water. Drain and add 4 cups of water. Add salt, turmeric and coriander. Bring to boil. Mix well by stirring gently. Lower the temperature; cover and cook over a gentle heat for 10-12 minutes until water is absorbed and rice and lentils are tender. Melt the butter in a skillet and fry onions until golden brown. Add chopped chilies and pour over cooked khichri. Serve with poppadums and chutney.

Shahi Pulao
(NUT AND RAISIN PULAO)

PREPARATION TIME: 5-6 minutes.

COOKING TIME: 10-15 minutes.

SERVES: 6 people

2 cups Basmati or long grain rice
4 tblsp ghee or butter
1 inch cinnamon stick
6 small cardamoms
2 large cardamoms
2 bay leaves
6 cloves
1 tsp salt
4 tblsp raisins
4 tblsp chopped mixed nuts
   (almonds, cashew, pistachio)

Wash rice in 4-5 changes of water, drain. Heat butter or ghee and fry cinnamon, cardamoms, bay leaves and cloves for half minute. Add drained washed rice, salt and 4 cups of water. Bring to boil gently. Stir once or twice. Reduce heat add raisins and nuts, cover and cook for 10-12 minutes or until water is totally absorbed and the rice is tender. Serve with meat or vegetable curry.

Jhinga Pulao
(PRAWN PULAO)

PREPARATION TIME: 6 minutes

COOKING TIME: 10-15 minutes

SERVES: 4-6 people

1 cup long grain or Basmati rice
1 onion, peeled and chopped
4 tblsp ghee or butter
1 inch cinnamon stick
1 bay leaf
6 small cardamoms
6 cloves
1-2 tsp ginger paste
1-2 tsp garlic paste
8 oz large shrimps, peeled and cooked
1 tblsp chopped fresh green coriander
   leaves
1 tsp garam masala powder
1-2 green chilies
¾ tsp salt

Wash rice in 3-4 changes of water. Drain and soak in 2 cups of water. Keep aside. Fry onion in ghee or butter until golden brown. Add cinnamon, bay leaf, cardamoms and cloves; fry for 1 minute. Add ginger and garlic pastes. Cook for ½-1 minute. Add shrimps and sprinkle with coriander and garam masala. Add green chilies and salt. Stir in soaked rice and water. Mix well and bring to boil. Reduce heat, cover and cook until water is absorbed and rice is tender (about 10-15 minutes). Do not stir during cooking. Serve with curry. To color pulao, add a few drops of red or orange food color 2-3 minutes before removing from heat. A pinch of saffron may be added along with the spices.

Pita

PREPARATION TIME: 10 minutes, and 1 hour for dough to rest

COOKING TIME: 30 minutes

MAKES: 16

2 tsp dried yeast
1 tsp fine granulated sugar
3½ cups wholewheat flour
Pinch salt
1½ tblsp butter or margarine

Mix yeast and sugar and add 2 tblsp tepid water. Cover and let it stand in a warm place until frothy. Sift flour and salt; add butter and yeast mixture. Knead with sufficient water to make a pliable dough. Cover and leave for 1 hour. Knead once again and divide into 16 even-sized balls. Roll each one out on a lightly-floured surface to a 6 inch oval or circle. Place on greased baking sheets. Bake at 375°F for 7-10 minutes.

Saag Paratha
(PARATHA MADE WITH A LEAFY VEGETABLE)

PREPARATION TIME: 10 minutes

COOKING TIME: 20 minutes

MAKES: 16-18

3½ cups wholewheat flour (Atta)
Pinch salt
¼ cup drained cooked spinach
Butter or ghee

Sift flour and salt; add spinach and 2 tblsp butter. Knead with sufficient water to make a soft, pliable dough. Knead well and allow to stand for 5 minutes. Heat a non-stick skillet or a Tawa. Make 16-18 even sized balls. Roll each ball out on a lightly-floured surface into a 6-7 inch circle. Place in the skillet or Tawa and cook for 1-3 minutes on low heat. Turn over and cook on the other side. Add a little butter or ghee to each side and shallow fry until light brown. Serve hot or cold.

Kulcha
Kulcha is a deep fried yeast bread.

PREPARATION TIME: 5-6 minutes, and 5-6 hours for yeast to rise.

COOKING TIME: 30 minutes

MAKES: 20-25

1 tsp dried yeast
1 tsp fine granulated sugar
4 cups rice flour
Pinch salt
3 tblsp ghee or butter
2 tblsp natural yogurt
Salad or olive oil

Mix yeast and sugar with 1 tblsp tepid water. Cover and let it stand in a warm place until frothy. Sift flour and salt. Add ghee or butter, and the yogurt. Knead with sufficient water to form a fairly hard dough. Make a well in the center; add yeast mixture and knead. Let it rest for 5-6 hours in a warm place, to rise. Knead once again to a soft, pliable dough. Make 20-25 even-sized balls. Roll each ball into a 2-2½ inch circle. Fry in hot oil for about 2-3 minutes, until lightly golden brown. Serve hot or cold with curry.

Stuffed Paratha

PREPARATION TIME: 10 minutes

COOKING TIME: 30 minutes

MAKES: 16-18

3½ cups wholewheat flour (Atta)
Pinch of salt
2 tblsp ghee or butter
Ghee or oil for frying

Filling
A few flowerets of cauliflower, finely
   chopped
Pinch of salt
1 tsp cumin seed
¼ tsp chili powder
1 tsp ground coriander

Sift flour and salt. Add ghee or butter and knead with sufficient water to make a soft, pliable dough. Make 16-18 even-sized balls. Mix the filling ingredients together. Take a ball of dough and make a slight depression in the center. Fill the center with 1 tsp of cauliflower mixture. Pull the surrounding dough from around the filling to gather at the top. Roll gently into a complete ball. On a lightly floured surface, roll each paratha into a 6-7 inch round. Place the paratha on a preheated non-stick skillet or Tawa. Let it cook for 2 minutes, until little brown specs appear. Flip over on to the other side and cook for 2 minutes. Take a little ghee or oil and shallow fry parathas on both sides. Cook each side on low heat, until golden brown. Serve hot or cold with a curry. Cook all the stuffed parathas in the same way.

Facing page: Biryani (top), Jhinga Pulao (center left) and Tahiri (bottom right).

Nan

The distinctive taste of Nan comes from baking the bread in a clay oven. Nan baked in gas or electric ovens does not have the same charcoal flavor.

PREPARATION TIME: 10-15 minutes and 2-3 hours for dough to rest

COOKING TIME: 30-40 minutes

MAKES: 16-17

2 tsp dried yeast
1 tsp fine granulated sugar
1½ tsp baking soda
1 tblsp sesame or onions seeds
3½ cups all-purpose flour
Pinch salt
4 tblsp melted butter
3 tblsp natural yogurt

Mix yeast and sugar and add 1 tblsp tepid water. Stand in a warm place until frothy. Sift flour and salt, and add baking soda. Make a well and add half the melted butter, yogurt and yeast mixture. Knead with sufficient water to give a smooth dough. Cover and leave to rise for 2-3 hours. Knead again and make 16-17 balls. Roll each ball into either an elongated flat bread – 6 x 10 inches or into a 6-7 inch circle – on a lightly-floured surface. Place on greased baking sheets. Brush with the remaining butter and sprinkle with a few onion or sesame seeds. Bake at 400°F, for 5-6 minutes. When ready the bread will have brown spots on it. Serve hot.

Sheermaal

PREPARATION TIME: 10 minutes

COOKING TIME: 30-40 minutes

MAKES: 10

3½ cups all-purpose flour
Pinch salt
2oz fine granulated sugar
4 tblsp butter or margarine
1 tblsp dried yeast
1 cup tepid water
Milk
Sesame seed

Sift flour and salt, and add all but 1 tsp of the sugar. Add butter or margarine. Mix yeast with the tepid water and remaining sugar mix and stand in a warm place until frothy. Add the yeast liquid to the flour and knead to make a soft dough. Let it rest. When risen to twice its volume, knead once again for 4-5

Below: Saag Paratha (top left), Stuffed Paratha (top right) and Kulcha (bottom).

minutes. Divide into 10 equal portions. Roll each one out into a round or oval shape, ¼ inch thick. Brush with milk and sprinkle with sesame seeds. Place on greased baking sheets. Bake at 375°F for 5 minutes. Turn over and bake for a further 5 minutes until light brown and cooked.

Paratha

Parathas are shallow-fried breads.

PREPARATION TIME: 10 minutes

COOKING TIME: 25 minutes

MAKES: 16-18

3½ cups wholewheat flour (Atta)
Pinch of salt
Ghee or butter for frying

Sift flour and salt. Add sufficient water to knead into a soft dough. Knead well and keep aside to rest for 5 minutes. Make 16-18 even-sized balls. Roll each ball out into a 2 inch circle. Put a ¼ tsp butter in the center. Fold in half; apply a little more butter, and fold in half again to make a triangular shape. On a floured surface, carefully roll each piece of folded dough into a 6

inch triangle. Heat a non-stick skillet or Tawa. Place the paratha on it. Cook for 1-2 minutes. Flip over and cook for 2 minutes. Add a little ghee or butter to the surface and flip over; fry first side again. Repeat for the second side. Both sides should be browned and pressed with a spatula to cook the corners. Cook all parathas in the same way and stack them. Serve hot or cold with curry.

Facing page: Sheermal (top), Nan (center) and Pita (bottom).

Roti/Chapati/Phulka

PREPARATION TIME: 6 minutes

COOKING TIME: 20 minutes

MAKES: 16-20

3½ cups wholewheat flour (Atta)
Pinch of salt
⅔ cup water

Sift flour and salt into a mixing bowl. Knead to a soft pliable dough with water and leave to rest for 5 minutes. Make 16-20 even-sized balls and roll one ball out on a lightly-floured surface to a 7 inch circle. Heat a non-stick skillet or Indian bread griddle known as a "Tawa". Place the rolled circle of dough on it. When little bubbles appear, turn over and cook for ½ minute. Broil on both sides until the roti puffs and swells. Make the rest in the same way and stack them. A little butter can be applied to each roti to keep it soft. Keep them well wrapped in a clean tea cloth or baking foil.

Alternative method:
The roti can be cooked for 1-1½ minutes on each side in the skillet until little brown specs appear. Make them puff up by pressing with a clean tea cloth to rotate the steam.

Puri
These are deep fried little round breads.

PREPARATION TIME: 6 minutes

COOKING TIME: 10 minutes

MAKES: 25-30

3½ cups wholewheat flour (Atta)
Pinch salt
3 tblsp ghee or
3 tblsp salad or olive oil
Salad or olive oil for deep frying

Sift flour and salt and add ghee or oil. Knead with sufficient water to make a soft, pliable dough. Knead well and allow to stand for 5 minutes. Make 25-30 small balls. Roll each ball out into a small circle 2-2½ inches in diameter. Heat oil. The oil is at the correct temperature when a piece of dough dropped into it rises to the surface immediately. If not, then wait for the oil to heat to the right temperature. Slide one puri into the oil. Press gently with a straining spoon. Turn over and the puri will swell. It may need a little pressing. Deep fry for 1-2 minutes until it is light brown. (The side of the puri which goes in first, always has a thin crust, the other side will always have a thick side. When this thick side is light brown the puri is cooked.) Drain. Fry all the puri in the same way and serve, hot or cold, with a curry or chutney, or both.

Roti/Chapati/Phulka (left),
Paratha (top left) and Puri
(above).

Sweets

Saboodana Kheer (SAGO PUDDING)

PREPARATION TIME: 10 minutes
COOKING TIME: 10 minutes
SERVES: 4-6 people

½ fresh coconut, grated and milk
    extracted (see below)
3¾ cups milk
½ cup fine granulated sugar
2 tblsp raisins
4 tblsp sago
8 smal cardamoms, seeds removed
    and crushed
2 tblsp flaked almonds

Grate coconut and liquidize with 1 cup water. Strain to remove coconut milk and discard the coconut. Boil milk to reduce to 2½ cups; add sugar and raisins. Add sago and simmer for 5-8 minutes. Remove from heat and add coconut milk. Pour into a dish and add the crushed cardamom seeds. Mix well and sprinkle with sliced almonds. Cool and serve.

Rasmalai

PREPARATION TIME: 15-18 minutes and overnight for paneer
COOKING TIME: 30 minutes
SERVES: 4 people

7½ cups milk
Lemon juice
2 tsp all-purpose flour
8 green cardamoms, seeds crushed
A few sugar cubes, cut in half

For milk sauce
2½ cups milk evaporated to 2 cups

For syrup
1¾ cups fine granulated sugar
⅔ cup water

For garnish
A few drops of kewra or rosewater
2 tblsp chopped pistachio nuts
2 tblsp chopped almonds

Bring the milk to the boil and add the lemon juice. Leave the milk to separate. Cool for 10 minutes. Strain the curds through a fine sieve or a muslin cloth. Hang overnight for the liquid to drain

from the paneer. Make the syrup by boiling sugar and water for 2-3 minutes. Mash the paneer with the palm of the hand for 5 minutes. Add flour and cardamom seeds, a little at a time, and continue mashing. Leave to rest for 2-3 minutes. Divide into 15-20 equal sized balls. Take a ball and put a piece of sugarcube in the center. Close the ball and make it smooth. Press gently to flatten it into a 1½ inch round. Make all rasmalai like this. Simmer syrup and dip rasmalai into it, a few at a time. Boil for 30 minutes. Put the milk sauce in a serving dish. Remove rasmalai from syrup and immerse in milk sauce. When all the rasmalai are in milk, sprinkle with rose or kewra water and chopped nuts. Cool and refrigerate before serving.

Gulab Jamun

PREPARATION TIME: 20 minutes
COOKING TIME: 30-40 minutes
SERVES: 6 people

2¼ cups fine granulated sugar
3 cups water
Kewra or rosewater
1½ tblsp all-purpose flour
2 tsp coarse semolina
1½ tblsp unsalted butter
9 tblsp powdered milk
8 small cardamoms, seeds removed
    and crushed
Pinch of saffron
Milk
Salad or olive oil for frying

Gently boil the sugar and water for 4-5 minutes to form a 1 string syrup. Add kewra or rosewater. Mix flour, semolina, butter, powdered milk, cardamom seeds and saffron and knead with milk to form a dough. Make 25-30 even-sized balls. Make the balls smooth and round, or oblong. Attention should be paid to the split edges as they may crack during cooking; make them smooth. Deep fry the gulab jamuns in hot oil on low heat until dark brown on all sides. Drain well and transfer them immediately to the syrup. When all the gulab jamuns are in the syrup, give the syrup a final boil. Cool before serving.

Jallebi

PREPARATION TIME: 20 minutes, and 24 hours
COOKING TIME: 30-40 minutes
SERVES: 6 people

Batter
1 cup all-purpose flour
⅔ cup baisen flour or cornstarch
3 tblsp natural yogurt
Yellow food coloring
Salad or olive oil for deep frying

Syrup
1½ cups fine granulated sugar
½ cup water
A few drops of lemon juice

Prepare a thick batter with the flour, baisen flour or cornstarch, yogurt, and a little warm water. Set aside for 24 hours to ferment. Make a 1 string syrup by boiling sugar and water; add lemon juice whilst syrup is boiling. Remove from heat. Take a piping paper and spoon in some of the batter. Pipe even sized rings of the mixture into the hot oil and deep fry for 3-4 minutes, until crisp. Remove from the oil, and drain thoroughly. Steep the jallebi in warm syrup for 3-5 minutes. Remove jallebi and arrange in a dish. Cook the remaining batter in the same way.

Shalu Tukra

PREPARATION TIME: 5 minutes
COOKING TIME: 10-15 minutes
SERVES: 6 people

6 medium size slices of white bread
Salad or olive oil for deep frying
¾ cup fine granulated sugar
¾ cup of water
Few drops of kewra or rosewater
4 tblsp condensed milk
⅔ cup heavy cream, whipped
1½ tblsp sliced pistachio nuts
1½ tblsp flaked almonds
6 small cardamoms, seeds removed
    and crushed

Deep fry the bread slices in oil until crisp and brown. Drain on kitchen paper. Boil sugar and water for 2-3 minutes to make a syrup. Add rose or kewra water. Arrange fried bread

on a flat serving dish, and pour sugar syrup evenly over the slices. Soak for 10 minutes. Pour condensed milk evenly over the center of each slice. Spread over the cream and sprinkle with nuts and cardamom seeds. Serve warm or cold.

Rasgullas (MILK BALLS IN SYRUP)

PREPARATION TIME: overnight
COOKING TIME: 30-40 minutes
SERVES: 6 people

5 cups milk
Juice of 1 lemon
Kewra or rosewater
2¼ cups fine granulated sugar
2½ cups water
2 tsp all-purpose flour

The day before, boil the milk and add the lemon juice. (The milk will separate into curds and whey.) Strain through a fine sieve or a clean muslin cloth. Discard the whey; suspend the curd in muslin, overnight, to drain off every single drop of liquid. Next day: boil the rosewater, sugar and water and let it simmer gently. With the palm of your hand mash the milk curds (paneer) for 5-6 minutes to break up the texture. Sprinkle on the flour, a little at a time, and mix well, mashing with your palm. Let it rest for 1-2 minutes. Make into 20-22 even-sized balls. Put a few at a time into the boiling syrup and boil for 10-12 minutes. Remove and place in a dish. Replace any water which is lost by evaporation, and repeat the process for the remaining balls. When all the rasgullas are done, pour the syrup over them. Cool and serve. If a large saucepan is used, all the rasgullas can be made in one go.

Facing page: Gulab Jamun (top), Shalu Tukra (center) and Saboodana Kheer (bottom left).

Facing page: Mohan Thaal (top), Coconut Barfi (left) and Rasmalai (bottom right).

Mohan Thaal

PREPARATION TIME: 10 minutes

COOKING TIME: 20-30 minutes

SERVES: 10 people

1 cup fine granulated sugar
½ cup water
1 cup baisen flour
¼ cup milk
¾ cup unsalted butter
6 small cardamoms, seeds removed and crushed
2 tblsp chopped pistachio nuts
2 tblsp chopped almonds

Make syrup by boiling sugar and water until thick (2 string consistency). Mix baisen flour, milk and half the butter; beat until smooth. Heat remaining butter, add baisen mixture, and cook for 5-6 minutes. Add sugar syrup, and mix well. Remove from heat and add crushed cardamom seeds. Pour into a greased dish and allow to set for 5 minutes. Sprinkle evenly with chopped nuts. Cut into pieces.

Balushahi

PREPARATION TIME: 15 minutes

COOKING TIME: 30-40 minutes

SERVES: 4-6 people

1¾ cups all-purpose flour
Pinch of salt
¼ tsp baking soda
3 tblsp unsalted butter
1½ tblsp natural yogurt
Seeds of 8 green cardamoms, crushed
Salad or olive oil for deep frying

Syrup
A generous cup fine granulated sugar
4 tblsp water
2 tblsp chopped pistachio nuts

Sift flour with salt and soda. Rub in butter. Add yogurt, crushed cardamoms, and sufficient cold water to make a soft dough. Divide into 16 equal-sized balls. Flatten each ball between palms of the hands to make 'cakes' 1½-2 inches in diameter, with the sides thinner than the centers. Lower into hot oil and deep fry on low heat for 8 minutes, without disturbing. Turn Balushahi and cook for another 8 minutes. Drain on kitchen paper. Make sugar syrup by boiling sugar and water for 2-3 minutes. Dip Balushahi in sugar syrup for 3-4 minutes. Arrange on a tray and sprinkle with chopped pistachio nuts.

Paneer Ki Kheer

PREPARATION TIME: 2-3 hours

COOKING TIME: 1 hour

SERVES: 6 people

To make paneer
3¾ cups milk
Lemon juice

Bring milk to the boil, add lemon juice. When the milk separates, strain through a fine sieve or muslin cloth. Discard the liquid and suspend the paneer for 3-4 hours to drain out all the moisture. Break into small lumps.

To make milk sauce
3¾ cups milk
½ cup fine granulated sugar
2 tblsp chopped mixed nuts
6 small cardamoms, seeds removed and crushed
Few drops of kewra or rosewater

Boil milk to reduce to 2 cups; dissolve sugar in the milk and cool. When cold, add the nuts and crushed cardamom seeds. Add the paneer and refrigerate for 30-40 minutes. Add rosewater or kewra water. Serve.

Above: Balushai (top left), Gajjar Ka Halwa (right) and Pooa Kheer (bottom left).

Coconut Barfi

PREPARATION TIME: 20 minutes

COOKING TIME: 40-50 minutes

SERVES: 10-12 people

1lb shredded coconut
2 cups evaporated milk
¾ cup fine granulated sugar
A generous cup unsalted butter
8 green cardamoms, seeds removed and crushed

Dry roast the coconut until pale brown. Remove from heat. Put the evaporated milk, into a non-stick pan with the coconut, sugar and butter. Cook on a gentle heat, stirring the mixture continuously until oil the separates (10-15 minutes). Add crushed cardamom seeds. Cook until the mixture is dry. Grease a flat dish. Pour in mixture and flatten it with a spatula dipped in cold water. Cool for 10 minutes and cut into squares or diamond shapes. Can be kept for 1 month in the refrigerator.

Gajjar Ka Halwa
(CARROT HALWA)

PREPARATION TIME: 15 minutes

COOKING TIME: 1 hour

SERVES: 6 people

2lbs carrots, peeled and grated
2 cups evaporated milk
¾ cup fine granulated sugar
1 inch cinnamon stick
1-2 bay leaves
½ cup unsalted butter
8 green cardamoms, seeds crushed
3 tblsp chopped blanched almonds
1½ tblsp pistachio nuts

Cook the grated carrots with the evaporated milk and sugar on a low heat. Add cinnamon and bay leaves and cook until the milk has almost completely evaporated. Add butter and cardamom seeds. Cook over a gentle heat, stirring continuously to stop mixture from sticking to the pan (the color should change from orange to deep red or brown; this should take 45-50 minutes). When the oil separates, spread on a flat dish. Sprinkle with chopped nuts and serve. Can be eaten hot or cold.

Pooa Kheer

PREPARATION TIME: 10 minutes

COOKING TIME: 15 minutes

SERVES: 6 people

1½ cups all-purpose flour
2 eggs
3 tblsp water
2 tblsp raisins
6 small cardamoms, seeds removed and crushed
Salad or olive oil
2 tblsp flaked almonds
2 tblsp sliced pistachio nuts
Few drops rosewater
3¾ cups milk, boiled and reduced to 2 cups
¼ cup fine granulated sugar

Mix flour, eggs, and water to make a smooth batter. Add raisins and keep aside for 2-3 minutes. Add crushed cardamoms and mix. Heat a little oil in a non-stick skillet. Fry spoonfuls of the batter to make 2 inch pancakes (pooas). Arrange all the pooas in a flat serving dish and sprinkle with almonds and pistachio nuts. Heat reduced milk with rosewater and sugar. Pour the milk over pooas. Serve after 5 minutes.

Glossary

Most of the items listed are readily available at most supermarkets, health-food shops and delicatessens. When they are not, substitutes can be made.

Aniseed (*Sauf*). These are the tiny seeds of the anise, and are different from Chinese staranise. The Chinese staranise is called anise only because of its similar smell. Aniseed is used in curry powders, in making liquorice, cordials and cough linctus.

Atta. This ordinary wholewheat flour is readily obtainable from most supermarkets, health-food shops and delicatessens. Whether white or brown, it is both nutritious and nourishing. The texture and color differ due to the variety of wheat used. Extra bran added to the flour makes Indian bread dry and coarse in appearance. Always knead the mixture and allow it to stand for 5 to 10 minutes for the gluten to work. Atta can also be used mixed with baisen flour, cornstarch, millet flour, or any other kind of flour.

Baisen. Baisen is the flour of Bengal gram or black chickpea, also known as channa. The special, black chickpea is dehusked and then ground to make flour. It is very high in protein and is gluten free. The split pulse is used for making daals and the flour is used for making batter for pakoras and also for making sweets.

Bayleaf (*Tej Patta*). These are the leaves of a tree belonging to the common laurel family. Bay trees are used as ornamental plants and grow to great heights. The dried leaves are sold in all good food stores. They are used in sweets and curries and for pickling. Bay leaves should not be eaten.

Cardamom (*Elaychi*). There are two varieties of Elaychi. The first is small, with green pods which are called cardamoms or chotyenaychi. The seeds inside are dark and sticky, with a beautiful smell. Cardamoms may be included in recipes for the aroma they give to the food, or chewed after the meal as a mouth freshener. The skin of the pod is always discarded. The larger variety is black in color

Sevian Ki Kheer

PREPARATION TIME: 5 minutes

COOKING TIME: 15 minutes

SERVES: 6 people

1½ tblsp unsalted butter
1 bay leaf
1 cup fine vermicelli
2½ cups milk reduced to 2 cups
⅓ cup fine granulated sugar
8 small cardamoms, seeds removed and ground
2 tblsp raisins
2 tblsp chopped almonds

Melt butter in a pan and fry bay leaf for 1-2 minutes. Add broken vermicelli and fry for 1 minute. Add milk, sugar and ground cardamom seeds. Simmer gently for 5-6 minutes. Add raisins. Gently stir pudding once or twice during cooking to stop it from burning. Remove from heat, pour into a serving dish, sprinkle with chopped almonds. Serve hot or cold.

Suji Halwa
(SEMOLINA PUDDING)

PREPARATION TIME: 5-6 minutes

COOKING TIME: 10 minutes

SERVES: 6 people

⅔ cup coarse semolina
½ cup unsalted, or clarified butter
3 tblsp chopped mixed almonds and cashew nuts
3 tblsp raisins
½ cup fine granulated sugar
1¼ cups water
8 small cardamoms, seeds removed and ground

It is important to use a large enough saucepan as semolina will increase to twice its volume. Dry roast the semolina in a non-stick pan for 2-3 minutes, until it turns light brown. Remove to a dish. Melt butter or clarified butter and add nuts and raisins. Fry for 1 minute, then add semolina. Add sugar and water. Sprinkle with ground cardamom seeds. Cover and cook on a low heat for 3-4 minutes. Mix well and stir fry for 1-2 minutes until dry. Serve hot or cold.

with a thick skin. The seeds inside are used in sweets and are very different in smell and flavor from the smaller, green variety. Black cardamom is an important ingredient in the making of many curry powders, while both small and large varieties are importnt constituents of whole or powdered forms of garam masala.

Chili *(Mirch).* There are many different varieties of chili, but they only really differ in strength. Chili powder is made by ripening the chili on the plant and then drying it out in the hot sun, both skin and seed being powdered. There are a few hybrids which have the flavor but not the same pungency. These varieties are sold in European markets. Green peppers, or capsicums, are the large, fleshy varieties of chili and are used as a vegetable. Paprika is made from red peppers, or capsicums. Dried and then browned, paprika has the red color and smell, but not the pungency, of chili.

Cinnamon *(Dalchini).* Cinnamon is obtained from the bark of an evergreen tree belonging to the laurel family and is chiefly cultivated in southern India, Sri Lanka and the East Indies. The outer bark is stripped then dried; it has a pleasant, sweet taste and aroma and is thought by some to possess aphrodisiac properties. It is extensively used in sweets, pilaus, meat and other curries. It can be bought in stick and ground form.

Cloves *(Lavang).* Cloves are aromatic and may be used whole or in ground form. It is one of the spices which goes to make whole garam masala. Cloves are used for both sweet and savory dishes. Oil of cloves is used in dentistry, to ease pain.

Coconut Milk. This is not, contrary to popular opinion, the liquid inside the fruit, which is more correctly termed coconut water. To extract the milk, break the shell and scoop or chisel out the white flesh. Cut the flesh into small pieces and blend with a little water in an electric blender. Let the pulp stand for five minutes. Squeeze the pulp through a sieve and collect the white liquid. This process may be repeated to produce progressively weaker milks. The used flesh should be discarded. If you cannot obtain fresh coconut, steep desiccated coconut in warm water and then strain.

Coriander *(Dhanai).* This is used to flavor nearly all curries. It is sold in seed and ground form, but fresh coriander leaves are also sold in some supermarkets and speciality food shops. The leaves are used for garnishing. Although coriander belongs to the parsley family it is different from both European and Chinese parsley in flavor.

Cumin *(Zeera).* Cumin belongs to the same family as aniseed. It has tiny, light brown seeds resembling caraway seeds. It is used in vegetable, meat and fish curries and in pickles. It is one of the most widely used spices. Cumin can also be bought in ground form.

Curry. For all curry preparations a range of spices is needed. It is advisable that you buy these individual spices and keep them in airtight containers. The flavor is in the aromatic ois that they possess. If the spices are to be used frequently then buy ready-powdered spices, otherwise buy in whole form and grind them freshly for use. Whole spices can be stored without losing much of their strength for surprisingly long periods of time. The overall flavor is better if you grind the spices yourself.

Garlic *(Lassan).* Garlic is sold in most food shops in either fresh, powdered, or granule form. The fresh cloves of garlic give the best results and flavor.

Ginger *(Adrak).* Ginger is eaten all over the world. It is sold in fresh root form, dried form (called sonth) and ready ground. For best results use the fresh root, peeled and crushed, or as directed.

Hing *(Asafoetida).* This is a gum resin and has a strong smell. It has medicinal properties and is used to combat nausea. Hing is always used with foods which ferment or are likely to produce gases, as it helps in digestion. Always buy it in a sealed jar or can. The powdered form loses its flavor much faster than the solid variety.

Jaggery. Sold in Oriental shops, this is the semi-solid stage of sugar-cane juice. It has a light yellow to dark orange color, and the flavor of molasses. Jaggery can always be substituted by soft brown sugar or ordinary granulated sugar.

Methi *(Fenugreek).* Fenugreek seeds are tiny, yellow seeds which are bitter to the taste. The leaves are eaten in curries as a leafy vegetable. Methi seeds are used in panch-phoran spice mixture and in many other curry powders.

Onion Seed *(Kalongi).* These are tiny, black seeds and are generally available only from Oriental shops. Onion seeds are used for curries and in pickling.

Rice. There are many varieties of rice, but they are roughly divided into three groups: long grained, like Basmati, American and Patna; medium grained, like Carolina, and glutinous, like Spanish and Chinese. For best results, the rice should be washed in three to four changes of water until the water runs clear, then soaked for ten to twenty minutes. To cook by the absorption method: measure rice with a cup and cook in twice as many cupfuls of water. This method is only good for long grained rice. The other varieties of rice should be cooked in large quantities of water and then strained. The rice should be drained and rinsed under hot running water. It is only loose rices which require washing and soaking; the pre-packed varieties do not.

Sugar Syrup. For various sweets different kinds of sugar syrups are needed. The strength is measured in 'strings'. Boil sugar and water for a few minutes, until it becomes thick. Take a drop of syrup between thumb and forefinger, press and separate; if the syrup forms one string it is called a 'one string syrup'. As it grows thicker it will form more strings. Three or four string syrups will be thick and sticky.

Tamarind. These are light brown pods which have a sour taste. To make tamarind pulp, take a little tamarind and break loose the pods. They sometimes have small, black seeds in them. Pour enough boiling water over the pods to submerge them. Leave for 10 to 15 minutes, then squeeze them well. The pulp around the seeds will dissolve in water, giving a darkish, thick, creamy extract. Strain this through a coarse sieve. This gives the first, and best, extract. For second and subsequent extracts, repeat the process. These later extracts are not as strong as the first. The trick is to make the first extract thick with the minimum of water and the remainder with varying strengths for future use. The extract does not last for more than four or five days and should be used within two for best results.

vegetable. Methi seeds are used in panch-phoran spice mixture and in many other curry powders.

Once the pulp has been extracted, the pods and seeds should be discarded. Tamarind pulp can be bought in concentrated form from shops, and should be diluted before use.

Composite Spices:

Ginger and Garlic Pastes. Since ginger is used extensively in most meat, fish and poultry dishes, it is advisable to prepare the paste in large quantities and store it in a refrigerator in an airtight container. On no account should it be kept in a metal container. Buy 4 oz root ginger. Peel and cut into smaller pieces. Place in a blender with ¼ cup of water. When reduced to a paste it will keep for up to a month in a normal fridge and much longer in the freezer. Wash the blender with a little vinegar or lemon juice before normal washing to get rid of the smell. Garlic paste can be produced in the same way using 4oz peeled garlic cloves.

Panch-Phoran. This is a mixture of five spices in whole form, mixed in equal quantities and on no account ground. To make a suitable quantity, which will keep for about six months, use: 1 tsp each of mustard seeds (red and yellow), cumin seed, onion seed, aniseed and fenugreek. Keep the mixture in an airtight jar and use as required. It will keep for up to six months.

Facing page: Sevian Ki Kheer (top) and Suji Halwa (bottom).

Index

FAMILY
COOKBOOK

Contents

Introduction

Being married, having looked after a family for a number of years and having worked for a long time as a professional cook, I felt there was a gap in the market for a cook book that would give well-balanced, nourishing meals for a growing family, without stretching the pocket too far.

In this book I have tried to provide a variety of recipes, as it is easy to get tied to a weekly routine of Sunday is chicken, Monday is stew, and so on, and then having your family tell you what day it is by what's on their plates.

There are times, of course, when you only have the two of you to cater for and, therefore, you can celebrate with a special meal, so I have included some extra special recipes that I hope you will find a joy to prepare and eat.

Always remember that presentation is a major part of any meal, and take time over this, setting a table to complement your meal. I have also included some of the more traditional recipes that, in this day and age of convenience foods, may have been forgotten.

This book, I hope, will help you enjoy cooking for your family, as opposed to just filling a gap when they are hungry.

Smoked Haddock in
French Mustard Sauce (top),
Chicken Curry (left) and
Poussin in White Sauce (right)

Meals for Two

Poussin in White Sauce

1 pkt sage and onion stuffing
2 poussins
Fat
1¼ cups milk
¼ cup all-purpose flour
2 tblsp soft margarine
Salt and pepper

Make the stuffing as directed on the packet and use to stuff the poussins. Place the poussins in a roasting pan with melted fat, and cook in the oven for 30-40 minutes at 350°F, until tender. Put the milk, flour, margarine and seasoning into a pan and bring gradually to the boil, beating all the time. Cook gently for 3 minutes, stirring. Serve with baked potatoes and corn with red peppers.
Serves two

Smoked Haddock in French Mustard Sauce

¾lb smoked haddock fillet, skinned
  and cut into two
A little milk
Salt and pepper
1 tblsp butter
2 tblsp flour
⅔ cup milk
1 tblsp French mustard
Chopped chives (optional)

Place the fish in an ovenproof serving dish. Pour a little milk over the fish and season. Cover and cook in the oven for 15-20 minutes

at 325°F. Heat the butter in a pan, stir in the flour and cook for 2 minutes. Allow to cool, then pour in the milk gradually. Bring to the boil, stirring. Season and stir in the French mustard. Spoon the sauce over the fish and garnish with chopped chives if desired. Serve with potato croquettes and broccoli.
Serves two.

Broiled Meats

2 sausages
Liver
2 pork chops
Tomatoes
Mushrooms, sliced if flat

Broil the sausages, liver, pork chop and tomatoes until tender. Boil mushrooms until soft. Serve with baby new potatoes.
Serves two.

Chicken Curry

2 tblsp butter
1 small chicken, jointed
1 small onion, peeled and chopped
1 small apple, peeled and chopped
1 tsp curry powder
1 tblsp flour
½ tsp curry paste
1¼ cups chicken stock
1 chili (optional)
Pinch of powdered ginger
Pinch of powdered turmeric
1 tsp chutney
Squeeze of lemon juice
Salt and pepper
Shredded coconut
White raisins

Garnish
Thin onion rings, lightly fried
Thin green pepper rings, lightly fried
Lemon rind, lightly fried

Heat the butter and fry the chicken pieces. Remove and drain on paper towels. Fry the onion and apple for 2-3 minutes, then add the curry powder, flour and curry paste. Cook briefly, then carefully blend in most of the stock, reserving ¼ cup. Bring to the boil and cook for a few minutes until it forms a thin sauce. Add the remaining spices, chutney, lemon juice and seasoning. Return the chicken pieces to the pan. Pour the remaining stock over the coconut and allow to stand for a few

minutes, then add the strained liquid to the curry. If preferred, fresh coconut or coconut milk can be used instead. Add the white raisins then cover and simmer for 2-3 hours. Garnish with onion, pepper and lemon rind to serve.
Serves two.

Plaited Lamb

1lb ground lamb
2 onions, peeled and chopped
2 tblsp breadcrumbs
1 tsp dried rosemary
1 tblsp tomato paste
1 tblsp Worcestershire sauce
2 eggs, beaten
Salt and pepper
8oz puff pastry

Mix together the ground lamb, onions, breadcrumbs, rosemary, tomato paste, Worcestershire sauce and one of the eggs. Add salt and pepper. Roll out the pastry into an oblong on a floured surface. Place the lamb mixture in the center and cut diagonal strips from the center to the edges along both sides. Brush all four sides with a little beaten egg. Fold the pastry at each end and then fold the strips over alternately so they meet in the center. Place the plaited lamb on a greased coohy sheet and brush with the remaining beaten egg. Cook in the oven for 15-20 minutes at 425°F. Then reduce the heat to 350°F, and cook for a further 30 minutes. Serve with new potatoes and a green vegetable.
Serves two.

Pasta Fish Pie

3 tblsp macaroni
Salt
8oz white fish

Cheese Sauce
1 tblsp butter or margarine
2 tblsp flour
⅔ cup milk
Salt and pepper
Pinch of dry mustard
3 tblsp Cheddar cheese, grated

Break the macaroni into small pieces (if using long macaroni), and cook in 2 pints of boiling, salted water until tender. Meanwhile, simmer the fish in a little salted water until tender. Lift the fish out and flake with a fork. Heat the

butter or margarine in a pan, stir in the flour, and cook the 'roux' for 2-3 minutes over a low heat. Remove the pan from the heat and gradually add the milk, seasoning and mustard. Bring to the boil and cook until thickened, then add the grated cheese. Put the drained macaroni and fish into a hot dish and top with the cheese sauce. Place for 2-3 minutes under a hot broiler until the cheese topping bubbles. Serve with green beans and corn.
Serves two.

Braised Beef

1 tblsp fat
12oz of brisket or chuck roast, cut into pieces
1 carrot, peeled and sliced
1 onion, peeled and sliced
1 turnip, peeled and sliced
1 leek, trimmed and sliced
2 sticks celery, trimmed and sliced
2 tblsp fat bacon, diced
Bouquet garni (mixture of fresh herbs, i.e. parsley, thyme, sage, in muslin bag)
Salt and pepper
⅔ cup beef stock
¼ cup red wine

Heat the fat in a flameproof casserole dish or large saucepan and brown the meat for 3 minutes. Lift the meat onto a plate. Brown the vegetables in the fat together with the diced bacon. Add the bouquet garni, seasoning, stock and wine then return the meat on top of the mixture. Cover tightly and cook very slowly for about 1 hour. Lift the lid from time to time and add more stock if the mixture appears to be running dry. Remove the bouquet garni. Sieve or blend the vegetables and stock to make a sauce and reheat with the meat. Serve with boiled potatoes.
Serves two.

Stuffed Mushrooms

Two large, flt mushrooms
2 tblsp butter
1 rasher of bacon, rinded and chopped
1 tblsp fresh breadcrumbs
1 tsp chopped parsley
Grated rind of ¼ lemon
½ tsp lemon juice
2 tblsp Cheddar cheese, grated
Salt and pepper
Parsley

Remove the stalks from the mushrooms and chop finely. Heat the butter and fry the mushroom stalks and the bacon for a few minutes. Remove from the heat and stir in the breadcrumbs, parsley, lemon rind and juice, and cheese. Season well. Place the mushroom caps on a greased cooky sheet, divide the filling between each cap and cook for 15-20 minutes at 325°F. Sprinkle with chopped parsley. Serve with corn and sauté potatoes.
Serves two.

Veal Cutlets Bonne Femme

2x8oz veal cutlets
Salt and pepper
¼ cup flour
¼ cup clarified butter or butter and oil mixed
½ cup boiled, cold potatoes, thinly sliced
4 tblsp onions
¼ cup sherry
⅔ cup demi-glace sauce
1 tblsp chopped parsley

Sprinkle the veal cutlets with salt and pepper and dredge with flour. Heat the butter, or butter and oil, in a skillet and gently fry the cutlets on both sides for a few minutes. Place the cutlets in an ovenproof dish and cook in the oven for 15-20 minutes at 350°F, until tender. Fry the potatoes in the same pan until golden brown; remove and keep warm. Fry the onions for two minutes. Transfer the onions to a saucepan of water and boil until soft. Drain off the butter and pour the sherry into the pan. Add the demi-glace sauce and bring to the boil, stirring continuously. Arrange the cutlets on a serving dish, surrounded by the fried potatoes and onions. Cover with the demi-glace sauce and decorate with chopped parsley.
Serves two.

Facing page: Plaited Lamb (top left), Pasta Fish Pie (top right) and Veal Cutlets Bonne Femme (bottom).

Bacon and Chestnuts

1lb joint of bacon, boned and rolled
2 tblsp butter
1 small onion, peeled and chopped
¼ cup chestnut pure'e
¼ tsp mixed herbs
¼ tsp mixed spice
1 tsp soft brown sugar
1 beaten egg
1lb puff pastry

Place the bacon in a saucepan, cover with cold water, bring to the boil and simmer for 1 hour. Remove the bacon from the pan and trim off any excess fat; leave until cold. Melt the butter and fry the onion until soft. Mix with the chestnut purée, herbs, spice, and sugar, and half the beaten egg to bind the mixture. Roll out the pastry to a circle large enough to wrap around the bacon joint. Spread the mixture over the top of the bacon. Fold the pastry up over the joint and seal with a little of the beaten egg. Place on a cooky sheet. Brush with beaten egg. Cook in the oven for 30-35 minutes at 425°F. Serve with carrots and broad beans.
Serves two.

Demi-Glace Sauce

2 tblsp dripping or butter
2 tblsp peeled and chopped onion
2 tblsp peeled and chopped carrot
¼ cup flour
1 rasher bacon, rinded and diced
2½ cups brown stock
1 tsp tomato paste
1 tsp mixed herbs
Salt and pepper

Heat the dripping or butter, fry the onion, bacon and carrot until very lightly browned. Do not overcook at this stage as burnt onion gives a bitter taste to the sauce. Add the flour and continue cooking slowly until a rich chestnut color. Draw the pan aside, add the stock and

This page: Braised Beef (top left), Broiled Meats (center) and Stuffed Mushrooms (bottom).

Facing page: Filled Jacket Potatoes (top left), Sausage and Mushroom Pie (top right), Bacon and Chestnuts (bottom right) and Stuffed Eggplant (bottom left).

Pork Fillets and Apricots

8oz pork fillet, cut into small pieces
1 tblsp seasoned flour
2 tblsp butter
7oz can of apricot halves
1 tblsp Worcestershire sauce
1 tblsp soft brown sugar
2 tsp wine vinegar
1 tsp lemon juice
½ tsp powdered cinnamon
4 tblsp water
½ cup long grain rice

Toss the pork pieces in the seasoned flour. Heat the butter in a flameproof casserole dish and fry the pork until lightly browned. Chop all but three of the apricot halves. Mix 4 tablespoons of the apricot syrup with the Worcestershire sauce, sugar, vinegar, lemon juice, cinnamon and water. Pour the apricot sauce and chopped fruit over the pork. Bring to the boil, stirring continuously. Reduce the heat, cover and simmer for 15 minutes. Meanwhile, cook the rice in boiling, salted water. Spoon the pork and sauce onto a serving dish and spoon the drained rice around the meat. Decorate with the reserved apricots. If required serve with a green vegetable.
Serves two.

when all the liquid has been incorporated, add the paste, herbs and seasoning to taste. Bring to the boil, skim thoroughly and simmer, covered, for 30 minutes. Strain through a fine-meshed strainer, pressing as much as possible of the vegetables through.
Makes 1 pint.

Sausage and Mushroom Pie

8oz pork sausages
2 tblsp butter
1 onion, peeled and sliced
3 tblsp flour
⅔ cup milk
⅔ cup brown stock
Salt and pepper
Pinch of mixed herbs
½ cup sliced mushrooms
8oz puff pastry
1 egg, beaten

Prick the sausages and broil them until golden. Heat the butter in a pan and fry the onion for 5 minutes. Stir in the flour and cook for a further minute. Gradually add the milk and stock and bring to boil. Stir until thickened then add the seasoning, herbs and mushrooms. Place the sausages in a pie dish and pour over the mushroom sauce. Roll out the puff pastry and use to cover the dish. Trim off any excess pastry. Glaze the top of the pie with the beaten egg and cook in the oven for 40 minutes at 390°F. Serve with new or boiled potatoes and a green vegetable.
Serves two.

Stuffed Eggplant

3 medium eggplant, washed and
    stalks removed
Salt
1¼ cups butter
1 medium onion, peeled and finely
    chopped
1 clove garlic, peeled and crushed
¾ cup ground beef
14oz can of tomatoes
1 tblsp chopped parsley
1 tsp dried marjoram
2 tsp tomato paste
Pepper
2 tsp cornstarch
½ cup Cheddar cheese, grated

Slice the eggplant in half lengthwise. Scoop out the flesh carefully and chop finely. Put the flesh on a large plate, sprinkle with salt and leave for 30 minutes. Blanch the eggplant skins in boiling water for 5 minutes. Remove and place on a serving dish. Heat the butter, add the onion and garlic and cook until soft. Stir in the ground beef and cook until brown. Add the tomatoes, parsley, marjoram and tomato paste. Season with pepper and bring to the boil. Blend the cornstarch with a little cold water and add to the beef and tomato mixture. Return to the boil, then remove from the heat. Drain the eggplant flesh in a sieve and rinse in cold water. Stir half the flesh into the beef and tomato mixture and use to stuff the eggplant halves. Top each one with grated cheese and cook in the oven for about 30 minutes at 350°F. (Use the left-over eggplant flesh in a Bolognese sauce or as a vegetable covered with a cheese sauce.) Serve the stuffed eggplant hot with a tossed green salad.
Serves two.

Hearts and Stuffing

2 lambs' hearts
Seasoned flour
1½ tblsp unsalted butter
1¼ cups brown stock
1 small onion
½ cup carrots
1 celery heart

Stuffing

2 shallots
1 stick celery
1oz belly pork
2 tblsp fresh breadcrumbs
1 rounded tblsp parsley
1 tsp curry powder
Salt and pepper
1½ tblsp melted butter

First make the stuffing. Peel and chop the shallots. Scrub and dice the celery stick. Grind or finely chop the pork. Place these ingredients in a bowl with the breadcrumbs, parsley, curry powder and seasoning. Bind together with the melted butter. Rinse the hearts. Cut out any tubes and discard, and fill the hearts with the stuffing. Sew up the openings and coat the hearts with seasoned flour. Melt the butter in a heavy pan and fry the hearts over a

high heat until brown. Lift the hearts into a casserole dish. Stir in enough seasoned flour to absorb the fat. Cook for 2-3 minutes then add the stock and bring to the boil. Pour over the hearts. Cover the casserole and cook in the oven at 325°F for 2 hours. After 2 hours peel and chop the onion, carrot and celery heart. Add to the casserole and continue to cook for a further 1 hour. Serve with boiled potatoes and green vegetables.
Serves two

Filled Jacket Potatoes

2 medium sized potatoes
2 tblsp butter
Salt and pepper

Cheddar Cheese Filling

¼ cup Cheddar cheese, grated
2 tblsp butter
A little milk
Salt and pepper
1 tblsp Parmesan cheese

Bacon Filling

6 tblsp bacon, rind removed, chopped
    and fried
2 tblsp butter
A little milk
Salt and pepper
1 small green pepper, cored, seeded
    and finely chopped

Sausage and Onion Filling

2 small pork sausages, chopped and
    broiled
2 tblsp butter
A little milk
Salt and pepper
1 small onion, peeled, chopped and
    fried

Liver and Zucchini Filling

6 tblsp lambs' liver, chopped and
    fried
2 tblsp butter
A little milk
Salt and pepper
2 small zucchini, diced and fried

Scrub the potatoes well. Prick them and dot their skins with butter. Sprinkle lightly with salt and pepper. Cook in the oven for 1-1¼ hours at 400°F. When cooked, cut in half lengthwise and scoop out the centers, keeping the skins intact. Mash the potato in a basin, adding one of the filling mixtures. Return the mixture to the potato skins. Cook for a further 15-20 minutes.
Serves two.

Lasagne

2 tblsp margarine
1 small onion, peeled and sliced
1 cup ground beef
7oz can of tomatoes
1 tsp tomato paste
⅔ cup beef stock
1 tsp dried marjoram
1 tsp mixed herbs
Pinch garlic salt
Salt and pepper
1 tsp cornstarch
6 tblsp lasagne
½ tblsp butter
2 tblsp margarine
¼ cup flour
1 cup milk
6 tblsp Cheddar cheese, grated

Heat the margarine and fry the onion until soft. Stir in the ground beef and cook until browned. Add the tomatoes, tomato paste, stock, herbs and garlic. Season well, cover and simmer for 30 minutes. Meanwhile, mix the cornstarch to a paste with a little cold water, stir into the meat sauce and bring to the boil, stirring continuously. Cook the lasagne in boiling, salted water, adding the ½ tblsp butter, for 10-15 minutes. Drain carefully. Heat the margarine, stir in the flour and cook for a few minutes. Allow to cool and gradually add the milk. Return to the heat and bring to the boil, stirring continuously. Stir in two-thirds of the cheese. Cover the base of a greased ovenproof dish with half the lasagne. Spoon over half the meat and tomato sauce. Cover with the remaining lasagne and spoon over remaining tomato sauce. Pour on the cheese sauce, sprinkle the Cheddar cheese on top and cook in the oven at 375°F for 30-35 minutes.
Serves two

Facing page: Lasagne (top left), Hearts and Stuffing (top right) and Pork Fillets and Apricots (bottom).

Family Meals

Cod in White Sauce

1½lb cod fillet
Salt and pepper
⅔ cup milk
2 tblsp lemon juice
2 tblsp butter

White Sauce
2 tblsp margarine
¼ cup flour
Milk
Salt and pepper
Pinch of paprika

Wash and skin the fish and cut into four pieces. Place the fish in an ovenproof dish and season well. Pour the milk and lemon juice over the fish and dot with some of the butter. Cover the dish and cook for 20 minutes at 400°F. Melt the margarine and remaining butter in a pan, stir in the flour and cook for 1 minute. Drain the liquid from the fish and add enough milk to make up to 1¼ cups. Stir the liquid slowly into the roux, bring to the boil and cook for 1 minute, stirring continuously. Add seasoning and paprika. Serve with new potatoes and broccoli.
Serves four.

Beef Surprise

1 onion, peeled and chopped
3 tblsp fat
¼ cup flour
1¼ cups brown stock
Pinch of mixed herbs
1lb ground beef
Salt and pepper

Cook the onion in the fat until transparent. Add the flour and cook for 5 minutes. Add the stock, bring to the boil and cook until the sauce thickens. Add the herbs, ground beef and seasoning. Stir continuously, cook until the meat is browned. Lower the heat and simmer gently for 1 hour, stirring frequently. Arrange on a hot dish. Garnish with tomatoes and creamed potatoes, and serve.
Serves four.

Chicken Pie

Pastry
2 cups flour
Pinch of salt
¼ cup margarine
¼ cup lard
Beaten egg and milk mixed together
    to glaze top of pie

Chicken Sauce
⅔ cup milk
1 tblsp margarine
1 tblsp all-purpose flour
Salt and pepper
1 cup cooked chicken, chopped
3 tblsp white wine (optional)

First make the sauce by placing the milk, margarine and flour in a small pan. Bring to the boil, beating continuously. Simmer for 2 minutes until the sauce thickens. Add seasoning, stir in the chopped chicken and add the wine, if desired. Sift the flour and salt into a bowl and rub in the margarine and lard until it looks like breadcrumbs. Add enough water to form a dough. Use half the dough to line a large, flat plate. Add the chicken mixture then cover with the remaining pastry, sealing the edges. Cut slits in the top. Brush the top of the pie with the beaten egg and milk mixture. Cook in the oven for 25 minutes at 400°F, until golden brown. Serve with creamed potatoes and carrots.
Serves four.

Spaghetti Bolognese

2 tblsp butter
1 tblsp olive oil
¼ cup mushrooms, chopped
1 onion, peeled and chopped
1 carrot, peeled and chopped
½lb ground beef
½ cup tomato paste
1¼ cups brown stock
8oz spaghetti
Parmesan cheese, to serve

Heat the butter and oil in a pan and fry the mushrooms, onions and carrot. Stir in the meat, cook for a few minutes then add the tomato paste and stock and simmer gently. Cook for one hour, until the mixture thickens, stirring occasionally. Meanwhile, place the spaghetti in boiling, salted water and cook for 15 minutes. Drain. Serve together with the Bolognese sauce and sprinkle with Parmesan cheese.
Serves four.

Beef Bake

1½lb stewing steak
¼ cup flour
Salt and pepper
2 tblsp lard
2 onions, peeled and chopped
2½ cups brown stock
1 tblsp tomato paste
3 tblsp red wine (optional)
2 carrots, peeled and sliced
2 tsp dried mixed herbs

Topping
¼ cup white breadcrumbs
¼ cup butter
2 cups all-purpose flour
2 tsp baking powder
1 tsp salt
Pepper
1 tsp garlic salt
1 tsp Parmesan cheese
3 tblsp oil
⅔ cup milk

Cut the meat into cubes and toss in seasoned flour. Melt the lard in a pan and fry the onions. Add the meat and fry for 5 minutes or until the meat is brown. Remove from the heat and blend in the stock, tomato paste and red wine. Add the carrots and herbs. Return to the heat and bring to the boil. Turn the mixture into an ovenproof dish, cover and cook in the oven for 2 hours at 325°F. Fry the breadcrumbs in the butter until golden brown, then lift out on to a plate. Sieve together the flour, baking powder, salt, pepper, garlic salt and Parmesan cheese, add the oil and milk and gradually mix to a dough. Drop large spoonfuls of the dough into the fried breadcrumbs and roll into balls. Arrange on top of the meat mixture. Return the casserole uncovered to the oven and cook for a further hour, or until the top is golden brown. Serve with peas and new potatoes.
Serves four.

Sweet and Sour Pork Chops with Rice

4 large pork chops

Sauce
14oz can of tomatoes
1 large green pepper, cored, seeded
    and chopped
2 tblsp cornstarch
3 tblsp wine vinegar
2 tblsp brown sugar
2 tblsp soy sauce
Salt and pepper

To make the sauce place the tomatoes and ⅔ cup of their juice in a saucepan and break down with a fork. Add the green pepper, bring to the boil and simmer for 10 minutes. Blend the cornstarch and vinegar together to form a paste. Add the paste to the tomato mixture. Add the remaining sauce ingredients and cook for 15 minutes. Meanwhile, cook the pork chops under a moderately hot broiler. Place the chops on a flat, flameproof serving dish and pour over the sauce. Place under a hot broiler for 2-3 minutes to heat through.
Serves four.

Pork Chops with Brussels Sprouts and Corn (far left, top), Beef Surprise (far left, bottom) and Cod in White Sauce (left).

Facing page: Spaghetti Bolognese (top), Chicken Pie (center left) and Shepherd's Pie (bottom).

Pork Chops with Brussels Sprouts and Corn

⅓ cup butter
1 large onion, peeled and chopped
1lb Brussels sprouts
½ cup frozen corn
4 pork chops (large)
1 tsp salt
1 tsp cayenne pepper
1 tsp chopped parsley

Melt 2 tblsp of butter in a saucepan. Add the chopped onion and fry lightly. Cook the Brussels sprouts in boiling, salted water for about 8 minutes until cooked but still firm. Also cook the corn. Drain both vegetables. Melt 2 tblsp of the butter and add the drained Brussels sprouts and corn and cook very gently, shaking the pan frequently. Melt the remaining butter. Sprinkle the pork chops with the salt and the cayenne pepper and fry them in the butter over a medium heat for about 5-10 minutes on each side. Remove the chops to a serving dish. Add 2 tablespoons of water to the juices in the pan and bring to the boil, stirring continuously. Arrange the vegetables round the chops and pour over the sauce. Sprinkle with the chopped parsley and serve. Serves four.

Chicken Casserole

2 tblsp lard
½ cup mushrooms, sliced
4 chicken joints
¾ cup flour
2 large carrots, peeled and sliced
1 potato, peeled and sliced
1¼ cups chicken stock
1¼ cups white wine
Salt and pepper
6 tblsp peas

Melt half the lard, fry the mushrooms, then place them in an ovenproof dish. Coat the chicken in the flour and fry in the remaining lard until golden brown. Transfer to the ovenproof dish and add the sliced carrots and potato. Put the leftover flour in a pan and add the stock and wine, stirring all the time. Add the seasoning, bring to the boil and pour over the chicken and vegetables. Cover and cook in the oven for 1 hour 35 minutes at 350°F. Add the peas 10

minutes before the end of the cooking time. Serve with new potatoes.
Serves four.

Shepherd's Pie

2 tblsp fat
1 onion, peeled and chopped
¼ cup mushrooms, chopped
2 tomatoes, skinned and chopped
12oz cooked beef or lamb, ground
Pinch of mixed herbs
Salt and pepper
1¼ cups brown stock
1lb mashed potato
¼ cup butter

Heat the fat and fry the onion for 3 minutes. Add the mushrooms and fry for another minute. Add the tomatoes and the meat and cook for 3 minutes. Stir in the herbs and seasoning and finally add the stock. Put the mixture into a pie dish and cover with the mashed potato. Dot small pieces of butter over the

mashed potato. Cook in the oven for 30-40 minutes at 400°F, until the top is crisp and brown. Serve with peas and leeks.
Serves four.

This page: Beef Bake (top left), Chicken Casserole (top right) and Sweet and Sour Pork Chops with Rice (bottom).

Country Chicken

4 chicken legs
Butter for frying
2 onions, peeled and chopped
2 tblsp cornstarch
A little milk
⅔ cup hot chicken stock
½ cup peas
½ cup corn

Fry the chicken legs in butter to seal. Set aside to drain on paper towels. Fry the onions until tender but not brown. Transfer the chicken and onions to an ovenproof dish. Blend the cornstarch with the milk. Add the chicken stock. Add the peas and corn to the casserole and pour the chicken stock over the vegetables but do not completely cover chicken. Cook in the oven, uncovered, for 20-30 minutes at 375°F. Serve with boiled potatoes. Serves four.

Liver With Oranges

12oz lambs' liver
¼ cup flour
Salt and pepper
Pinch of mustard
½ cup butter
1 tblsp olive oil
1 onion
1 tsp garlic salt
½ tsp brown ketchup sauce
⅔ cup brown stock
2 oranges, peeled and sliced, to garnish
Creamed potatoes, to serve

Trim the liver and cut into 3-4 slices. Season the flour with salt, pepper and the mustard. Dip the liver into the seasoned flour. Melt half the butter and 1 tsp of oil. Fry the liver in the butter and oil, cooking each side for 2-3 minutes. Remove the liver to a warmed dish and keep hot. Add the remaining butter to the pan and cook the onion until soft. Add the garlic salt and brown sauce. Stir in the stock. Simmer until the mixture thickens and add extra seasoning if desired. Place the liver on a serving dish, pour over the sauce and garnish with slices of orange. Pipe creamed potatoes round to make a border. Serves four.

Beef and Dumplings

1-1½lb chuck roast
Salt and pepper
¼ cup flour or
1½ tblsp cornstarch
2 tblsp fat
3¾ cups brown stock

Pinch of mixed herbs
2 onions, peeled and chopped
4 carrots, peeled and sliced

Dumplings
1 cup all-purpose flour
1 tsp baking powder
Pinch of salt
¼ cup suet
Water to mix

Wipe the meat and cut into small pieces. Remove excess fat. Coat the meat in seasoned flour or cornstarch and fry in the fat for a few minutes to seal. Add the stock, herbs and vegetables, and bring to the boil. Transfer to an ovenproof dish and cover. Cook in the oven for 2½ hours at 350°F. Meanwhile, make the dumplings. Sieve the flour, salt and baking powder into a basin. Add the suet and blend with a knife. Stir in enough water to bind. The dumpling mixture should be just soft enough to form into balls. Divide into 8 portions and roll into balls with lightly floured hands. If necessary thicken the casserole with extra cornstarch or flour, blended with a little cold water. Twenty minutes before the end of the cooking time put the dumplings into the simmering liquid. Leave uncovered, unless there is plenty of space between the dumplings and the lid to allow them to rise well. Serve with boiled potatoes.
Serves four-six.

Liver with Oranges (facing page), Beef and Dumplings (center) and Country Chicken (left).

Toad in the Hole

½lb sausages (pork or beef)
1 tblsp lard
1 cup all-purpose flour
½ level tsp salt
Pinch of garlic salt
1 egg
1¼ cups milk

Put the sausages into a large, shallow pan or dish. Add the lard and place in the oven at 450°F. Sieve the flour, salt and garlic salt into a bowl. Add the egg and a little milk and beat until smooth. Add the rest of the milk a little at a time, beating well, to make a batter. Pour the batter into the pan. Cook for 30-45 minutes. Serve with mixed vegetables and duchesse potatoes. Serves three.

Meat Loaf

2 slices of bread
1lb prime ground beef
1 onion, peeled and chopped
1 tsp Worcestershire sauce
Salt and pepper
1 egg, beaten

Grate the bread or place in a blender to produce crumbs. Mix the ground beef, onion, Worcestershire sauce, salt and pepper and breadcrumbs. Add the egg and bind the mixture together. Put the mixture into a greased loaf pan and cover with wax paper. Cook in the oven for 50-60 minutes at 390°F. When the meat loaf is cooked the juices should run clear when a skewer is inserted. Turn the loaf out onto a flat serving dish. Garnish with cooked vegetables such as carrots, runner beans, peas and Brussels sprouts. Serves four.

Black Pudding or Bratwurst with Apple

1lb potatoes, peeled
3 large tart apples
3 tblsp oil
2 tblsp butter
1lb black pudding or bratwurst, sliced
1 tsp chopped parsley

Boil and mash the potatoes and keep them warm. Peel and core the apples and cut each one into 8

segments. Heat half the oil and all the butter in a pan. Add the apple, cover and cook for 5 minutes on a low heat. Drain and keep warm. In another pan heat the remaining oil and add the sliced black pudding or bratwurst. Fry on both sides until it is slightly crisp and heated through. Remove and drain. Place the mashed potato in the center of a heated serving dish and surround it with alternate portions of black pudding or bratwurst and apple. Sprinkle the potato with the chopped parsley. Serve with a green vegetable and fresh tomatoes.
Serves four.

Wine Coated Ham

2lb ham
Salt and pepper
1 cup carrots, peeled and cut into sticks
1 cup turnips, peeled and cut into sticks
1 cup green beans
1 cup frozen peas
1 tblsp soft brown sugar
⅔ cup red wine
¼ cup butter

This page: Wine Coated Ham (top), Black Pudding or Bratwurst with Apple (center right), Gammon Rounds with Onion Sauce (bottom left). Facing page: Steak and Kidney Pudding (top left), Crunchy Lamb Pie (top right), Meat Loaf (center left) and Toad in the Hole (bottom right).

Cover the ham with cold water and soak for 4 hours, changing the water frequently. Place the ham in a large pan, cover with cold water and simmer for 40 minutes. Bring a large pan of salted water to the boil, add the vegetables and cook for about 10 minutes. When the vegetables are cooked drain them, rinse with cold water and drain them again. Lift the ham from the pan. Peel off the rind and place the ham in an ovenproof dish. Sprinkle the ham with sugar and place in the oven for 5 minutes at 375°F. Pour the wine over and return to the oven for 5 minutes, basting frequently. Melt the butter in a pan and add the drained vegetables, salt and pepper. Heat through, stirring continuously. Place the

ham on a large serving dish with the vegetables and serve with the sauce from the cooking. Serve with new potatoes if required.
Serves four.

Gammon Rounds in Onion Sauce

4 gammon rounds
3 onions, peeled and sliced
¼ cup butter or margarine
½ cup flour
Salt and pepper
2½ cups milk

Broil the gammon rounds until tender. Boil the onions until soft, then drain. Melt the butter or margarine, remove from the heat and stir in the flour. Return to the heat and cook gently for a few minutes. Remove the pan from the heat and gradually stir in the milk. Bring to the boil and cook, stirring with a wooden spoon until smooth. Season well. If any small lumps have formed beat thoroughly. Stir in the boiled onions and serve with the gammon. Serve with potatoes in their jackets and green beans. Serves four.

Crunchy Lamb Pie

2 tblsp margarine
1 onion, peeled and chopped
½ packet parsley sauce mix
⅔ cup milk
1 tblsp half and half cream or top of the milk
¾ cup cold cooked lamb, minced
½ packet instant potato
2 tblsp Lancashire or Cheddar cheese, grated

Heat the margarine and fry the onion until soft. Make the parsley sauce as directed on the packet, using the milk, and stir in the cream, or top of the milk and the onion. Add the lamb to the sauce. Mix well and turn into a greased pie dish. Make the instant potato as directed on the packet and spread over the meat mixture. Sprinkle the cheese over the potato. Cook in the oven for 30 minutes at 400-425°F. Serve with a green vegetable or baked onions. Serves two.

Steak and Kidney Pudding

1½lb stewing steak
2 lambs' kidneys
1 tblsp flour
Salt and pepper
⅔ cup stock

Suet Crust Pastry

2 cups all-purpose flour
2½ tsp baking powder
½ tsp of salt
A pinch of pepper
½ cup shredded suet
⅔ cup water

To make the suet crust pastry, sift flour, baking powder and seasoning into a mixing basin. Add the suet and stir in enough water to mix to a firm dough. Turn out onto a floured board and use as required. Trim and cut the steak into strips. Cut the kidneys into small pieces. Mix the steak and kidney together. Put the flour and seasoning on a plate and use to coat the meat. To line a basin with the pastry, cut off ¼ of the dough and reserve for the lid. Roll out the rest of the pastry into a large, thin round. Lower into the basin. Add the meat and enough stock to come two-thirds of the way up the basin. Roll out pastry for the lid and place in position. Seal the edges. Cover with either wax paper or foil, or a muslin cloth dipped in boiled water and then floured. Fix securely round the basin rim with string. Put the pudding in a steamer, stand this over a saucepan of boiling water and steam for 4 hours. Add more boiling water when necessary. Serve with creamed potatoes and Brussels sprouts. Serves four.

Breast of Lamb and Onion Stuffing

1½lb breast of lamb, boned
1 tblsp oil
1 tblsp butter
Salt and pepper
Lamb seasoning
⅔ cup chicken stock
1 tblsp cornstarch, blended in a little cold water

Stuffing

2 tblsp long grain rice
1 tblsp butter
2 onions, peeled and chopped
Salt and pepper
Pinch of mixed spice
½ tsp lamb seasoning

First make the stuffing. Cook the rice in boiling salted water, rinse and drain. Heat the butter and fry the onion. Mix the rice and onion together with the salt and pepper, mixed spice and the lamb seasoning. Spread the stuffing on the lamb; roll and tie. Brush with the oil and butter, season and sprinkle with lamb seasoning. Roast in the oven for 20 minutes at 400°F. Reduce the heat to 350°F. Pour the stock into the roasting pan and cover with foil. Cook for a further hour. Remove the meat from the pan and thicken the gravy with the cornstarch to accompany the meat. Serve with roast potatoes, turnips and mixed vegetables.
Serves four.

Peppered Mackerel with Gooseberry Sauce

8oz mackerel fillets, washed
¼ cup flour
¼ cup oil
2 tsp peppercorns

Marinade

3 tblsp oil
Grated rind and juice of 1 lemon
1 tblsp soy sauce
1 clove garlic, peeled and crushed
1 tblsp wine vinegar
1 tblsp sugar

Gooseberry Sauce

½lb gooseberries, topped and tailed
1 apple, peeled, cored and diced
¼ cup sugar
Sprig of mint
1¼ cups water
Pinch of salt
1½ tblsp arrowroot (optional)

To make the marinade, liquidize all the ingredients in a blender. Soak the fish fillets in the marinade for 15 minutes. Drain them and dry on kitchen paper, then dip them in the flour. Discard the marinade. Brush the fillets with the oil and place on a greased broiler rack. Broil for 3 minutes on each side, then remove and sprinkle with peppercorns. Arrange on a hot dish and keep warm. Place the gooseberries in a saucepan with the diced apple, sugar, mint and half the water. Boil for 8 minutes, then remove the mint. Work the gooseberry mixture in a blender or rub through a sieve to a purée. Add a pinch of salt. Reheat the purée in a saucepan and thicken, if liked, with the arrowroot mixed to a paste with a little cold water. Boil for 4 minutes until clear and thick. Serve the broiled mackerel with the gooseberry sauce. Serve with new potatoes and mushrooms.
Serves four.

Lamb Cobbler

¼ cup oil
1 onion, peeled and sliced
1½lb ground lamb
2 tblsp flour
2 tblsp tomato paste
1¼ cups brown stock
Salt and pepper
Pinch of rosemary
1 tsp dry mustard
2 tblsp Worcestershire sauce

Topping

2 cups all-purpose flour
Pinch of salt
2 tsp baking powder
¼ cup butter
¼ cup water
1 tblsp milk

Heat the oil in a pan and fry the onion until soft. Add the lamb and cook for 5 minutes. Stir in the flour and tomato paste and cook for 5 minutes. Then add the stock, seasoning, rosemary, mustard and Worcestershire sauce. Make the topping by sifting the flour and salt together, and cut in the butter. Add enough water to form a dough. Roll out the dough to ¼ inch thick. Cut into rounds to form small scones. Arrange the scones around the top of the dish. Brush the scones with milk. Bake in the oven for 30 minutes at 375°F, until the scones are browned. Serve with creamed potatoes and Brussels sprouts.
Serves four.

Peppered Mackerel with Gooseberry Sauce (top), Lamb Cobbler (center right) and Breast of Lamb and Onion Stuffing (bottom).

Quick Meals

Sausage Rolls

Basic Pastry
4 cups all-purpose flour
Pinch of salt
½ cup lard
½ cup margarine
¼ cup Parmesan cheese

Filling
Salt and pepper
½ cup Cheddar cheese
1lb sausage meat
A little beaten egg and milk, beaten together to glaze the pastry

To make the pastry, sift the flour and salt into a basin. Add the Parmesan cheese and cut in the fat. Mix with enough water to form a dough. Roll out into two rectangles 12"x10". Cut each rectangle in half lengthwise. Mix the salt and pepper and Cheddar cheese into the sausage meat and roll out with the hands into four lengths the same as the pastry. Place on the pastry. Brush the edges of the pastry with water, fold over and seal. Cut into 3" lengths and mark the top with a knife. Brush with the milk and egg mixture. Place on a greased cooky sheet in the oven for 20 minutes at 400°F. Serve with French fries and peas or a mixed salad.

Fisherman's Pie

1lb white fish fillets, steamed
1lb mashed potato
2 tblsp butter or margarine
¼ cup Cheddar cheese (optional)

Sauce
2 tblsp butter
¼ cup flour
1¼ cups milk
Pinch of salt
1 tsp dried parsley

Flake the cooked fish and place in a pie dish. Make the sauce. Heat the butter gently, remove from the heat and stir in the flour. Return to the heat and cook gently for a few minutes but do not let the 'roux' brown. Remove from the heat and blend in the milk, stirring well. Add salt and parsley. Cover the fish with the sauce, then spread

mashed potato over the top of the fish. Dot with small pieces of butter or margarine and sprinkle with Cheddar cheese, if desired. Cook in the oven for 25-30 minutes at 400°F.
Serves four.

Savory Eggs

1lb ground beef
1 large onion, peeled and grated
2 tblsp white breadcrumbs
1 tblsp Worcestershire sauce
Salt and pepper
2 eggs, beaten
4 hard-boiled eggs, shelled
Dried breadcrumbs
Oil for deep frying

Mix together in a bowl the ground beef, grated onion, breadcrumbs and Worcestershire sauce. Season and bind the mixture with one of the eggs. Divide the mixture into

four portions and mold round each of the hard-boiled eggs. Dip the covered eggs in the rest of the beaten egg then coat with breadcrumbs. Heat the oil in a deep fat fryer or deep skillet. When hot, fry the savory eggs for 5-10 minutes, until crisp and golden brown. Serve hot or cold with a green or mixed salad.
Serves four.

Chicken Marengo

1 large roasted chicken
¼ cup butter
½ cup flour
2½ cups chicken stock
2 tblsp tomato paste
Salt and pepper
1 beef stock cube
Pinch of mixed herbs
1½ tblsp butter or margarine
1 onion, peeled and chopped
½ cup sliced mushrooms
1 tblsp sugar

Skin and bone the cooked chicken and cut the meat into small pieces. Melt the butter in a pan and stir in the flour to make a roux. Allow to cool. Add the chicken stock and the tomato paste and bring to simmering point, stirring continuously. Add seasoning, beef stock cubes and mixed herbs. Fry the onions and mushrooms in the butter or margarine. Place the chicken, mushrooms and onions in an ovenproof dish. Pour the sauce over chicken mixture and fold through. Cover and cook in the oven for 15 minutes at 450°F. Serve with saute' potatoes and green beans.

Cornish Pasties

1lb round steak
2 potatoes, peeled
2 onions, peeled
2 small carrots, peeled
2 tblsp frozen peas
Salt and pepper
Pinch of mixed herbs
3 tblsp brown stock
A little milk and egg beaten together to glaze

Basic Pastry
4 cups flour
½ cup margarine
½ cup lard
Pinch of salt
⅓ cup water

First make the basic pastry. Sieve the flour and salt into a bowl. Cut in the fat until it looks like breadcrumbs and mix with enough water to form a dough. Divide into four and roll out into rounds. Cut the meat, potatoes, onions and carrots into cubes and mix with the peas. Add seasoning and the herbs, add the stock and spoon onto the

This page: Sausage Rolls (top), Chicken Marengo (left) and Savory Eggs (bottom right).

Facing page: Cornish Pasties (top), Cheesy Pizza (center right) and Fisherman's Pie (bottom left).

pastry rounds. Brush the edges of the pastry with a little water, bring the edges together and seal. Lift the pasties onto a greased cooky sheet and brush with the egg and milk mixture. Cook in the oven for 25 minutes at 425°F. Lower the heat to 350°F for a further 25 minutes to cook the meat and the vegetables thoroughly. Serve with French fries, mushrooms and peas.
Serves four.

Picnic Burgers

¼ cup butter or margarine
1 onion, peeled and chopped
¼ cup flour
⅔ cup stock
Salt and pepper
1½ cups ground meat, cooked
6 tblsp white breadcrumbs
Pinch of mixed herbs
2 tsp chopped fresh parsley
1 beaten egg
3 tblsp dried breadcrumbs
¼ cup fat

Heat the butter or margarine and fry the onion until soft. Stir in the flour and cook for a few minutes, then gradually stir in the stock, bring to boil and cook until thickened. Add seasoning. Stir in the ground meat and the breadcrumbs. Add the mixed herbs and parsley. Allow the mixture to cool, then form into 8 flat cakes. Coat with beaten egg and breadcrumbs. Fry in hot fat until crisp and golden brown. Drain on paper towels. Serve hot between buttered rolls or with vegetables.
Serves four.

Welsh Rarebit

2 tblsp butter
¼ cup flour
⅔ cup milk
1 tsp made mustard
Salt and pepper
1 cup cheese, grated
1 tblsp Worcestershire sauce
4 large slices of buttered toast

Melt the butter in a saucepan, stir in the flour and cook for several minutes. Allow to cool. Gradually add the milk, bring to boil, stirring, and cook until thick and smooth. Add the mustard, seasoning, most of the cheese and the Worcestershire sauce. Heat

steadily, but do not boil, until the cheese has melted. Spread over hot, buttered toast and sprinkle with the remaining cheese. Brown under a hot broiler. Serve hot with French fries.
Serves four.

Scotch Eggs

4 hard-boiled eggs, shelled
1 lb sausage meat
1 egg, beaten
¼ cup breadcrumbs
1 tsp mixed herbs
1 tblsp flour
Oil

Using floured hands, coat the eggs with the sausage meat. Brush with the beaten egg. Combine the breadcrumbs and the mixed herbs. Roll the eggs in the breadcrumb and herb mixture. Fry the eggs in moderately hot oil for 10 minutes. Remove the eggs from the oil and drain well. Serve with bird's nest potatoes.
Serves four.

Cheesy Pizza

Pizza Dough
½ tsp superfine sugar
⅓ cup warm water
1 tsp dried yeast
1 cup all-purpose flour
Pinch of salt
1 tblsp lard
2 tsp oil

Topping
14oz can of tomatoes
¼ cup mushrooms, sliced
2 bacon rashers, rinded and chopped
½ tsp dried marjoram
½ cup Cheddar cheese, grated
Stuffed olives, sliced

Dissolve the sugar in the water and sprinkle with the yeast. Leave in a warm place until frothy. Sieve the flour and salt into a bowl and rub in the lard. Blend the yeast liquid and the oil with the flour until a dough is formed. Turn the dough onto a floured board and knead well. Return the dough to the bowl and cover until it has doubled in size. Knead the dough again. Use the dough to line a 9″ pizza plate. Before it starts to rise, brush with oil and cover with the topping. Drain the tomatoes and break them up with a fork. Spread over the dough and cover with

mushrooms and bacon. Sprinkle with the majoram. Top with Cheddar cheese and olives. Leave the pizza for 15 minutes before baking. Cook in the oven for 25 minutes at 400°F. Serve with a salad.
Serves three-four.

Hamburgers and Tomatoes

1 lb ground beef
¼ cup breadcrumbs
⅔ cup tomato ketchup
1 large onion, peeled and chopped
½ tsp mixed herbs
½ tsp dried parsley
1 tsp Tabasco sauce
Salt and pepper

Put all the ingredients into a bowl and mix well together. Form into eight rounds and chill in the refrigerator for 2 hours. Cook on an oiled broiler or fry in a little oil for 5 minutes on each side. Serve with creamed potatoes and beans.
Serves four.

Saucy Chump Chops

4 lamb chump chops
2 tblsp seasoned flour
3 tblsp oil
3 onions, peeled and sliced
3 tomatoes, skinned, deseeded and chopped
Pinch of garlic salt
⅔ cup white wine
⅔ cup chicken stock
Salt and pepper
4 zucchini, sliced
1 lb potatoes, peeled
1¼ cups white sauce
6 tblsp Cheddar cheese, grated
1 tsp Parmesan cheese

Coat the lamb chops with the seasoned flour. Heat the oil and fry the chops until browned on both sides. Remove from the pan and place in the bottom of an ovenproof dish. In the same oil fry the onions; add the chopped tomatoes and garlic salt. Pour in the wine and stock, add seasoning and simmer for 10 minutes. Blanch the zucchini in boiling water for 3-4 minutes. Drain and scatter over the chops. Pour the tomato mixture over the top. Blanch the potatoes in boiling water for 5 minutes. Slice and arrange them over the top of

the tomato mixture. Heat the white sauce and stir in ¼ cup of the Cheddar cheese and all the Parmesan cheese. Blend and pour over the potatoes. Sprinkle with the remaining Cheddar cheese. Cook in the oven for 1 hour at 325°F.
Serves four.

Party Hamburgers

1 lb ground beef
2 medium onions, peeled and grated
1 medium potato, peeled and grated
Pinch of mixed herbs
Salt and pepper
1 beaten egg
A little fat
Sweet roll or slices of bread
Butter (optional)

To Garnish
Rings of raw onion
Slices of apple dipped in lemon juice
Olives
Glacé cherries
Chopped scallions
Yogurt
Parsley

Mix together the ground beef, onion, potato, herbs and seasoning. Bind with the beaten egg. Form into 4 round or square hamburger shapes. Either fry in a little hot fat, turning carefully, for about 15 minutes, or cook on a well-greased tray in the center of the oven for 25 minutes at 400°F. Toast the rolls or bread, and butter if desired. Put the cooked hamburgers on the rolls or toast and keep warm until required. Garnish with raw onion rings, slices of apple dipped in lemon juice, olives, glacé cherries on cocktail sticks, chopped spring onions, yogurt and parsley. Serve hot, with vegetables or cut small to eat with fingers.
Serves four.

Facing page: Hamburgers and Tomatoes (top right), Scotch Eggs (center left) and Saucy Chump Chops (bottom right).

Sausage and Tomato Quiche

½lb chipolata sausages
6 tblsp Cheddar cheese, coarsely
   grated
2 tomatoes, skinned and sliced
2 eggs
1 cup milk
Salt and pepper
½ tsp dried basil

Basic Pastry
¾ cup all-purpose flour
Pinch of salt
½ cup fat
2 tblsp cold water

Make the basic pastry. Sift the flour and salt into a bowl. Cut in the fat until it looks like breadcrumbs and add enough water to make a dough. Roll out and line a flan case or pie plate with the pastry. Prick the base and sides and bake blind in the oven for 20 minutes at 400°F. Fry or broil the sausages until lightly browned. Sprinkle the cheese over the base of the cooked pastry case. Arrange the cooked sausages in a wheel design, and put tomato slices in-between the sausages. Beat the eggs, stir in the milk, add seasoning and the basil. Pour over the quiche filling. Reduce the oven temperature to 350°F, and cook for a further 30-35 minutes. Serve hot or cold, with rice or salad.
Serves four.

Beef Shapes

2 tblsp fat
1 medium onion, peeled and chopped
½lb ground cooked beef
Salt and pepper
Fat for deep frying

Sauce
2 tblsp butter or margarine
¼ cup flour
1¼ cups stock

Coating
1 tblsp flour
Salt and pepper
1 egg, beaten
Dried breadcrumbs

Garnish
Watercress
Tomatoes

Heat the fat in a small skillet. Add the onion and beef, and cook gently for about 3 minutes until the beef turns brown, stirring with

a fork. Cook gently for 10 minutes, until the onion is tender. Drain off any liquid. To make the sauce, melt the butter or margarine in a saucepan, blend in the flour and cook for 2-3 minutes. Add the stock gradually, stirring all the time. Bring the sauce to the boil and cook for 3 minutes. Add the beef mixture and mix well. When cool enough to handle, divide the mixture into 8 portions. Roll in seasoned flour, dip in beaten egg and coat with breadcrumbs. Heat the fat in a deep fat frier or deep skillet, and fry the shapes until golden brown. Drain on paper towels. Garnish with watercress and tomatoes. Serve hot with vegetables, or cold with a salad.
Serves four.

Boston Baked Beans

1½ cups dried haricot beans
Cold water
2 medium onions, peeled and thinly
   sliced
1-1½ cups fat salt pork cut into 1"
   cubes
2-4 tblsp dark molasses
2 tsp dry mustard
1 tsp salt
Pepper

Wash the beans, cover with cold water and soak overnight. Drain, reserving the liquid and making up to 1¼ cups. Fill an ovenproof dish with the beans, onion and pork. Heat and mix the liquid with the remaining ingredients, including plenty of pepper. Pour into the ovenproof dish and cover. Cook in the oven for 5-6 hours at 275°F, or for 4 hours at 300°F. Stir occasionally, and add more water if the beans start to dry out while cooking. Serve with boiled potatoes.
Serves four-six.

Pork Sausage Croûtes

12 pork sausages
3 bacon rashers
A little fat
2 dessert apples, peeled, cored and
   sliced
6 bread rounds
2 tomatoes, sliced
Parsley to garnish

Fry the sausages until golden brown, without using extra fat. When cooked, place in a warm dish and keep hot. De-rind and

halve each bacon rasher and roll and secure with a cocktail stick. Fry in a little fat, or without fat, until crisp. Keep warm with the sausages. Fry the sliced apples in hot fat until golden brown on both sides. Toast the bread. Place the sausages on top of the bread, then add the apple rings and uncooked tomato. Garnish with parsley and arrange the bacon rolls round the dish. Serve with baked beans or creamed potatoes and with a green vegetable.
Serves four-six.

Fish Pasties

4 plaice fillets
Salt and pepper
A little lemon juice
¼-½ cup mushrooms, thinly sliced
1 egg, beaten
4 tomatoes to garnish

Basic Puff Pastry
2 cups all-purpose flour
Pinch of salt
½-¾ cup fat, cut into small cubes
1 tsp lemon juice
½ cup cold water

Make the basic puff pastry. Sieve the flour and salt into a bowl. Cut in the fat. Mix the lemon juice with the water and mix into the flour to make a dough. Roll out the pastry, fold and roll again, three times in total. Finally, roll into a large, fairly thick square and divide into four. Lay a plaice fillet crosswise on each piece, season, and sprinkle with lemon juice. Cover with sliced mushrooms, damp the pastry edges and fold over to form a triangle. Press together and trim. Brush with beaten egg and bake in the oven for about 10 minutes at 375-400°F, or until the pastry is risen. Reduce the heat slightly and cook until brown. Cut the tomatoes into halves, place in an oiled dish and bake in the oven for 5 minutes. Put the egg left over from glazing into a separate ovenproof dish and bake for about the same time. When set, chop and place a spoonful on each tomato half. Put the pasties on a hot dish to serve and garnish with tomatoes and egg.
Serves four.

Chicken Risotto (left), Sausage and Tomato Quiche (below) and Boston Baked Beans (bottom).

Potato and Scrambled Egg

1lb potato or
½lb instant mashed potato
A little milk
A stick of butter
Salt and pepper
2 eggs
⅔ cup milk
4 tblsp Cheddar cheese, grated
Pinch of dry mustard

Cook or prepare the potatoes and mash them with a little milk, half the butter and seasoning. Place the eggs, milk, cheese and mustard in a bowl with seasoning. Beat together. Melt the remaining butter in a small pan and add the egg mixture, stirring continuously until all the fat is absorbed. Stir in the potatoes and egg mixture and mix together. Spread onto a large, flat surface and cut into shapes using assorted cutters. Place the potato shapes on an oiled broiler and place under a hot broiler for 10 minutes, until browned. Serve with fresh or canned tomatoes.
Serves four.

Savory Sausage Tournedos

1lb chuck roast, ground
Salt and pepper
1 tsp mixed herbs
1 large onion
1 beaten egg
¼ cup fat
1lb can of baked beans with pork
sausages and tomato sauce
1 large tart apple

Mix the chuck roast with seasoning and the herbs. Peel the onion and cut into four even slices. Remove the centers from the onion rings. Finely chop the centers and remainder of the onion. Add the chopped onion to the chuck roast, and bind with beaten egg. Divide the mixture into 4 rounds (tournedos). Heat the fat and fry the tournedos gently for 8 minutes on each side. Remove to a serving dish and keep hot. Heat the beans and sausages in a saucepan. Peel and core the apple and cut into four slices. Cook gently in the skillet with the onion rings until the onion is golden brown and crisp, and the apples are tender but not broken. Place an onion ring on the tournedos, then a layer of baked beans and top with an apple

ring. Place two sausages inside the apple ring. Add the remaining baked beans and serve with creamed potatoes.
Serves four.

Risotto with Chicken

2 small onions, peeled and chopped
¼ cup butter
15oz can of tomatoes
1 tblsp tomato paste
1½ cups long grain rice
3¾ cups chicken stock
4 tblsp Parmesan cheese
1lb cooked chicken, diced
½ cup mushrooms, chopped
Pinch of cayenne pepper

Fry the onion in the butter, add the tomatoes and tomato paste, and cook for 5 minutes, stirring continuously. Add the rice. Heat the stock to boiling point. Add the

stock to the rice and tomato mixture, cover and cook for 10 minutes. Remove from the heat and add the Parmesan cheese, cooked chicken, mushrooms and cayenne pepper. Cook gently for another 15 minutes, until all the liquid is absorbed.
Serves four.

Potato Figures

1lb potatoes, peeled
A little milk
¼ cup butter
Salt and pepper

Cook the potatoes in boiling, salted water for 20 minutes or until cooked. Drain the potatoes, add a little milk, the butter and seasoning and mash thoroughly. Spread the potato onto a large, flat surface and cut into shapes using assorted

cutters. Place the potato shapes on a greased cooky sheet and cook in the oven for 20 minutes at 350°F. Serve with sausages and canned spaghetti.

Fish Cakes

1 cup potatoes, peeled and cut into
even-sized pieces
4oz white fish fillets
8oz potatoes
1 tblsp butter or margarine
Salt and pepper
Oil for frying
1 sprig of parsley to garnish (optional)

Coating
Flour
1 egg, beaten
Dried breadcrumbs

Cook the potatoes in a pan and cover with cold water, adding a little salt. Boil for 25 minutes until cooked. Steam the fish for 15 minutes until cooked. Mash the cooked potato, flake the fish and add to the potatoes with the butter or margarine and seasoning. Divide the mixture into six and shape into round fish cakes. Coat each cake with flour, beaten egg and finally breadcrumbs. Heat the oil in a skillet and fry the fish cakes carefully, cooking them on each side. Drain well on paper towels. Serve on a shallow dish and garnish with a sprig of parsley if desired. Serve with boiled potatoes and peas.
Serves six.

This page: Savory Sausage Tournedos (top), Fish Pasties (center right) and Pork Sausage Croûtes (bottom left).

Facing page: Potato Figures (top), Fish Cakes (center right) and Potato and Scrambled Egg (bottom left).

The Family Roast

Lamb

ROASTING TIME: 25 minutes per 1lb + 25 minutes at 325°F.

Place in the center of a preheated oven. If a covered roasting pan is used basting is not necessary, but if the joint is uncovered or pot-roasted, the meat should be basted every 20-30 minutes. The meat should be turned over, using 2 metal spoons, halfway through the cooking. Transfer the meat from the pan to a hot, flat dish large enough to allow for carving. Keep hot. As accompaniments: medium brown, thickened gravy, mint or cranberry sauce. Serve with new potatoes, peas, French or green beans.

Veal

ROASTING TIME: 225 minutes per 1lb + 25 minutes at 325°F.

Place in the center of a preheated oven. If a covered roasting pan is used basting is not necessary, but if the joint is uncovered or pot-roasted, the meat should be basted every 20-30 minutes. The meat should be turned over, using 2 metal spoons, halfway through cooking. Transfer the meat from the tin onto a large, flat carving dish. Keep hot. As accompaniments: medium brown, thickened gravy, veal forcemeat stuffing, squeeze of lemon, bacon rolls. Serve with green vegetables, onions, tomatoes, baked or boiled potatoes.

Turkey

ROASTING TIME: For a 6-8lb turkey cook for 15 minutes at 400°F, then reduce temperature to 350°F and allow 15 minutes per 1lb + 15 minutes.

If the bird is frozen it must be allowed to thaw out completely before cooking. Stuff the bird, sprinkle with salt and place in a roasting pan. Brush the bird with melted dripping, butter or oil. The bird may be wrapped in foil, but the cover should be removed for the last 20-30 minutes to brown the skin. If left unwrapped the bird should be basted frequently.

Transfer to a large carving dish when cooked. As accompaniments: sausages, chestnut, sausage meat or veal forcemeat stuffing, bacon rolls, cranberry or celery sauce, thickened gravy. Serve with roast, fried or boiled potatoes, onions, peas or Brussels sprouts.

This page: Turkey (top), Pork (center right) and Lamb (bottom).

Facing page: Mutton (top), Steak (center left), Veal (center right) and Duck (bottom).

Beef

ROASTING TIME: 15 minutes per 1lb + 15 minutes at 350°F.

Place in the center of a preheated oven. If a covered roasting pan is used basting is not necessary, but if the joint is uncovered or pot-roasted, the meat should be basted every 20-30 minutes. The meat should be turned over, using 2 metal spoons, halfway through the cooking. Transfer the meat from the pan to a hot, flat dish large enough to allow for carving. Keep hot. As accompaniments: thin, dark brown gravy, Yorkshire pudding, horseradish sauce, roast parsnips. Serve with baked or boiled potatoes and any vegetable.

Baked Whole Gammon

ROASTING TIME: 30 minutes per 1lb + 30 minutes at 350°F.

Spread gammon with a little melted butter or margarine and wrap in foil. Place in a roasting pan in the center of a preheated oven. Transfer the meat from the pan when cooked, remove the foil and put the gammon onto a large, flat carving dish. Keep hot. As accompaniments: thin, dark brown gravy, sage and onion stuffing, apple sauce. Serve with baked or boiled potatoes, cabbage, celery, Brussels sprouts or cauliflower.

Pork

ROASTING TIME: 30 minutes per 1lb + 30 minutes at 350°F.

Place in the center of a preheated oven. If a covered roasting pan is used basting is not necessary, but if the joint is uncovered or pot-roasted, the meat should be basted every 20-30 minutes. The meat should be turned over, using 2 metal spoons, halfway through the cooking. Transfer the meat from the tin to a hot, flat dish large enough to allow for carving. Keep hot. As accompaniments: thin, dark brown gravy, sage and onion stuffing, apple sauce. Serve with boiled potatoes, cabbage, cauliflower, celery, onion, spinach or Brussels sprouts.

Duck

ROASTING TIME: For a 2-3lb duck, cook for 15 minutes per lb. + 15 minutes at 350-375°F.

If the bird is frozen it must be thawed out completely before cooking. Stuff the bird with sage and onion stuffing, and place in a roasting pan. Brush the bird with melted dripping, butter or oil. Duck must be well pricked all over the breast to allow the fat to run out and leave the breast skin crisp and succulent. Transfer to a large carving dish when cooked. As accompaniments: apple sauce; thin gravy, flavored with orange juice if

liked. Serve with roast potatoes, peas, carrots and any green vegetable.

Steak

Season steak before cooking. Steak can be broiled, fried or roasted until tender and cooked to one's liking. Serve with baked or boiled potatoes and any vegetable.

Mutton

ROASTING TIME: 25 minutes per 1lb + 25 minutes at 325°F.

Place in the center of a preheated oven. If a covered roasting pan is used basting is not necessary, but if the joint is uncovered or pot-roasted, the meat should be basted every 20-30 minutes. The meat should be turned over, using 2 metal spoons, halfway through the cooking. Transfer the meat from the pan onto a large, flat carving dish. Keep hot. As accompaniments: medium brown, thickened gravy, redcurrant, cranberry or mint sauce. Serve with baked or boiled potatoes and any vegetable.

Chicken

ROASTING TIME: 15 minutes per 1lb + 15 minutes at 400°F.

If the bird is frozen it must be allowed to thaw out completely before cooking. Stuff the bird, sprinkle with salt and place in a roasting pan. Brush the bird with melted dripping, butter or oil. The bird may be wrapped in foil, but the cover should be removed for the last 20-30 minutes to brown the skin. If left unwrapped the bird should be basted frequently. Transfer the bird to a large carving dish. As accompaniments: veal forcemeat, bread sauce, bacon rolls and thin gravy. Serve with baked, fried or boiled new potatoes, and green vegetables.

Beef (top), Chicken (far left) and Baked Whole Gammon (left).

Vegetables

about 15 minutes at 400-425°F, until brown and crisp on the edges. An alternative to duchesse potatoes is to make birds' nests. Pipe the potato into rings and cook the same as for duchesse potatoes. Fill with vegetables.

Baked Potatoes

Peel potatoes and cut out any eyes and green parts. Cut into slices. Melt fat in an ovenproof dish and place potatoes in the dish. Cook in the oven at 425°F, for about 1 hour. Serve as required.

Potato

Potatoes (Boiled)
New Potatoes

Scrub potatoes well, then scrape. Cook in salted water for 10-20 minutes according to size. Drain well, toss in butter and serve.

Creamed Potatoes

Peel potatoes and cut out any eyes and green parts. Cook in salted water for 15-20 minutes. When cooked, drain well. Using a potato masher or a fork, mash the potatoes in a pan until smooth and free of lumps. To each pound of potatoes add 2 tblsp butter, a little milk and seasoning. Beat the mixture until light and fluffy. Serve as required.

Sauté Potatoes

Peel potatoes and cut out any eyes and green parts. Cook in salted water until they are almost cooked, drain well and allow to cool slightly. Cut into slices. Fry the potato slices in hot fat, turning them until crisp and golden brown on both sides. Serve as required.

Duchesse Potatoes

1 lb cooked potatoes
2 tblsp butter
1-2 egg yolks, beaten
A little hot milk if the egg yolks are small
2 tsp salt
Pinch of pepper
A little egg and water mixed together to glaze

Put the hot, cooked potato through a sieve. Melt the butter in a saucepan. Add the beaten egg yolks and hot milk, if used. Beat well and add seasoning. Allow to cool slightly. Put into a piping bag with a star vegetable nozzle. Pipe in crowns onto a greased cooky sheet. Brush with egg and water glaze. Cook in the top of the oven for

This page: Baked Potatoes (top left), Creamed Potatoes (center right) and Sauté Potatoes (bottom).

Facing page: Boiled Potatoes (top left), Duchesse Potatoes (top right), Birdsnest Potatoes (center) and Potato Croquettes (bottom).

Potato Croquettes

1lb cooked potato
2 tblsp butter
A little milk
2 tsp salt
Pepper to taste
1 beaten egg
Breadcrumbs

Mash the cooked potato with the butter and a little milk. Add seasoning and leave to cool. Divide the mixture into even-sized portions. Roll each portion into a ball, using a little flour on the hands to prevent sticking. Using a palette knife and the hand, shape the balls into cork shapes, with flat ends. Coat with beaten egg and breadcrumbs. Fry in deep, hot fat until golden.

Old Potatoes

Peel potatoes and cut out any eyes and green parts. Cook in salted water for 15-20 minutes until soft. Drain well and serve.

Bubble and Squeak

1½lb potatoes, peeled
A little milk
Knob of butter
1lb green cabbage, trimmed and
  roughly chopped
1 small onion, peeled and chopped
Salt and pepper
1 egg

Cook the potatoes in salted water until soft. Drain and mash with a little milk and butter. Plunge the cabbage into boiling, salted water. Cook for 5 minutes, drain well and chop finely. Mix the potato and cabbage with the onion, add seasoning and the egg. Put the mixture in a skillet and fry in a little fat until golden brown.

This page: Bubble and Squeak (top), Potatoes Normandie (center) and Jacket Potatoes (bottom).

Facing page: Brussels Sprouts (top), Mushrooms (center left) and Glazed Carrots (bottom right).

This page: Creamed Spinach (top left), Peas (fresh) (top right) and Green Beans (bottom).

Facing page: Cauliflower Cheese.

Glazed Carrots

¼ cup butter
1lb young carrots, scraped and
    quartered lengthwise
Salt and pepper
Pinch of sugar

Garnish
Knob of butter
Chopped fresh parsley

Melt the butter in a pan. Add the carrots, seasoning, sugar and enough water to cover. Cook slowly without a lid for about 15 minutes, until the carrots are soft and the water has evaporated, leaving the carrots with a slight glaze. Serve in a warm dish. Garnish with a knob of butter and chopped parsley.

Mushrooms

Baked
Remove the stalks and peel off the outer skin, beginning from the edge and pulling towards the center. Place in an ovenproof dish with a little butter, and cook for 10-15 minutes in the oven at 350°F.

Broiled
Prepare the mushrooms as above. Put a knob of butter the size of a pea on each mushroom in the hollow where the stalk was attached. Cook under a medium broiler for 7-10 minutes.

Fried
Prepare mushrooms as above. Fry in butter for about 7-10 minutes until tender.

Cauliflower Cheese

1 cauliflower, washed and trimmed
2 tblsp butter
¼ cup flour
1¼ cups milk
½ cup Cheddar cheese, finely grated
Salt and pepper
2 tblsp fresh white breadcrumbs

Cook the cauliflower in boiling, salted water for about 10 minutes. Drain and place in an ovenproof dish. Melt the butter in a pan, add the flour and cook for a few minutes. Allow to cool before gradually adding the milk. Bring to the boil. Stir in 6 tblsp of the cheese and season well. Pour the sauce over the cauliflower. Mix the remaining cheese and breadcrumbs together and sprinkle over the top.

Brown in the oven for 5-10 minutes at 400°F and serve.

Green Beans

Top, tail and remove any tough strings. Shred the beans finely. Cook in boiling, salted water for 10-20 minutes until tender. When cooked, drain. Toss in butter and serve.

Creamed Spinach

3lb fresh spinach, washed and coarse
   stalks removed
2-4 tblsp butter
3 tblsp light cream
Salt and pepper
Pinch of powdered nutmeg

Put the washed spinach in a
saucepan with a little water. Heat
gently, turning the spinach
occasionally. Bring to the boil and
cook gently for 10-15 minutes until
very soft. Drain thoroughly and
pass through a sieve or use a
blender. Add butter, cream,
seasoning and nutmeg to the
purée. Return to the pan and
reheat. Serve in a warmed dish.

Jacket Potato

Scrub the potato until the skin is
clean. Remove any eyes and
discolored parts. Prick the skin,
(this prevents the potato from
bursting in the oven). Brush over
with oil. Place on a cooky sheet in
the middle of the oven. Cook for
between 1-2 hours, according to
size of potato, at 350-375°F, until
tender.

Potatoes Normandie

3 tblsp butter
1½lb potatoes, peeled and thinly
   sliced
Salt and pepper
1¼ cups milk

Use a little of the butter to grease
an ovenproof dish. Layer the slices
of potato in the dish, seasoning
between each layer. Pour the milk
over the potatoes. Dot the
remaining butter over the top.
Cook in the oven for 1-1½ hours
at 350°F, until the potatoes are soft.
Serve with roast beef, lamb or
pork.

Peas (Fresh)

Shell the peas. Cook in boiling,
salted water with 1 tsp salt, 1 tsp
sugar and a sprig of mint, for 10-15
minutes. Remove the mint, strain
well and serve.

Beets (Boiled)

Boil beets in a saucepan for 1-1½ hours. Do not damage the skin before cooking. The skin will peel off easily once the beets are cooked.

Braised Celery

2 tblsp butter
2 medium-sized carrots, peeled and diced
8 sticks celery, scrubbed, trimmed and cut in half lengthwise
1¼ cups chicken stock
Salt and pepper
Chopped parsley to garnish

Heat the butter and fry the carrots for a few minutes. Add the celery and cook for a further 2 minutes. Place the vegetables in an ovenproof dish and pour on the stock. Season well. Cover and cook in the oven for about 1-1¼ hours at 350°F. Garnish with chopped parsley.

Collards or Greens

Wash well. Shred finely before cooking in boiling, salted water for 10-15 minutes. When cooked, drain well. Toss in butter, if liked, and serve.

Leeks

1½lb fresh leeks, washed, trimmed and halved
Butter
Pepper

Cook the prepared leeks in boiling, salted water for 10 minutes. Drain and toss in butter and add pepper.

Roast Parsnips

1lb parsnips, peeled, quartered and sliced

Garnish
Chopped fresh parsley

Cook the prepared parsnips in boiling, salted water for about 5 minutes. Drain well. Place in the fat around the joint and cook for about 45 minutes. Garnish with chopped parsley.

Brussels Sprouts

Cut a cross in the stalks and remove the outer leaves. Cook in boiling, salted water for between 7-15 minutes. When cooked, drain, toss in butter and serve.

Corn on the Cob

Strip off the husks and remove the silky threads. Cook the corn on the cob in boiling water for about 10-15 minutes, adding a little salt at the end of the cooking time. When cooked, drain. Serve with melted butter.

Broccoli

Thoroughly wash the broccoli and remove any withered leaves. Cook in boiling, salted water for 25-30 minutes. When cooked, drain and serve as required.

This page: Leeks (top), Roast Parsnips (center left), Boiled Beets (center right) and Broccoli (bottom).

Facing page: Braised Celery (top left), Collards or Greens (top right) and Corn on the Cob (bottom).

Meals with Salads

French Dressing

1 tblsp sugar
¼ tsp salt
¼ tsp dry mustard
⅔ cup vinegar
1¼ cups corn oil

Blend the sugar, salt and mustard with the vinegar. Gradually beat in the oil, a little at a time. Taste and adjust the seasoning if necessary. Pour the dressing into a screw-topped jar. Shake vigorously before using, as the oil and vinegar will separate if left to stand.

Cheese and Ham Pie

Packet white sauce mix
½ cup cheese, grated
½ cup cooked ham, finely chopped
A little milk or beaten egg

Basic Pastry
2 cups flour
½ cup shortening
1 tsp salt
2 tblsp cold water

First make the pastry. Sieve the flour and salt together in a bowl. Cut the fat into pieces and cut into the flour until it looks like breadcrumbs. Add the water to make a dough. Roll out enough pastry to line a shallow pie dish or pan. Make up the white sauce mix as directed on the packet. Mix the cheese and ham with the sauce and pour into the lined pie dish or pan. Roll out the remaining pastry to make a lid for the pie. Place on top, seal, and brush the top with milk or beaten egg. Place in the oven at 450°F for 15 minutes. Reduce the temperature to 350°F until cooked. Serve with a mixed salad.

Chunky Herrings

6-8 rollmop herrings
1lb small new potatoes, cooked
Small piece of cucumber, diced
Cooked peas
Sage or parsley to garnish

Vinaigrette Dressing
6 tblsp oil
3 tblsp wine vinegar
¼ tsp chopped fresh herbs, e.g. tarragon, chervil
4-5 capers, chopped
Salt and pepper
Pinch of dry mustard

Remove the herrings from their liquid, drain well. Arrange the herrings on a flat dish. Blend together all the ingredients for the vinaigrette dressing. Mix the potatoes, cucumber and peas and toss with the dressing. Put the mixture round the herrings and garnish with sage or chopped parsley. Serve with a mixed salad.
Serves six

Mushroom Salad

Salt and pepper
Pinch of dry English mustard
9 tblsp oil
3 tblsp wine vinegar
1 tblsp chopped fresh parsley
1 garlic clove, peeled and crushed
12oz mushrooms, sliced

Put the salt, pepper, mustard, oil, vinegar, parsley and garlic into a screw-topped jar and shake well. Pour over the mushrooms in a bowl. Leave to stand for 1 hour then serve.

Egg and Bacon Pie (far left), Chunky Herrings and Cheese and Ham Pie (above).

Egg and Cheese Open Pie

½ cup cheese, grated
2 eggs
⅔ cup milk
¼ tsp mixed mustard

Basic Pastry
2 cups flour
1 tsp salt
½ cup shortening
2 tblsp cold water

Make the basic pastry. Sieve the flour and salt together into a bowl. Add the fat cut into pieces and cut into the flour until it is like breadcrumbs. Add the water to make a dough. Roll out and use to line a pie pan. Prick the base. Sprinkle with the cheese. Beat the eggs, add the milk and mustard. Pour the egg mixture over the cheese. Cook the open pie in the oven for 15 minutes at 450°F. Reduce the temperature to 325°F and cook for about 30 minutes or until the open pie is cooked. Serve with a mixed salad.

Dressed Crab

1 large cooked crab
Parsley to garnish

Pull off all the crab claws and wipe the shell. Turn the crab onto its back and firmly pull the body from the main shell. Remove and discard the stomach bag which lies behind the head and gray feathered gills or 'fingers' as these must not be eaten. Take out all the meat with a skewer or small spoon, putting dark and white into separate basins, then crack the top of the shell and remove pieces so there is a flat cavity to fill. Scrub inside the shell thoroughly under cold water. Dry and brush with oil. Crack the claws and remove the meat, adding it to the light meat. Arrange dark and light meat alternately in the shell and garnish with parsley. Serve with a mixed salad.

Kidney Beans and Onion

Salt and pepper
Pinch of dry English mustard
½ tsp dried basil
1 garlic clove, peeled and crushed
3 tblsp olive or corn oil
1 tblsp wine vinegar
1 small onion, peeled and sliced
14oz can of red kidney beans, drained
Chopped parsley to garnish

Combine the salt, pepper, mustard, basil, garlic, oil and vinegar in a screw-topped jar. Lay the onion rings on a plate and sprinkle with salt. Leave for 30 minutes. Drain and rinse in cold water. Place the beans in a bowl, add the onion and toss in the dressing. Garnish with the chopped parsley and serve.

This page: Apple and Nut Salad (top), Kidney Beans and Onion (center right) and Mushroom Salad (bottom). Facing page: Dressed Crab (top), Chicken Legs in Breadcrumbs (center left), Tuna and Mackerel Loaf (center right) and Chicken and Tomato Salad (bottom).

Chicken Legs in Breadcrumbs

Chicken legs as required
1 beaten egg
Dried breadcrumbs
6 tblsp oil or butter

Coat the chicken legs with the beaten egg and breadcrumbs. Heat the oil or butter in a pan. Fry the chicken fairly quickly until brown all over, then lower heat and cook slowly to cook right through. When pierced with a skewer the juices should run clear. Drain on crumpled paper towels. Serve with fried tomatoes and mushrooms and a green salad or other cooked vegetables.

Cucumber and Tomato Salad

1lb tomatoes, chopped
½ cucumber, finely diced
2 tblsp French dressing
Watercress to garnish

Toss the cucumber and tomato in the French dressing. Garnish with watercress.

Tuna and Mackerel Loaf

2lb whole-wheat loaf bread, one day old, refrigerated for 24 hours
2oz powdered gelatin
1¼ cups white sauce
5oz canned tuna, drained
8oz mackerel fillets, drained
½ cup cooked potato, diced
¼ cup cooked peas
¼ cup green beans, diced
¼ cup corn
¼ cup cooked red peppers, diced
12 capers
2 tblsp small pickled cucumbers, diced
1oz chopped onion
Salt and pepper
Pinch of cayenne pepper
Juice and grated zest of ½ lemon
⅔ cup mayonnaise

Cut the crust off the loaf at one end and reserve. With a long bread knife cut round inside the crust and remove the bread from the center. Scoop out any remaining crumbs. Dissolve the gelatin in a cup of hot water. Bring the white sauce to the boil, add the gelatin and simmer gently for 10 minutes until thick. Blend the tuna and mackerel fillets to a smooth paste. Add the paste to the thickened sauce and blend well. Mix in the rest of the ingredients except the mayonnaise. Cool and then add the mayonnaise. Fill the crust shell with the mixture. Replace the reserved crust, stand the loaf on a plate, place in the refrigerator and leave overnight to set. Serve by cutting into slices with a bread knife dipped in hot water. This is ideal for picnics or served with a mixed salad.

Bean Salad

6oz can kidney beans, drained
14oz can sliced green beans, drained
1 small onion, peeled and chopped
1 stalk celery, peeled and chopped
3 tblsp wine vinegar
1 tblsp oil
Few drops of sugar substitute
Salt and pepper

Mix together the beans, chopped onion and chopped celery. Mix the vinegar, oil, sugar substitute and seasoning together and pour over the salad. Leave to marinate in the dressing for a few hours, stirring occasionally. Serve well chilled with cold, lean meat.

Pineapple, Cheese and Celery Salad

½ cup pineapple pieces
½ cup cheese, diced
¼ head of celery, coarsely sliced
Mayonnaise for dressing
Lettuce
Watercress to garnish

Drain the pineapple and cut into small cubes. Toss with the other ingredients. Serve on a bed of lettuce, garnished with watercress.

Rice Salad

½ cup patna rice
6 tblsp pineapple pieces
5oz corn
2 radishes, finely sliced
¼ red pepper, cored, seeded and finely sliced
¼ green pepper, cored, seeded and finely sliced
French dressing
Watercress or cucumber slices to garnish

Boil the rice in salted water for 15 minutes. Drain well and cool. Drain the pineapple thoroughly and cut into small cubes. Mix all the ingredients together in a bowl and toss in French dressing. Garnish with watercress or slices of cucumber.

Prawn Salad

6 tblsp thick mayonnaise
1 tblsp tomato paste
2 tblsp lemon juice
1 tblsp Worcestershire sauce
1 tsp grated lemon zest
1 tsp grated onion
2 tsp chopped fresh parsley
Salt and pepper
½ cup prawns

Mix the mayonnaise, tomato paste, lemon juice, Worcestershire sauce, lemon zest, onion, parsley and seasoning together thoroughly. Leave for 4 hours before using. Check the flavor before mixing the prawns with the sauce. Serve with a mixed salad.

Apple and Nut Salad

Salt and pepper
Pinch of dry mustard
3 tblsp corn or olive oil
1 tblsp wine vinegar
3 red eating apples, peeled and cored
8 sticks of celery, scrubbed and chopped
¼ cup chopped peanuts
Chopped fresh parsley to garnish

Put salt, pepper, mustard, oil and vinegar into a screw-topped jar and shake well. Put the apples and celery in a bowl with the chopped nuts. Pour the dressing over the apples and celery and toss well. Spoon into a serving dish and garnish with chopped parsley.

Chicken and Tomato Salad

1 lettuce, washed and cut into small pieces
2 cooked chicken breasts, sliced or
½ cup bought sliced chicken
2 tomatoes, peeled and quartered
¼ cup frozen corn, cooked and cooled
¼ cup frozen green beans, cooked and cooled

French Dressing
Salt and pepper
Pinch of dry English mustard
3 tblsp olive oil
1 tblsp wine vinegar

Make a French dressing by shaking together the salt, pepper, mustard, oil and vinegar in a screw-top jar. Place the lettuce pieces in a salad bowl, add the tomato, corn and beans. Toss with the French dressing. Serve the chicken with the salad.

Cucumber and Tomato Salad
(left), Rice Salad (below) and
Pineapple, Cheese and Celery
Salad (bottom).

Mix the ingredients thoroughly together in a large bowl and dress with the mayonnaise. Garnish with watercress.

Pasta Salad

4oz spaghetti
1 tblsp of butter
2 carrots, peeled and coarsely grated
2 tblsp raisins
6 radishes, finely sliced
¼ green pepper, cored, seeded and finely sliced
¼ red pepper, cored, seeded and finely sliced
2 tblsp French dressing
Watercress to garnish

Boil the spaghetti in salted water for 10-15 minutes. Drain well, toss in the butter and leave to cool. Put all vegetables and raisins together in a bowl and mix well. Toss in the French dressing. Garnish with watercress.

Winter Salami Risotto

½lb salami, thinly sliced
4-6oz liver sausage, garlic sausage and luncheon meat, thinly sliced
2 green peppers
1 red pepper
4 large, ripe tomatoes
½ cup green beans, cooked
8 stuffed olives
8-10 tblsp medium or long grain rice, cooked
3-4 tblsp vinaigrette dressing

Chop some of the meats and roll the remainder. Chop most of the vegetables, leaving a few large pieces for garnish. Slice the stuffed olives. Blend the rice with the vinaigrette dressing, chopped meat, vegetables and olives and put in the bottom of a shallow dish. Top with the larger pieces of vegetables and rolls of meat. Serve with a green salad.

Spanish Pâté

1 cup chicken livers, ground
1lb pig's liver, ground
1 cup ground beef
1¼lb pork, ground
12oz bacon fat, ground
1 tblsp salt
Pepper
1 tsp ground mace
1 tblsp chopped, fresh mixed herbs
2 tblsp sherry
¼ cup brandy
3 garlic cloves, peeled and crushed
6 tblsp stuffed green olives

Mix together all the ingredients,

except the olives, until well blended. Divide the patê mixture between two well-greased terrines or loaf pans, adding the olives throughout the páte, at different levels. Cover with foil and put in a roasting pan containing 2″ water. Cook for 2 hours in the oven at 300°F. Leave to cool. Place the pâté in the refrigerator for 1-2 hours, then turn into a serving dish. Serve with a mixed salad.

Coleslaw

1 cup cabbage, finely shredded
2 radishes, finely sliced
¼ cucumber, finely diced
1 stick celery, finely diced
¼ green pepper, cored, seeded and finely sliced
¼ red pepper, cored, seeded and finely sliced
1 apple, peeled and finely sliced
1 large carrot, peeled and coarsely grated
Watercress
Mayonnaise for dressing

This page: Bean Salad (top right), Coleslaw (center left) and Pasta Salad (bottom). Facing page: Winter Salami Risotto (top), Prawn Salad (center left) and Spanish Pâté (bottom).

Meals without Meat

Macaroni Cheese

6oz quick cooking macaroni
2 quarts water

Cheese Sauce
3 tblsp butter
6 tblsp flour
1¾ cups milk
Salt and pepper
½ cup Cheddar cheese, grated

Topping
2-4 tblsp Cheddar cheese, grated
2 tblsp dried breadcrumbs

Garnish
1 tomato
Parsley

Boil the macaroni in salted water
for about 7 minutes. Add a little
pepper if desired. Melt the butter
in a saucepan, stir in the flour and
cook for 2 minutes. Cool.
Gradually blend in the milk, bring
to the boil and cook until
thickened and smooth. Add
seasoning, and the cheese. Strain
the macaroni and blend with the
sauce. Put into a 2½ pint dish, top
with the cheese and breadcrumbs
and brown under a hot broiler.
Garnish with tomato and parsley.

Cheese and Potato Whirls

¼lb instant potato powder or 1lb of
    potatoes, cooked
2 tblsp butter and a little milk, if
    using cooked potatoes
2 cups grated cheese
1 egg
Salt and pepper
Mixed mustard
Egg, beaten to glaze

Basic Puff Pastry
2 cups all-purpose flour
½ tsp salt
¾ cup shortening
2 tsp wine vinegar or lemon juice
⅔ cup ice-cold water

First make the pastry. Sieve the
flour and salt into a bowl. Cut
shortening into ½" dice. Toss
through the flour. Add vinegar or
lemon juice to the water. Add to
the flour and mix to a soft dough.
Turn onto a floured board. Roll
into a square. Fold the side edges
to the middle, top and bottom to
middle, then fold in half. Press
gently together. Leave to rest in
refrigerator for 15 minutes.
Remove and roll the pastry once
again into a square, fold the side
edges to the middle, top and
bottom to middle, then fold in half.
Make the instant potato as
directed on the can or packet or
mash the cooked potato with the
butter and milk. Add the cheese,
egg, seasoning and mustard. Roll
the pastry into a square, spread
with the cheese and potato
mixture. Roll up as for a jelly roll
and brush with egg to glaze. Cut
into the required number of slices
and cook on a cooky sheet in the
oven for 20-25 minutes at 440°F.

Cheese Crust Vegetable Pie

Cheese Pastry
1½ cups flour
Pinch of salt
½ cup shortening
6 tblsp Cheddar cheese, grated
2-3 tblsp cold water to mix

Filling
¼ cup butter
1 onion, peeled and sliced
7oz can corn
3 carrots, peeled and sliced
¼ cup mushrooms, sliced
2oz packet of leek soup
2 sticks celery, scrubbed and sliced
Pepper
1 egg, beaten to glaze

Sift the flour and salt into a mixing bowl. Cut the shortening into the flour and stir-in the cheese. Bind together with the water. Melt the butter in a pan and fry the vegetables for a few minutes. Drain on paper towels. Make up the packet of leek soup as directed, but using only 1¼ pints of water. Stir the vegetables into the leek soup, season with pepper and pour into a 3¾ cup pie dish. Roll out the pastry to top the pie. Trim and crimp the edges. Use any leftover pastry to decorate the pie top. Brush with beaten egg. Cook in the oven for 15 minutes at 400°F. Reduce the heat to 350°F and cook for a further 20 minutes. Serve with new potatoes.

Cheese Crust Vegetable Pie (top), Cheese and Potato Whirls (far left) and Macaroni Cheese (above left).

Corn Quiche

Pastry
1½ cups all-purpose flour
Pinch of salt
6 tblsp fat
2 tblsp water to mix

Filling
7oz can corn
2 eggs, beaten
1¼ cups milk
½-¾ cup cheese, grated
Salt and pepper

Garnish
Parsley
Tomato

Sieve the flour and salt into a bowl. Cut the fat into pieces and cut into the flour until it looks like breadcrumbs. Mix with enough water to make a dough. Roll out and use to line a pie pan. Drain the corn and mix with the eggs. Add the milk, cheese and seasoning. Pour into the pastry case. Cook in a hot oven for 15 minutes at 425°F. Reduce the heat to 375°F and cook for a further 10 minutes. Garnish with parsley and wedges of tomato. Serve hot or cold.

Cheese Crowns

2½ cups milk
½ wheatena
½ cup Parmesan cheese
2 tsp made mustard
1 tblsp Worcestershire sauce
Dash of cayenne pepper
Lettuce to garnish

Coating
1 eg, beaten
6 tblsp dried breadcrumbs
Fat for frying

Grease a cake pan and set aside. Heat the milk to near boiling point. Stir in the wheatena, bring to the boil and cook, stirring vigorously, for 3-4 minutes. Remove the pan from the heat, add the remaining ingredients and pour into the prepared cake pan. When the mixture is cold, turn onto a floured board, and divide into 8 wedges. Brush with beaten egg and coat with breadcrumbs. Heat the fat, carefully add the wedges and shallow fry on both sides until crisp and golden brown. Drain on paper towels. To serve, stand on end, top with cutlet frills and serve on a bed of lettuce.

Savory Egg Pie

Pastry
1½ cups all-purpose flour
Pinch of salt
6 tblsp fat
1½ tblsp water

Filling
1 onion, peeled and chopped
2 tblsp fat
1¾ cups milk
¼ cup soft, white breadcrumbs
3 large eggs, beaten
Few drops of Worcestershire sauce
Salt and pepper
Watercress to garnish

Sieve the flour and salt into a bowl. Cut the fat into pieces and cut into the flour until it looks like breadcrumbs. Mix with enough water to make a dough. Roll out the pastry and use to line a pie plate. Crimp the edges. Fry the onion in the fat, and spread over the pastry. Warm the milk, add the breadcrumbs and eggs. Stir in the Worcestershire sauce and seasoning. Pour the mixture into the pastry case. Cook in the oven for about 20-25 minutes at 400°F, until the pastry is crisp and the filling is set. Garnish with watercress and serve hot or cold with salad.

Cheese Loaf

2 cups all-purpose flour
2 tsp baking powder
Pinch of salt
Pinch of dry mustard
¼ cup shortening
6 tblsp cheese, grated
1 egg
7 tblsp milk

Grease a small loaf pan and line the bottom with wax paper. Sieve the flour, salt and mustard together and cut in the margarine. Add the cheese. Beat the egg and milk together and reserve a little to brush the top. Pour the rest into

Cheese Bread Pudding

4 large slices of buttered bread
½-¾ cup Cheddar cheese, grated
Salt and pepper
1 tsp Worcestershire sauce
Pinch of dry mustard
2 eggs
1¾ cups milk

Cut the crusts off the bread and cut each slice into 6 squares. Fill a greased, 3¾ cup pie dish with layers of bread, cheese, seasoning, Worcestershire sauce and mustard. Reserve a little cheese. Beat together the eggs and milk and pour over the layers. Sprinkle the top with the reserved cheese and cook in the oven for 40-45 minutes at 325°F. Serve with potato croquettes.

Cheese Hot Pot

1¼lb potatoes
6oz onions
6oz carrots
9oz grated cheese
Salt and pepper
⅔ cup water
Chopped parsley to garnish

Peel the potatoes, onions and carrots, and cut into thin slices. Put in layers into a deep dish with the cheese and a little seasoning between layers. Continue until all the vegetables are used, finishing with a layer of cheese. Pour the water into the dish to moisten. Cover with a greased lid and cook in the oven for 30 minutes at 450°F. Reduce to 375°F and cook for a further 1½ hours. Remove the lid and allow to brown for about 5 minutes. Garnish with chopped parsley.

the dry ingredients and mix to a soft dough. Shape into a loaf and put into the pan. Cook in the oven on a shelf above the center for about 35 minutes at 400°F, until well risen and golden brown. Cool on a wire tray. Serve, sliced and buttered, the same day. If kept to the next day, serve toasted and buttered.

Egg and Potato Omelette

¼ cup butter
2 small cooked potatoes, diced
4 eggs
½ tsp salt
Pinch of pepper

Heat the butter in a frying or omelette pan. Add the potatoes and cook until golden. Beat the eggs and season. Add the eggs to the potato and cook quickly until the mixture is set. Fold over and serve at once. Serve with a green vegetable.

Kedgeree Fish and Mushrooms

¾ cup cooked smoked haddock
1 hard-boiled egg, shelled
1 cup cooked, long grain rice
Pinch of cayenne pepper
Pinch of salt
½ cup mushrooms
A little butter
Chopped fresh parsley

Flake the fish coarsely with a fork. Chop the egg white, sieve the yolk and put the yolk to one side for garnishing. Using a fork mix the flaked fish, chopped egg white, cooked rice and seasoning in a saucepan over moderate heat until hot. Cook the mushrooms in a little butter. Pile the mixture into a hot dish and garnish with chopped parsley and sieved egg yolk. Serve at once with the cooked mushrooms.

Facing page: Cheese Hot Pot (top), Cheese Crowns (center left), Corn Quiche (center right) and Savory Egg Pie (bottom).

This page: Kedgeree Fish and Mushrooms (top), Cheese Bread Pudding (center left), Cheese Loaf (center right) and Egg and Potato Omelette (bottom).

Meals for Special Occasions

to cool completely. Drain the apricots, reserving the juice. Garnish the loaf with apricot halves and the stuffed olives. Mix the cornstarch with a little of the apricot juice, then add the rest of the juice and the wine. Heat, stirring, until thickened. Cool, then brush over the meat loaf and serve the rest separately in a jug. Serve the meat loaf on a bed of lettuce leaves, with potato croquettes and vegetables.
Serves eight-ten.

Boeuf en Croûte

1 tblsp oil
3lb beef round roast
2 tblsp butter
1 onion, peeled and chopped
½ cup mushrooms, chopped
2 tblsp freshly chopped parsley
Salt and pepper
10oz bought or home-made basic
  puff pastry
A little milk
Few sprigs of watercress to garnish

Heat the oil in a large pan and fry the meat quickly on all sides to seal the juices. Transfer the oil and the meat to a roasting dish. Cook in the oven for 45 minutes at 400°F. Leave to cool. Melt the butter in a pan and fry the onions until soft. Add the mushrooms, parsley and seasoning. Cover and fry for 5 minutes. Roll out the pastry to make a rectangle large enough to cover the meat. Spread ⅓ of the stuffing over the center of the pastry and place the meat on top. Spread the rest of the stuffing over the meat. Dampen the edges of the pastry and fold them over the meat

Turkey and Apricot Loaf

1½lb uncooked turkey meat, ground
¾ cup fresh white breadcrumbs
1 onion, peeled and finely chopped
1 tblsp Worcestershire sauce
1 egg, beaten
Pinch of mixed herbs
Pinch of allspice
Salt and pepper

15oz can apricot halves
½ cup stuffed, green olives, sliced
2 tsp cornstarch
⅔ cup dry white wine

Grease a 1lb loaf pan and set aside. In a large bowl, mix together the turkey, breadcrumbs, onion, Worcestershire sauce, egg, herbs, allspice and seasoning, and combine well. Spoon the mixture into the loaf pan, making sure the corners are well filled, smooth over the top and bang the pan on a flat surface to release any air bubbles. Cook in the oven for about 90 minutes at 350°F, or until the meat loaf is cooked through. The juices will run clear when a skewer is inserted. Remove from the oven, allow to cool in the pan for 30 minutes, then turn out and leave

This page: Sweet and Spicy Noisettes (top), Veal in Orange (center left) and Peppered Steak (bottom right).

Facing Page: Boeuf en Croûte (top), Turkey and Apricot Loaf (center left) and Stuffed Trout with Almonds (bottom).

like a parcel. Trim as necessary. Place the meat, pastry joins downwards, in a roasting pan. Roll out any pastry trimmings and cut into leaf shapes, to decorate the top. Brush the top with a little milk. Increase the oven temperature to 425°F, and cook the beef for about 40-45 minutes until the pastry is golden. Place the meat on a serving dish and garnish with watercress. Serve with baked potatoes, Brussels sprouts and carrots.
Serves six-eight.

Veal in Orange

1½-2lb veal fillet
1 onion
2½ cups white stock
Salt and pepper
2 oranges
4 small, young carrots
1 cup long grain rice
¼ cup butter
6 tblsp flour
Pinch of powdered saffron
⅔ cup heavy cream
Parsley to garnish

Dice the veal. Peel the onion and keep it whole. Put the veal, onion, stock and seasoning into a pan. Bring to the boil. Lower the heat and simmer for 40 minutes until the meat is tender. Remove the onion. Cut away the peel from 1 orange, remove the white pith, then cut the orange flesh into narrow strips. Soak in ⅔ cup water for 30 minutes. Peel the carrots, cut into neat matchsticks, put with the orange rind and a little seasoning and simmer in a covered pan for 20 minutes. Remove the carrots and orange rind and cook the rice in remaining salted water. Heat the butter in a pan, stir in the flour and cook for several minutes. Add the strained veal stock and bring to the boil. Cook until thickened. Add the orange rind, carrots, cooked rice and any liquid left, together with the pinch of saffron powder and the cream. Stir over a low heat until smooth. Add the cooked veal and mix thoroughly. Arrange a border of rice with the remaining orange cut into slices on a serving dish. Spoon the veal mixture in the center of the dish and sprinkle with parsley. Serve with potatoes and vegetables of your own choice.
Serves six.

Veal with Cucumber

8-12oz fillet veal, cubed
Salt and pepper
1 tblsp cornstarch
¼ cup butter
½ cup mushrooms
2 eating apples, peeled cored and sliced
1 cucumber, peeled and diced
1 green pepper, cored, and deseeded and sliced
1 red pepper, cored and deseeded and sliced
½ cup cooked rice

Sweet and Sour Sauce
1 tblsp cornstarch
2 tblsp sugar
2 tsp soy sauce
3 tblsp vinegar
⅔ cup chicken stock

Toss the veal in seasoned cornstarch and fry in the butter until golden. Remove and keep warm. Fry the mushrooms, apple slices and cucumber. Fry the peppers. Return the meat to the pan. Cover and cook for 10 minutes until the meat is tender. Stir in the cooked rice. Transfer to a serving dish and keep hot. Mix the sweet and sour sauce ingredients together, add to the pan and, stirring gently, boil for 2-3 minutes, until the sauce is transparent. Pour the sauce over the veal and cucumber mixture. This can be served as a meal in its own right, or served with a vegetable if required.
Serves four.

Sweet and Spicy Noisettes

1 tsp honey
1 tsp dry mustard
Salt and pepper
1 garlic clove, peeled and crushed
2 tsp lemon juice
6 noisettes of lamb
3 canned pineapple rings with juice
2 tblsp butter
1½ tblsp chopped mint
1 tomato, quartered
3 glacé cherries

Combine the honey, mustard, seasoning, garlic and lemon juice and spread the noisettes with the mixture. Leave to stand for 20 minutes. Place ¼ cup of the pineapple juice in a pan, add the butter and bring to the boil. Boil until reduced by half and add the mint. Keep warm. Broil the noisettes, basting them occasionally with the pineapple mixture. When the meat is cooked, arrange it on a

warmed serving dish and decorate with the tomatoes and the pineapple rings. Garnish with the glacé cherries. Serve with fried mushroom rings and bird's nest potatoes.
Serves three.

Stuffed Trout with Almonds

Salt and pepper
2 medium trout, filleted
8-10 tblsp butter
¼ cup blanched almonds

Stuffing
¾ cup fresh, white breadcrumbs
2 tblsp chopped fresh parsley
1 medium onion, peeled and finely chopped
Salt and pepper
2 tsp mixed dried herbs
1 tart apple, peeled and finely chopped
1 small egg, beaten
A little water

Season the fish lightly and fry for about 10 minutes in the butter, until tender. Transfer to a hot dish. For the stuffing mix together the breadcrumbs, parsley, onion, seasoning, herbs and apple. Stir in the beaten egg, and water if necessary, to give a soft consistency. Stuff the fish with this mixture. Fry the almonds for about 5 minutes, adding extra butter if necessary. Scatter the almonds over the fish. Garnish with parsley, and serve with sauté potatoes and a vegetable.

Three Ring Rice

1 red pepper
A stick of butter
1 cup cooked rice
2 medium onions, peeled and chopped
½ green pepper, cored, deseeded and chopped
1 small garlic clove, peeled and crushed
1 cup ground beef
6oz can of concentrated tomato paste
1 tsp salt
½ tsp chili powder
4oz packet of frozen peas

Core, deseed and cut the red pepper into strips. Arrange at intervals in the bottom of a ring mold. Melt half the butter. Stir in the rice and spoon into the mold over the pepper. Fry the onion and green pepper together with the

garlic in the remaining butter until soft. Add the ground beef and cook until brown. Stir in the tomato paste, salt and chili powder. Cook the peas, strain, put on top of the rice, then cover with the beef mixture. Press down each layer firmly. Place the mold in a shallow pan of hot water. Cook in the oven for about 20 minutes at 350°F, or until firm to the touch. Turn out onto a hot dish. Serve with corn or a side salad.

Veal with Cucumber (above right) and Three Ring Rice (below right).

herbs. Pour over the juice from the tomatoes and finish with a layer of potato slices. Pour water in to come halfway up the dish and dot the butter over the top. Cover tightly and cook in oven for 90 minutes at 350°F. Remove the lid and cook for a further 30 minutes to brown the potatoes. Serve with boiled carrots tossed in butter and chopped parsley.
Serves six.

Gammon with Mixed Fruit

4-5lb gammon hock
2 tblsp apricot jam
2 tblsp made mustard
Cloves for decoration
1 small, fresh pineapple, peeled
1 tblsp chutney
5 tblsp unsweetened pineapple juice
2lb canned apricot halves, drained

Cover the gammon with cold water and soak for 4 hours. Drain the gammon and wrap in foil. Place in a roasting pan and cook in the oven for 2 hours at 375°F. Remove the rind from the gammon and score the surface of the meat. Mix half the apricot jam with the mustard and spread the mixture over the gammon. Stud the meat with the cloves in a decorative pattern and return the meat to the oven for about 30 minutes. Cut the pineapple into slices and remove the core from each slice. Heat the remaining apricot jam with the chutney and pineapple juice in a wide pan. Glaze the pineapple slices and the apricot halves in this mixture. Place the finished gammon joint in a serving dish and garnish with the glazed pineapple slices and apricot halves. Serve with an exotic salad.
Serves ten.

Crown Roast of Lamb

2 best ends of lamb, chined
2 tsp butter
1 tart apple, peeled, cored and chopped
8oz pork sausage meat
2 tblsp fresh breadcrumbs
1 tblsp chopped fresh parsley
1 tblsp finely chopped mint
Glacé cherries

Trim the skin and fat from the ends of the rib bones so that 1 inch of the bone protrudes. Place the two joints back-to-back with the bones curving upwards and outwards.

Secure with kitchen thread. Heat the butter and sauté the apple, add the sausage meat, cook for 2-3 minutes and then stir in the rest of the ingredients. Place the stuffing in the cavity of the crown. Cover the tips of the bones with foil and roast in the oven for 30 minutes per 1lb plus 30 minutes at 350°F. Decorate the bone ends with cutlet frills and glacé cherries and serve with roast potatoes and a green vegetable.
Serves six-eight.

Pork Provençal

2lb pork fillets
15oz can tomatoes
1½lb potatoes, peeled and thinly sliced
1½ cups onions, peeled and thinly sliced
Salt and pepper
¼ tsp dried mixed herbs
2 tblsp butter

Slice the meat and trim off any surplus fat. Butter an ovenproof dish then arrange the tomatoes, meat, onions and potatoes in layers. Season each layer and add

This page: Pork Provençal (top) and Turkey Roast with Fruit Sauce (bottom).

Facing page: Crown Roast of Lamb (top), Egg and Melon Salad (bottom left) and Gammon with Mixed Fruit (bottom right).

Egg and Melon Salad

1 small cabbage
1 firm, ripe melon
1 orange
Salt and pepper
2 carrots, peeled and grated
4 hard-boiled eggs
Few sprigs of watercress
Few leaves of Belgian endive
8 radishes

Cooked Salad Dressing
1 tsp flour
1 tblsp sugar
Salt and pepper
½ tsp mustard powder
1 large egg, beaten
2 tblsp water
2 tblsp vinegar
1 tsp butter

To prepare the dressing, combine the flour, sugar, mustard and seasoning in a heavy-based saucepan. Mix in the egg to form a smooth paste. Add the water, vinegar and butter and stir over a low heat until the sauce begins to thicken. Remove from the heat, stir thoroughly and, if necessary, strain to remove any lumps. Cool in the refrigerator. Chop the cabbage very finely. Cube the melon. Peel the orange and cut the segments into pieces. Combine these ingredients with the grated carrots in a mixing bowl. Season as required. Pour over the cooled dressing and spoon the salad mixture onto a large salad dish. Shell and slice the hard-boiled eggs and arrange them with the watercress and Belgian endive leaves round the salad. Cut the radishes into floral shapes and garnish the salad and serve.
Serves four.

Barbados Turkey

¼ cup flour
1 tsp powdered ginger
1 tsp curry powder
4oz turkey escalopes
6 tblsp butter
¼ cup rum
¼ cup shredded coconut
3 tblsp pineapple juice
5 tblsp chicken stock
¼ cup heavy cream
Salt and pepper
Few sprigs of parsley
6-8 slices canned pineapple

Mix together the flour, ginger and curry powder and use to coat the turkey. Heat the butter and fry the escalopes for about 10 minutes each side until cooked and golden. Add the rum and set alight. When the flames subside, remove the escalopes and keep hot. Add the coconut to the pan and brown quickly. Then stir in the pineapple juice and stock. Boil for 5 minutes, reduce the heat and stir in the cream and seasoning. Arrange the escalopes in a serving dish and cover with the sauce. Garnish with the parsley and pineapple. Serve with boiled rice and green vegetables.
Serves four.

Crown of Chicken

Salt and pepper
¼ cup flour
2lb potatoes
3 tblsp milk
2-4 tblsp butter
6 or 8 chicken legs
4 tblsp olive oil
1 can cherry fruit pie filling
Watercress to garnish

Coat the chicken legs in seasoned flour. Peel the potatoes and cook in boiling, salted water. Drain and mash the potatoes with the milk and butter and keep hot. Meanwhile, fry the chicken in the olive oil until cooked and golden brown. Drain on paper towels and keep hot. Drain excess oil from the frying pan, add the cherry pie filling and heat gently. Place the creamed potatoes in the center of a hot serving dish, stand the chicken legs round the edges. Pour over the hot cherry sauce. Garnish with watercress and serve with a green salad.

Duck and Orange Sauce

1 large duck, e.g. 3lb
1 orange
1¼ cups bought Espagnole sauce
1 tblsp lemon juice
2 tblsp white wine
⅔ cup water
Orange segments to garnish

Place the duck in an open roasting pan. No fat is necessary. Cook in the oven at 300°F. Cook for 25 minutes for every 1lb in weight and 30 minutes over. Prick the breast skin after 30 minutes with a fine skewer. Pare the rind from the orange, cut into wafer-thin strips and simmer in water for about 10 minutes. Strain the Espagnole sauce carefully, reheat with the orange rind, orange juice, lemon juice and wine. Garnish the duck with orange segments and serve with the orange sauce. Serve with potato croquettes, broccoli and roast turnips.
Serves four.

Peppered Steak

Steak, as required
A little oil or butter
Peppercorns

Brush the steak with oil or melted butter and broil until tender, or as required. When the steak is cooked, place on a serving dish and sprinkle with the peppercorns. Tap with a steak hammer to crush the peppercorns into the steak. Serve with French fries, potato croquettes, onion rings or broccoli, or a mixed side salad.

Turkey Roast with Fruit Sauce

2 tblsp butter
5½lb white turkey roast
1 red pepper
1 small green pepper
1 onion
8oz can mandarin oranges
8oz canned corn

For the Sauce
2 tsp cornstarch
1 tblsp vinegar
1 tsp sugar
1 tsp Worcestershire sauce
1-2 tblsp sherry

Spread the butter over the turkey roast then wrap in foil to make a parcel. Place in a roasting pan and roast in the oven for 90 minutes at 375°F. Core, deseed and chop the peppers. Peel and chop the onion. Drain the mandarins and corn, reserving the juices. Mix the mandarins, corn, peppers and onion together. To make the sauce, mix the cornstarch with a little water to make a smooth paste. Blend the juices from the mandarins and corn with the vinegar, sugar, Worcestershire sauce, sherry and cornstarch and heat until thickened, stirring well. Add the fruit and vegetables. Remove the turkey roast from the oven and unwrap the foil. Pour a little of the sauce all over and round the turkey and cover again with the foil. Cook the turkey for a further 1-1½ hours or until the turkey is tender and cooked through. Unwrap the turkey and place on a serving dish. Surround with fruit sauce and serve the rest of the sauce separately. Serve with roast potatoes and vegetables of your own choice.
Serves six-eight.

Crown of Chicken (right),
Duck and Orange Sauce
(below) and Barbados
Turkey (bottom).

Index

CAKES &

CAKE DECORATION

Contents

Introduction

Cake decorating is both rewarding and interesting. It is hoped that this book will show how simple it can be and encourage those who use it to improve on their basic skills.

Starting with the simplest frostings, such as butter frosting, which is easy to use and can create elaborate novelty cakes, the book gradually introduces the more complex techniques required to master the frosting and decoration of wedding and other celebration cakes.

Always try to avoid last-minute rushes; many of the decorations can be made in advance and stored. Try to plan ahead when you know that you will be making a special cake and remember that frosting and decorating can take time and patience. If you have not had much

practice, start with the simpler designs before trying to tackle a royal-frosted celebration cake. You will be anxious that the result should be stunning, so practice first!

Never push the frosting design straight onto the cake, as you may ruin the surface you have created. If you are using a complex design, apply it first in white frosting then go over it in color. This way, if you make a mistake, you will not have not stained the surface of the cake. The cakes in this book will certainly give you some new ideas and may encourage you to design versions of your own.

Cakes and their decoration is an absorbing hobby. By following and practising some of the designs suggested, it is hoped you will be able to produce a highly professional result – cakes for every occasion.

Note:
All eggs are size 2.
All spoon measures are level.
Cooking times may vary as they depend upon the efficiency of your oven. Dishes should always be placed in the center of the oven unless otherwise stated. Fan-assisted ovens may cook slightly quicker, so follow the manufacturer's instructions.
Always preheat the oven to the specified temperature.

Basic Cakes and Icing

Lining Cake Pans
All pans must be greased and lined unless you are using a non-stick cake pans, in which case follow the manufacturer's instructions.
If using a shallow pan, only the base needs to be lined for beaten sponges and the quick cake mixture.
If you are making a fruit cake, which will take longer to bake, then the sides as well as the base need lining using a double thickness of wax paper.

To Grease the Pan
Brush with melted lard, margarine or oil. Grease the wax paper with melted fat or oil; if you are using non-stick silicone paper do not grease it. In the preparation of pans, it is necessary to grease and dust them with flour if you are not lining them.

Round Pans
To line a deep, round pan, draw with a pencil round the edge of the cake pan on double thickness wax paper and cut the resulting shape out.
Using a piece of string, measure round the pan. Use another piece of string to measure the height plus 1 inch. Cut out one long strip or two shorter lengths of wax paper to the equivalent of these measurements. If making two lengths, add on a little extra for them to overlap. Make a fold ¼ inch deep along one edge and cut into the fold at regular intervals at a slight angle. Place one of the circles of paper in the bottom of the pan, followed by the side pieces and, finally, the second paper circle which will cover the slashed edges.

Square Pans
To line a deep, square pan follow the instructions above as for a round pan, but fold the long strips so they fit into the corners of the pan.

Rich Fruit Cake

CAKE SIZES	5in round 4in square	6in round 5in square	7in round 6in square	8in round 7in square	9in round 8in square	10in round 9in square
APPROX COOKING TIME:	2½ hours	2¾ hours	3¼ hours	3¼ hours	4 hours	4¼-4½ hours
OVEN:	275°F	275°F	275°F	275°F	275°F	275°F
Note for all recipes: First ⅔ of cooking time at 300°F.						
Butter	¼ cup + 1 tblsp	6 tblsp	½ cup	½ cup + 2 tblsp	¾ cup + 2 tblsp	1 cup + 2 tblsp
Eggs	2	2	3	4	5	6
Flour	¾ cup	1 cup	1½ cups	1¾ cups	2¼ cups	2¾ cups
Dark soft brown sugar	⅓ cup	⅓ cup + 1 tblsp	10 tblsp	¾ cup	1 cup	1¼ cups
Molasses	½ tblsp	½ tblsp	1 tblsp	1 tblsp	1 tblsp	1 tblsp
Ground almonds	2 tblsp	2 tblsp	3 tblsp	¼ cup	5 tblsp	⅓ cup
Ground mixed spice	¾ tsp	¾ tsp	1 tsp	1¼ tsp	1½ tsp	1¾ tsp
Grated lemon rind	½ lemon	½ lemon	1 lemon	1 lemon	1 lemon	2 lemons
Grated orange rind	½ orange	½ orange	1 orange	1 orange	1 orange	2 oranges
Grated nutmeg	¼ tsp	¼ tsp	¼ tsp	½ tsp	½ tsp	¾ tsp
Chopped almonds	¼ cup	⅓ cup	½ cup	¾ cup	1 cup	1¼ cups
Currants	1 cup	1¼ cups	1⅔ cups	2 cups	2⅔ cups	3¼ cups
Raisins	¼ cup	½ cup	¾ cup	1 cup	1¼ cups	1½ cups
White raisins	⅔ cup	1 cup	1¼ cups	1¾ cups	2 cups	2⅓ cups
Chopped mixed candied fruits	1oz	1½oz	2oz	2½oz	3½oz	4oz
Candied cherries	1oz	1½oz	2oz	2½oz	3½oz	4oz
Orange juice	1¼ tblsp	1¼ tblsp	1¼ tblsp	1¼ tblsp	2¼ tblsp	2¼ tblsp
Brandy	1¼ tblsp	1¼ tblsp	1¼ tblsp	1¼ tblsp	2¼ tblsp	3¼ tblsp

Jelly Roll Pans (Long, Shallow Pans)
Grease and line a shallow pan so that the cake may be easily removed. Line the sides of the pan with paper at least 1½ inches longer than the pan, cutting into each corner.

Loaf Pans
When lining a loaf pan the method is again the same, but the paper should be 6 inches higher than the top of the pan.

11in round 10in square	12in round 11in square
5¼ hours	6 hours
275°F	275°F
1⅓ cups	1½ cups + 2 tblsp
7	8
3½ cups	4 cups
1½ cups	1¾ cups
1½ tblsp	2 tblsp
7 tblsp	½ cup
1¾ tsp	2½ tsp
2 lemons	2 lemons
2 oranges	2 oranges
¾ tsp	1 tsp
1½ cups	1¾ cups
3⅓ cups	3½ cups
1¾ cups	2 cups
2¾ cups	3 cups
5oz	6oz
5oz	6oz
2¼ tblsp	3¼ tblsp
3¼ tblsp	4¼ tblsp

Oiling and lining cake pans.

Rich Fruit Cake

This is a traditional recipe which cuts well and is rich, dark and moist. Traditional fruit cake improves with keeping and is used for celebration cakes – weddings, birthdays and Christmas – with almond paste and royal frosting. Prepacked dried fruit is ready washed, but if you are buying your fruit loose rinse it through with cold water and dry it well with kitchen paper or clean cloths. Then spread it out on a tea towel placed on a cooky sheet in a warm (not hot) place for 24 hours. Do not use wet fruit in a cake as the fruit will sink.

Mix the white raisins, currants and raisins together. Cut the glacé cherries into quarters, rinse in warm water and dry with kitchen paper. Add the cherries to the fruit together with mixed peel, almonds, and grated orange and lemon rind. Sift the flour with a pinch of salt, ground cinnamon and mixed spice. Cream the butter until soft, then add the sugar, and cream until light and fluffy (do not overbeat). Add the eggs one at a time, beat well and after each egg add a spoonful of flour. Add the dark molasses, orange juice and brandy, if desired. Spread the mixture evenly into a greased and double-lined pan. Use the back of a spoon to make a slight hollow in the center of the cake so it will be flat when cooked. Tie two thicknesses of brown paper round the pan then bake in the center of the oven at 300°F, (see chart for the suggested time). With large cakes turn the oven down to 275°F, after two-thirds of the cooking time. To test the cake, push a toothpick into the center. It should come out clean if the cake is cooked. When the cake is cooked, remove the pan from the oven and leave the cake in the pan to cool. Turn the cake onto a wire rack and remove the lining paper. Spike the top of the cake with a skewer and spoon a few tablespoons of brandy or other spirit over the top. To store the cake, wrap it in cheesecloth and foil. If possible, repeat the spooning over of brandy or spirit every few weeks. The cake can be allowed to mature for 2-3 months.

Quick Mix Cake

This is a quick cake, which is ideal for novelty cakes, and the mixture is firm enough to cut into any shape; it is moist and crumbly and can be filled with cream, butter or jam.

Put the margarine, sugar, eggs, sifted flour and baking powder in a bowl. Mix together all the ingredients with either a wooden spoon or electric mixer. Beat for 1-2 minutes until the mixture is smooth and glossy. In a food processor this will take 30 seconds-1 minute. Put the mixture in a prepared pan. Level the top with the back of a spoon and bake in the center of the oven at 325°F (see chart for the suggested time). When baked, the cake will be firm to the touch and shrink away from the sides of the pan. Loosen the sides of the cake from the pan and leave it to cool on a wire rack. Turn the cake right way up onto another wire rack.

Beaten Sponge Cake

This cake mixture is ideal for afternoon tea and the cake may be filled with cream, butter frosting or fruit. It does not keep well and is best eaten the same day it is made, although it can be kept in the freezer for up to 2 months.

Put the eggs and sugar in a

heatproof bowl over a saucepan of hot, not boiling, water. The bowl must not touch the water. Beat the mixture until it becomes thick enough to leave a trail when lifted. Sift the flour and baking powder together and fold into the egg mixture with a metal spoon, taking care not to knock the air out. Pour the mixture into a prepared pan and gently shake the mixture level. Bake in the center of the oven (see chart for oven temperature and suggested time). Remove from the pan and cool on a wire rack. When making a jelly roll, turn out the

cake onto a sheet of wax paper sprinkled with confectioners' sugar. Quickly peel off the lining paper and trim the cake edges. Fold and roll the cake up without cracking it. Let it cool a little, then unroll and remove the wax paper. Fill and re-roll the cake.

Madeira Cake

Madeira cake is a moist cake that can be covered with almond paste and then frosted with royal frosting or any other frostings.

PREPARATION TIME: 15 minutes
COOKING TIME: 1 hour 15 minutes to 1 hour 30 minutes
OVEN TEMPERATURE: 325°F

¾ cup butter
¾ cup sugar
Grated rind of 1 lemon
3 eggs
2 cups flour
2 tsp baking powder
2 tblsp warm water

Cream the butter and sugar until they are light and fluffy. Beat the

eggs in one at a time, adding a spoonful of flour after each egg. Sift in the remaining flour and fold it into the mixture with lemon rind and juice. Turn into a prepared cake pan and bake in the oven for 1¼-1½ hours. When cooked, the cake should be firm to the touch. Leave it in the pan to cool for 5-10 minutes, then turn onto a wire rack and remove the lining paper.

Beaten Sponge Cake

CAKE SIZES	2 x 7in cake pans	8in cake pan 7in square cake pan	11 x 7in jelly-roll pan	18 sponge drops	8in round cake pan	2 x 8in cake pans
APPROX COOKING TIME:	20-25 minutes	25-30 minutes	10-12 minutes	5-10 minutes	35-40 minutes	20-25 minutes
OVEN:	350°F	350°F	375°F	375°F	350°F	350°F
Eggs	2	2	2	2	3	3
Fine white sugar	⅓ cup	⅓ cup	⅓ cup	⅓ cup	½ cup	½ cup
Cake flour	½ cup	½ cup	½ cup	½ cup	¾ cup	¾ cup
Baking powder	¾ tsp	¾ tsp	¾ tsp	¾ tsp	¾ tsp	¾ tsp

Quick Mix Cake

CAKE SIZES	2 x 7in cake pans	18 paper cake cases or small tart tins	8in cake pan / 8in ring mold / 7in deep square cake pan	*1¾ pint pudding mold / *add 3 tblsp cornstarch sifted with the flour	About 26 paper cases of small tart tins	2 x 8in cake pans
APPROX COOKING TIME:	25-30 minutes	15-20 minutes	35-40 minutes	about 50 minutes	15-20 minutes	30-35 minutes
OVEN:	325°F	325°F	325°F	325°F	325°F	325°F
Shortening	½ cup	½ cup	½ cup	½ cup	¾ cup	¾ cup
Fine white sugar	⅔ cup	⅔ cup	⅔ cup	⅔ cup	1 cup	1 cup
Eggs	2	2	2	2	3	3
Flour	1 cup	1 cup	1 cup	1 cup	1½ cups	1½ cups
Baking powder	1¼ tsp	1¼ tsp	1¼ tsp	1¼ tsp	1½ tsp	1½ tsp
Vanilla essence	4 drops	4 drops	4 drops	4 drops	6 drops	6 drops

For Victoria Sponge see "Tea Time Treats."

Variations

Chocolate Victoria Sponge
Replace 1oz flour with 1oz sifted cocoa powder. Add this to the other flour.

Coffee Victoria Sponge
Replace the water with coffee essence, or dissolve 2 tsp instant coffee powder in 1 tblsp boiling water.

Lemon Victoria Sponge
Add the very finely grated rind of 1 lemon.

11 x 7 x 1½in cake square	12 x 9in jelly-roll pan
30-35 minutes	12-15 minutes
350°F	400°F
3	3
½ cup	½ cup
¾ cup	¾ cup
¾ tsp	¾ tsp

9in cake pan	11 x 7 x 1½in cake square 8in round cake pan 8in square cake pan	2½ pint pudding mold	11½ x 8½ x 1½in cake square	9in round cake pan 9in square cake pan	12 x 10 x 2in cake square
about 25 minutes	35-40 minutes	about 1 hour	about 40 minutes	about 1 hour	50-60 minutes
325°F	325°F	325°F	325°F	325°F	325°F
¾ cup	¾ cup	¾ cup	1 cup	1 cup	1¼ cups
1 cup	1 cup	1 cup	1⅓ cups	1⅓ cups	1⅔ cups
3	3	3	4	4	5
1½ cups	1½ cups	1½ cups	2 cups	2 cups	2½ cups
1½ tsp	1½ tsp	1½ tsp	2 tsp	2 tsp	2¼ tsp
6 drops	6 drops	6 drops	8 drops	8 drops	10 drops

Basic Frosting Recipes and Their Uses

Quick Frosting

This is an easy white frosting which is a quick version of the traditional American frosting. A sugar thermometer is not required for this recipe, but the frosting must be used very quickly before it sets.

PREPARATION TIME: 7-10 minutes

1 egg white
¾ cup confectioners' sugar
Pinch of salt
2 tblsp water
Pinch of cream of tartar

Put all the ingredients into a heatproof bowl and mix. Put the bowl over a pan of simmering water and beat the mixture. If possible, use an electric mixer until the frosting peaks. Remove the frosting from the heat and pour it over the cake, spreading it quickly. This will cover a 7 inch cake.

Chocolate Fudge Frosting

PREPARATION TIME: 10 minutes

This is a delicious chocolate frosting which is quick and easy to make.

¼ cup butter
3 tblsp milk
1 cup confectioners' sugar, well sifted
2 tblsp cocoa powder, sifted

Melt the butter in a small saucepan with the milk. Add the confectioners' sugar and cocoa and beat well until smooth and very glossy. Cool until lukewarm and pour over cake. This is enough to fill and frost the top of a 8 inch cake.
NB: if the frosting is too thick to pour, reheat gently to thin. This frosting can also be made in a small bowl over a pan of gently simmering water.

Sponges: Beaten Sponge, Madeira Cake.

Marzipan or Almond Paste

This is a paste which is made firm and rollable, and is traditionally used as a base cover for fruit cakes before coating with royal frosting or any other decorative frosting. Prepare the cake by levelling the top, if necessary. Dust a work surface with confectioners' sugar and roll out half the almond paste 1 inch larger than the top of the cake. Brush the top of the cake with the apricot glaze, or the egg white and brandy. Invert the cake onto the almond paste and, using a palette knife, draw up the top of the almond paste around the cake. Put the top of the cake down on a board and brush the sides of the cake with apricot glaze. Cut two pieces of string or thread, one the height of the cake and the other equal in length to the circumference. Roll out the remaining almond paste into a strip, equal in width and length to the circumference of the cake, using the strings as a guide, or cut two short strips of paste instead. Carefully wrap the almond paste round the cake, pressing firmly round the sides and joins. For a square cake, cut the string into four lengths, equal to the sides of the cake and cut the paste to match. Press lightly on the paste when it is placed round the cake in order to produce sharp corners. When covered, leave the cake for 24 hours to dry. Wedding cakes should be left for up to 1 week before frosting, otherwise almond oil will stain the frosting if the cake is kept after the wedding.

Marzipan or Almond Paste

PREPARATION TIME: 15 minutes

½ cup sugar
½ cup confectioners' sugar
1 cup ground almonds
1 tsp lemon juice
A few drops almond essence
1 or 2 egg yolks, beaten

Mix the sugars and the ground almonds in a bowl. Make a well in the center and add the lemon juice, almond essence and egg yolk or yolks to the mixture and form into a pliable dough. Lightly dust the work surface with confectioners'

Guide to Almond Paste Quantities Required for Cakes

Square	Round	Almond Paste/ Marzipan
5 inch	6 inch	12oz
6 inch	7 inch	1lb 4oz
7 inch	8 inch	1½lb
8 inch	9 inch	1½lb
9 inch	10 inch	2lb
10 inch	11 inch	2¼lb
11 inch	12 inch	2½lb
12 inch		3lb

sugar and turn out the dough. Knead until smooth. The almond paste can be stored in a polythene bag or wrapped in foil for 2-3 days before use. Makes 1lb.

Apricot Glaze

PREPARATION TIME: 10 minutes

This glaze can be stored in an airtight container for up to 1 week, if kept in the refrigerator. Re-boil the glaze and cool before applying to the cake.

6-8oz apricot jam
2 tblsp water

Put the jam and water in a saucepan and heat until the jam has melted, stirring occasionally. Pour the jam through a sieve and return it to a clean saucepan. Re-boil and simmer until you have a slightly thickened consistency. Cool before applying to the cake.

How to Royal Frost

It does not matter whether you frost the top or the sides first, the important point to remember is that the frosting should be applied in several thin coats. Try frosting a section first, rather than doing all of it in one go. Your aim is to achieve a smooth surface and you must let each coat dry before applying another. Most cakes require 2 coats on the top and sides, with maybe 3 on the top for a very smooth finish. Wedding cakes require three coats all over and the bottom tiers need 4 coats. For a 2 or 3-tier cake apply 4 coats to the bottom tier; for a 4-tier cake apply 4 coats to the bottom 2 tiers.

Method for Frosting a Cake – Frosting the Sides of a Round Cake

A flat-sided scraper is essential for producing smooth sides. Put plenty of frosting on the side of the cake and, using a small palette knife, move it back and forth to get a relatively smooth surface and to remove little air pockets. For round cakes, put your arm round the back of the cake and move the scraper forwards on the cake as this will help you to get a smooth, sweeping movement without stopping. The scraper should be upright against the side of the cake. Move the scraper off the cake at an angle so the join is not noticeable. If you use a turntable, it will make frosting larger cakes easier. Hold the scraper to the side of the cake and use the other hand round the cake so the turntable moves round quickly and smoothly in one revolution. Scrape off any extra frosting with a small palette knife. Wipe the cake board and allow each coat to dry for 2-3 hours or overnight before frosting the top.

Frosting the Top

When frosting the base tier of a wedding cake, remember not to add glycerine. Spread the frosting on the cake and, using a metal, or firm plastic, ruler held at a 30° angle, draw it gently across the cake with a positive movement. Try not to press down too hard or the frosting will be too thin. Remove any surplus frosting from the sides of the cake with a clean palette knife. Leave the frosting to dry for at least a day. Remove any rough edges round the joins with clean, fine-graded sandpaper. If the coating is not enough, repeat this 2-3 times. Wait 24 hours before applying frosting decoration onto the cake.

Frosting a Square Cake

Ice 2 opposite sides first, then the other 2 sides to produce sharp corners. Hold the palette knife parallel with the side of the cake when frosting.

Royal Frosting

The consistency of royal frosting depends upon its use. For rosettes and flat frosting it should be quite firm, whereas for applying latticework and writing it should be a little thinner. When frosting is required for any flooding and runouts, it should be thin and smooth. Royal frosting can be made in any quantity in the proportion of 1 egg per cup of sieved confectioners' sugar. Keep the frosting bowl covered with a damp cloth to keep it moist. As an egg substitute, egg albumen (white) can be bought in specialist cake decoration shops and the instructions for use are given on the packet. The addition of glycerine will aid the softening of the frosting when it is dry. This makes it easier to cut.

Wedding Cakes

When frosting wedding cakes, do not add glycerine to the two top layers of frosting on the bottom tier, so the cake can support the other tiers. Made frosting can be stored in an airtight container in a cool atmosphere for 2 days. Before use the stored frosting should be stirred well.

Beat the egg whites with a wire whisk until frothy, making sure that the bowl is clean and dry first. Gradually beat in half the confectioners' sugar using a wooden spoon. Beat in the remaining half of the confectioners' sugar with the glycerine and, if using lemon juice, add it now. Beat the mixture thoroughly until smooth and white. Beat in enough icing sugar to give the mixture a consistency which is stiff and stands in peaks. Add the color, if required. Cover the bowl with a damp cloth and leave the frosting to stand for several hours. This allows any air bubbles to rise to the surface of the frosting and burst. Before using, stir well with a wooden spoon. Do not overbeat. Note: if you are using an electric mixer, use the slowest speed and leave the frosting for 24 hours as this will incorporate more air and will need longer to stand.

Facing page: covering with almond paste, and using apricot glaze.

Guide to Royal Frosting Quantities Required to Flat Frost in Two Thin Coats

Square	Round	Icing Sugar
5 inch	6 inch	1½lb
6 inch	7 inch	2lb
7 inch	8 inch	2½lb
8 inch	9 inch	3lb
9 inch	10 inch	3½lb
10 inch	11 inch	3½lb
11 inch	12 inch	4½lb
12 inch		4½lb

Molding Frosting

PREPARATION TIME: 20 minutes

This is also known as kneaded fondant. It is very easy to use and can be rolled out like pastry. It is ideal for covering novelty cakes and even rich fruit cake. The frosting sets and becomes firm. Molding frosting can be used to cover a cake directly or over almond paste. If using almond paste first, allow the paste to dry before covering with the frosting, which can also be used to make flowers and other decorations.

2 cups confectioners' sugar
1 egg white
¼ cup liquid glucose
Food coloring or flavoring, if desired

Sift the confectioners' sugar into a mixing bowl and add the egg white and the liquid glucose to the center of the sugar. Beat the ingredients with a wooden spoon, gradually incorporating the confectioners' sugar to result in a stiff mixture. Knead the frosting until you have a pliable paste. This icing can be stored by placing it into a bag, wrapping it in plastic wrap or sealing it in a plastic container and storing it in a cool place for up to 3 days. If adding a color, sprinkle with a little more sifted confectioners' sugar to keep the frosting the same consistency.

To Apply Molding or Gelatin Frosting

Brush either the cake with apricot glaze or the almond paste with egg white. Roll out the frosting on a surface dusted with confectioners' sugar or cornstarch, or between two sheets of dusted polythene. Roll out the frosting at least 3 inches larger than the top of the cake. Support the frosting on a rolling pin and drape it over the cake. Dust your hands with cornstarch or confectioners' sugar and rub the surface of the cake, working in circular movements with the palms of your hands to make the frosting thinner and ease it down the sides of the cake. Smooth out any folds in the frosting and cut off the excess. If frosting a square cake, mold the corners so that the square keeps its shape. Leave to dry.

Gelatin Frosting

PREPARATION TIME: 20 minutes

This frosting can be used in the same way as molding frosting, but when it dries it becomes quite brittle. The frosting can be used to make decorations such as flowers and leaves.

2 tsp gelatin powder
2 tblsp water to dissolve the gelatin
2 cups confectioners' sugar
1 egg white

Put the gelatin powder into the water, which is contained in a small, heatproof basin held over a saucepan of hot water. Stir until the gelatin has dissolved. Sift the confectioners' sugar into another bowl and add the dissolved gelatin and egg white. Stir well until firm, then knead with the fingers until smooth. Dust with extra confectioners' sugar, if necessary. If adding food coloring, sprinkle with more confectioners' sugar to keep the frosting to the same consistency. This frosting can be stored for 2 to 3 days before use. To do so, wrap it in plastic wrap or a polythene bag and keep it in a sealed container. If it begins to dry, place the frosting in its sealed polythene bag and dip briefly in hot water. Leave for 1 hour and knead well before use.

Glacé Frosting

PREPARATION TIME: 10 minutes

Probably the quickest frosting to make, it is used on sponges, small cakes and cookies. To keep the frosting liquid, place the bowl over a pan of hot water.

1 cup confectioners' sugar
2 tblsp warm water
Various flavorings and colorings

Sift the confectioners' sugar into a mixing bowl and gradually add the water. The frosting should be thick enough to coat the back of a spoon when it is withdrawn from the mixture. Add the flavoring and the coloring, if desired. This quantity will frost 18 small cakes and half the amount will frost the top of a 8 inch cake.

Variations

Coffee
Replace 1 tblsp warm water with 1 tblsp coffee essence.

Orange or Lemon
Replace 1 tblsp warm water with 1 tblsp orange or lemon juice. Add the grated rind of one orange or lemon and a few drops of food coloring.

Chocolate
Sift 3 tblsp cocoa powder with the confectioners' sugar.
NB: you must be careful not to keep the frosting in too hot a bowl of water, otherwise it will lose its gloss. Also, if a newly-frosted cake is moved around without being given a chance to set, the glacé frosting could crack and spoil the smooth surface.

Buttercream Frosting

This frosting is good for covering sponge and quick cake mixture cakes. Butter frosting is ideal for covering novelty cakes, as it can be flavored and colored easily and is no problem to use.

PREPARATION TIME: 10 minutes

½ cup butter
1 cup sifted confectioners' sugar
2 tblsp milk
Flavorings (see 'Variations')

Beat the butter and some of the confectioners' sugar until smooth. Add the remaining confectioners' sugar with the milk and flavoring. Beat until creamy. This frosting will cover and fill a 8 inch 2-layer cake. Store in an airtight container in the refrigerator, for several weeks if necessary.

Variations

Lemon or Orange
Add the grated rind of 1 lemon or orange to the butter. Replace the milk with lemon or orange juice. Add a few drops of orange or lemon coloring.

Molding frosting, Royal frosting, Butter frosting, American frosting and Buttercream frosting.

Chocolate
Blend 2 tblsp cocoa powder with 2 tblsp boiling water. Cool, then add to the mixture with 1 tblsp milk.

Coffee
Replace 1 tblsp milk with 1 tblsp coffee essence.

Crème au Beurre

PREPARATION TIME: 15 minutes

2 egg whites
½ cup confectioners' sugar, sifted
½ cup unsalted butter
Flavorings (see 'Variations')

Place the egg whites and confectioners' sugar in a bowl over a pan of simmering water. Beat until the mixture holds its shape. Cool. Cream the butter until soft

then beat into the egg white mixture, a little at a time. Flavor or color as required.

Variations

Chocolate
Melt 2oz plain chocolate in a bowl over a pan of hot water. Cool and beat into the egg white mixture.

Coffee
Add 1 tblsp coffee essence to the egg white mixture.

Praline
Gently heat ¼ cup of both sugar and blanched almonds in a small pan until the sugar turns brown round the nuts. Turn the mixture onto an oiled cooky sheet, cool and crush with a rolling pin. Add the 3 tblsp of this crushed praline to the egg white mixture.
NB: this frosting can be stored in an airtight container in the

refrigerator for several weeks.

Confectioners' Custard

PREPARATION TIME: 10-15 minutes

3 egg yolks
¼ cup sugar
¼ cup all-purpose flour
1¼ cups milk
2 tblsp butter
1 tblsp sherry

Put the egg yolks and sugar in a bowl and beat until smooth and creamy. Stir in flour and mix well. Heat the milk until hot, but not boiling, and stir into the egg mixture. Return the mixture to the pan and stir, bringing it gently to the boil. Remove from the heat

and beat in the butter and the sherry. Pour into a bowl, stirring occasionally to prevent a skin forming. Makes 1¾ cups of custard. NB: the custard can be stored in the refrigerator for up to 48 hours.

Basic Equipment and Practising Skills
You will probably have most of the basic pieces of equipment needed for decorating simple cakes: various-sized bowls and basins, measuring cups, measuring spoons, wooden spoons, spatula, pastry brush, rolling pin, kitchen scales, airtight containers, cocktail sticks, artist's brush and a wooden skewer, to name but a few. However, special frosting equipment is often required, so it is wise to invest in a good, basic selection. You can extend your range as the need

arises. Palette knives are ideal for smoothing and spreading frosting. They come in various sizes and one would prove most useful. A frosting ruler is essential for flat icing the tops of cakes. Choose a firm, not flexible, ruler – at least 12 inches long, but preferably 14 inches. A frosting rule is even better. A frosting turntable is invaluable for frosting and decorating large cakes. There are several types of frosting scraper and these are used for pulling round the sides of the cake until it is smooth. Frosting cones come into the same category and have serrated teeth of various sizes.

Decorating Tips

Decorating tips come in various forms, the metal types giving the best definition. Try to start with a few basic tips. The range available starts from size 00. A basic frosting tip kit should consist of a fine, a medium and a thick writing tip; a shell tip; a leaf and a scroll tip; a ribbon tip (which is also used for basketwork); a forget-me-not and an 8-point and 10-point star tip. Tips are available in two styles: plain or screw-on types. Screw-on tips are used in conjunction with nylon pastry bags and a screw connector. Plain tips can be used with paper or nylon pastry bags. With this type of tip remember that the frosting has to be removed in order to change a tip. You can either make your own, or use a nylon pastry bag or frosting pump. To make a paper pastry bag, cut a piece of good quality wax paper or non-stick silicone paper into a 10 inch square. Fold in half to form a triangle. Fold the triangle in half to make a yet smaller triangle. Open out the smaller triangle and re-shape into a cone. Turn over the points of the cone so that it stays conical. Secure the join with a little sticky tape. Cut about ½ inch off the tip of the bag and push in a tip.

Nylon Pastry Bags

Nylon bags are sold in various sizes and can be easily filled. These bags are used with a screw connector. The connector is pushed into the bag and protrudes through the hole at the tip of the bag. This allows the tip to be placed at the end and secured with a screw-on attachment, allowing the tip to be changed without emptying the pastry bag.
Nylon pastry bags are most useful for gâteaux as they can be filled with cream, and a meringue tip (a large decorative tip) can be attached to make rosettes.

Frosting Pumps

These are bought as part of a frosting set; some are made of metal and others of plastic. They consist of a tube with a screw attachment for the screw-on type of tip. The frosting is controlled with a plunger which is unscrewed to refill the tube. Unfortunately, pumps are difficult to use for delicate work as you cannot feel the movement of the frosting to help control it.

Decorations

Frosting Decorations

Stars

Stars can be made with various-shaped tips ranging from 5 to 8, or more, points. With the 5-point star, use a tip number 13 or 8. These are the most useful sizes. Place the star nozzle in the bag and fill with frosting. Hold the bag upright and push out enough frosting to form a star. Remove the tip from the surface of the star swiftly. Stars should be fairly flat without a point in the center.

Rosettes

These are made with a star tip, but using a circular movement. Start at one side of the circle and finish slightly higher than the surface of the frosting in the middle of the circle.

Shell

Use either a star tip or a special shell tip No. 12. Shell tips give fatter shells. Hold the pastry bag at an angle to the surface on which the shell is required and start pushing out frosting towards the center of where the shell will rest. First move the tip away from you and then towards you. Push out more frosting for the thicker parts of the shell. Link the shells together by starting the second shell over the tail of the first.

Leaves

Use a leaf tip, which is No. 10 and has a pointed tip, or sometimes an indentation in the center of the point. Leaves can be decorated straight onto the cake or on non-stick silicone paper, left to dry and then placed onto the cake for decoration. Two or three overlapping movements can be used to give the leaf some form.

Basket Weaving

See 'Tracy Rose Wedding Cake'.

Templates

These are patterns made of paper or card which are used to transfer the pattern onto the top of a cake. It is easy to create your own or, for simple decorations, i.e. circles and squares, draw round a saucepan lid or plastic storage container. On the 21st birthday cake we use a round template. Draw a circle of the required size onto a piece of wax paper and cut it out with a pair of scissors.
Fold the circle in half, into quarters and into eighths, ending with a flattened cone shape. Draw a line in a concave shape from one point to another and cut it out. When the circle is opened, the edge of it will be scallop shaped.

Frosted Flowers

Use a large, medium or fine petal tip, depending on the size of flower required, and a frosting nail, or a piece of waxed paper cut into squares and attached to a cork. Once made, leave the flowers to dry for at least 1 day before transferring them to a cake.

Rose

Hold the pastry bag with the thin part of the tip upright. Push out a cone of frosting, twisting the nail quickly through the fingers and thumb. Push out frosting to make three, four or five petals round the center of the rose by curving them outwards.

Forget-me-nots

Push out the frosting straight onto the cake, using a No. 2 writing tip for the petals, by joining five or six dots together round the edge of the frosting nail and frosting a curved petal in the center. Alternatively use a forget-me-not tip.

Holly Leaves

Color some almond paste green, roll out onto waxed paper and cut into rectangles. Using a frosting tip, cut each holly leaf into shape by cutting first two corners of the rectangle and working your way down the sides until you have a holly leaf shape. Mark the 'veins' with a knife point. Roll out a little more almond paste and color it red for the holly berries.

Christmas Roses

Cover the top of an essence bottle with a little foil and take a piece of molding frosting the size of a pea and dip it into cornstarch and roll it into a ball. Shape another piece into a petal (see 'Molded Roses'). Repeat until you have five petals. Place the small ball in the foil and surround it with the petals, overlapping them. Leave to dry. Remove from the foil and paint the center yellow with a little food coloring.

Mistletoe

Roll out a little molding frosting or almond paste colored green. Cut into tongue shapes and round the ends. Mark a definite vein down the middle of the leaf with a knife and leave it to dry. Make small, pea-sized balls out of either natural almond paste or white molding frosting.

Molded Roses

Make a cone with a little colored molding frosting and press it out at the base so that it stands. Place a piece of frosting the size of a pea in a little cornstarch and roll it into a ball. Using a hard-boiled egg, flatten the frosting in your hand with quick strokes into a petal shape. Use more cornstarch if it gets too sticky. Gently try to get the frosting very thin. Carefully wrap the petals round the cone and turn the edges outwards. Repeat the process until a fully shaped rose is achieved. Leave the rose to dry and cut off the base. It may be necessary to use a cocktail stick to curl the petals.

Chocolate Leaves

Break the chocolate into small pieces and place in a bowl over a pan of hot water. Gently heat until the chocolate melts. Do not overheat the chocolate or let any water dilute it. With an artist's small paintbrush, paint the underside of the freshly-picked, undamaged and washed rose leaf, making sure that the chocolate spreads evenly over the surface of the leaf. Allow the chocolate to set and, when hard, carefully peel the leaf away from the chocolate, starting from the tip.

Facing page: a variety of cake decorations.

Novelty Cakes

These are fun cakes enjoyed by all ages, but particularly by children. There follows a variety of designs which can be used for every occasion. It is suggested that you use the quick cake mixture or maderia cake for these. Hopefully, this will inspire you to design your own novelty cakes which might be more appropriate for a specific occasion. If you find it difficult to find a cake board for an unusual cake, make your own by covering a sheet of thick card with silver foil.

Birthday Box

12x10x2 inch quick mix cake
Recipe apricot glaze
8oz almond paste (optional) – this makes the cake a little smoother
Recipe molding frosting
Thin 12x10 inch cake board or piece of thick card
Food coloring – yellow
8oz candies
8oz royal frosting
Egg white, beaten, for attaching molding frosting

Put the cake on a larger cake board. Brush with apricot glaze and cover, if desired, with a thin layer of almond paste. Color the molding frosting and save 4oz in a plastic bag. Brush the cake with egg white, roll out the molding frosting and use it to cover the almond pasted cake. With a knife or ruler press lines diagonally into the frosting. Roll out the reserved 4oz of molding frosting and cover the white side of a thin, rectangular, silver cake board (the same size as the top of the cake). Fit a pastry bag with a small star tip and fill with royal frosting. Pipe shells round the bottom edge of the cake. Put the lid on a basin and apply frosted shells round the edge of the lid. Decorate the lid with either fresh or piped flowers and a bow secured with royal frosting. Place the candies on top of the cake and put the lid on, leaving them partially revealed.

Clown

1lb molding frosting
*   6 tblsp colored pale orange*
*   ¾ cup colored yellow*
*   ⅔ cup colored red*
*   ¼ cup colored green*
1 large jelly roll
4 small jelly rolls
2 Lady fingers (sponge fingers)
1 marshmallow
1 recipe apricot glaze
1 recipe royal frosting, colored red

Using the orange molding frosting, break off 2 small rounds and gently flatten them. Make 4 cuts halfway into the balls to make fingers. Roll out the remaining orange frosting into a strip which is 8x3 inches. Brush the ends of the jelly roll with the apricot glaze and use the orange strip to cover the ends of the jelly roll. Brush the rest of the jelly roll with the glaze and with a third of the yellow frosting rolled out into a strip 8x5 inches, cover the glazed area of jelly roll. Squeeze the join of the yellow and orange frosting so that it forms a head and body. Stand the jelly roll upright on a cake board with something for support. Put the small jelly rolls lengthways for the legs and brush with glaze. Take a small ball of yellow molding frosting and roll it out into a 4x1 inch width. Divide it into 2 and cut slashes in each

This page: Birthday Box.

Facing page: Clown.

halfway up. These will be used for the hair (reserve). Brush the sponge fingers with glaze and cover them with yellow fondant. Stick them with jam onto the sides of the body. Roll out the remaining yellow frosting into a strip 8x5 inches and cut it down the middle. Use each strip to cover the legs. Roll out a small piece of red frosting and mold it over the marshmallow and leave to dry. Roll out 2 pea-sized balls of red frosting and use them as buttons. Roll out another small piece of red frosting and cut with a pastry cutter. Divide the green frosting into two balls, rolling out one and cutting with the same round pastry cutter. Using a cocktail stick, create folds in the circles which radiate from the center. Work your way round. Cut one of the circles in two and the other into four. Roll out the red frosting into an oblong 7x3 inches and attach it to the legs in thin strips. Using the reserved green frosting, flatten it a little and cut it into two, shaping each half into an oval. Stick them upright on to the end of the legs as boots. Put half red and half green frills round the neck of the clown, securing them with a little apricot glaze. Put quarter frills round his wrists and ankles, with a little glaze to attach them to the hands. Secure the hair

to his head with glaze. Do the same with the hat. Fill a pastry bag fitted with a writing tip with the red frosting and pipe features onto the clown's face. Surround him with sweets or put balloons in his hand.

Giant Sandwich Cake

12x10x2 inch quick mix cake
Food colorings – brown, green, yellow, pink, red
Recipe molding frosting
Egg white to brush almond paste
½ x recipe butter cream frosting
8oz almond paste, if required

Cut the cake diagonally so you have 2 triangles. Color half of the frosting pale brown. Divide a further quarter into four and color the pieces green, yellow, salmon pink and red. Remember to keep frosting in a plastic bag when you are not using it, to prevent it from drying out. For the lettuce, roll out an irregular shape with the green frosting and crinkle it up using a cocktail stick so it looks like ruched material. Reserve on a sheet of non-stick silicone paper. To make the ham, roll out the pink frosting with a pinch of white frosting, making sure the colors stay separate. Roll out into an oval shape and reserve. For the cheese, roll the yellow frosting into a 4 inch square and reserve. For the tomato slices, roll the red frosting into a 4 inch square and with a small, plain round pastry cutter cut rounds. Roll out the pale brown frosting into 6 strips all 2 inches wide: two

12 inches long, two 10 inches long, two 16 inches long. Use the egg white to brush the sides of the triangles. Stick the brown strips onto the appropriate length sides. Roll out the remaining white frosting into a triangle large enough to cover the top of one triangular cake piece. Brush the top of the cake triangle and fix on the molding frosting triangle. Spread the top of the other cake, the one without white molding frosting, with a little butter frosting to make the bottom half of the sandwich and make sure it is on either a presentation plate or a cake board. Around the edges of the bottom triangle lay the lettuce, ham, tomato and cheese so they spill out of the cake. Stick together with the frosted triangle. Fit a pastry bag with a star tip and fill with the remaining butter frosting. Frost irregular swirls in between the lettuce, tomato, cheese and ham. Dust the top of the triangular cake with a little confectioners' sugar.

Birthday Breakfast

Rich fruit cake (measure the size of your skillet and bake a cake that will fit)
Recipe apricot glaze
4oz white molding frosting
Food colorings – brown, pink
15oz can apricot halves

Transfer the fruit cake to the frying pan. Brush the top with apricot glaze. Roll out the white molding frosting and cut into several irregular shapes, rounding off any sharp corners. Roll the remaining frosting into sausage shapes and brush them with a little brown and pink food coloring. Drain the can of apricot halves. Place the irregular white molding frosting shapes on top of the cake, putting an inverted apricot half on each one. Put the sausages in the pan. Brush the sausages and the apricot halves with a little apricot glaze.

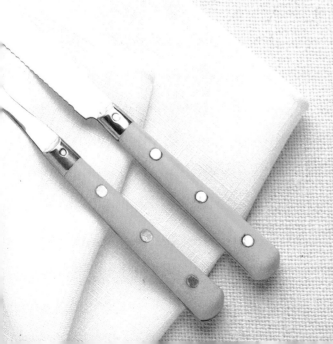

Giant Sandwich Cake (top left) and Birthday Breakfast (bottom left).

Camelot Castle

2 8 inch square 6-egg Victoria sponges
Recipe butter cream frosting
Recipe apricot glaze
4 ice cream cones
4 miniature jelly rolls
1 rectangular plain cooky
1 water cooky
½ cup granulated sugar
4oz molding frosting
Recipe royal frosting
Sugar flowers
Silver balls
3 or 4 small paper flags
Food colorings – pink, green, red

Toffee Water (To Fill Moat)
1 cup granulated sugar
⅔ cup water
Blue food coloring
Sugar thermometer, if available

Cut a 2 inch wide slice from one cake. Put the other cake towards the back of the cake board. Stick the large section of cake to the cake on the board with some butter frosting. Make sure it sits towards the back of the base cake. With apricot glaze, secure the 2 inch slice on the front edge of the cake board. Using apricot glaze, brush the ends of the small jelly rolls and place them in the four corners of the cake, placing the ice cream cones on top. Cover the small jelly rolls, ice cream cones and the top and sides of the cake with butter frosting. Also frost the 2 inch slice. Put the water cooky on the front side of the cake between the 2 jelly roll towers. Put the granulated sugar, with a few drops of pink food coloring, in a bowl and stir well until the sugar takes up the color. Sprinkle the colored sugar over the ice-cream cones, the top of the castle and the grounds. Fit a star tip to a pastry bag and fill with royal frosting. Pipe round the top of the castle walls and over the front surface of the water cooky. When the stars are just drying, go round the top of the walls and frost another row of stars on top of each alternate star. Put a silver ball in the center of each of the stars round the edge of the door and 2 for doorknobs. Color a little of the royal frosting green, and a little red, and frost the green vine with red stars for flowers. You can also use sugar flowers.

To Make the Water to Fill the Moat
Color the molding frosting green and roll it out to form a long sausage which will go round the edge of the board. Use the frosting

with a pastry wheel. With a little water, attach the ribbons of fondant to the inside of the shoes approximately halfway between the toe and heel. With a cocktail stick, gently mark round the top of the shoe, then the sole. Cut two 6 inch long, string-width strips of fondant and make a little bow out of each and put them in place. As an alternative, pink satin ribbon can be used in place of fondant. Fill the shoes with the candies.

Football Boot

10x8 inch quick mix cake
Jam for filling
Recipe apricot glaze
Recipe molding frosting
Recipe butter frosting
¼ cup shredded coconut
¼ cup chocolate chips
Food coloring – red, yellow, black and
    green
Medium star tip and pastry bag
2 liquorice laces
12 inch square cake board
1 cocktail stick

Cut the cake horizontally and stick together with jam for filling. Put the cakes on the board. With a cocktail stick mark out the outline of the boot. When you are happy with the outline, cut it out with a sharp knife and brush with apricot glaze. Divide the molding frosting into two, remembering to keep the frosting in a plastic bag when not in use. Roll out half the frosting into an oblong and cover the boot shape (top and sides). Do not frost the leg. Cut the frosting at the ankle to indicate the top of the boot. Divide the remaining frosting into two, coloring half red and the rest yellow. Draw out the shapes for the patches, tongue of the boot and the flash on some wax paper. Draw a large 'E' with a double line and cut it out. This should be used as a template to guide you when you roll out the red frosting to cover the ankle and the flash for the side of the boot. Roll out the yellow molding frosting and cut the

to form a wall and stick it down by smoothing it onto the board, then leave it to dry for one hour. Heat the sugar and water so the sugar dissolves and boils. Continue to boil the mixture until it reaches 'soft crack' point, that is, just before it starts to color. If a sugar thermometer is available, the reading should be 270-290°F. Pour the sugar mixture into the moat. Put the sugar flowers on the green banks of the moat and lay the cooky across from the castle to the land to form a drawbridge. Use the flags to decorate.

Ballet Shoes

2 jelly rolls
12 inch square cake board
2lb fondant frosting
Food coloring – pink
Recipe apricot glaze
Cornstarch to dust
4 tblsp jam
1 yard pink satin ribbon (as an
    alternative to fondant ribbons)

To Make Shoes
Cut the edge of one end of the cake into a point. Then cut the tip of the point. This will be the toe end of the shoe. Repeat for the other shoe and place them both on

the cake board. Cut the other end of the cake, rounding it slightly. Cut out a long oval towards the heel end of the cake. Press the cake in firmly, but gently, to create an instep. Color all the fondant pale pink. Brush the cake with the glaze. Roll out the fondant on the cornstarch-dusted work surface. Press the fondant down and smooth out any cracks. Mold it gently round the toe and take special care to squeeze and tuck it into the inside of the shoe. Cut off any excess and re-mold it into a ball. Roll out. Cut 4 long strips 1 inch wide and cut the shortest ends with pinking shears or cut

This page: Camelot Castle.

Facing page: Ballet Shoes (top) and Football Boot (bottom).

same shapes, but smaller, to go on top of the red. Cut the liquorice laces and tie into a bow. With a little frosting place it at the ankle. Mix half of the butter frosting yellow and half red. Fill a pastry bag with the red butter frosting and pipe a band about 6 stripes wide, then repeat with the yellow frosting. Work your way up the leg until you have 3 red bands and 2 yellow. Put rows of chocolate chips on the side of the boot to represent studs. Put the shredded coconut in a bowl and add a few drops of green food color. Stir in and use to sprinkle on the board to represent grass.

Shirt and Tie

15x3½x¾ inch quick mix cake
2 x recipe butter cream frosting
4oz colored fondant, if using design
  with tie
1 small packet round candies, e.g.
  jellies
Food coloring – red

In a clean bowl reserve ¼ of the butter cream frosting and with the food coloring make up a darker shade of the color previously used. Wash the pan used for baking the cake and, if the pan is old or marked, line with foil so that it is totally covered both inside and out. Alternatively, you could make or use a cardboard shirt box. Put the cake into the cake pan or box, and spread with the lighter frosting. If the cake fits snugly into its box or pan, only frost the top; if not, frost all the visible cake. Make the neck and collar shaping by first marking it out. Draw a line in the frosting with a cocktail stick 3 inches from one end of the cake. (The 9 inch sides are top and bottom.) This marks the shoulder line, so use this line to guide you when building up the collar with more frosting. Half the collar (front and back) should be on either side of the faint line. Fill the pastry bag with the darker frosting and with a writing tip outline the collar and shoulder seam. Roll out a thin strip of fondant 1½ inches wide and 14 inches long, pinch it in to form the tie knot and place on the cake. If you are using the design with center placket (shirt front) pocket and sleeves use the darker frosting in the pastry bag and frost the shirt front, pocket and sleeves. Put the candies in position as buttons.

Artist's Palette

9 inch square quick mix cake
Recipe apricot glaze
¾lb molding frosting
½ cup granulated sugar
Food colorings – red, blue, green,
  yellow, orange, violet and brown

Cut a kidney shape out of the cake and carefully cut a circle slightly off center. Place the cake on the cake board and brush with apricot glaze. Color all except 2oz of the molding frosting pale brown. Roll out and use to cover the palette, pushing in gently at the hole so that the frosting coats the inner wall of the circle. Push down to reveal the cake board. Using a dry brush, dip gently into the brown food coloring and drag hesitantly across the palette. Wipe the brush with kitchen paper to absorb some of the food coloring and continue to cover the palette with the wood grain. Leave to dry. Color 1 tblsp of granulated sugar with each of the food colorings. This is done by adding a few drops and stirring until the sugar absorbs the color. Roll out the remaining molding frosting into a long sausage shape and cut in half. Make a point at the end of one sausage and leave to dry and gently flatten the end of the other.

To Make the Pencil and Paintbrush
When the molding frosting shapes are dry, copying a pencil, color the one with the pointed end by painting in the lead and the outside. Copy the brush you are using and place them next to the palette. When the palette is dry, put little mounds of the colored sugar on the top.

Pugwash at Sea

11½x8½x1½ inch quick mix cake
Recipe royal frosting
Recipe butter frosting
8oz molding frosting
Recipe apricot glaze
1 packet of mints with a hole
1 black liquorice candy
1 tiny paper flag on a cocktail stick
Food colorings – including blue

Cut a 4 inch slice from the shortest side of the cake. From the smallest cake cut 2 inch slice from one end. Cut a point out of the remaining rectangle measuring 6½x4 inches.

Artist's Palette (left) and Shirt and Tie (below).

Place the remaining 8½x7 inch cake on a cake board. Stick the pointed cake to the top of the large cake then stick the 2 inch strip on top of that to form a cabin. Brush the two pieces of cake with apricot glaze. Color the molding frosting with your favorite color and roll it out to cover the ship. Using a pastry bag fitted with a writing tip and filled with royal frosting, write the name of the ship and pipe on the doors and windows. Use a little frosting to secure the liquorice candy on top of the cabin as a funnel. Cotton wool may be used to simulate smoke. Color the butter frosting with a little blue food coloring and spoon it over the large cake to form waves. Use a fork to peak the frosting, but do not overmix or the frosting will go green! Put the flag at the front of the boat and with a little frosting, stick the mints onto the deck to represent life belts.

Radio

8 inch round quick mix cake
Recipe apricot glaze
Recipes gelatin or molding frosting
6oz jam
Food coloring – brown, pink, black, non-toxic gold
1 egg white, beaten
Recipe royal frosting

Cut a crescent off one side of the cake so it will stand up on its side. Place the cake on a 9-inch square cake board. Brush the cake all over with apricot glaze. Tint the frosting pink and roll it out. Cover the cake completely and leave to dry. Take the remaining frosting, re-mold it and tint it a little darker. Roll it out into a rectangle and cut into 6 strips to make the starburst. Cut two circles for the knobs and a semi-circle for the dial. Stick all the decoration on the cake with egg white. Fill a pastry bag with royal frosting and fit it with a writing tip. Frost the mesh by decorating

diagonally between the starburst. Decorate on the lines for the dial, tuner knob and 'on/off' switch. Finally, pipe a decorative triangle on the board under each knob, with another smaller triangle over the top. Leave the frosting to dry. Using a small paintbrush, paint the mesh and trim with non-toxic gold food coloring and the inside of the mesh with diagonal lines of black food coloring.

House on the Hill

2 11½x8½x1½ inch quick mix cakes
2 recipe apricot glaze
1½ recipe molding frosting
Food colorings – red, green
Recipe butter frosting
Recipe royal frosting
16oz almond paste
Sugar flowers

Coconut mushrooms, if available
¼ cup shredded coconut
Candle and holder

Put the cakes on top of one another. Cut them in an irregular 'T' shape with a round top. Use the butter cream to layer the cakes together. Stand the cakes up so they resemble a 'T' shape on a 9 inch heart-shaped cake board. Brush the layered cakes with the apricot glaze. Roll out the almond paste and cover the cake with a thin layer. Divide the molding frosting into two and color half red. Roll out the red molding frosting, reserving 2oz to cover the top bar of the 'T', and use egg white to brush the almond paste so the frosting will adhere. Roll out the white frosting, reserving 4oz, and use it to cover the non-frosted section of the cake. Roll out the reserved 4oz of white molding frosting and cut small circles. Dot them on the red roof. Roll out the 2oz of the red molding frosting and cut 2 circles, 1 inch in diameter, for windows and a rectangle for a door. Color a little royal frosting green and decorate with leaves on the side of the house. Make frosted curtains on the windows and the arch round the door. Use the sugar flowers to decorate the house and garden. Put the shredded coconut in a bowl with a few drops of green coloring, mix well and use the coconut to decorate the board like grass. Stand the coconut mushrooms on the grass and put the candle holder with candle on the roof to represent the chimney.

Snowman

1¾ pint) pudding basin quick mix cake
⅔ pint pudding basin quick mix cake; use a 2½ pint mixture altogether
Recipe American frosting
A few round candies or liquorice candies for buttons and features
8 inch length of ribbon
Paper hat, optional

When the cakes have cooled on a wire rack, trim the smaller cake

This page: Radio Cake. Facing page: House on the Hill (top) and Pugwash at Sea (bottom).

round the wider edge to round it off. Spread the jam on the top of the larger cake and sit the smaller on top of the larger cake to form the head and body on the cake board. Cover the cakes completely with the American frosting. Select the candies or liquorice assortment candies for features and buttons. Decorate with a hat and a ribbon scarf.

Kitchen

8 inch square Madeira cake
Recipe royal frosting
Recipe apricot glaze
1lb molding frosting
Food colorings – red, green, orange, silver

Toffee Water
1 cup granulated sugar
⅔ cup water
Sugar thermometer, if available

Cut the cake in half and form an 'L' shape on a 12 inch cake board. Halfway along one piece of cake, cut a 1 inch square hole. Roll out half the molding frosting, brush the cake with apricot glaze and use the frosting to cover the 'L' shape. Color three-quarters of the remaining frosting red and use half rolled out and laid on the inside of the rectangle of the 'L'. Using a knife, mark ½ inch squares and press down gently. Do not cut through the frosting. Roll out the remaining red frosting and cut into small squares to form tiles for the work surface. Spread the rectangle of cake without the hole cut into it with a little royal frosting and stick down the small squares with a little frosting surrounding each. Cut two 2 inch squares and use one to line the hole, gently pushing in the corners. Place the other square alongside as a draining board. Use a knife to indent the board.

To Make Faucets
Take a pinch from the remaining white frosting and roll out into a small sausage shape. Cut in half, and with a small pair of scissors snip lengthways down the end once and again crossing the cut. Splay out the 4 pieces. Curl the other end of the sausage to form the waterspout. Repeat with the other small sausage shape and leave them both to dry.

To Make the Vegetables
Take a pinch from the remaining

white molding frosting. Color it green and shape about two-thirds into a small ball for the heart of the cabbage. Shape the remainder into 8 leaves and arrange the leaves around the heart, overlapping each one. Press gently so that they adhere to one another. Taking another pinch from the white, color it orange and shape into small cones. Make a little piece green and cut out some stalks. Press them to the tops of the carrot. To make the peas, shape any small pieces of green molding frosting into balls. Color a small pinch of molding frosting red and form into small balls. Make more green stalks and, with a cocktail stick, dent the top of each ball and push in a little green stalk to make tomatoes.

To Make Plates
Roll out any odd pieces of colored molding frosting into tiny balls. Mold a few round the end of a pencil and flatten some gently. Reserve them until you have made the sugar water. Color a little royal frosting red and use to fill a pastry bag fitted with a writing tip. Frost the knobs and drawers on the inside of the kitchen. Using a small paintbrush, paint the faucets with silver non-toxic coloring. Leave them to dry.

To Make the Sugar Water
Heat the sugar and water so that the sugar dissolves and boils. Continue to boil the mixture until it reaches a soft crack point – that

is, just before it starts to color. If a sugar thermometer is available, the reading should be 270-290°F. Pour the sugar mixture into the sink and push in the plates and dishes before it sets. Using a little royal frosting, put the faucets into place.

The Mouse that got the Cheese

8 inch square Madeira sponge
2 x recipe butter frosting
2 eyes, as used in dollmaking
1 yard pink cord
2 inch diameter teardrop shapes of pink paper
1 jelly candy
2 cocktail sticks
Food coloring – black

Mouse
Cut the cake diagonally and stand it upright on the diagonal line. Round the top of the triangle to give the mouse a smooth back. With a little black food coloring, color half the butter frosting so it is light grey. Cover all the exposed areas of the cake and peak it gently with a fork. Cut 12 inches of pink cord and attach it to one end for a tail. Cut 6 inch lengths and knot them all in the middle. Push them onto the front of his face, placing the jelly sweet on the knot. Attach the tear drop shapes to the side of his head for ears using the cocktail sticks. Place an eye on each side of his head.

Cheese
Put the remaining triangle on one end and, with a melon baller, scoop out little holes. Cover the cake with the remaining butter frosting and smooth gently with a palette knife.

Christmas Pudding

This makes a quick, non-frosted Christmas cake which acts as a centerpiece for a party, or for a family Christmas.

9 inch recipe for rich fruit cake baked in a 1¾ pint ovenproof pudding basin
6 tblsp brandy
8oz almond paste
Recipe apricot glaze
½ recipe royal frosting
Holly to decorate

After cooking, soak the fruit cake with the brandy. As the cake is not frosted this will keep it moist. Put the cake on a cake board or plate. Roll out the almond paste into a circle and push it into an irregular shape, like a little island with coves. Brush the top and a little way down the cake with the apricot glaze. Cover the top and the sides of the cake with the almond paste. Fit a pastry bag with a large star tip and fill with royal frosting. Decorate with large frosted stars round the base of the cake. Decorate with real almond paste or artificial holly.

This page: Kitchen (top) and The Mouse that got the Cheese (bottom).

Facing page: Snowman and Christmas Pudding Cake.

Tea Time Treats

Baking at home is not as difficult as some might expect and in very little time one can create some appetizing treats for the tea table. Here are lots of recipes which may tempt you to try them for yourself at picnics, birthdays and tea parties.

Biscuits

PREPARATION TIME: 15 minutes

COOKING TIME: 10-15 minutes

OVEN TEMPERATURE: 400°F

2 cups all-purpose flour
1 tsp cream of tartar
½ tsp bicarbonate of soda
Good pinch of salt
3 tblsp butter or margarine
6 tblsp superfine sugar
3 tblsp white raisins
1 tblsp sugared ginger pieces
1 tblsp sunflower seeds
2 eggs, plus a little milk if required
1 egg, beaten or a little milk for
  glazing

Sieve the dry ingredients twice. Cut in the fat, add sugar, white raisins, ginger pieces and sunflower seeds and mix to a soft dough with eggs. Knead lightly on floured surface. Roll out to approximately ½ inch thickness. Place on floured cooky sheet and brush the top with beaten egg or milk. Bake in the oven for 10-15 minutes.

Walnut Cake

PREPARATION TIME: 15 minutes

COOKING TIME: 35 minutes

OVEN TEMPERATURE: 350°F

4 eggs
¾ cup superfine sugar
1 cup all-purpose flour, sifted
1 tblsp oil
½ cup walnuts, finely chopped
Recipe butter cream
Walnut halves to decorate

Grease and line two 8 inch cake pans. Place the eggs and sugar in a heatproof bowl and beat over a pan of hot, but not boiling, water until thick (see beaten sponge method). Partially fold in the flour, add the oil and chopped walnuts and fold in gently. Divide the mixture between the prepared pans and bake in the oven for 35 minutes. When the cake is cooked it will spring back when touched. Turn onto a wire rack to cool. Split each cake in half and fill with butter cream. Swirl the remaining butter cream on top of the cake and decorate with walnut halves.

Welsh Cakes (above), **Walnut Cake** (right) and **Biscuits** (far right).

Welsh Cakes

PREPARATION TIME: 15 minutes

COOKING TIME: 8 minutes (4 minutes per side)

OVEN TEMPERATURE: 275°F

1 cup all-purpose flour
1 tsp baking powder
3 tblsp sugar
3 tblsp butter or margarine
½ tsp ground nutmeg
3 tblsp currants
1 egg, plus a little milk if required
Pinch of salt

Sieve the flour, baking powder and salt. Cut in the fat and stir in sugar, nutmeg and currants. Mix to a pastry consistency with egg. Roll out to ¼ inch thickness and cut with a ¼ inch small biscuit cutter. Cook on baking stone or large greased pan. Switch oven off for 15 minutes then grease and reheat for second batch. Dredge with superfine sugar and serve. Makes 10.

Flapjacks

PREPARATION TIME: 15 minutes
COOKING TIME: 30 minutes
OVEN TEMPERATURE: 350°F

½ cup margarine
½ cup soft brown sugar
6 tblsp corn syrup
1 cup rolled oats

Melt the margarine, sugar and syrup in a bowl over a pan of hot water. Stir in the rolled oats and mix thoroughly. Grease a shallow 8 inch square pan. Turn the mixture into the pan and smooth down the top. Bake in the oven for 30 minutes until golden. Cool in the pan for 3 minutes before cutting into fingers. Remove from pan when cool. Makes 16.

Coconut Specials

PREPARATION TIME: 20 minutes
COOKING TIME: 30 minutes
OVEN TEMPERATURE: 325°F

8oz puff pastry
A little jam, melted
4 tblsp melted butter
½ cup shredded coconut
½ cup sugar
2 eggs

Roll out the puff pastry. Using a round cooky cutter, cut rounds and use to line a patty pan. Using a pastry brush, coat the pastry with a little jam. Beat together the butter, coconut, sugar and eggs. Divide the coconut mixture between the patty pans. Bake in the oven for 30 minutes until golden brown. When cooked, remove from pan and cool on a wire rack. Makes 14.

Victoria Sponge

PREPARATION TIME: 30 minutes
COOKING TIME: 20-25 minutes
OVEN TEMPERATURE: 375°F

A stick of butter or margarine
½ cup sugar
2 eggs
1 cup cake flour, sifted with a pinch of salt
1¼ tsp baking powder
1 tblsp hot water

3 tblsp jam
⅔ cup heavy cream, whipped
Confectioners' sugar

Grease and line two 7 inch cake pans. Cream the fat and sugar until light and fluffy. Beat in the eggs singly and fold in 1 tblsp of flour with each egg. Fold in the remaining flour, then add the hot water. Divide the mixture between the pans and bake in the oven for 20-25 minutes until the cakes are golden. When the cakes are cooked they will spring back when lightly pressed. Turn the cakes onto a wire rack to cool. Stick the cakes together with jam and cream. Sprinkle the top with confectioners' sugar.

Chocolate Fudge Triangles

PREPARATION TIME: 25 minutes

COOKING TIME: 30 minutes for base, 10 minutes for topping
OVEN TEMPERATURE: 350°F

A stick of butter
¼ cup superfine sugar
1½ cups all-purpose flour

Fudge Topping
A stick of butter
¼ cup superfine sugar
2 tblsp corn syrup
⅔ cup condensed milk
4oz plain chocolate

Cream the butter and sugar together until fluffy. Add the flour and stir until the mixture binds. Knead until smooth. Roll out and press into a shallow 8 inch square pan. Prick with a fork and bake in the oven for 30 minutes. Cool in the pan. Put the ingredients for the topping in a heavy saucepan and stir until dissolved. Slowly boil and stir for 7 minutes. Cool the

topping a little and spread over the cooky base. Leave it to set. When set, cut into squares, then cut diagonally to make triangles.

Lemon July Cake

PREPARATION TIME: 30 minutes
COOKING TIME: 25 minutes
OVEN TEMPERATURE: 375°F

Base
A stick of butter or margarine
½ cup sugar
1 egg, beaten
1½ cups flour
2 tsp baking powder

1st Topping
⅔ cup water
3 tblsp sugar
1 tblsp cornstarch
Juice of two lemons

2nd Topping
⅔ cup milk
1 tsp cornstarch
2 tblsp butter
6 tblsp sugar
Shredded coconut to sprinkle

Base
Cream the butter and sugar, add the egg and flour and pour into a pan and press down. Bake in the oven for 20 minutes.

1st Topping
Mix the water with the cornstarch to make a paste. Boil with the other ingredients until the mixture begins to thicken, stirring constantly. Spread on the cooked cake base while the mixture is still warm.

2nd Topping
Boil milk and cornstarch until it thickens. Add the the butter and sugar, creamed. Mix well and spread on top of the July. Sprinkle with the shredded coconut, cut into fingers and serve.

This page: Chocolate Brownies (top), Chocolate Fudge Triangles (bottom) and Flapjacks (center).

Facing page: Victoria Sponge (top right), Lemon July Cake (center left) and Coconut Specials (bottom).

Chocolate Brownies

PREPARATION TIME: 25 minutes

COOKING TIME: 35 minutes

OVEN TEMPERATURE: 350°F

1 cup all-purpose flour
½ tsp baking powder
4oz plain chocolate
¼ cup butter
½ cup soft brown sugar
2 eggs
6 tblsp walnuts
6 tblsp mixed fruit

Frosting
4oz plain chocolate
1 tblsp butter

Sift the flour and baking powder together in a bowl. Melt the chocolate in a bowl over a small saucepan of hot water. Cream the butter for the brownies with the sugar until light and fluffy. Beat in the eggs separately, adding the flour with the second egg. Beat the melted chocolate into the mixture, then fold in the walnuts and fruit. Grease and line a shallow 8 inch square pan and bake in the oven for 35 minutes. Cut into squares while still warm and cool in the pan.

Spiced Cookies

PREPARATION TIME: 20 minutes

COOKING TIME: 15 minutes

OVEN TEMPERATURE: 350°F

1 cup wholewheat flour
½ tsp bicarbonate of soda
1 tsp ground cinnamon
1 tsp mixed spice
¼ cup rolled oats
6 tblsp sugar
6 tblsp butter or margarine
1 tblsp corn syrup
1 tblsp milk

Put the flour, bicarbonate of soda, cinnamon, mixed spice, oats and sugar into a bowl. Melt the butter in a small saucepan with the syrup and milk. Pour the liquid into the dry ingredients and beat until smooth. Make the mixture into little balls and place them a little apart on a lightly-greased cooky sheet. Flatten each one. Bake in the oven for 15 minutes until golden, and cool on the cooky sheet.

Macaroons

PREPARATION TIME: 20 minutes

COOKING TIME: 20 minutes

OVEN TEMPERATURE: 350°F

1 cup superfine sugar
10 tblsp ground almonds
1 tblsp rice flour
2 egg whites
Rice paper
20 split almonds

Mix the sugar, almonds and rice flour together. In a separate bowl, beat the egg whites lightly and add the ready-mixed dry ingredients. Let the mixture stand for 5 minutes. Line a cooky sheet with rice paper. Mold the mixture into little balls and place them on the lined cooky sheet slightly apart. Gently flatten the macaroons and put an almond on each one. Bake in the oven for 20 minutes, then cool on cooky sheet. Makes 20.

Almond Slices

PREPARATION TIME: 20 minutes

COOKING TIME: 20 minutes

OVEN TEMPERATURE: 400°F

Pastry Base
2 cups all-purpose flour
½ cup butter
¼ tsp salt
Cold water to mix

Topping
4 tblsp jam
½ cup sugar
½ cup confectioners' sugar
¾ cup ground almonds
1 egg, plus 1 egg white
A few drops almond essence
2 tblsp flaked almonds to decorate

Chocolate Frosting
6oz plain chocolate
2 tblsp light cream

To Decorate
1 packet chocolate chips
6 tblsp whole nuts

Sift together the dry ingredients into a bowl and make a well in the center. Add the sugar, syrup, eggs, oil and milk and beat until smooth. Grease and line a 9 inch cake pan and pour in the cake mixture. Cook in the oven for 45-50 minutes; leave in the pan for a few minutes before turning out the cake onto a wire rack.

To Make the Chocolate Frosting
Put the chocolate and cream into a small, heavy pan and heat gently until melted. Cool the mixture slightly and pour over the cake. Decorate with chocolate chips, or nuts.

Harvest Crunchies

PREPARATION TIME: 20 minutes

COOKING TIME: 15 minutes

OVEN TEMPERATURE: 375°F

¾ cup all-purpose flour
½ tsp mixed spice
¾ cup wholewheat flour
2 tblsp oatmeal
½ cup butter or margarine
¼ cup soft brown sugar
2 tblsp white raisins
2 tblsp milk

Sift the flour and spice into a bowl. Stir in the wholewheat flour and oatmeal. Cut the fat into the mixture until it resembles a stiff dough by adding the milk. Flour a work surface and turn the dough out onto it. Lightly knead the dough and roll it out until very thin. With a 3 inch fluted cooky cutter, cut out rounds and place them on a lightly-greased cooky sheet. Bake in the oven, then cool on a wire rack. Makes 20.

Sift the flour and salt into a bowl and cut in the butter until it resembles fine breadcrumbs. Add enough water to mix into a pliable dough. Roll out the dough onto a floured surface and use to line a greased or dampened shallow 10x6 inch baking pan. Pinch the long edges to form a border. Cover the base with jam. In a clean bowl, mix together the sugars and almonds. Beat well and then add the whole egg, egg white and almond essence. Use the almond mixture to cover the jam, spreading evenly with a knife. Sprinkle with almonds. Bake in the oven for 20 minutes until well risen and golden. When cooked, cut in the pan and leave to cool for 10 minutes. Then remove from pan and leave to finish cooling on a wire rack.

Viennese Fingers

PREPARATION TIME: 20 minutes

COOKING TIME: 15 minutes

OVEN TEMPERATURE: 350°F

¾ cup butter or margarine
¼ cup confectioners' sugar
Grated rind of 1 orange
1 cup all-purpose flour
6 tblsp cornstarch

Cream together the butter, sugar and orange rind until fluffy. Sieve the flour and cornstarch together and beat well into the mixture. Fill a pastry bag fitted with a 1 inch fluted tip and pipe 3 inch fingers, well separated, onto a sheet of non-stick silicone paper. Bake in the oven for 15 minutes and, when cooked, transfer to a wire rack to cool. If required, two fingers can be sandwiched together with a little apricot jam. Makes 12.

Chocolate Fudge Cake

PREPARATION TIME: 15 minutes

COOKING TIME: 45-50 minutes

OVEN TEMPERATURE: 325°F

1¾ cups all-purpose flour
1 tsp bicarbonate of soda
1 tsp baking powder
2 tblsp cocoa powder
10 tblsp soft brown sugar
2 tblsp corn syrup
2 eggs
¾ cup oil
1¼ cups milk

Facing page: Macaroons (top), Spiced Cookies (right) and Harvest Crunchies (bottom left). This page: Chocolate Fudge Cake (top), Viennese Fingers (left) and Almond Slices (bottom).

Celebration Cakes

round the bottom of the cake. With a medium, plain tip make bulbs between each of the stars on the inner edge of the cake. Make another row of bulbs on the side of the cake above the stars. Colour a little of the frosting pink and fit a pastry bag with a writing tip. Make a row of dropped loops from each of the bulbs on the top of the cake. From the point of alternate stars on the top edge of the cake make a row of dropped loops. Go round the cake again making loops on the stars omitted on the first round. Make a bulb on the point of each of the stars. With the pink frosting, make a scallop on the cake board round the stars. Write the message with swirls round it in the shape of 'S's and 'C's on the top of the cake and place the flowers, a little fern and the ribbon in position.

Boy's Birthday Cake

8 inch square, rich fruit cake
Recipe apricot glaze
1¾lb almond paste
Royal frosting, made with 3lb
*   confectioners' sugar*
Food coloring – blue
8 silver leaves for the top
16 silver leaves for the side panels

Brush the top of the cake with the apricot glaze. Cover the cake with the almond paste and leave it to dry. Attach the cake to the board with a little frosting. Flat frost the sides and top of the cake and let it dry. Fit a pastry bag with a large tip and make a continuous 'S' pattern on the top edge and the base of the cake. Make 4 bars horizontally across and down the corners of the cake. At each of the 4 corners, and

Mother's Day Cake

7 or 8 inch square or round cake
Recipe apricot glaze
1½lb almond paste
Royal frosting, made with 2lb
*   confectioners' sugar*
Food colorings – green, yellow
Green ribbon
Frosted flowers

Brush the top and sides of the cake with apricot glaze and cover with almond paste; leave to dry. With a little frosting, attach the cake to the cake board and flat frost the top and sides; leave to dry. Using a pastry bag fitted with a leaf tip, make a row of leaves in white frosting facing outwards around the bottom of the cake. Then make an overlapping circle of white leaves around the top edge of the cake. Fill another pastry bag with green-colored frosting and make a row of leaves facing outwards on top. Finally, make an overlapping circle of green leaves on the top. Fill a pastry bag with a little yellow-colored frosting and fit a medium writing tip and write 'Mother' on the top surface of the cake. Attach the frosted flowers on the top surface with a dab of frosting and, using the pastry bag with green frosting and the leaf tip again, make a few leaves around the flowers to finish. Decorate with the green ribbon.

Girl's Birthday Cake

8 inch round, rich fruit cake
Recipe apricot glaze
1¾lb almond paste
Royal frosting, made with 3lb
*   confectioners' sugar*
3 frosted flowers
Food coloring – pink
Pink ribbon
Frond of asparagus fern

Brush the top and sides of the cake with apricot glaze. Cover the cake with the almond paste. Attach the cake to the board with a little frosting. Flat frost the top and the sides of the cake. Fit a pastry bag with a large star tip and make a circle of stars round the top edge of the cake. Make a row of stars

This page: Girl's Birthday Cake and Boy's Birthday Cake.

Facing page: Mother's Day Cake.

on the top of the cake, make a single line from the flat surface of the cake crossing the continuous 'S' and ending in the corner. Fit a small star tip and frost vertically down the corners of the cake, covering the ends of the bars. Frost the decorative lines on the top of the cake, starting with a long line with a dot at each end and working out and down with shorter lines towards the outer edge. Write the name in the center of the cake. Color a little of the frosting blue and fit a writing tip onto the pastry bag. Make 2 rows of scallops on the top edge of the cake, a row on each side of the continuous 'S', ending at the corner where the corner bars start. Go over the name in blue. Make a dropped loop round the base of the cake, with the point of the loops at each of the corners. Attach 2 silver leaves at the base corners of each of the 4 side panels, and 2 silver leaves on the top of the cake at each of the 4 corners attached to the flat surface of the cake.

Silver Wedding Anniversary Cake

8 or 9 inch square, rich fruit cake
Recipe apricot glaze
1¾-2lb almond paste
Royal frosting, made with 2½lb confectioners' sugar
8 silver leaves
Silver non-toxic coloring

Brush the top and the sides of the cake with apricot glaze and cover with almond paste. Leave the cake to dry. Attach the cake to the board with a little frosting. Flat frost the top and sides of the cake, giving 2 or 3 coats. Fit your pastry bag with a medium writing tip. Using a saucepan lid or a round template, draw a circle in the center of the top of the cake. Using a medium-sized five-star tip, pipe a continuous swirl round the bottom edge of the cake and finish off each corner with a shell. With a smaller star tip, pipe a small dot on the top edge of the cake in the center of the top edge of each of the side panels and divide the space between the original dot and the corner of the cake with a further

It is most important that a celebration cake should feed the desired number of guests, so here is a guide:

Round	Square	Portions
6 inch	5 inch	20-30
7½-8 inch	7 inch	40-45
10 inch	9 inch	70-80
11 inch	10 inch	100-110
12 inch	12 inch	130-140

NB: for decorating simple cakes, candies can be utilised and are easily applied to butter frosting. These are much used in novelty cake designs.

dot. You should have 3 dots on each of the top sides of the cake. Using these as a guide, join them together by making a scallop, with the dots marking the points of the scallop. Using a writing tip, pipe with a scribbling line between the scallop on the sides of the cake and the template circle drawn on the top of the cake. The scribbling should be done with a continuous line that never crosses itself. Using the same tip, overfrost the template-drawn circle with a continuously twisting line. On the side panels and on the corners of the cake, create three beads in

descending size below each of the points of the scallop. Overfrost the continuous swirls round the bottom of the cake with a plain, continuous swirl beginning and ending with an 'S' shape. Make the '25' in the circle on top of the cake, then – when dry – overfrost this again with white. Fit your pastry bag with a medium star tip and, having positioned the silver leaves, secure them with a frosted rosette. Using a fine paintbrush, gently paint the continuous swirl overfrost on the circle on the top surface of the cake and also the top of the '25' with a single silver line.

Silver Wedding Anniversary Cake.

Golden Wedding Cake

10 inch)round, rich fruit cake
Recipe apricot glaze
2¼lb almond paste
Royal frosting, made from 3lb
   confectioners' sugar
Food coloring – yellow
6 gold leaves
Yellow ribbon

Brush the sides and top of the cake with the apricot glaze. Cover the cake with the almond paste and leave to dry. Attach the cake to the board with a little frosting. Flat frost the top and sides of the cake. Fit a pastry bag with a large star tip and make a row of shells round the top of the cake. Create a row of shells round the bottom of the cake. Fit the pastry bag with a smaller star tip and create continuous 'C's on the shells on the top of the cake. Fit the pastry bag with a medium-sized plain tip and make a scallop on the top of the cake round the shells. Round the bottom of the cake, on the board, make a scallop round the shells. Repeat the scallop on the side of the cake under the shells on the top edge of the cake. Colour a little of the frosting yellow and, using a writing tip, repeat the pattern of continuous 'C's on the top edge of the cake. Make a dropped loop on top of the shell at the base of the cake. Fit the same pastry bag with a leaf tip and make inverted leaves between the shells at the base of the cake, with the point of the leaves creeping up the sides of the cake. With a writing tip, write the words and surround them with 'S's and 'C's. Decorate with a real rose or any other flower, or frosted flowers and/or gold leaves.

Diana Wedding Cake

Two-Tier Round Cake
10 inch round, rich fruit cake
6 or 7 inch round, rich fruit cake
2 x recipe apricot glaze
3lb almond paste
Royal frosting, made from 3½lb
   confectioners' sugar
Silver cake boards: 13 inch and 8 or
   9 inch
32 silver leaves
8 frosted flowers
4 round pillars

Brush the top and sides of the cake with apricot glaze and cover with almond paste. Leave the cake to dry. Attach the cake to the board

with a little frosting. Flat frost the top and sides of the cake, giving three coats and an extra coat on the base cake. Fit a pastry bag with a large star tip and make shells round the bottom of each of the cakes. Using the same tip, mark the cake surface lightly at the edge as though it were square – treat it as though it had four corners, putting a dab of frosting in each of the four corners and a smaller dab at the center of each of the four sides. From each of the dabs which mark the center of the sides make an inverted 'S', finishing at the corner mark. Repeat this from where you started and mirror the original shape towards the other corner point. Repeat this round the cake. Make a 'C' facing the center of the cake, with its back marking the center point of the side. Overpipe all the decorative swirls, the 'S's and 'C's twice. Fit a pastry bag with a medium-sized plain tip and make a continuously twisting scallop on the upper edge of the sides of the cakes. Repeat this pattern on the cake board around the shells. With the same tip, frost over the decorative swirls, 'S's and 'C's on the tops of the cakes. Make a scallop on the top surface of the cake, encompassing the 'C's in the curves; three curves to each imaginary side. Make dropped loops under the continuously twisting scallop on the sides of

This page: Golden Wedding Cake. Facing page: Diana Wedding Cake.

Lindsey Jane
Wedding Cake.

cakes. On the sides of the cake below the loops, attach the flowers and leaves with a little frosting, four flowers per cake below each 'C' and a frosting rosette to attach the other leaves between each of the flowers. Assemble the cake using the pillars and decorate the top with flowers.

Lindsey Jane Wedding Cake

Two-Tier Square Cake
6 inch square, rich fruit cake
10 inch square, rich fruit cake
2 x recipe apricot glaze
3¼lb almond paste
Royal frosting made with 4lb
* confectioners' sugar*
28 pink frosted roses, to decorate
Asparagus fern, to decorate
Silver cake boards, 8 inch and 12
* inch*
4 square pillars
2 narrow ribbon bows

This design is suitable for a 1, 2 or 3-tier cake. The roses are chosen to match the bridal attire.
Brush the sides and tops of the cakes with apricot glaze and cover with almond paste. Leave to dry. Attach the cakes to the cake boards with a dab of frosting. Flat frost the cakes, giving two or three coats all over. Fit a pastry bag with a medium-sized shell tip and decorate shells on the top edge of the cakes, the bottom edge and up each of the corners. Apply with frosting on the top of the cakes in each corner 2 shells facing each other. Fit the pastry bag with a medium-sized plain tip and create a shallow scallop round the top side of the cake. Create an 'S'-shaped swirl, filling each of the small scallops. On the bottom tier, put a cluster of roses in the middle of the cake, surrounded by fern, two roses in each of the corners and one rose

at the base of each of the corners. On the top tier, repeat but with a single rose at the top of each corner and the ribbon bows on top of the cake. Assemble the cake using the pillars.

Christening Cake

8 inch round, rich fruit cake
Recipe apricot glaze
1¾lb almond paste
Royal frosting, made with 3lb
* confectioners' sugar*
Food coloring – blue
½oz almond paste
1 narrow, white ribbon bow

Brush the top and sides of the cake with the apricot glaze. Cover the cake with the almond paste and leave it to dry. Attach the cake to the board with a little frosting. Flat frost the top and sides of the cake with the royal frosting. Fit a pastry bag with a large star tip. With a frosting comb, comb the sides of the cake with a swirling line and make a row of shells round the top of the cake. Fit a pastry bag with a small star tip and make a scallop round the top of the shells. Make a graduated rope round the bottom of the cake with a large, dropped loop round the rope. Fit the pastry bag with a small plain tip and make a scallop on the top of the cake next to the shells. Write the name of the baby on the top of the cake. Color a little royal frosting blue. Using a writing tip, make beads at the points of each of the tips. Make another scallop onto the silver board. Go over the name with the blue, making small 'C's and scrolls. To make the bootees, color a little molding frosting pale blue and shape two. Press a small hole towards the end of each of the oval shapes. With a writing tip, pipe round the holes, making a little bow at the front. Decorate with a silver ball and put the small bow between the bootees.

Tracy Rose Wedding Cake

Three-Tier Square
5 inch square, rich fruit cake
8 inch square, rich fruit cake
11 inch square, rich fruit cake
3 x recipe apricot glaze
5lb almond paste
Royal frosting, made with 8lb
  confectioners' sugar
2 x recipe molding frosting, peach
  color (to make 60 molded roses)
3 cake boards: 7 inch, 10 inch and 14
  inch
Food colorings – green, peach (brown)
8 square cake pillars
2 rectangular silver boards

Brush the top and sides of the cakes with apricot glaze and cover with almond paste; leave to dry. Attach the cakes to the silver cake boards with a dab of frosting. Flat frost the tops of the cakes with the peach colored royal frosting. Cut the thin, rectangular cake boards lengthways down the middle and then cut each widthways with a sharp knife. Cut the corners off each piece diagonally so that they will go together to form a square with a square hole in the center. Place each on a sheet of wax paper and flat frost onto the white side with a palette knife; leave to dry. Fit a pastry bag with a medium writing tip and the other with a basket weave tip. Hold the basket weave tip sideways and on the side of the first cake pipe 3 lines, evenly spaced, one above the other and all of the same length. Pipe a vertical line using the writing tip along the edge of the basket weaving. Continue this process until the cake is covered. Repeat the basket weave method on each of the cardboard lids. To make the molded flowers see chapter on decorations. Color a little of the royal frosting green and fit a pastry bag with a leaf tip. Color a little more royal frosting a dark peach and use it to fill a bag fitted with a star tip. Continue to use the writing tip filled with the tinted peach royal frosting as used in the basket weave. Position the molded frosting roses facing outward round the top edges of the 2 bottom tiers and in a radiating pattern on the small top tier. Make frosted dark peach stars between each of the roses and dot the center of each star using the tinted peach royal frosting. Make frosted leaves at random round the flowers. Place the pillars on a tray and frost small

stars dotted with tinted peach for the center of the flower. Again, frost leaves at random and leave to dry.

To Assemble the Cake
Place the basket lids round the outer edge of each of the cake's bottom two tiers and, with a little frosting, secure them to the top of

the cake. Make sure that there is enough room in the square at the center of each cake for the four pillars.
Note: the cake board can be frosted with a palette knife to surround each of the cakes, if required.

This page: Christening Cake.

Facing page: Tracy Rose Wedding Cake.

and, with inverted 'S's and 'C's, pipe little swirls around the words. Create the starbursts round the cross. Decorate with the ribbon.

Fiona Anne Wedding Cake

Three-Tier Round
6 inch round, rich fruit cake
8 inch round, rich fruit cake
10 inch round, rich fruit cake
3 x recipe apricot glaze
4lb almond paste
Royal frosting, made with 7lb confectioners' sugar
60 silver leaves
30 frosted sugar roses, painted with non-toxic silver food coloring
Silver cake boards: 8 inch, 10 inch and 13 inch
8 round cake pillars

Brush the top and the sides of the cake with apricot glaze, cover with almond paste and leave to dry. Attach the cakes to the cake boards with a dab of frosting. Flat frost the cakes, giving three coats all over and an extra coat for the tops. Fit a pastry bag with a large star tip and create inverted shells with the tail of the shell going up the side of the cake. With the same tip, create 'C's round the top edge of each of the cakes and leave to dry. Pipe a further 'C' on top of the first. Fit the pastry bag with a medium plain tip and create a further 'C' on top of the original two. Working along the side edge of the cakes, pipe a dropped loop with a swirling action to create a graduated rope. With a plain writing tip, create a dropped loop round the tail of each of the base shells, missing out a shell as you pipe. When you have gone round the cake, repeat the process, crossing the dropped loop from the tail of the shell that you missed out on the first round. On the tops of the cakes, create a scallop round each of the 'C' shapes. Fit the pastry bag with the medium plain tip and create a bead to conceal the tail of each of the base shells.

Confirmation Cake

8 or 9 inch square, rich fruit cake
Recipe apricot glaze
1¾-2lb almond paste
Royal frosting, made with 2½lb confectioners' sugar
Food coloring – violet
Violet ribbon

Brush the top and the sides of the cake with apricot glaze and cover with almond paste. Leave the cake to dry. Attach the cake to the board with a little frosting. Flat frost the top and the sides of the cake, giving 2 or 3 coats. Fit a pastry bag with a medium-sized 5-point tip and make a row of graduated ropes round the top edge of the cake. To do this, start from the center of one side and mark with a small dot of frosting. Divide the area between the corners of the cake and the original dot with another dot and work your way round each of the sides of the cake. You now have 3 dots on each side of the cake. Frost between each of the dots in a continuous swirl which gets thicker at the halfway mark and decreases in size towards the end. Repeat the graduated ropes round the bottom edge of the cake. Fit the pastry bag with a smaller star tip and make a scallop round each of the graduated ropes. You should have 4 on each side of the cake on both the top edge and the bottom. On the flat surface of the cake, make a scallop using the same tip as before, but facing outwards, so you have concave and convex scallops on the top edge of the cake. Fit the pastry bag with a plain writing tip and go over the first scallop with a continuously twisting line. Fit another pastry bag with a little violet-colored frosting and, towards one side of the top of the cake, make the outer line of the cross with a continuous line. Take a little white frosting and thin it with a small amount of lemon juice until it flows. When the violet-colored outline of the cross is dry, flood the shape with the liquid icing. Burst any bubbles and leave it to dry. With the violet icing and writing tip, write the words 'God Bless'

This page: Confirmation Cake.

Facing page: Fiona Anne Wedding Cake.

To Decorate

Reserve 15 roses for the bottom cake, 10 for the middle tier and 5 for the top tier. Reserve 30 silver leaves for the bottom cake, 20 for the middle tier and 10 for the top tier. Space the decorations as follows: 1 rose, with twinned silver leaves on either side, with a frosted forget-me-not (using a forget-me-not tip) to secure the leaves and a single rose placed slightly lower down on the side of the cake, followed by another rose and surrounded by twin silver leaves. Assemble the cake using the pillars and decorate the top with flowers.

Valentine Cake

8 or 9 inch round, rich fruit cake, cut
   to a heart shape
Recipe apricot glaze
1½lb almond paste
Royal frosting, made with 3lb
   confectioners' sugar
Red and cream molded roses
Food coloring – green
Red ribbon

Brush the top and sides of the cake with apricot glaze and cover with almond paste; leave to dry. With a little frosting, attach the cake to the cake board and flat frost the top and sides; leave to dry. Make two rows of shells around the base of the cake in white frosting. Attach the red and cream molded roses with a dab of frosting on the top surface of the cake. Colour a little frosting with the green food coloring and, using a leaf tip, make a few leaves round the molded roses. Make a bow with the red ribbon and attach to the top surface of the cake to finish.

Good Luck Cake

8 inch round, rich fruit cake
Recipe apricot glaze
1¾lb almond paste
Royal frosting, made with 2lb
   confectioners' sugar
Food colorings – violet, pink
1oz black molding frosting
2 silver leaves
1 silver horseshoe, small
1 narrow, black bow

Brush the top and the sides of the cake with the apricot glaze. Cover the cake with the almond paste and let it dry. Flat frost the top and sides of the cake, having first attached the cake to the board with a little frosting. With a small star tip, make a row of shells round the top edge of the cake. Create a row of graduated ropes round the top edge of the side of the cake. Using the same tip, make a double row of shells round the bottom of the cake. Color a little frosting pink and, with a writing tip, make a loose scallop round the inside edge of the cake on the top surface. Make frosted dropped loops over the 2 rows of shells at the bottom of the cake. Color a little frosting violet and, with a writing tip, make a scallop pattern round the outer edge of the top of the cake. Repeat the pattern on the board round the cake. Make a small bulb on the side of the cake on the point of the pink dropped loops. Write the words 'Good Luck' or 'Best Wishes' on the top of the cake using a writing tip and violet-colored frosting. With the pink frosting, pipe a line under the words and pipe a bulb at the point of the violet dropped loops. Roll out the black molding frosting and either cut out the shape of a cat, using a sharp knife, or draw the cat onto a piece of greaseproof paper and use it as a guide. When the cat has been cut out, let it dry and put it in place with a little frosting. Arrange the leaves and the ribbon.

21st Birthday Cake

This design can also be used for a golden wedding or silver wedding anniversary cake. Just omit the '21' and change the color used: either yellow balls for a golden wedding or silver balls for a silver wedding, writing your message on the top of the cake.

8 or 9 inch square, rich fruit cake
Recipe apricot glaze
1¾-2lb almond paste
Royal frosting, made with 2½lb
   confectioners' sugar
Food coloring – violet
4 medium-sized silver horseshoes

Brush the sides and top of the cake with apricot glaze. Cover the cake with the almond paste and leave to dry. Attach the cake to the board with a little frosting. Flat frost the top and the sides of the cake. When the frosting is dry, make a template. Alternatively, draw a circle round a small saucepan lid or fluted jelly mold, onto a piece of wax paper. Use either of these templates to mark out the top of the cake. Fit a pastry bag with a large star tip and make shells round the base of the cake. Using a plain writing tip filled with white frosting, mark a point 1 inch from the top edge of the cake on each of the side panels. Make a further point halfway between the first mark and the corner of the cake. You will now have 3 dots on each of the side panels. Use them as a guide to enable you to make inverted scallops. The dots mark the points of each scallop and also the corner of the cake. Using your template and the same tip, make the decorative shape on the top surface of the cake. Fit your pastry bag with a forget-me-not tip. Make random forget-me-nots between the scallop on the side of the cake and the template-drawn pattern on the top. Fit the pastry bag with a medium, plain writing tip and make an inner circle on the flat surface of the cake echoing the shape drawn with the use of the template. Write the figures '21' and the name, if required. Color a little of the frosting violet and, using a medium tip, dot the center of each flower. Using the violet frosting make a scallop shape on the cake board, curving round each of the shells. Using a small writing tip, go over the original template-drawn line with a continuously twisting line. Go over the '21' and the name with the violet frosting. This can be done with half straight and half continuous twists. Using a little white frosting, attach the horseshoes in the center of each of the side panels of the cake.

Flower Birthday Cake

7 inch or 8 inch round, rich fruit cake
   or Madeira cake
Recipe apricot glaze
1½lb almond paste
Recipe pink molding frosting
Selection of molded flowers
Ribbon – color of your choice

Brush the top and sides of the cake with apricot glaze and cover with almond paste; leave to dry. With a little frosting, attach the cake to the cake board and cover with the pink molding frosting; leave to dry. Attach the molded flowers with a dab of frosting. Decorate with the ribbon.

Flower Birthday Cake and Good Luck Cake.

Engagement Cake

8 or 9 inch square, rich fruit cake
Recipe apricot glaze
1¾-2lb almond paste
Royal frosting, made with 2½lb
  confectioners' sugar
Three frosted flowers
Food colorings – pink, blue
Pink ribbon

Brush the cake with the apricot glaze. Cover the cake with the almond paste and let it dry. Attach the cake to the board with a little frosting. Flat frost the top and the sides of the cake. Fit a pastry bag with a medium star tip and make shells round the base of the cake. Using the same tip, make 'C's at the corners of the cake on the top surface of the cake. Pipe another 'C' on top of the first. On the edge of the top of the cake, create a continuous 'S' pattern and repeat it on the top of the first row. With the same tip, make a line on the flat surface of the cake. Using a writing tip, make another line on the inside of the first line. Color some of the frosting blue and, with a writing tip, make another line round the top edge of the cake. Go over over the 'C's in the corners of the cake and make dropped loops over the shells at the bottom of the cake. Fit another pastry bag with a medium-sized plain tip. Color a little icing pink and use it to make continuous loops, starting and ending with an 'S'. Write the message on the top of the cake and make bulbs between each of the shells where each of the blue loops point. With the blue frosting, make – using a writing tip – small, decorative, inverted 'C' and 'S' shapes round the message. Attach the frosted flowers and the ribbon.

This page: 21st Birthday Cake.

Facing page: Valentine Cake and Engagement Cake.

Easter and Christmas Cakes

Special cakes are traditionally used for the celebration of religious festivals; the most popular being the traditional Christmas cake and the simnel cake at Easter. Not everybody enjoys rich cake, so there are sponge variations in this book for both Easter and Christmas.

Simnel Cake

PREPARATION TIME: 40 minutes

COOKING TIME: 3 hours

OVEN TEMPERATURE: 325°F reduced to 300°F

8 inch round, rich fruit cake mixture
1¾lb almond paste
2 tblsp apricot glaze
1 egg white, beaten
Ribbon to decorate

Place half the mixture in a prepared, deep cake pan. Roll out a quarter of the almond paste into a 8 inch circle and lay it on top of the mixture. Spread the remaining mixture on the top of the almond paste. Bake in the oven for 1 hour, lower the temperature and bake for a further 2½ hours. Leave in the pan for 5 minutes and turn onto a wire rack to cool. Roll out a third of the remaining almond paste into a 8 inch circle. Brush the top of the cake with apricot glaze. Press the almond paste circle on top of the cake and brush with beaten egg white. Shape the remaining almond paste into balls and place round the edge. Brown under a hot broiler and allow to cool. Decorate with ribbon.

Daffodil Cake

9 inch round Madeira cake
Recipe vanilla-flavored butter frosting
Molding frosting daffodil
3 tblsp apricot jam
1 tblsp cocoa powder

Slice the cake and spread with the jam. Use half of the butter frosting and sandwich the cake together. Spread the top of the cake with a ¼

of the remaining butter frosting. Smooth it with a palette knife. Fill a pastry bag with the remaining butter frosting and fit it with a 5-point star tip. Make shells round the edge of the cake. Put the daffodil on the cake. Mix a little butter frosting with cocoa powder. With a pastry bag fitted with a writing tip, write 'Easter' on the cake below the daffodil.

Easter Nest

8 inch round lemon sponge (beaten or Victoria)
1 box orange-flavored chocolate sticks
½ cup candy-coated chocolate speckled eggs
Recipe lemon-flavored butter frosting

Put the cake on a plate or cake board. Cover the cake with lemon-flavored butter frosting. Put a

This page: Daffodil Cake (top) and Simnel Cake (bottom).

Facing page: Easter Cake with Chicks (top) and Easter Nest (bottom).

ribbon round the side of the cake and make a bow. Lay the orange-flavored chocolate sticks at angles round the sides of the cake, leaving an uncovered area in the center of the cake. Fill the center with eggs.

Fruit Easter Cake with Chicks

PREPARATION TIME: 45 minutes
COOKING TIME: 1 hour
30 minutes to 1 hour 45 minutes
OVEN TEMPERATURE: 325°F

¾ cup butter
¾ cup sugar
3 eggs
1 cup flour
¾ cup mixed dried fruit
1¼ cups cake flour
1½ tsp baking powder
¼ cup chopped mixed candied fruit
¼ cup candied cherries, halved
Grated rind of 1 orange
5 tblsp orange juice
1 crushed sugar cube

To Decorate
Fluffy chicks
Yellow ribbon

Cream the butter and sugar together until light and fluffy. Beat in the eggs singly, adding a little flour after each. Toss the fruit in the remaining flour and add to the mixture with the orange rind and juice. Grease and line a 7 inch cake pan. Fill with the mixture and smooth with the back of a spoon. Sprinkle with some of the crushed sugar cube. Bake in the oven for 1½- 1¾ hours. Turn out and cool on a wire rack. Decorate with yellow ribbon, chicks and fresh or artificial flowers. Sprinkle top of cake with remaining sugar cube.

Festive Garland

If you prefer you can make edible decorations for this cake.

8 inch quick mix cake, baked in a ring mold
Recipe apricot glaze
Recipe butter frosting
1 round cake board
Holly leaves, berries, Christmas roses, mistletoe, candle and ribbon (color of your choice)

Split the cake and sandwich together with the glaze. Put the cake on the plate or cake board and cover with the frosting, peaking it as you go around. Press the roses, holly leaves, berries and mistletoe into the cake, leaving a gap for the bow. When the frosting is dry and hard, place a candle in the center of the ring and attach the bow in the space reserved.

Christmas Bells

7 inch or 8 inch square Christmas cake
Royal frosting, made with 2½lb confectioners' sugar
½ recipe white molding frosting
½ cup granulated sugar
4 sprigs of holly, real or artificial
1 yard narrow, white satin ribbon
Food coloring – pink

Put the cake on a silver cake board. Royal frost the cake and leave to dry between coats. Roll out the molding frosting and, using a bell shape cutter, cut 10 bells and leave them to dry on non-stick silicone paper. Mix the granulated sugar and pink food color well until the sugar becomes pink. Sprinkle over the bells and leave to dry. Fill a pastry bag, fitted with a medium-sized star tip, with the royal frosting. Make a row of shells round the bottom of the cake. Make a border of shells round the top of the cake and a line of shells up each of the 4 corners of the cake and allow the frosting to dry. Make 5 bows with the narrow, white ribbon. With a little frosting sugar secure two frosting bells on each side panel of the cake. The tops of the bells should be nearest to each of the 4 corners. Two of the bells should be placed in the center of the top of the cake, with the tops of the bells together. Put a ribbon bow above each of the bells. Position the sprigs of holly in each of the four corners on top of the cake.

Christmas Tree

8 inch square quick mix cake or rich fruit cake mix
Recipe apricot glaze
Recipe almond paste, if using fruit cake
Recipe butter frosting, if using quick mix cake
1lb molding frosting

To Decorate
1 cake board
Silver balls
Shredded coconut to sprinkle
Recipe royal frosting

8oz molding frosting, white
Chocolate sticks
Gold or silver non-toxic food coloring
Food coloring – red, blue, green, yellow
8oz molding frosting

Cut the cake diagonally and place the outer edges of the square next to one another, i.e. back-to-back to produce a triangular shape. If using a fruit cake, brush with apricot glaze and cover with almond paste. If using a butter frosting on a quick cake mixture, cover the cake with the butter frosting and leave on the cake board. Roll out the molding frosting and, using a fluted pastry cutter, cut circles and then cut each one in half and use to stick onto the butter frosting. Start at the bottom edge of the cake and overlap slightly until you reach the top. With the remaining frosting, make some small presents and a square tub for the tree. Cover the tree trunk with a little of the remaining butter frosting and lay the chocolate sticks vertically on the tree trunk. Use any remaining frosting to frost the leaves of the tree, or make the leaves if desired. Decorate with the silver balls and sprinkle with shredded coconut. With the white frosting to decorate, color small pinches in various colors and, with the white royal frosting, make strings around the various colored shapes to make more little parcels. Roll out the remaining white frosting and cut it into a star. Color with a little non-toxic gold or silver food coloring.

Traditional Christmas Cake with Holly and Roses

7 inch round Christmas cake
Recipe apricot glaze
1½lb almond paste
Royal frosting, made with 2lb confectioners' sugar

To Decorate
Silver balls
Christmas roses
Almond paste holly leaves and berries, small snowman or Santa, if available
Ribbon

Brush the cake with apricot glaze. Cover with the almond paste and leave to dry. Flat frost the top and sides of the cake with royal frosting and leave to dry again. Use a pastry bag fitted with a 5-star tip and make shells around the top edge of the cake and then on the top,

round the sides of the cake and, finally, around the bottom edge of the cake. When dry, make a further row between the top 2 rows using the 5-star tip upright to make stars. Decorate the top of the cake with almond paste holly and frosted or molded Christmas roses and a small snowman or Father Christmas, if desired. Tie the ribbon round the cake and make a bow. Push a silver ball into the center of each of the stars.

Christmas Tree (right) and Festive Garland (below).

Frosted Mistletoe Cake

This is a quick and easy Christmas cake, which can be made either round or square. Any bought decorations can be used to complement the design.

7 inch or 8 inch square or round
*   Christmas cake*
Recipe apricot glaze
1½lb almond paste
2lb green molding frosting
12 mistletoe leaves and berries made
*   from almond paste*
2ft x 2 inch length of green ribbon
Food coloring – green

Put the cake on a silver cake board. To decorate, roll out the green molding frosting. With a small, sharp knife cut out several mistletoe leaves. Make them long and narrow with rounded ends and mark them with a knife to indicate the veins. With the uncolored molding frosting roll small, pea-sized balls of frosting to represent the berries. Use the mistletoe to decorate the top of the cake. With the ribbon, tie a large bow and attach it to the top of the cake with a little royal frosting. Fill a shaker with a little frosting sugar, or put it through a small sieve and shake it gently round the edge of the cake, dusting some of the mistletoe.

Christmas Candles

2 jam-filled jelly rolls
1lb green molding frosting
4oz white molding frosting
Recipe apricot glaze
Rectangular silver cake board
Food colorings – red, yellow, blue
Red ribbon
3 cocktail sticks

Cut one jelly roll ¾ of the way down. Brush the jelly rolls with apricot glaze. Roll out the green molding frosting and cover the jelly rolls. Stand them upright with something for support. In a small, heavy saucepan stir to dissolve half to three-quarters of the white molding frosting. Roll out the

This page: Christmas Bells Cake (top) and Traditional Christmas Cake with Holly and Roses (bottom).

Facing page: Frosted Mistletoe Cake.

remaining white frosting on a surface dusted with confectioners' sugar or cornstarch and cut out 3 flame shapes. Leave on non-stick silicone paper to dry. When dry, paint a blue dot near the bottom; surround by yellow and edge with red. Reserve to dry. Pour the liquid molding frosting over the candles in a drizzle so that it dries like wax. Stick a flame in to the top of each candle, using a cocktail stick to support them. Decorate with ribbons.

Postbox

This makes a quick and easy festive cake for those who do not like traditional Christmas cake.

1 chocolate jelly roll
8oz red molding frosting
Recipe royal frosting
Recipe apricot glaze

Roll out the molding frosting and cut out two circles to cover the ends of the jelly roll. Roll out the remaining frosting to cover the rest of the jelly roll. Brush the jelly roll with the apricot glaze and cover with molding frosting. Fit a pastry bag with a writing tip and fill with some royal frosting. Frost the detail onto the postbox and leave to dry. With the remaining frosting, spoon half on top of the postbox and the remainder at the bottom. Dust with a little confectioners' sugar.

Icicles with Holly

7 inch or 8 inch square or round, rich fruit cake
Recipe apricot glaze
1½lb almond paste
Royal frosting, made with 2lb confectioners' sugar
Blue ribbon
Almond paste holly leaves and berries

Brush the top and sides of the cake with apricot glaze and cover with almond paste; leave to dry. With a little frosting, attach the cake to the cake board and flat frost the top and sides. Leave it to dry between and after coats. Using a pastry bag fitted with a shell tip, make a circle of shells on the top edge of the cake and again round the bottom of the cake. Fit the pastry bag with a plain or fine-band tip. Place the ribbon round the sides of the cake. Make the icicles down and over the ribbon, varying them in length and width. Fit the pastry bag with a writing tip and go over to make smaller icicles, which should hang free of the cake. Use the remaining frosting to secure the holly in a pattern on top of the cake.

This page: Postbox and Christmas Candles. Facing page: Icicles with Holly.

Gâteaux

Minted Lime Gâteau

PREPARATION TIME: 35 minutes
COOKING TIME: 20 minutes
OVEN TEMPERATURE: 375°F

½ cup sugar
3 eggs
¾ cup cake flour
3 tblsp melted butter
Grated rind of 1 lime
Flesh of 1 lime, de-pipped

Decoration
1¼ cups heavy cream
1 fresh lime
Grated chocolate (optional)

Beat the sugar and eggs together in a basin, over a saucepan of hot water, until the mixture is thick. Sieve the flour twice and fold into the beaten mixture. Mix in the lime flesh and grated rind. Grease and flour an 8 inch cake pan and fill with the mixture. Bake in the oven for 20 minutes. Cool on a wire rack.

To Decorate
Whip the cream and spread over the gâteau, reserving a little for decorating. Fill a nylon pastry bag with the remaining cream and, using a star tip, shape rosettes to decorate the gâteau. Sprinkle the sides with chocolate, if desired, and decorate with slices of lime.

Gâteau St Honoré

PREPARATION TIME: 1 hour 30 minutes
COOKING TIME: 30 minutes
OVEN TEMPERATURE: 325°F

This is a fantasy choux pastry dessert. Also known as a croquembouche, it can be built directly onto a serving stand or onto a meringue or basic pastry base, and is a French favorite for weddings. If making the choux pastry a day in advance, the buns can be crisped by heating in a preheated oven at 350°F for 5 minutes. Cool before filling and assembling.

Choux Pastry
6 tblsp butter
¾ cup water
1 cup flour
Pinch of salt
3 beaten eggs

Filling
2½ cups heavy cream
2 tblsp milk
2 tblsp sifted confectioners' sugar
2 tblsp raspberry liqueur

Caramel
1 cup granulated sugar
⅔ cup water

Sift the flour and salt together. Melt the butter in a heavy saucepan, with the water, and bring to the boil. Remove from heat. Add flour and salt mixture to the pan as soon as liquid has boiled. This should be carried out rapidly. Beat with a wooden spoon until glossy. The mixture should be the right consistency to form small balls at this stage. Turn out onto a plate and spread out to cool. Return it to the pan and gradually beat in the eggs. Fill a pastry bag with the choux paste. Attach a ¾ inch plain tip. Shape the choux paste into small balls onto a greased cooky sheet. Make sure they are well apart. Bake in the oven for 25 minutes until well risen and golden brown. They should be firm to touch. Pierce each bun to allow the steam to escape and return them to the oven for 2 minutes. Cool on a wire rack.

Filling
Whip half the cream with the milk, fold in the confectioners' sugar and the raspberry liqueur. Whip the remaining cream and use half to form a mound in the center of the serving plate or stand. With the other half, fill a pastry bag fitted with a star nozzle and reserve. Use the raspberry cream to fill another pastry bag fitted with a plain tip and fill each of the choux buns. Stick the choux buns round the cream mound so that it is completely covered and shape rosettes between each bun using the plain cream.

For the Caramel
Melt the sugar gently in a saucepan with the water and boil until it turns brown and caramelizes. Cool until the caramel begins to thicken but not set and pour quickly, but gently, over the gâteau. Leave to set and chill for ½ hour before serving.

Raspberry Gâteau

PREPARATION TIME: 40 minutes
COOKING TIME: 35 minutes
OVEN TEMPERATURE: 375°F

4 eggs
½ cup sugar
¾ cup flour
2 tblsp melted butter
3 tblsp cornstarch
Grated rind of ½ lemon

Filling
1lb raspberries, fresh (or drained, if tinned)
6 tblsp sherry
1¾ cups heavy cream, whipped
Finely-grated chocolate or chocolate vermicelli

Put the sugar, eggs and lemon rind in a basin over a pan of hot water and beat until pale and thick. Remove from the heat and continue to beat until cool. Sieve the flour and cornstarch together. Fold the flour and melted butter into the mixture using a metal spoon. Bottom line and grease an 8 inch square cake pan, fill with mixture and bake in the oven for 35 minutes. When cooked, turn out and cool on a wire rack. Cut the cake in half horizontally and sprinkle with sherry. Spread the bottom layer with whipped cream and reserve a little cream for decoration. Cover the cream with half the raspberries. Put the top layer of the sponge onto the raspberry filling and cover the sides of the cake with a thin layer of cream using a palette knife. Press the chocolate over the sides of the cake. Cover the top of the cake with a thin layer of cream and fill a nylon pastry bag fitted with a large tip with the remaining cream.

Shape a cream border round the top of the cake. Fill the top with the remaining raspberries.

Apricot Meringue

PREPARATION TIME: 30 minutes
COOKING TIME: 1 hour to 1 hour 15 minutes
OVEN TEMPERATURE: 275°F

6 egg whites
1½ cups sugar
2 cups heavy cream, whipped
6 apricot halves, sliced

Line a cooky sheet with non-stick paper. Beat the egg whites in a clean, dry bowl until stiff. Continue to beat and add the sugar, 1 tblsp at a time, until the mixture is very stiff and glossy. Fit a large star tip to a pastry bag and pipe 8 swirls onto the cooky sheet. Bake in the oven for 1-1¼ hours until crisp and dry. Leave to cool and peel from the paper. Lay half the meringue swirls onto a presentation plate and fill a pastry bag, fitted with a star tip, with the whipped cream. Shape a line of cream onto each swirl and layer with slices of apricot. Shape with cream again. Stick together with another meringue swirl and shape with cream around the edge of the top meringue and decorate the cream with further slices of apricot.

Facing page: Gâteau St. Honoré (top left), Minted Lime Gâteau (top right) and Raspberry Gâteau (bottom).

Black Forest Gâteau

PREPARATION TIME: 35 minutes
COOKING TIME: 40 minutes
OVEN TEMPERATURE: 375°F

3 eggs
½ cup sugar
¾ cup flour
1 tblsp cocoa powder

Filling
15oz can black cherries, pitted
1 tblsp arrowroot
2 tblsp Kirsch
1¼ cups heavy cream
Grated chocolate or chocolate flakes
  to decorate

Place the eggs and sugar in a basin and beat over a saucepan of hot water until thick. Remove from the heat and continue to beat until cool. Sieve the cocoa powder and flour together and gently fold into the mixture using a metal spoon. Grease and line the bottom of an 8 inch cake pan. Pour the mixture into the pan and bake in the oven for 40 minutes. Turn out and cool on a wire rack.

Filling and Decoration
Drain the juice from the cherries into a pan and blend with a little arrowroot. Bring to boil and stir until it thickens. Add the cherries to the syrup and allow to cool. Cut the cake in half and sprinkle the base with a little kirsch. Whip the cream and use it to fill a nylon pastry bag fitted with a large star tip. Shape a circle of cream into the border edge of the base cake. Fill with half the cherry mixture. Sprinkle the top of the cake with a little kirsch and place on top of the filling. Spread a little cream on the sides of the gâteau and press the grated chocolate onto it using a palette knife. Shape swirls of cream on top of the gâteau and fill the center with the remaining cherries. Sprinkle with a little chocolate.

Walnut and Banana Galette

PREPARATION TIME: 45 minutes
COOKING TIME: 25 minutes
OVEN TEMPERATURE: 350°F

½ cup butter
1½ cups flour
½ cup sugar
½ cup chopped walnuts
Grated rind of ½ lemon

Filling and Decoration
1¼ cups heavy cream
2 tblsp confectioners' sugar
4 bananas

Cream the butter, sugar and lemon rind until fluffy. Fold the flour in and knead it until you have a soft dough. Put the dough in a polythene bag and chill for ½ hour in the refrigerator. Grease and flour 3 cooky sheets and mark a 7 inch circle on each. To make the circles, use a saucepan lid as a guide. Divide the dough into 3 and place a piece of dough on each circle. Press it out until it fills the circle. Sprinkle the top of each circle with chopped walnuts and bake in the oven for 25 minutes. When cooked, allow to cool before turning onto a wire rack.

Filling and Decoration
Whip the cream and fold in the confectioners' sugar. Slice the bananas and sprinkle them with a little lemon juice, which prevents them from discoloring. Stick the layers together with some cream sprinkled with banana slices. Using a nylon pastry bag filled with the remaining cream and fitted with a large star tip, shape the decoration around the top of the galette and decorate with slices of banana. Allow the galette to stand for 30 minutes before serving.

Brandied Chestnut Roll

PREPARATION TIME: 35 minutes
COOKING TIME: 12 minutes for the base, 10 minutes for the filling
OVEN TEMPERATURE: 425°F

3 eggs
½ cup sugar
2 tblsp brandy
1 cup flour

Filling
1 tblsp sugar
1¼ cups heavy cream
1 tblsp sugar
8¾oz can chestnut purée (crème de marron)
6oz plain chocolate
1 tblsp butter
2 tblsp brandy

Beat the eggs and sugar until thick. Gently fold in the sieved flour and the brandy with a metal spoon. Line and grease (bottom only) a 9x13 inch jelly roll pan. Pour the mixture into the pan and bake in the oven for 12 minutes. Cover a clean, damp cloth with a sheet of wax paper. Sprinkle the paper with 1 tblsp sugar. Turn the cake out onto the paper and remove the wax used to line the pan. The edges of the cake will be crisp, so trim with a sharp knife. Roll up the cake by putting a clean sheet of wax over the cake. Cool on a wire tray.

Filling
Whip the cream and sugar until stiff and stir half the cream into the chestnut purée. The chestnut purée mixture must be smooth before use. Gently unroll the cake and remove the wax paper rolled with it. Spread the chestnut cream on the inner side of the cake and re-roll. Melt the chocolate in a bowl over a pan of hot water, adding the butter and brandy. Cover the cake completely with the chocolate mixture. Mark the chocolate-coated cake with a fork when half set. Pipe the whipped cream with a large tip into whirls on top of the cake.

Ginger Ice Cream Gâteau

PREPARATION TIME: 1 hour
COOKING TIME: 25 minutes
OVEN TEMPERATURE: 325°F

Ice Cream
⅔ cup milk
1 egg
6 tblsp sugar
¼ cup green ginger wine
1¼ cups heavy cream

Almond Base
3 egg whites
10 tblsp sugar
6 tblsp cornstarch
½ cup ground almonds

Topping
⅔ cup heavy cream
4 tblsp apricot jam, sieved
3 pieces stem ginger, chopped
¼ cup whole or flaked almonds, toasted

Ice Cream
Put the milk, egg and sugar into a basin over a pan of hot water. Stir continuously until the custard mixture begins to thicken. When it will coat the back of the spoon, remove it and let it cool. Stir in the ginger wine and cream. Pour into a rigid, shallow freezer container and partially freeze. When the ice cream is partially frozen, remove from the freezer and pour into a bowl. Beat until smooth and creamy. Line an 8 inch cake pan with plastic wrap and pour in the ice cream. Return to the freezer until frozen.

Almond Base
Beat the egg whites in a clean bowl until they are stiff. Add the sugar and beat again. Gently fold in the cornstarch and ground almonds. Line the bottom of a cooky sheet. Fill a nylon pastry bag fitted with a ½ inch tip with some of the almond mixture. Spread the mixture in an 8 inch circle and smooth evenly. Bake in the oven for 25 minutes.
Place the almond base on a flat plate. Carefully lift the ice cream out of the pan and peel off the plastic wrap. Place the ice cream on the almond base.

For the Topping
Whip the cream, fold in the jam, stem ginger and almonds and spread over the ice cream.

Brandied Chestnut Roll (left), Walnut and Banana Galette (below) and Black Forest Gâteau (bottom).

Peach and Almond Gâteau

PREPARATION TIME: 60 minutes

COOKING TIME: 60 minutes for cake, 20 minutes for confectioners' custard

OVEN TEMPERATURE: 350°F

4 eggs, separated
½ cup sugar
1 cup cake flour
1¼ tsp baking powder
2 tblsp corn oil
3 tblsp boiling water
1 tsp almond essence

Filling
2 tblsp apricot jam, warmed

Confectioner's Custard
3 egg yolks
¼ cup sugar
¼ cup flour
1¼ cups milk
2 tblsp butter
1 tblsp sherry

To Decorate
1¼ cups heavy cream
¼ cup flaked almonds, toasted
14½oz can sliced peaches, drained

Grease and line an 8 inch loose-bottomed, deep cake pan. Place the egg yolks, sugar, flour, oil, water and almond essence in a bowl and beat for 2 minutes with a wooden spoon. Stiffly beat the egg whites and fold into the cake mixture using a metal spoon. Pour the mixture into a prepared pan and cook in the oven for about 60 minutes until well risen. Remove cake from pan and cool on a wire rack. Remove paper when cake is cold.

For the Confectioners' Custard
Put egg yolks in a bowl and beat until smooth and creamy. Stir in the flour and mix well. Heat the milk until hot, but not boiling, and stir into the egg mixture. Return the mixture to the pan and stir, bringing it gently to the boil. Remove from the heat and beat in the butter and the sherry. Pour into a bowl, stirring occasionally to prevent a skin forming.

Assembling the Gâteau
Cut the cake into 3 layers, placing the bottom layer on a serving plate. Spread the cake with 1 tblsp of jam and half the confectioners' custard. Place the second layer on top and spread with the remaining jam and

custard. Put the top of the cake onto the filling. Spread the cake with half the cream and arrange the peaches on the top. Fit a pastry bag with a medium star tip and shape the remaining cream to decorate the gâteau. Sprinkle on the toasted almonds.

Chocolate Torte

PREPARATION TIME: 35 minutes

COOKING TIME: 1 hour 30 minutes

OVEN TEMPERATURE: 300°F

6oz plain chocolate
1 tblsp strong black coffee
¾ cup butter
¾ cup sugar
4 eggs, separated
1¼ cups cake flour
1½ tsp baking powder

Filling and Icing
Cherry jam
6oz plain chocolate
2 tblsp strong black coffee
¾ cup confectioners' sugar
⅔ cup heavy cream or
½ cup chocolate shavings
14½oz can black cherries, pitted

Melt the chocolate and coffee over a basin of hot water. Allow it to cool. Cream the butter and sugar together until light and fluffy. Slowly beat in the egg yolks and the cooled chocolate mixture. Fold in the flour using a metal spoon. Beat the egg whites in a clean, dry bowl until stiff, then fold into the mixture. Line and grease the base of an 8 inch cake pan and bake in the oven for 1½ hours. Allow the cake to cool in the pan for 10 minutes before turning onto a wire rack. Cut the cake horizontally and stick together with the cherry jam. Melt the chocolate and coffee for the frosting in a basin over a saucepan of hot water and remove from the heat. Beat in the confectioners' sugar. Pour the chocolate frosting over the cake, working it over the sides of the cake with a palette knife. When set, decorate with either the whipped cream or chocolate shavings and drained cherries.

Avocado Cheesecake

PREPARATION TIME: 30 minutes plus chilling

Crumb Base
8oz chocolate Graham crackers
6 tblsp butter, melted

Filling
2 ripe avocado pears
½ cup cream cheese
6 tblsp sugar
Juice of ½ a lemon
Grated rind of 1 lemon
2 tsp gelatin powder
2 egg whites
⅔ cup heavy cream, whipped

Decoration
⅔ cup heavy cream, whipped

Crush the crackers into fine crumbs and stir in the melted butter. Use the mixture to line a 7½ inch springform pan. Press it down to line the base and the sides. Chill well.

For the Filling
Peel and stone the avocados and save a few slices for decoration. Put the remainder into a basin and mash well. Mix in the lemon juice and grated rind, cream cheese and sugar. Beat until smooth. Dissolve the gelatin in 2 tblsp of hot water and stir into the mixture. Beat the egg whites in a clean, dry bowl and fold into the mixture with the whipped cream. Pour onto a prepared cracker base and chill thoroughly until set.

To Decorate
Carefully remove the cheesecake from the pan. Fill a nylon pastry bag, fitted with a star tip, with the cream reserved for decoration. Decorate a border of cream round the edge of the cake. Decorate with the avocado slices.
NB: sprinkle the avocado with lemon juice to prevent it from discoloring. This is useful when reserving the slices for decoration.

This page: Chocolate Torte (top) and Apricot Meringue (bottom).

Facing page: Avocado Cheesecake (top), Ginger Ice Cream Gâteau (center left) and Peach and Almond Gâteau (bottom).

Index

MICROWAVE
COOKING

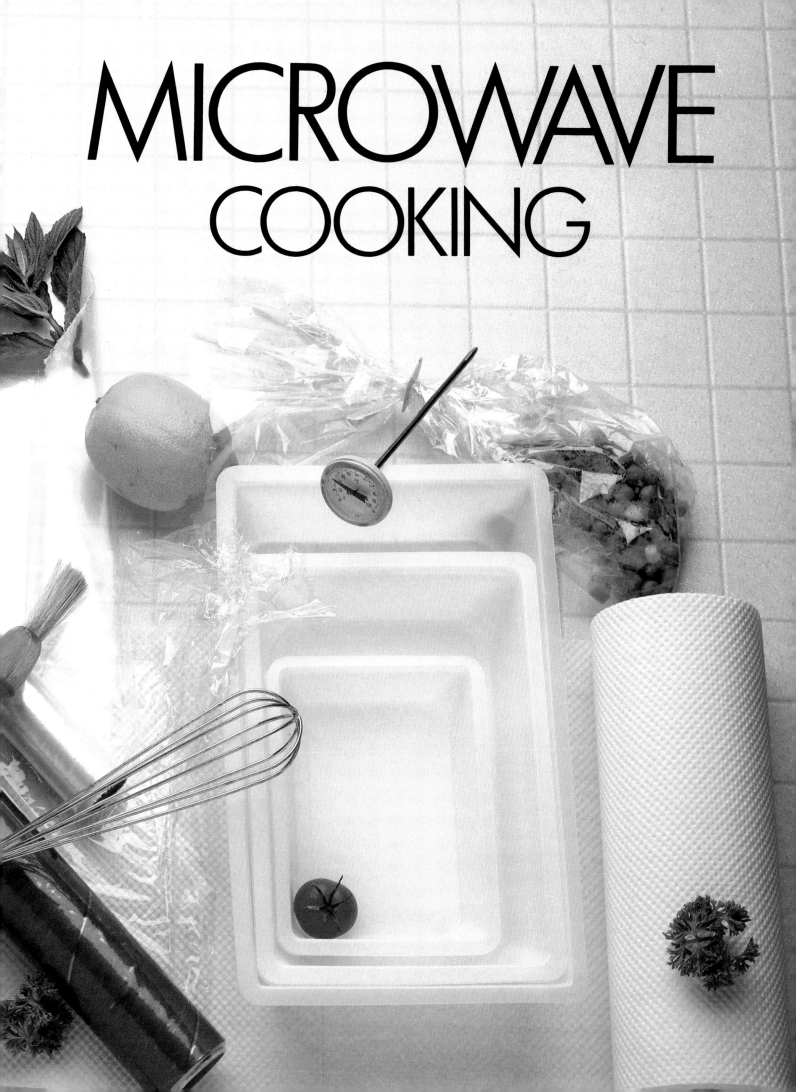

Contents

Introduction

The microwave oven is one of the most exciting kitchen appliances available. It may be used to defrost, reheat, and cook foods, and is therefore more versatile than a conventional oven; in fact it can cope with 75% of your normal cooking needs.

The theory behind microwave cooking must be learned and fully understood before a microwave oven can be used to its full extent. It is a very different method of cooking, which is clean, quick, efficient, labor saving and economical.

The Principles of Microwave Cookery

Electricity is converted into microwave energy inside the oven by the magnetron. The 'microwaves' are transferred into the oven cavity where they bounce off the metal interior and penetrate the outer 1"-1½" of the food. They pass through non-metal containers as though they were not there, and simply cause the molecules in the food to vibrate very fast indeed. The heat that is created passes by conduction through to the center of the food and the food is cooked by friction heat. As a rough guide, cooking times by the microwave method are about ⅓ to ¼ of the conventional times.

Different Types of Microwave Ovens

A microwave oven may be either free standing or built-in. If built-in, it is placed in a housing unit, with a conventional oven situated above or below the microwave.

Convected Hot Air and Microwave Combined

These ovens are now widely available. They are more expensive than an ordinary microwave oven as they combine two units in one. The most common criticism of food cooked in a microwave is that it does not appear 'brown'. This is because there is no dry heat available to caramelise or 'brown' the food. Some people prefer to buy the combination ovens, which use traditional cooking methods and microwave cooking combined. In some models both cooking methods may be used simultaneously, whilst in others the

microwave and the hot air ovens are used one after the other.

Broilers
Some microwave ovens offer a browning broiler.

The Output of the Microwave
The cooking time for each dish/recipe is governed by the electrical output of the microwave oven, and the output also controls the running costs of the appliance. The output is measured in watts. A 700w microwave oven consumes about 1.3k per hour and is, therefore, a most economical method of cooking. Microwave ovens are available in a variety of power ratings and the cooking, re-heating and defrosting times vary according to the output. A 3lb chicken takes 21 minutes in a 700w microwave and 28 minutes in a 500w.

There is no pre-heating before use, and no cooling down after cooking.

Versatility
A microwave oven may be used to defrost, cook and reheat food. It is also well suited to the many different methods of cooking – a microwave oven can poach, shallow fat fry, braise, roast, boil and bake. It will even dry herbs for winter use, and may be used to sterilize jars. The oven and cooking containers stay cool, and microwave ovens are, therefore, perfectly safe for elderly people to use, and for households where there are children.

Cleaning
As the oven cabinet does not get very hot, all that is necessary is a

wipe with a clean dish cloth. Should smells cling e.g. curry or fish, simply squeeze a lemon into 1¾ cups of water and bring to the boil. Wipe the oven with the acidulated water. Food does not bake onto the containers so they are easier to wash up.

Turntables

Manufacturers choose different methods of ensuring that the food cooks evenly. Go by personal recommendation wherever possible. Hidden turntables are popular as they do not restrict the shape of dish used. Some ovens offer stirrer fans and turntables.

Standing Times

Standing, or equalizing, time is simply the time that the food takes to finish cooking. The heat is passed from the outside to the center by conduction. The standing time will vary according to the size and density of the food. Standing time may take place either inside or outside the microwave oven; it is an important part of microwave cookery which must be used. It is just as important after defrosting.

Containers for Use in the Microwave Oven

Special containers are available for microwave cookery, but they are not essential. The heat is localized in the food, and not in the container, so the dish itself does not usually become hot. Some plastics, Pyrex, china, glass, and even paper and basketware, may be used. Be guided by the length of time the food will stand in the microwave, and by the temperature that it will reach.

Plastic wrap is a boon to the microwave owner, as it may be used in place of a lid to cover foods and prevent splashing. Do remember to pierce plastic wrap and roasta bags to allow steam to escape.

Metal – including tin foil – may damage the heart of the microwave oven, the magnetron, and should not be used unless specifically directed by the manufacturer.

Browning Dish or Skillet

A browning dish is a special dish which, when preheated in the microwave oven, will become very hot over the base. Several shapes and sizes are available, either with a lid or without. The dish is used to brown such foods as chops, sausages, hamburgers, bacon, eggs etc. The food must be turned to brown on the other side. The deep browning dishes with lids are also used as casserole dishes. *These containers must not be used in conventional ovens.*

**Herby Roast Chicken (left),
Devilled Pork Chops (below)
and Chicken Breasts in Garlic
Cream Sauce (right).**

Variable Power Chart

MICROWAVE POWER LEVEL	DESCRIPTION AND SUGGESTED USE
10 or Full–High	Microwave energy constant at full wattage. For cooking vegetables, poultry, fish and some sauces, start joints.
8 or Roast	Power on for 13 seconds, auto cut-out for 2 seconds. Repeated continually for time selected, for reheating some joints.
7 and 6 – Medium	Power is on for about 10 seconds, off for 5 seconds, for chops, meat balls, chicken pieces, cakes.
4 and 5 – Simmer	Power is on for 6 seconds, off for 9 seconds, for completing casseroles, defrosting large joints, egg and cheese dishes.
3 – Defrost	Generally for defrosting (allow a standing time afterwards), for melting chocolate, and for delicate sauces.
2 – Very Low	Power is on for 3 seconds, off for 12 seconds. Keep cooked food warm for up to ½ hour. Soften butter and cream cheese from refrigerator.

Please note that this chart is given only as a guide. The variable power dial differs slightly from manufacturer to manufacturer.

Cooked food reheats remarkably quickly without drying out. A chart is provided to give some of the most common foods. Allow a few minutes standing time, after reheating, and before serving.

GENERAL RULES FOR REHEATING.
1. Cover food, allowing steam to escape, unless told specifically not to cover.
2. Stir foods such as casseroles, baked beans, stewed fruits, halfway through reheating.
3. Allow a short standing time – 3-5 minutes before removing covering and serving.
4. Reheat small items, such as sausage rolls or sausages, arranged in ring fashion on outside edge of plate. Reheat on Power 4, or Simmer.

Re-heating Chart

TYPE OF FOOD & WEIGHT	COVER	STIRRING	POWER LEVEL	TIME
1 Plated Meal	Plastic Wrap	–	Full	3-4 minutes
1 Large Macaroni Cheese	Plastic Wrap	Yes, once	Power 7 or Roast	10 minutes
2 Bowls Soup	–	Yes, once	Full	5 minutes
Baked Beans 4ozs	–	–	Power 7 or Roast	2 minutes
Baked Beans 16ozs	Yes	Yes, twice	Power 7 or Roast	7 minutes
Chicken Pieces 8ozs	Yes	–	Full	3-4 minutes
Beef Casserole For 4	Yes	Yes, twice	Full	10-12 minutes
Cooked Vegetables 4ozs	Yes	–	Full	45 seconds
Cooked Vegetables 1lb	Yes	Yes, once	Full	2 minutes
1 Family Meat Pie	No	No	4 or Simmer	7-8 minutes
6 Mince Pies	No	No	4 or Simmer	4 minutes
4 Bread Rolls	Kitchen Roll	No	4 or Simmer	2 minutes
Christmas Pudding 1½lb	Plastic Wrap	No	Power 7 or Roast	3 minutes
Sauce ½ pt	Plastic Wrap	Yes, twice	Full	2 minutes
Fish 12ozs	Plastic Wrap	–	Full	2 minutes

Defrosting Chart

FOOD TO BE DEFROSTED AND WEIGHT	POWER LEVEL	MICROWAVE TIME	STANDING TIME
Ground Meat 1lb	4 or defrost	6 minutes	15 minutes
Chicken 3lb	4 or defrost	30 minutes	30 minutes
Joint of Beef 3lb	4 or defrost	20 minutes	30 minutes
Shepherd's Pie 1lb	4 or defrost	8 minutes	10 minutes
Large Lasagne	6 or simmer	20 minutes	15 minutes
Chops 1lb	4 or defrost	6 minutes	10 minutes
Sausages 1lb	4 or defrost	6 minutes	10 minutes
Cod 8ozs	4 or defrost	6 minutes	10 minutes
Raspberries 8ozs	4 or defrost	4 minutes	15 minutes
1 Victoria Sandwich (2 egg)	4 or defrost	2-3 minutes	15 minutes
Large Sliced Loaf	4 or defrost	7 minutes	10 minutes
Cheese Sauce ½ Pint	4 or defrost	7 minutes	7 minutes
Chicken in Sauce for 4	Simmer	12 minutes	10 minutes
Family Apple Pie	4 or defrost	8 minutes	5 minutes
Family Meat Pie or Quiche Lorraine	4 or defrost	6-7 minutes	10 minutes

The microwave oven makes a perfect partner for your freezer as it enables you to defrost frozen foods in a fraction of the time that it would normally take. Remember to turn or stir the foods, for more even defrosting, and remember that a standing time is very important.

ALTERING TIMINGS

The recipes given in this book can be cooked in any model of variable power microwave oven that is available today. Each of these recipes was tested in a 700W microwave oven. Convert the timings in the following way, if the output of your oven is other than 700W:–

If using an oven of 500W, add 40 seconds for each minute stated in the recipe.

If using an oven of 600W, add 20 seconds for each minute stated in the recipe.

If using an oven of 650W plus, you will only need to allow a slight increase in the overall time.

Stirring and Turning

Stirring and turning are methods used to equalize the heat in the food, i.e. the cooking of the food. The amount of stirring or turning will be governed by the type of food to be cooked, the cooking time and the even distribution of energy in the microwave oven. The recipes in this book give you a guide as to when to stir and turn. Adjust, if necessary, according to your own particular oven. Arrange foods such as baked apples or jacket potatoes in a ring fashion, leaving a space in the center.

Starting Temperature of Food

The starting temperature of food will alter the cooking time. It may be at average room temperature, at cold room temperature or taken from the refrigerator or cold larder. Please note that the timings in this book are calculated for food at average room temperature, unless otherwise stated.

Can You Cook a Complete Meal by Microwave?

The easiest way to use a microwave oven is to employ stage cookery.

The microwave oven cooks according to weight and time, not by temperature, and different types of food require different cooking times. During the standing time of the denser foods, such as joints and jacket potatoes, the less dense items, such as vegetables and sauces, are completely cooked. Foods of similar density may be cooked together, e.g. potatoes and carrots, but remember that the total energy available in the microwave oven must be shared between the foods introduced. If carrots and potatoes are cooked simultaneously, the resulting weight must be checked, and the cooking time calculated accordingly.

Some Things Cannot be Done

Do not try to cook Yorkshire puddings or other batter recipes, boil eggs, deep fat fry, or produce really crisp foods such as roast potatoes, as none of these will be successful. *Pastry* – baking blind, suet crust and some puff pastry recipes work beautifully, but do not try to cook the top of an apple pie.

Soups and Starters

Vegetable Soup

PREPARATION TIME: 10 minutes
MICROWAVE TIME: 21-26 minutes
SERVES: 4 people

2 tblsp butter
1lb young leeks, cleaned and sliced
1 medium onion, peeled and sliced
1½ cups potato, peeled and diced
1 carrot, peeled and diced
Salt and freshly ground black pepper
  to taste
1¼ tblsp chopped fresh parsley
1¾ cups homemade chicken stock
1¼ cups milk

Melt the butter in a 3 quart casserole dish. Microwave on Full Power for 1 minute. Stir in all the prepared vegetables, salt and pepper, parsley and 4 tblsp of the stock. Cover the dish, piercing the plastic wrap if used. Microwave on Full Power for 12 minutes. Stir. Set aside, covered, for 5 minutes. Transfer the vegetables into the food processor bowl or blender goblet; add the milk and blend or process until smooth. Return to the casserole dish and stir in the remaining stock. Microwave on Full Power, covered, for 3-5 minutes. Stir well before serving.

Asparagus with Mayonnaise

PREPARATION TIME: 10 minutes
MICROWAVE TIME: 10-12 minutes
SERVES: 4 people

1lb frozen asparagus spears
1 cup corn oil
2 tblsp butter
1 egg
1 egg yolk
⅔ cup olive oil
Salt and freshly ground black pepper
  to taste
2½ tblsp lemon juice
Chopped fresh parsley

Arrange the asparagus in a roasta bag in a suitable dish. Add 4 tblsp water to the bag, with the butter. Seal the bag with a rubber band.

Pierce the bag once at the base. Microwave on Full Power for 10-12 minutes, turning the bag over once halfway through cooking time. Set aside. Put the egg and egg yolk into the goblet of a food processor or blender with the salt and pepper. Blend on maximum. Add the oil, in a steady trickle, blending to a smooth mayonnaise. Add the lemon juice. Carefully drain the asparagus and arrange on a heated serving dish. Sprinkle with the parsley and serve accompanied by the mayonnaise. Serve immediately.

Soured Cream Prawns

PREPARATION TIME: 5 minutes
MICROWAVE TIME: 7-8 minutes
SERVES: 4 people

4 tblsp butter
2 cups peeled shrimps
Freshly ground black pepper to taste
1 egg yolk
⅔ cup soured cream
Paprika

Butter 4 ramekin dishes and divide the shrimps among them. Season well with black pepper. Combine the egg yolk and soured cream and spoon over the shrimps. Dot with the remaining butter. Microwave all 4 ramekins together on Power 4, or Simmer, for 7-8 minutes. (The dishes should be arranged in a ring, leaving a space in the centre.) Serve immediately sprinkled with paprika.

Corn Starter

PREPARATION TIME: 5 minutes
MICROWAVE TIME: 15 minutes
SERVES: 4 people

4 corn cobs
Sprigs of fresh savory
Salt and freshly ground black pepper
  to taste
A stick of butter

Arrange the cobs in a suitable dish. Add 3 tblsp cold water and a few sprigs of savory. Season. Cover with plastic wrap and pierce.

Microwave on Full Power for 6 minutes. Turn each cob over. Re-cover and microwave on Full Power for 6 minutes. Set aside. Put the butter into a 1¼ pint jug and microwave on Power 4 or Simmer for about 3 minutes or until melted. Transfer the cooked cobs to a serving dish. Pour over the butter and sprinkle with extra chopped savory before serving.

Individual Frozen Pizzas

PREPARATION TIME: 2 minutes
MICROWAVE TIME: 6½-8½ minutes
SERVES: 1 person

Preheat a browning dish, without the lid, for 5-7 minutes. Put 1¼ tblsp of oil and 1 individual pizza onto the dish. Microwave uncovered for approximately 1½ minutes on Full Power. Allow to stand for 1 minute before serving. As many pizzas as will fit onto your dish may be microwaved at the same time; increase the microwave time accordingly. Pizzas may be heated directly from the freezer, without the browning dish, on an ordinary non-metallic plate but the base will not be as crisp.

Chestnut Soup

PREPARATION TIME: 15 minutes
MICROWAVE TIME: 34 minutes
SERVES: 4 people

2 tblsp butter
1 stalk celery, chopped
2 large onions, chopped
3¾ cups homemade chicken stock
  (hot)
8oz unsweetened chestnut puree
Salt and freshly ground black pepper
  to taste
4 rashers bacon, de-rinded

Put the butter, celery and onions into a 3 quart casserole dish; cover with a lid and microwave on Full Power for 4 minutes. Stir. Mix 1¼ cups stock with the chestnut puree, in a 2½ pint mixing bowl. Stir into the onion mixture. Season

with salt and black pepper; cover and microwave on Full Power for 7 minutes. Stir in the remaining stock and microwave on Full Power for 20 minutes. Allow to stand whilst preparing the bacon. Arrange the bacon on a microwave roasting rack, or on 2 sheets of absorbent kitchen paper. Microwave, uncovered, on Full Power, for about 3 minutes. Serve the soup sprinkled with the crumbled crispy bacon.

Tomato Baskets

PREPARATION TIME: 5 minutes
MICROWAVE TIME: 5½-6½ minutes
SERVES: 6 people

6 large firm tomatoes
8oz packet frozen mixed vegetables
4 tblsp butter
Salt and freshly ground black pepper
  to taste
Few sprigs of fresh mint

Cut the top off each tomato and reserve. Using a grapefruit knife or a teaspoon, carefully scoop out the centre flesh. (Use in a soup or sauce recipe). Pierce the pouch of frozen vegetables once and place in a dish. Microwave on Full Power for 3½ minutes, turning the bag once halfway through the cooking time. Set aside. Stand the prepared tomatoes upright on a serving dish, in a ring. Dot with half the butter.

Asparagus with Mayonnaise (top), Vegetable Soup (center) and Soured Cream Prawns (bottom).

Microwave on Full Power for about 2-3 minutes until very hot. Mix the drained, cooked vegetables with the remaining butter and salt and pepper and spoon into the tomato shells. Top with the reserved lids, and garnish with sprigs of mint. Serve immediately.

Quick Flat Bun Pizzas

PREPARATION TIME: 10 minutes

MICROWAVE TIME: 6½-7½ minutes

SERVES: 4 as a main meal, 8 as a snack

4 flat buns
1 medium onion, finely chopped
1¼ tsp tomato paste
1¼ tsp dried oregano
8oz can tomatoes, chopped
1¼ tsp French mustard
Salt and freshly ground black pepper to taste
1¼ cups Cheddar cheese, thinly sliced or grated
Stuffed olives, sliced

Tomato Baskets (right), Quick Flat Bun Pizzas (below) and Individual Frozen Pizza (far right).

Cut the flat buns in half and arrange in a ring on a suitable cooky sheet. Place the onion in a 2½ pint mixing bowl; cover and microwave for 1½ minutes on Full Power. Stir in the tomato paste, oregano, chopped tomatoes and the mustard. Season with salt and pepper. Divide among the flat buns, and cover with the cheese. Decorate with the sliced olives. Microwave on Power 4 for 5-6 minutes, until the cheese has melted. Serve immediately.

Garlic Prawn Starter

PREPARATION TIME: 30 minutes
MICROWAVE TIME: 20 minutes
SERVES: 4 people

1½lb zucchini, cleaned, topped and tailed
Salt and freshly ground black pepper to taste
12oz peeled prawns
1¼ tblsp chopped chives
2½ tblsp dry white wine
2 cloves garlic, crushed
1¼ tblsp lemon juice
4 tblsp butter

Garnish
Unpeeled prawns

Slice the zucchini thinly into a colander, sprinkling them generously with salt. Cover with a plate and weigh down; leave to stand for 20 minutes. Rinse well under cold running water. Drain thoroughly. Arrange the zucchini in

a vegetable dish. Season with salt and pepper. Cover and microwave on Full Power for 12 minutes. Stir. Set aside, covered. Put the peeled prawns, chives, wine, garlic, lemon juice and butter into a 2½ pint casserole dish . Cover with a lid. Microwave on Power 4, or Simmer, for 8 minutes. Stir once halfway through cooking time. Drain the excess liquid from the zucchini. Top with the heated prawns and their juices. Garnish with the unpeeled prawns and serve immediately.

Egg and Tuna Starter

PREPARATION TIME: 10 minutes

MICROWAVE TIME: 10 minutes

SERVES: 4 people

7oz can tuna fish in oil, drained
2 hard boiled eggs, cooked
*   conventionally and chopped*
1 cup milk
2 tblsp butter
Salt and freshly ground black pepper
*   to taste*
¼ cup all purpose flour
1¼ tsp made mustard
½ cup grated Cheddar cheese

Garnish
Stuffed olives, sliced

Flake the tuna fish and divide between 4 ramekin dishes. Top with the egg. Melt the butter in a 1 litre jug for 1 minute on Full Power, or until very hot. Stir in the flour and gradually stir in the milk. Microwave on Full Power for 2 minutes. Beat well with a wire whisk. Microwave on Full Power for 2 minutes. Beat well with a wire whisk. Beat in salt and pepper and cheese. Divide the sauce among the ramekins. Garnish with sliced olives. Microwave all 4 ramekins together for 5 minutes on Power 4 or Simmer. Serve immediately.

Mackerel Pate

PREPARATION TIME: 10 minutes, plus chilling

MICROWAVE TIME: 3 minutes

SERVES: 6 people

1 onion, finely chopped
4 tblsp butter
1½ cups cream cheese
2½ tblsp lemon juice
2½ tblsp chopped fresh parsley

¾lb smoked mackerel fillets
1¼ tsp coarse French mustard
Freshly ground black pepper to taste
4 tblsp soured cream
2½ tsp tomato paste

Garnish
Lemon wedges
Fresh parsley and cucumber slices

Put the onion into a soup bowl. Cover with plastic wrap and pierce. Microwave on Full Power for 1 minute. Set aside. Flake the fish into the food processor or blender goblet, discarding skin and bones. Add the onion. Place the butter in the bowl used for the onion and microwave on Power 4, or Simmer, for 2 minutes. Add to the processor or blender with all the remaining ingredients. Process or blend until smooth. Pour into a dampened loaf pan; smooth the surface. Chill until firm. Turn out onto a serving dish and garnish with wedges of lemon, crimped cucumber slices and parsley.

This page: Corn Starter (top), Garlic Prawn Starter (bottom).

Facing Page: Chestnut Soup (top left), Egg and Tuna Starter (top right) and Mackerel Pate (bottom).

Vegetables

All types of vegetables, both frozen and fresh, microwave exceptionally well. They keep their color, flavor and shape. Follow a few simple rules and use the charts to help you.

Helpful Hints
1. If you want to add salt, dissolve it in a little water beforehand. Adding salt can cause some vegetables to dry; to be on the safe side season with salt after cooking.
2. Always cover vegetables – roasta or freezer bags are very useful, but remember to pierce them.
3. Stir at least once during the cooking time or, if using a bag, turn it over.
4. Add only the amount of water necessary.
5. Cut the vegetables into even sized pieces.
6. Allow a standing time after cooking and before serving.
7. Cook frozen vegetables from frozen, do not defrost them first.

Fresh Vegetable Chart

VEGETABLE AND WEIGHT	ADDITION	MICROWAVE TIME	STANDING TIME
Sliced Green Beans 1lb	4 tblsp water	8 minutes	5 minutes
Broad Beans 1lb	4 tblsp water	8 minutes	5 minutes
Broccoli Spears 8ozs	4 tblsp water	7 minutes	4 minutes
Sliced Carrots 1lb	2½ tblsp water	7-8 minutes	4 minutes
Cauliflower Flowerets 1lb	4 tblsp water	7-8 minutes	5 minutes
Chopped Celery 8ozs		7 minutes	4 minutes
Zucchini 1lb	2 tblsp butter	10 minutes	3 minutes
Leeks 1lb	2½ tblsp water	7-8 minutes	3 minutes
Mushrooms (Sliced) 8ozs	2 tblsp butter	2 minutes	2 minutes
Sliced Summer Squash 1lb	2 tblsp butter	7 minutes	3 minutes
New Potatoes 1lb	2½ tblsp water	7 minutes	4 minutes
Old Potatoes 1lb	4 tblsp water	9 minutes	5 minutes
Sliced Onions 1lb	2½ tblsp water	8-9 minutes	4 minutes
Brussels Sprouts 1lb	2½ tblsp water	6-7 minutes	4 minutes
Diced Swede 1lb	2½ tblsp water	13 minutes	6 minutes

Baked Stuffed Summer Squash

PREPARATION TIME: 20 minutes

MICROWAVE TIME: 22 minutes

SERVES: 4 people

1 medium size summer squash
2 tblsp butter
1 onion, peeled and finely chopped
1lb raw, lean ground beef
2 tblsp all purpose flour
1½ tsp dried basil or oregano
1 egg, beaten
1 beef stock cube, crumbled
Salt and freshly ground black pepper to taste
1¼ tblsp tomato paste

Wipe the summer squash with a damp cloth. Cut both ends off the summer squash and keep on one side. Scoop out the seeds with a spoon and discard. Melt the butter in a 2 quart mixing bowl for 1 minute on Full Power. Stir in the onion. Microwave on Full Power for 1 minute. Stir in all the remaining ingredients. Mix well. Secure one end of the summer squash with wooden cocktail sticks. Stuff the summer squash with the mixture. Secure the remaining end in place with wooden cocktail sticks. Place the summer squash on a meat roasting rack and cover with plastic wrap. Pierce. Microwave on Full Power for about 20 minutes, turning the summer squash once halfway through cooking time. Allow to stand, covered with foil, for 5 minutes before serving. Cut into rings, and serve piping hot.

Brussels Sprouts with Chestnut and Bacon

PREPARATION TIME: 15 minutes

MICROWAVE TIME: 8 minutes

SERVES: 4 people

1lb fresh Brussels sprouts
1¼ tblsp lemon juice
1½ tsp dried mixed herbs
2½ tblsp cold water
Salt and freshly ground black pepper to taste
6 tblsp butter
8oz canned whole chestnuts, drained
3 rashers bacon, de-rinded, cooked and chopped (see Garlic Mushrooms recipe)

Peel the sprouts and make a cross in the base of each one. Put the sprouts into a 2½ pint casserole dish, or into a roasta bag. Add the lemon juice, herbs, water, and salt and pepper. Cover with a lid, or pierce the bag if used. Microwave on Full Power for 5 minutes. Stir or turn once, halfway through cooking time. Set aside for 5 minutes. Put the butter into a ¾ pint jug and microwave on Power 4 or Simmer until melted (about 3 minutes). If using a roasta bag, tip the sprouts into serving dish. Add the chestnuts to the Brussels sprouts, stirring gently. Cover with a lid. Microwave on Full Power for 1 minute. Coat with melted butter, sprinkle with chopped bacon, and serve.

Brussels Sprouts with Chestnut and Bacon (top), Carrot and Parsnip Puree (center) and Baked Stuffed Summer Squash (bottom).

Frozen Vegetable Chart

VEGETABLE AND WEIGHT	AMOUNT OF WATER	COOKING TIME	STANDING TIME
Asparagus 8ozs	2½ tblsp	7 minutes	5 minutes
Broccoli 8ozs	4 tblsp	10 minutes	5 minutes
Brussels Sprouts 8ozs	2½ tblsp	4 minutes	3 minutes
Carrots 8ozs	2½ tblsp	6 minutes	3 minutes
Cauli Flowerets 8ozs	2½ tblsp	3 minutes	2 minutes
Zucchini 8ozs	Nil	4 minutes	2 minutes
Leeks 8ozs	2½ tblsp	6-7 minutes	2 minutes
Mixed Vegetables 8ozs	2½ tblsp	4 minutes	3 minutes
Mushrooms 8ozs	2 tblsp butter and herbs	4 minutes	2 minutes
Baby Onions 8ozs	2 tblsp butter	5 minutes	4 minutes
Peas 8ozs	Nil	4 minutes	2 minutes
Spinach 8ozs	Nil	5 minutes	3 minutes
Corn 8ozs	Nil	4 minutes	2 minutes

Carrot and Parsnip Puree

PREPARATION TIME: 15 minutes
MICROWAVE TIME: 13 minutes
SERVES: 4 people

8oz carrots, peeled
8oz parsnips, peeled
1 level tsp dried basil
4 tblsp well-flavored stock
2½ tblsp heavy cream
Salt and freshly ground black pepper to taste
Pinch grated nutmeg

Garnish
Carrot curls

Dice the peeled carrots and parsnips and place in a roasta bag in a 2½ pint casserole dish. Add 2½ tblsp water and the basil. Snip the bag once at the base. Microwave on Full Power for 8 minutes, turning the bag over once halfway through cooking time. Set aside for 5 minutes. Empty the contents of the roasta bag into the goblet of a food processor or blender. Add the stock and process until smooth. Add cream, salt and pepper, and nutmeg. Process just to blend. Return to the casserole dish and cover with a lid. Microwave on Power 4, or Simmer, for 5 minutes. Garnish with carrot curls and serve.

Zucchini Choice

PREPARATION TIME: 40-45 minutes
COOKING TIME: 10 minutes
SERVES: 4 people

1lb young zucchini, topped, tailed and washed
Salt and freshly ground black pepper to taste
1lb large firm tomatoes, skinned and sliced
1 tsp dried tarragon
1 clove garlic, crushed
2 tblsp butter

Arrange the sliced zucchini in a colander. Sprinkle generously with salt and leave to stand for 30 minutes. (This draws out the bitter juices.) Rinse well under cold running water. Drain. Layer the zucchini and tomatoes in a 2½ pint casserole dish, starting and finishing with zucchini. Season each layer with salt, pepper, tarragon and garlic. Dot the top with small knobs of butter. Cover tightly with a lid. Microwave on Full Power for 10 minutes. Allow to stand for 3 minutes before serving.

Cauliflower Cheese

PREPARATION TIME: 10 minutes
MICROWAVE TIME: 12 minutes
SERVES: 4 people

1 cauliflower, trimmed and divided into flowerets
1½ tblsp cornstarch
1¼ cups milk
1¼ tsp made mustard
Salt and freshly ground black pepper to taste
¾ cup grated Cheddar cheese
2 tblsp butter
½ red pepper, de-seeded and chopped

Arrange the flowerets of cauliflower in a roasta bag. Add 3 tblsp water. Pierce the bag, and place in a 2½ pint casserole dish. Microwave on Full Power for 7-8 minutes, turning the bag over once halfway through cooking time. Set aside, covered. Cream the cornstarch with a little of the milk to a smooth paste. Stir in the mustard and salt and pepper to taste. Heat the remaining milk in a 2¼ pint jug for 2 minutes on Full Power. Pour the heated milk onto the cornstarch mixture, stirring continuously. Return to the jug and microwave on Full Power for 2 minutes or until boiling. Beat in the cheese and butter, and any liquid from the cauliflower. Transfer cauliflower flowerets to a warmed serving dish. Pour the sauce over evenly. Sprinkle with the red pepper and serve immediately. The red pepper may be heated in a cup in the microwave for 1 minute on Full Power, if liked.

Ratatouille

PREPARATION TIME: 40 minutes
MICROWAVE TIME: 22-24 minutes
SERVES: 4 people

½lb zucchini
1lb eggplant
Salt and freshly ground black pepper to taste
4 tblsp butter
1 medium onion, peeled and sliced
1 large clove garlic, crushed
A little oil
1 red pepper, de-seeded and sliced
15oz can tomatoes, chopped
½ tsp dried oregano
½ cup crumbled Danish Blue cheese

Wash the zucchini and eggplant. Cut off the ends and discard. Slice into ¼ inch slices and layer with a generous sprinkling of salt in a colander. Top with a plate and a weight and set aside to drain for 15 minutes. Rinse well under cold running water and drain. Put the butter in a 1¼ pint measuring jug. Microwave on Full Power for 1-2 minutes until melted. Stir in the onion and garlic. Grease the sides and base of a 2-3 quart casserole or souffle dish with oil. Layer the eggplant, zucchini and red pepper

Ratatouille (top), Zucchini Choice (center left) and Cauliflower Cheese (bottom).

in the dish with the tomatoes, oregano, onion and garlic. Season each layer with salt and pepper. Cover with a lid. Microwave on Full Power for 20-22 minutes, removing the lid for the last 8 minutes. Turn the dish ¼ turn twice during the cooking time, if necessary. Top with the crumbled cheese and serve immediately.

Buttery Mashed Potato

PREPARATION TIME: 10 minutes
MICROWAVE TIME: 17 minutes
SERVES: 4-5 people

2lb old potatoes, peeled
4 tblsp milk
4 tblsp butter
Salt and freshly ground black pepper
  to taste
2½ tblsp light cream
Chopped fresh parsley

Cut the potatoes into small, even sized pieces and put into a roasta bag with the milk and butter. Season. Secure the bag with an elastic band and stand in a 2 quart mixing bowl. Pierce the bag once at the base. Microwave on Full Power for 17 minutes, turning the bag over once halfway through the cooking time. Allow to stand for 5 minutes. Turn the potatoes and their liquid into the bowl and mash with a fork. Beat with a wooden spoon adding the cream. Turn into a serving dish. Fork up and sprinkle with the parsley. Serve.

Potatoes Gratinee

PREPARATION TIME: 20 minutes
MICROWAVE TIME: 26 minutes
SERVES: 4 people

1½lb old white potatoes, peeled and
  thinly sliced
1¼ cups pouring white sauce
½ cup grated cheese
4 tblsp milk
Salt and freshly ground black pepper
  to taste
2 tblsp butter
1 Recipe quantity of Crispy Topping
  (see recipe)

Soak the potato slices in cold water for a few minutes. Heat the sauce in a large jug for 1 minute on Full Power. Beat in the grated cheese, milk, and salt and pepper to taste. Grease a shallow dish with the butter. Arrange the drained potato slices, overlapping slightly, in the

Spinach Fiesta (top), Buttery Mashed Potato (far left) and Potatoes Gratinee (left).

base of the dish. Pour the sauce evenly over the top. Cover with plastic wrap and pierce. Microwave on Power 7, or Roast, for 25 minutes. Stir once, gently, halfway through cooking time. Serve after 5 minutes standing time, sprinkled with the crispy topping.

Stuffed Baked Peppers

PREPARATION TIME: 10 minutes

MICROWAVE TIME: 14½-15½ minutes

SERVES: 4 people

4 large even-sized peppers, about 8oz each
3 tblsp water
¾lb cooked chicken, pork or turkey
3 tblsp drained, canned corn kernels
5 tblsp soured cream
¾ cup chopped mushrooms
Salt and freshly ground black pepper to taste

Cut the tops off the peppers and reserve. Scoop out the seeds and discard them. Stand the peppers upright in an oblong or round casserole dish. Add the water; cover and microwave on Full Power for 3½ minutes. Set aside. Combine all the remaining ingredients to make the filling and mix well. Drain the water from the peppers and divide the filling among them. Replace the tops. Cover with plastic wrap and pierce. Microwave on Full Power for 11-12 minutes. Stand for 3 minutes before serving.

Garlic Mushrooms

PREPARATION TIME: 20 minutes

MICROWAVE TIME: 12½-14½ minutes

SERVES: 4 people

6 tblsp butter
2 cloves garlic, crushed
¾lb mushrooms, stalks removed
4 rashers bacon, de-rinded
1 cup cream cheese
Salt and freshly ground black pepper to taste
1½ tblsp natural yogurt or soured cream
¾ tsp dried parsley

Garnish
Chopped fresh parsley

Place the butter and garlic into a small bowl and microwave on Power 4, or Simmer, for 3 minutes, or until melted. Using a pastry brush, brush the mushrooms all over, inside and out, with the melted butter. Arrange on a dinner plate, or cooky sheet, in a circular fashion, leaving a space in the centre. Arrange the bacon on 2 sheets of absorbent kitchen paper, on a dinner plate, fat to outside. Cover with 1 piece absorbent kitchen paper. Microwave the bacon on Full Power for 2½-3 minutes. Set aside. Transfer the cream cheese to a 2½ pint mixing bowl. Microwave, uncovered, on Defrost for 2 minutes. Stir in salt and pepper to taste, yogurt, dried parsley and chopped bacon. Soften the chopped onion in a cup for 45 seconds on Full Power. Stir into the cream cheese mixture. Fill the mushrooms with the cheese mixture. Microwave, uncovered on Roast, or Power 7, for 4-6 minutes. Serve immediately garnished with chopped parsley, on croutons of fried bread.

Spinach Fiesta

PREPARATION TIME: 20 minutes

MICROWAVE TIME: 22 minutes

SERVES: 4 people

1¾ cups long grain rice
Salt and freshly ground black pepper to taste
3 frozen cod steaks
½lb frozen spinach
2 tblsp butter
3 tblsp milk
3 tblsp canned tuna fish, drained
½ cup Cheddar cheese, cubed
Chopped fresh parsley

Put the rice into a 2-3 quart mixing bowl. Pour on 1¼ pints boiling water. Add ¾ tsp salt. Cover lightly with plastic wrap and pierce once in the centre. Microwave on Full Power for 12 minutes. Set aside. Snip the fish packets open and microwave all 3 together, arranged on a dinner plate in a ring, for 6 minutes on Defrost. Turn each packet over, halfway through cooking. Set aside. Pierce the . packet of spinach and place in a vegetable dish. Microwave on Full Power for 6 minutes. Set aside. Slip the cod steaks out of their packets and arrange on a pie plate in a ring. Dot with butter. Season and spoon over the milk. Cover with plastic

wrap and pierce. Microwave on Full Power for 4 minutes. Drain the spinach. Chop and fork into the cooked rice. Add the tuna fish to the rice with the cheese. Drain the cooked cod and flake into the rice. Pile onto a warmed dish and serve, sprinkled with plenty of chopped parsley.

JACKET POTATOES WITH FILLINGS

Plain Jacket Potatoes

PREPARATION TIME: 15-20 minutes

MICROWAVE TIME: 15 minutes

SERVES: 4 people

4 x 7oz potatoes, scrubbed clean

Prick the potatoes with a fork and arrange in a ring on a dinner plate. Microwave uncovered, on Full Power, for 15 minutes. Wrap in a clean tea towel and set aside for 10-15 minutes. (The potatoes will continue to cook). Meanwhile prepare one of the fillings (all fillings serve 4 people).

Cottage Cheese with Prawns and Chives

Instead of pricking the potatoes, make a cross in the top of each one before baking.
2 cups cottage cheese
2 tblsp chopped chives
1 cup peeled prawns
2 tblsp soured cream
1½ tsp tomato paste
Sliced cucumber and whole prawns to garnish

Blend all the ingredients together, apart from the cucumber and prawns. Using a cloth, carefully push up each hot potato from the base, to form a water lily. Divide the filling between the potatoes. Garnish with the cucumber and whole prawns before serving.

Pilchards with Corn

3 tblsp natural yogurt or mayonnaise
Salt and freshly ground black pepper to taste
12oz pilchards in tomato sauce
4 tblsp drained canned corn kernels
4 scallions, chopped

Cut the potatoes in half and carefully scoop out the flesh, leaving the skin intact. Put the potato flesh into a 2 quart mixing bowl. Mash well with a fork, adding the yogurt or mayonnaise and salt and pepper to taste. Open each pilchard and remove the backbone. Flake the pilchards into the potato; mix well, adding the corn and chopped scallions. Pile the mixture back into the potato shells. Arrange in a serving dish. Cover with plastic wrap. Microwave on Full Power for 4 minutes.

Baked Beans with Edam Cheese

16oz can baked beans in tomato sauce
2 cups Edam cheese, cubed
Salt and freshly ground black pepper to taste

Garnish
Watercress

Empty the beans into a 2 pint casserole dish. Add the cheese and salt and pepper to taste. Cover with a lid and microwave on Power 7, or Roast, for 2½ minutes. Stir gently. Microwave on Power 7, or Roast, for 2½ minutes. Halve the potatoes after their standing time. Spoon the beans and cheese onto the potatoes. Garnish with watercress and serve.

Stuffed Baked Peppers (top), Jacket Potatoes with Fillings (center) and Garlic Mushrooms (bottom).

Supper Dishes

Shish Kebabs

PREPARATION TIME: 10 minutes
MICROWAVE TIME: 8 minutes
SERVES: 3-4 people

12oz raw ground lamb
1 onion, finely chopped
2½ tsp lemon juice
3 tsp hot curry powder
1½ tblsp soured cream
½ egg, beaten
¼ cup all purpose flour
3 tblsp finely chopped fresh parsley
½ tsp salt
2 tblsp tomato sauce

Mix all the ingredients together. Form the mixture into small balls. Arrange the meatballs on a microwave roasting rack in a ring. Microwave, uncovered, on Power 7, or Roast, for 8 minutes. Serve hot with yogurt sauce.

Yogurt Sauce

PREPARATION TIME: 5 minutes
SERVES: 4 people

⅔ cup natural yogurt
1½ tsp granular mustard
3 tsp tomato paste
1½ tsp concentrated mint sauce
1½ tsp lemon juice
1½ tsp superfine sugar
2½ tblsp soured cream

Mix all the ingredients together until well blended. Refrigerate until required. Serve with Shish Kebabs.

Pasta Shells with Cheese and Bacon

PREPARATION TIME: 15 minutes
MICROWAVE TIME: 24 minutes
SERVES: 4 people

6oz dried pasta shapes
½ tsp salt
1¼ tblsp oil
8oz packet frozen mixed vegetables
1¼ tsp cornstarch
1¼ cups milk
1¼ tsp made mustard

Salt and freshly ground black pepper to taste
¾ cup grated mild hard cheese
2 bacon chops
1 Recipe Crispy Topping (see recipe)

Place the pasta in a 3-4 quart mixing bowl. Add the salt and the oil. Pour on 2 quarts boiling water. Cover tightly with plastic wrap and pierce once in the centre. Microwave on Full Power for 8 minutes. Set aside, covered. Microwave the pierced packet of vegetables in a suitable dish, for 4 minutes on Full Power, turning the packet over once halfway through the cooking time. Blend the cornstarch with 1½ tblsp milk until smooth. Put the remaining milk into a 2¼ pint jug and microwave on Full Power for 3 minutes. Beat the blended cornstarch into the hot milk together with the mustard and salt and pepper to taste. Microwave on Full Power for 2 minutes. Beat well adding the cheese. Microwave the bacon chops on 2 sheets of absorbent kitchen paper (with the fat facing outwards). Microwave on Roast for 4 minutes. To assemble the dish: drain the pasta and pile onto a serving dish; drain the vegetables and add to the pasta; chop the bacon and mix into the pasta and vegetables. Pour the cheese sauce evenly over the top and top with crispy crumbs. Microwave on Power 5, or Roast, for 3 minutes. Serve immediately.

Fish Fingers

PREPARATION TIME: 5 minutes
MICROWAVE TIME: 14 minutes
SERVES: 3-4 people

2½ tblsp cooking oil
8 frozen cod fish fingers

Preheat a large browning dish, without a lid, for 7 minutes, on Full Power. Put the oil into the heated dish. Microwave on Full Power for 1 minute. Carefully press the fish fingers into the oil. Microwave, uncovered, on Full Power for 3

minutes. Turn each fish finger over and microwave on Full Power for 3-4 minutes. Drain on absorbent kitchen paper and serve immediately (brown side uppermost).

Crispy Topping

PREPARATION TIME: 10 minutes
MICROWAVE TIME: 8 minutes

5 tblsp butter
1 cup fresh brown breadcrumbs
½ cup oatmeal

Put the butter into a 2 quart mixing bowl and microwave on Full Power for 1½ minutes. Stir in the breadcrumbs and oatmeal. Microwave on Full Power for 2½ minutes. Stir with a fork. Microwave on Full Power for 2 minutes. Stir. Microwave on Full Power for 2 minutes. Allow to stand for 5 minutes before using. Alternatively, the topping may be cooled and stored in an air tight container. Serve as a crispy finish for sweet and savory dishes.

Kidney and Sausage Supper Dish

PREPARATION TIME: 20 minutes
MICROWAVE TIME: 18 minutes
SERVES: 4 people

1lb chipolata sausages
2½ tblsp oil
8oz lambs' kidneys, skinned, halved and cored
3 tblsp tomato sauce
1½ tblsp Worcestershire sauce
Salt and freshly ground black pepper to taste
4 large, ripe tomatoes, skinned and chopped
8oz frozen peas
2½ tsp cornstarch

Preheat the deep browning dish, without the lid, for 4-7 minutes according to size. Prick the sausages and cut into 1 inch pieces. Add the oil and the pieces of sausage to the preheated dish, pressing the sausage against the sides of the browning dish. Microwave on Full

Power for 2 minutes. Stir in the kidneys, tomato sauce and Worcestershire sauce. Cover with the lid and microwave on Power 7, or on Roast, for 5 minutes. Season with salt and pepper and stir in the tomatoes and peas. Mix the cornstarch to a smooth paste with 5 tblsp water and stir in. Microwave on Full Power for 2 minutes. Stir. Microwave on Full Power for a further 2 minutes. Stir and serve immediately.

Cowboy Supper

PREPARATION TIME: 15 minutes
MICROWAVE TIME: 13 minutes
SERVES: 4 people

16oz can baked beans
7oz can corned beef, chilled
Freshly ground black pepper to taste
½ beef stock cube, crumbled
½ cup Cheddar cheese, cubed
1 French loaf

Empty the baked beans into a 2 quart casserole dish. Cover with a lid. Microwave on Power 6 for 5 minutes. Gently stir in the corned beef and season with pepper. Add the stock cube. Cover and microwave on Power 6 for 5 minutes. Add the cheese just before serving.
To warm the bread, cut the bread into pieces and arrange in a bread basket, between absorbent paper napkins. Microwave on Power 4, or Simmer, for 3 minutes. Serve immediately.

Shish Kebabs with Yogurt Sauce (top), Pasta Shells with Cheese and Bacon (center right) and Kidney and Sausage Supper Dish (bottom).

Poached Eggs on Cheese on Toast

PREPARATION TIME: 10 minutes

MICROWAVE TIME: about 10 minutes

SERVES: 4 people

4 eggs
Salt and freshly ground black pepper to taste
Softened butter
4 slices toast
1¼ cups grated cheese
Chopped chives

Put 1½ tblsp cold water into each of the 4 hollows of a microwave muffin pan or into 4 ramekin dishes. If using ramekins, arrange them in a ring on a dinner plate.

Microwave on Full Power until the water boils. Carefully crack 1 egg into each hollow or dish. Prick each yolk once with a cocktail stick. Season with salt and pepper. Microwave on Simmer for about 4 minutes until the whites are just set. Leave aside. Butter the toast and top with the grated cheese. Microwave on Power 5, or Simmer, for about 4 minutes until melted. Slide the toasted cheese onto a serving dish and place an egg on top of each one. Sprinkle with chopped chives and serve immediately.

Cod and Prawn Supper Dish

PREPARATION TIME: 15 minutes

MICROWAVE TIME: 15½ minutes

SERVES: 4 people

4 x 3oz frozen cod steaks, thawed
4 tblsp butter
Salt and freshly ground black pepper to taste
¼ cup flour
1¼ cups milk
¾ cup grated Cheddar cheese
1 cup peeled prawns
1 Recipe Crispy Topping (see recipe)

Garnish
Tomato wedges
Parsley

Arrange the fish steaks in a ring on a dinner plate. Divide half the butter into 4; put a small knob onto each fish steak. Season with salt and pepper and cover with plastic wrap. Microwave on Full Power for 3½ minutes. Set aside. Microwave the remaining butter in a 2¼ pint jug for 1 minute on Full Power. Stir in the flour and then gradually stir in the milk; season to taste. Microwave on Full Power for 2 minutes. Beat well. Microwave on Full Power for a further 2 minutes. Beat in the cheese. Cut the fish into bite-size pieces and arrange in a suitable dish with the prawns. Pour the sauce evenly over the fish. Sprinkle with the crispy crumbs. Microwave on Power 4 for 7 minutes. Serve immediately, garnished with tomato and parsley.

Chicken with Ham

PREPARATION TIME: 15 minutes

MICROWAVE TIME: 13 minutes

SERVES: 4 people

3 cups cooked chicken, roughly chopped
1 cup cooked ham, chopped
5 tblsp drained canned corn kernels with peppers
2 tblsp butter
4 tblsp flour
Salt and freshly ground black pepper to taste
1¼ cups well flavored chicken stock
¾ cup grated cheese
4 tblsp light cream

Garnish
Sliced tomato and parsley

Arrange the chicken, ham and corn in a suitable dish. Melt the butter in a large jug for about 1 minute on Full Power. Stir in the flour and salt and pepper to taste. Stir in a little of the stock, blending it in well. Add the remaining stock. Microwave on Full Power for 2 minutes. Beat well with a wire whisk. Microwave on Full Power for 2 minutes. Beat well. Beat in the cheese and the cream. Pour the sauce evenly over the meat. Microwave on Power 4, or Simmer, for about 8 minutes. Serve immediately, garnished with the tomato and parsley.

Sweet and Sour Pork

PREPARATION TIME: 25 minutes

MICROWAVE TIME: 29 minutes

SERVES: 4 people

1¼ tblsp oil
½ red pepper, de-seeded and chopped
1 carrot, peeled and cut into strips
1 large onion, sliced
4 inch cucumber, seeded and cut into strips
1 stalk celery, chopped
1lb pork fillet, cubed
14oz can pineapple pieces in natural juice
2½ tblsp soya sauce

Fish Fingers (top right), Poached Eggs on Cheese on Toast (far left) and Chicken with Ham (left).

2½ tsp tomato paste
1¼ tblsp wine vinegar
Salt and freshly ground black pepper
   to taste
2½ tsp cornstarch

Preheat the deep browning dish
without the lid for 4-7 minutes

according to size on Full Power. Put
the oil, pepper, carrot, onion,
cucumber and celery into the dish.
Stir well. Cover and Microwave on
Full Power for 4 minutes. Stir in all
remaining ingredients, apart from
the cornstarch. Cover and
microwave on Full Power for 3

minutes and then on Power 4, or
Simmer, for 20 minutes. Cream the
cornstarch with a little water and
stir into the pork mixture.
Microwave on Full Power for 2
minutes. Stir and then serve
immediately on a bed of rice.

**Cowboy Supper (top) and
Sweet and Sour Pork (bottom).**

Fish Dishes

Plaice with Lemon

PREPARATION TIME: 12-15 minutes

MICROWAVE TIME: 9 minutes

SERVES: 4 people

4 plaice fillets (about 3½oz each), skinned
Salt and freshly ground black pepper to taste
Juice of ½ a lemon
3 tblsp milk
1 cup mushrooms, sliced
2 tblsp butter
½ cup soured cream

Lay the plaice fillets out flat; season with salt and pepper and sprinkle with lemon juice. Roll up and secure with wooden cocktail sticks. Arrange the fillets close together in a dish and spoon over the milk; cover and microwave on Full Power for 5 minutes. Set aside. Put the mushrooms and butter into a small dish. Cover and microwave on Full Power for 2 minutes. Add the soured cream and stir in the juices from the fish. Microwave on Full Power for 2 minutes. Arrange the fish on a warmed serving dish. Pour over the sauce and serve immediately.

Curried Prawns with Chicken

PREPARATION TIME: 15 minutes

MICROWAVE TIME: about 22 minutes

SERVES: 4 people

4 tblsp butter
1 medium onion, finely chopped
5 tsp flour
5 tsp mild curry powder
2½ tsp tomato paste
3¾ cups boiling chicken stock
1¼ tblsp apple chutney
1 banana, thinly sliced
¼ cup raisins
Salt and freshly ground black pepper to taste
8oz peeled prawns
8oz cooked chicken, chopped
2½ tblsp lemon juice

Place the butter in a 3 quart

casserole dish. Microwave on Full Power for 1-2 minutes. Stir in the onion. Microwave on Full Power for 1½ minutes. Stir in the flour and curry powder. Microwave on Full Power for 2 minutes. Stir in the tomato paste and gradually add the stock. Add the apple chutney, banana, raisins and salt and pepper to taste. Cover and microwave on Full Power for 12 minutes. Stir in the peeled prawns, chicken and lemon juice. Microwave on Full Power for 3-4 minutes.

Curried Prawns with Chicken (top left), Scampi Italienne (top right) and Plaice with Lemon (bottom).

Scampi Italienne

PREPARATION TIME: 10 minutes	
MICROWAVE TIME: 10 minutes	
SERVES: 4 people	

½ red pepper, de-seeded and sliced
½ green pepper, de-seeded and sliced
4 tblsp butter
1 small onion, finely chopped
1 clove garlic, crushed
⅔ cup dry white wine
1½ tblsp lemon juice
Salt and freshly ground black pepper
  to taste
1lb frozen shelled scampi, thawed

Garnish
Lemon butterflies
Savory

Put the red and green peppers, butter, onion and the garlic into a 2 quart casserole dish. Cover with the lid. Microwave on Full Power for 3 minutes. Stir in the white wine, lemon juice, salt and pepper to taste and the scampi. Cover and microwave on Full Power for 6-7 minutes, stirring once halfway through. Serve immediately, garnished with lemon butterflies and savory.

Special Fish Pie

PREPARATION TIME: 15 minutes	
MICROWAVE TIME: 15 minutes	
SERVES: 4 people	

1lb young leeks, washed and cut into
  1½ inch lengths
4 large, firm tomatoes, skinned and
  sliced
3 tsp mixed dried herbs
2 tblsp butter
Salt and freshly ground black pepper
  to taste
¾lb cod, skinned and filleted
3 tblsp frozen corn kernels, thawed
½ cup grated Cheddar cheese
1½ tblsp tomato sauce
1lb potatoes, peeled, cooked and
  mashed

Arrange the leeks and tomatoes in the base of a casserole dish; sprinkle with half the herbs. Dot the butter over the surface and season well with salt and pepper. Cover and microwave on Full Power for 5 minutes. Cut the fish into 1 inch pieces. Arrange evenly over the vegetables and season once again. Cover and microwave on Full Power for 7 minutes. Drain off excess liquid and add the corn. Add the cheese, tomato sauce and remaining herbs to the potato; beat well. Pile or pipe the potato on top of the fish and vegetables. Microwave, uncovered, on Full Power for about 3 minutes. Brown under a pre-heated broiler, if desired, and serve immediately.

Mackerel with Apple Sauce

PREPARATION TIME: 30 minutes	
MICROWAVE TIME: 15 minutes	
SERVES: 4 people	

4 fresh mackerel, heads and fins
  removed, and filleted (approx. 6oz
  per fish)
1 cup fresh brown breadcrumbs
1 eating apple, peeled, cored and
  chopped
½ cup shredded suet
1½ tsp lemon juice
3 tsp finely chopped fresh parsley
1 onion, peeled and finely chopped
Salt and freshly ground black pepper
  to taste
1 egg, beaten
3 tblsp apple juice

Sauce
1½lb cooking and eating apples
  (mixed), peeled, cored and sliced
2½ tsp lemon juice
3 tsp superfine sugar
1 tblsp butter

Put the breadcrumbs, apple, suet, lemon juice, parsley and onion into a mixing bowl. Season to taste with salt and pepper. Mix with the beaten egg to bind. Divide the stuffing among the fish, pressing it well into each cavity. Make an incision with a sharp knife in the thickest side of each fish. Arrange the fish, nose to tail, in a shallow dish. Pour over the apple juice. Cover tightly with plastic wrap and pierce. Microwave on Full Power for 8 minutes. Stand on one side while preparing the sauce. Put the apples into a 2 quart mixing bowl with the lemon juice and sugar. Cover. Microwave on Full Power for 6-7 minutes. Allow to stand for 3 minutes. Beat together with the butter and the juices from the cooked fish. Serve immediately with the fish.

Trout with Almonds

PREPARATION TIME: 10 minutes	
MICROWAVE TIME: about 19 minutes	
SERVES: 4 people	

4 rainbow trout, cleaned and gutted
  (approx 8oz per fish)
5 tblsp butter
1 clove garlic, crushed
Salt and freshly ground black pepper
  to taste
1 cup heavy cream
½ cup flaked almonds

Garnish
Fresh parsley

Use a very small amount of foil to mask the tail of each fish. Make 2 incisions in the thick side of each fish. Put 4 tblsp of the butter into a suitable shallow dish and microwave on Full Power for 1½ minutes. Stir the garlic and salt and pepper into the butter. Arrange the fish, nose to tail, in the flavored butter. Cover with plastic wrap and pierce. Microwave on Full Power for 8 minutes. Turn each fish over once during cooking. Stand aside, covered. Put the almonds and the remaining butter into a soup bowl. Microwave on Full Power for 2 minutes. Stir. Microwave on Full Power for a further 2 minutes. Pour the cream over the fish, and microwave on Power 4 or, Simmer, for 5 minutes. Serve immediately sprinkled with the toasted nuts and garnished with parsley.

Devilled Herrings

PREPARATION TIME: 15-20 minutes	
MICROWAVE TIME: 6-7 minutes	
SERVES: 4 people	

2½ tblsp dry mustard
1¼ tblsp brown sugar
1¼ tblsp malt vinegar
4 fresh herrings, about 8oz each
½ cup white wine
1 medium onion, finely chopped
1½ tblsp finely chopped fresh parsley
Salt and freshly ground black pepper
  to taste
2 tblsp butter

Blend together the mustard, sugar and vinegar. Cut the heads and the tails off the fish and remove the back-bones; flatten each fish. Spread the mustard mixture inside the herrings and roll up. Secure with cocktail sticks. Arrange the fish in a suitable dish. Add the wine, parsley and salt and pepper to taste. Dot with butter. Cover tightly with plastic wrap or a lid. Pierce if using plastic wrap. Microwave on Full Power for 6-7 minutes. Stand for 3 minutes before serving.

Smoked Haddock with Scrambled Eggs

PREPARATION TIME: 5-10 minutes	
MICROWAVE TIME: 11 minutes	
SERVES: 3-4 people	

1lb smoked haddock fillet
Salt and freshly ground black pepper
  to taste
⅔ cup milk
4 tblsp butter
4 eggs
1½ tblsp finely chopped fresh parsley

Arrange the fish in a shallow container. Season with salt and pepper and add 2½ tblsp of the milk. Dot the fish with half the butter. Cover with plastic wrap and pierce. Microwave on Full Power for 7 minutes. Set aside, covered. Make the scrambled egg: beat the eggs with the remaining milk in a 2 quart mixing bowl; season to taste and add the remaining butter. Microwave on Full Power for 2 minutes; beat well, using a wire whisk. Microwave on Full Power for 2 minutes until light and fluffy. Carefully arrange the fish on a serving dish. Spoon the scrambled eggs either side of the fish. Sprinkle with the chopped parsley and serve immediately.

Special Fish Pie (top), Mackerel with Apple Sauce (center) and Trout with Almonds (bottom).

Prawns Creole

PREPARATION TIME: 15 minutes
MICROWAVE TIME: 18 minutes
SERVES: 4 people

1¾ cups long grain rice
2½ cups boiling chicken stock
2 medium size onions, chopped
½ red pepper, de-seeded and chopped
½ green pepper, de-seeded and chopped

8oz peeled prawns
15oz can pineapple segments in natural juice, drained
¼ cup seedless raisins
Salt and freshly ground black pepper to taste

Put the rice into a 2-3 quart mixing bowl. Pour on the boiling stock. Cover tightly with plastic wrap and pierce once in the centre. Microwave on Full Power for 12 minutes. Set aside, covered with a clean tea towel. Put the onion and red and green pepper into a 2 pint mixing bowl. Cover with plastic wrap and pierce. Microwave on Full Power for 3 minutes. Stir. Fork up the rice after 10 minutes standing time, and add the onions, peppers, prawns, pineapple, raisins and salt and pepper. Cover with plastic wrap and pierce. Microwave on Full Power for 3 minutes to reheat. Serve immediately.

Smoked Haddock with
Scrambled Eggs (below left),
Prawns Creole (below) and
Devilled Herrings (below
right).

Meat Dishes

Sausagemeat Stuffing

PREPARATION TIME: 15 minutes

MICROWAVE TIME: 10 minutes

SERVES: 4 people

1lb pork sausagemeat
¾ cup parsley and thyme mixed
1¼ tblsp tomato sauce
1¼ tsp made mustard
1 small onion, finely chopped
Salt and freshly ground black pepper
    to taste
⅔ cup boiling water

Put the sausagemeat into a 2 quart mixing bowl. Add all the remaining ingredients. Leave to stand for 3 minutes. Knead toether until well mixed. Using dampened hands, form the sausagemeat mixture into 20 balls. Arrange on a large roasting rack, or in a ring on a large circular dish, on 2 sheets of absorbent kitchen paper. Microwave on Power 7, or Roast, for 10 minutes.

Savory Ground Meat with Dumplings

PREPARATION TIME: 20 minutes

MICROWAVE TIME: 23 minutes

SERVES: 4 people

2 rashers bacon, de-rinded and
    chopped
1 medium onion, chopped
½ green pepper, de-seeded and
    chopped
1½lb raw ground beef or pork
1 beef stock cube, crumbled
1 tsp mixed dried herbs
⅔ cup water
1½ tsp chive mustard
Salt and freshly ground black pepper
    to taste
16oz can navy beans (or white
    kidney beans)

Dumplings
1 cup all purpose flour
1½ tsp baking powder
½ cup suet
½ tsp dried tarragon

Put the bacon, onion and pepper into a soup bowl. Cover with plastic wrap and pierce. Microwave on Full Power for 2 minutes. Put the ground meat into a 2 quart casserole dish. Microwave on Full Power for 4 minutes. Break down with a fork and stir in the onion mixture, stock cube, herbs, water and mustard. Season well with salt and pepper. Microwave on Power 6, or Roast, for 12 minutes. Stir in the beans. Set aside. To prepare the dumplings: mix together the flour, baking powder, suet and tarragon. Bind with sufficient cold water to make an elastic dough. Divide into 6 dumplings and arrange on top of the ground meat. Cover with a lid and microwave on Power 7 for 4-5 minutes. Stand for 3 minutes before serving.

Mixed Meat Loaf

PREPARATION TIME: 30 minutes

MICROWAVE TIME: 27 minutes

SERVES: 6-8 people

1 clove garlic
6oz lean bacon, de-rinded
1lb raw ground beef
8oz raw ground pork
6oz lambs' liver, finely chopped
6oz Canadian bacon, de-rinded and
    finely chopped
½ cup shredded suet
½ cup fresh brown breadcrumbs
½ tsp dried oregano
½ tsp mixed dried herbs
Salt and freshly ground black pepper
    to taste
4 tblsp sherry
1 egg, beaten

Glaze
2½ tblsp apricot jam or marmalade,
    sieved
1 tsp French mustard
½ tsp meat and vegetable extract

Rub a 2 quart plastic meat loaf pan with the clove of garlic. Lay the bacon in the meat loaf pan to line the base and the sides. In a large mixing bowl, mix the ground beef with the pork, liver, Canadian bacon, suet, breadcrumbs and herbs. Season to taste. Beat together the sherry and the egg; add to the mixture and bind together. Transfer to the prepared loaf pan. Smooth the top. Cover and microwave on Power 6, or Roast, for 27 minutes. Turn the dish ½ a turn twice during this time. Allow to stand for 10 minutes. Pour off the excess fat and carefully unmold the loaf. Mix all ingredients together for the glaze and brush over the top and sides of the meat loaf. Delicious hot or cold.

Cheesey Beef Cobbler

PREPARATION TIME: 30 minutes

MICROWAVE TIME: 20 minutes

SERVES: 4 people

1lb raw ground beef
1 onion, chopped
8oz can tomatoes, chopped
1 beef stock cube, crumbled
1¼ tblsp bottled brown sauce
Celery salt and freshly ground black
    pepper to taste
2½ tblsp frozen peas

Scone Topping
2 cups flour, sieved with 1½ tsp
    baking powder
4 tblsp margarine or butter, chilled
½ cup grated Cheddar cheese
1 tsp mixed dried herbs
1 egg, mixed with ½ cup milk
1½ tsp meat and vegetable extract

Put the ground meat and onion into a 7 inch souffle dish. Cover and microwave on Full Power for 4 minutes. Stir well with a fork. Stir in the toatoes, stock cube, brown sauce and celery salt and pepper. Cover and microwave on Power 7, or Roast, for 10 minutes. Stir in the peas and set aside. Put the flour and baking powder into a 2 quart mixing bowl. Blend in the margarine or butter. Mix in the cheese and herbs. Add the beaten egg and milk and mix to a soft dough. Knead lightly. Roll the dough out to a thickness of ½ inch. Using a 2 inch pastry cutter, cut the dough into scones. Arrange the scones on top of the ground meat. Cook, uncovered, on Full Power for 6 minutes. Serve immediately. Note: to improve the color of the scones mix the meat and vegetable extract with a little water and use to brush the scones prior to cooking.

Lamb Curry

PREPARATION TIME: 20 minutes

MICROWAVE TIME: about 45
    minutes

SERVES: 4 people

2 carrots, peeled and chopped
1 medium onion, chopped
2 tblsp butter
¼ cup all purpose flour
4-5 tsp mild curry powder
1lb lamb fillet, cubed
1¾ cups boiling chicken stock
1¼ tblsp shredded coconut
¼ cup white raisins
1 medium sized eating apple, peeled,
    cored and chopped
1 peach, peeled, stoned and roughly
    chopped
1¼ tomato paste
2½ tblsp lemon juice
Salt and freshly ground black pepper
    to taste

Preheat a large browning dish, without the lid, for 3 minutes on Full Power. Put the carrots, onion and butter into the preheated dish. Microwave on Full Power for 2 minutes, covered. Stir in the flour, curry powder and meat. Microwave on Full Power for 4 minutes. Gradually add the stock, stirring all the time. Stir in the coconut, white raisins, apple, peach, tomato paste, lemon juice and seasoning to taste. Cover and

Lamb Curry (top left), Savory Ground Meat with Dumplings (top right) and Mixed Meat Loaf (bottom).

microwave on Full Power for 7 minutes. Stir. Microwave on Power 4, Simmer or Defrost, for 30-35 minutes. Stir twice during this time. Serve immediately.

Pasta with Pork and Liver

PREPARATION TIME: 15 minutes

MICROWAVE TIME: 25 minutes

SERVES: 4 people

2½ tblsp oil
1 medium onion, sliced
12oz raw ground pork
4oz chicken livers, ground
1 cup mushrooms, chopped
8oz can tomatoes, chopped
4 tblsp sherry
Salt and freshly ground black pepper to taste
1 beef stock cube, crumbled

6oz dried pasta shells
Chopped fresh parsley

Heat the browning dish, without the lid, for 4-6 minutes on Full Power, according to size. Put half the oil, the onion and ground meats into the preheated dish. Stir well. Microwave on Full Power for 4 minutes. Stir in all the remaining ingredients, apart from the pasta and the parsley. Cover with the lid and microwave on Full Power for 3 minutes. Stir. Microwave, covered, on Power 5, or Simmer, for 10 minutes. Allow to stand whilst preparing the pasta. To cook the pasta, place the remaining oil and the pasta into a 3-4 quart bowl. Add 2 quarts water and ½ tsp salt to the pasta. Cover and microwave on Full Power for 8 minutes. Allow to stand for 5 minutes. Drain the pasta and arrange on a serving dish. Spoon the meat sauce evenly over the pasta, and garnish with chopped parsley. Serve immediately.

Pasta with Pork and Liver (far left), Cheesey Beef Cobbler (below) and Sausagemeat Stuffing (below right).

Chicken Breasts in Garlic Cream Sauce

PREPARATION TIME: 10 minutes

MICROWAVE TIME: 17 minutes

SERVES: 4 people

4 tblsp butter
1 clove garlic, crushed
1 medium onion, sliced
2 rashers bacon, de-rinded and chopped
½ cup mushrooms, sliced
½ tsp dried basil
Salt and freshly ground black pepper to taste
4 chicken breasts, skinned and boned (about 5oz each)
1 cup heavy cream

Garnish
Savory
Toasted flaked almonds

Melt the butter in a 2 quart casserole dish for 1-2 minutes on Full Power. Stir in the garlic, onion, bacon, mushrooms, basil and salt and pepper to taste. Cover and microwave on Full Power for 2 minutes. Arrange the chicken breasts on top of the vegetables. Cover and microwave on Power 7, or Roast, for 10 minutes. Season the cream and pour evenly over the top to coat. Garnish with savory and almonds. Serve immediately.

Chicken Casserole

PREPARATION TIME: 15 minutes

MICROWAVE TIME: about 40 minutes

SERVES: 4 people

4 chicken portions, skinned (about 8oz each)
2 tblsp butter
1 onion, finely chopped
2 stalks celery, chopped
2 carrots, chopped
2 tblsp drained canned corn kernels
2 tsp cornstarch
1¼ cups chicken stock
Salt and paprika to taste

Put the butter into a 3 quart casserole dish. Microwave on Full Power for 1 minute. Stir in the onion, celery and carrots. Cover with a lid and microwave on Full Power for 3 minutes. Pour the stock into the casserole, and add salt to taste. Arrange the chicken pieces on top of the vegetables, keeping the thickest part to the outside of the dish. Sprinkle each chicken piece with a little paprika. Microwave, covered, on Full Power for 4 minutes. Stir. Microwave on Power 4, Simmer or Defrost, for a further 30 minutes. Using a draining spoon, transfer the chicken to a warmed serving dish. Cover with a piece of foil and set aside. Cream the cornstarch with a little water and stir into the casserole dish. Microwave on Full Power for 2-3 minutes, until boiling and thickened. Stir in the corn. Serve the chicken pieces with the vegetable sauce spooned over the top.

Sausage Suet Pudding

PREPARATION TIME: 30 minutes

MICROWAVE TIME: 21 minutes

SERVES: 4 people

Filling
8oz pork sausages, cut into 1 inch pieces
8oz chicken livers, roughly chopped
¼ cup seasoned flour
1 tblsp oil
1 medium onion, chopped
½ green pepper, de-seeded and chopped
1¼ cups well flavored boiling stock
Salt and freshly ground black pepper to taste

Suet Pastry
2 cups all purpose flour
½ tsp salt
2 tsp baking powder
1 cup finely grated (or shredded) suet
⅔ cup water

Toss the sausages and chicken livers in the seasoned flour. Put the oil into a 2 quart mixing bowl. Microwave on Full Power for 2 minutes. Stir in the onion and green pepper. Microwave on Full Power for 2 minutes. Stir the chicken livers and sausage into the onion. Cover and microwave on Power 8, or Roast, for 5 minutes. Carefully stir in the boiling stock and salt and pepper to taste. Microwave on Full Power for 2-3 minutes, until thickened. Stir and set aside while preparing the pastry. Sieve the flour, salt and baking powder into a bowl. Stir in the suet and mix to a soft dough with the water. Knead lightly. Roll out ⅔ of the pastry and use to line a greased 2 pint boilable plastic pudding basin. Roll the remaining pastry into a circle. Fill the pastry-lined basin with the filling mixture. Dampen the pastry rim with cold water and top with the circle of pastry. Seal edges. Cut a small slit in the top to allow the steam to escape. Cover loosely with absorbent kitchen paper or plastic wrap. Microwave on Power 7, or Roast, for 9 minutes. Stand for 5 minutes before serving.

Herby Roast Chicken

PREPARATION TIME: about 35 minutes

MICROWAVE TIME: about 36 minutes

SERVES: 6 people

¾ cup fresh brown breadcrumbs
½ cup shredded suet
1 tsp finely chopped fresh parsley
1 tsp finely chopped fresh tarragon
1 eating apple, peeled, cored and chopped
1 tsp lemon juice
Salt and freshly ground black pepper to taste
1 small onion, finely chopped
1 egg, beaten
4lb chicken, giblets removed

Coating
4 tblsp butter
2 tsp chicken seasoning
1 tsp paprika
½ tsp mixed dried herbs

Garnish
Watercress

To make the stuffing, combine the breadcrumbs, suet, parsley, tarragon, apple, lemon juice and seasoning to taste. Put the onion into a small bowl and microwave on Full Power for 1 minute. Add the onion to the other ingredients. Bind together with the beaten egg.

Chicken Casserole (top right), Herby Roast Chicken (top left), Chicken Breasts in Garlic Cream Sauce (bottom right) and Sausage Suet Pudding (bottom left).

Roasting Meats

TYPE OF MEAT	MICROWAVE POWER LEVEL	TIME PER 1lb	INTERNAL TEMPERATURE AFTER MICROWAVING	INTERNAL TEMPERATURE AFTER STANDING
Chops 1. Lamb	Power 7 or Roast (Use pre-heated browning dish)	7-8 minutes	Turn the chops over once during cooking time.	
2. Pork	Power 7 or Roast (Use pre-heated browning dish)	9-10 minutes	Allow to stand for 5-10 minutes before serving.	
Beef (Boned & Rolled)	Power 7 or Roast	5-6 minutes *Rare* 7-8 minutes *Medium* 8-10 minutes *Well done*	130°F 150°F 160°F	140°F 160°F 170°F
Beef on the Bone	Power 7 or Roast	5 minutes *Rare* 6 minutes *Medium* 8 minutes *Well done*	130°F 150°F 160°F	140°F 160°F 170°F
Poultry (Unboned)	Full Power	7 minutes	185°F	190°F
Pork	Power 7 or Roast	10-11 minutes	180°F	185°F
Lamb	Power 7 or Roast	8-9 minutes	170°F	180°F

1. Have joints boned and rolled for best results.
2. Use a <u>microwave</u> meat thermostat to gauge when the meat should be removed from the microwave oven.
3. Any joint which is 3lbs or over will brown in the microwave oven, to increase the colouring, use a browning agent before cooking, or flash the meat under a pre-heated hot broiler after standing time.
4. Turn the joint over once during the cooking time.
5. Use a microwave roasting rack, or an upturned saucer, placed in a suitable dish so as to allow the juices to drain.

Stuff the neck end of the bird with the stuffing. Truss. Weigh the stuffed bird and calculate the cooking time accordingly (7 minutes per 1lb). Use small amounts of foil to mask the wings and the stuffed area, to prevent overcooking. Arrange the chicken in a suitable roasting dish, on two upturned saucers, or on a microwave roasting rack. Melt the butter in the microwave for 1 minute on Full Power. Brush the butter all over the chicken. Combine the chicken seasoning, paprika and herbs together and sprinkle all over the chicken. Cover with a split roasta bag. Microwave on Full Power for the calculated time. Allow the chicken to stand, covered with a tent of foil, before serving. Garnish with watercress.

Devilled Pork Chops

PREPARATION TIME: 10 minutes

MICROWAVE TIME: 16 minutes

SERVES: 4 people

2½ tblsp oil
4 loin pork chops (about 6oz each)
A stick of butter
1¼ tblsp dry mustard
2½ tblsp fresh breadcrumbs
1¼ tblsp soya sauce
2½ tsp Worcestershire sauce
1¼ tblsp tomato chutney
Salt and paprika to taste

Preheat the browning dish (without the lid) for 4-7 minutes, according to size, on Full Power. Put the oil into the heated dish and microwave on Full Power for 1 minute. Put the 4 chops into the dish, pressing them down well. Microwave on Full Power for 2 minutes. Turn the chops over and microwave on Power 7, or Roast, for 10 minutes. Combine all the remaining ingredients in a mixing bowl. Spread over the partly cooked chops. Microwave on Power 7, or Roast, for a further 3 minutes.

Beef or Pork Burgers

PREPARATION TIME: 20 minutes

MICROWAVE TIME: 6-7 minutes

SERVES: 4 people

1lb raw ground beef or pork
1 small onion, finely chopped
½ cup fresh breadcrumbs
1 stock cube, crumbled
½ tsp dried parsley
Salt and freshly ground black pepper to taste
1½ tblsp tomato sauce
1¼ tsp made mustard
2 eggs, beaten
4 buns

Mix the ground beef or pork, onion and breadcrumbs together. Add the stock cube and all the other ingredients, apart from the buns. Mix well. Divide the mixture into 4 and form into burgers. Arrange on a microwave roasting rack, or other suitable dish, in a ring. Microwave on Full Power for 6-7 minutes, turning each burger over once halfway through cooking time. Split the buns and fill with the burgers.

Glazed Leg of Lamb

PREPARATION TIME: 25 minutes

MICROWAVE TIME: about 50 minutes

SERVES: 6 people

4lb leg of lamb
2-3 cloves peeled garlic, cut into thin strips
Salt and freshly ground black pepper to taste
2½ tblsp tomato sauce
1¼ tsp dry mustard
1¼ tsp brown sugar
1 tsp mixed dried herbs

Devilled Pork Chops (top right), Beef or Pork Burgers (center left) and Glazed Leg of Lamb (bottom).

Make incisions all over the joint with a sharp knife; push a strip of garlic into each one. Season with salt and pepper. Combine the tomato sauce, mustard, brown sugar and herbs, and spread evenly over the joint. Arrange the joint on a roasting rack. Cover with a roasta bag. Microwave for 12 minutes on Full Power. Turn the joint over and microwave on Power 4, or Simmer, for 30-40 minutes or until the meat thermometer registers 160°F. Remove the joint. Cover with a tent of foil and allow to stand for 15 minutes before serving.

Rolled Rib Roast of Beef

PREPARATION TIME: 18 minutes

MICROWAVE TIME: 30 minutes

SERVES: 6-8 people

4lb piece rib roast, boned and rolled
Salt and freshly ground black pepper
* to taste*
1½ tblsp tomato sauce
1½ tsp soft brown sugar

Stand the joint on the microwave roasting rack, in a suitable dish, keeping the fat side of the meat underneath. Season with salt and pepper. Microwave for 7 minutes, on Full Power. Turn the joint over and microwave on Roast, or Power 7, for 21 minutes. Remove from the microwave. Cover loosely with a tent of foil and allow to stand for 15 minutes. Spread the tomato sauce and brown sugar all over the fat. Microwave on Full Power for 2 minutes. (Check temperatures with a microwave thermometer. See chart).

Barbecue Lamb Chops

PREPARATION TIME: 10 minutes, plus marinating time

MICROWAVE TIME: 16 minutes

SERVES: 6 people

Marinade
2½ tblsp wine vinegar
5 tblsp pure orange juice
1¼ tblsp tomato sauce
1¼ tsp soft brown sugar
1¼ tsp French mustard
½ tsp dried tarragon
1¼ tsp mild curry powder
Salt and freshly ground black pepper
* to taste*
1¼ tsp oil
6 loin chops, each about 5oz

**Rolled Rib Roast of Beef (top)
and Barbecue Lamb Chops
(left).**

Blend all the ingredients together for the marinade, apart from the oil. Lay the chops in a large shallow dish and pour over the marinade. Cover and chill for at least two hours. Turn the chops over in the marinade, once or twice. Preheat a large browning dish for 7 minutes on Full Power. Put the oil and the drained chops into the dish, pressing the chops against the hot dish. Microwave, uncovered, on Full Power for 5 minutes. Turn the chops over. Microwave on Roast, or Power 7, for 3-4 minutes. Serve immediately.

Shepherd's Pie

PREPARATION TIME: 30 minutes

MICROWAVE TIME: 38 minutes

SERVES: 4 people

1 tblsp cooking oil
2 zucchini, thinly sliced
1 small onion, finely chopped
1lb raw lean ground beef
1 tblsp flour
Salt and freshly ground black pepper
* to taste*
1 tblsp tomato paste
4 tblsp water
1 beef stock cube, crumbled
2lb potatoes
½ cup milk
1 egg
1 tblsp butter
2 tblsp mild hard cheese, grated

Preheat a small browning dish on Full Power for 3½ minutes (if using a large browning dish preheat on Full Power for 5 minutes). Add the oil, zucchini and onion, and stir. Cover with a lid and microwave on Full Power for 2 minutes. Add the meat and microwave on Full Power for 3 minutes, stirring once. Add the flour, salt and pepper to taste, tomato paste, water and stock cube. Stir well and cover. Microwave on Power 7, or Roast, for 12 minutes, stirring after the first 4 minutes. Remove from the microwave oven and leave to stand. Meanwhile prepare the potatoes. Peel and dice the potatoes. Put them into a roasta bag with 4 tblsp of the milk. Put the bag into a 2 quart bowl. Secure with a rubber band and pierce once at the base. Microwave on Full Power for 17 minutes (turn the bag over once during this time). Stand, covered, for 5 minutes. Drain the potatoes and mash them together with the egg, remaining milk and the butter. Pile the potato onto the meat mixture and sprinkle with the cheese. Microwave on Full Power for 3-4 minutes, until the cheese has melted and the pie is very hot. To speed this recipe up you can use reconstituted powdered potato.

Pork with Leeks and Grapes

PREPARATION TIME: 20 minutes
MICROWAVE TIME: 53 minutes
SERVES: 4-5 people

2½ tblsp oil
1 carrot, peeled and sliced
1 stick celery, chopped
8oz potato, peeled and diced
1lb young leeks, washed and sliced
1½lb boned shoulder of pork, cut into 1 inch cubes
¼ cup all purpose flour
Salt and freshly ground black pepper to taste
1¼ cups well flavored chicken stock
1 cup seedless white grapes

Preheat the browning dish for 4 or 7 minutes, according to size. Add the oil, carrot, celery, potato and leeks to the heated dish. Cover with the lid. Microwave on Full Power for 4 minutes. Using a perforated spoon, transfer the vegetables to a dinner plate. Return the browning dish to the microwave, without the lid, for 1 minute on Full Power. Toss the meat in the flour and seasoning; stir into the dish, turning so that all sides come in contact with the hot skillet. Microwave, uncovered, for 3 minutes on Full Power. Stir in the drained vegetables, stock and extra seasoning to taste. Cover with the lid. Microwave, covered, on Power 5, or Simmer, for 40 minutes. Stir in the grapes and serve after a standing time of 5 minutes.

Turkey Fricassee

PREPARATION TIME: 20 minutes
MICROWAVE TIME: 12 minutes
SERVES: 4 people

2 tblsp butter
¼ cup flour
1¼ cups chicken or turkey stock
Salt and freshly ground black pepper to taste
1 cup mushrooms, sliced
½ red pepper, de-seeded and chopped
4 rashers bacon, de-rinded and chopped

1 medium onion, chopped
12oz cooked turkey, chopped
1 cup stuffed olives, halved
2 tblsp light cream
1 egg yolk

To make the sauce: melt the butter in a 2¼ pint jug for 1 minute on Full Power. Stir in the flour to make a smooth paste. Gradually stir in the stock, mixing well. Season with salt and pepper. Microwave on Full Power for 2 minutes. Beat well with a wire whisk. Microwave on Full Power for 2 minutes. Beat in the sliced mushrooms. Put the red pepper, bacon and onion into a 2½ pint mixing bowl. Cover and microwave on Full Power for 2 minutes. Stir. Arrange the cooked turkey in a serving dish. Add the pepper mixture and most of the halved olives (reserve a few for decoration). Beat the cream and egg yolk into the sauce. Pour the sauce evenly over the vegetables and turkey. Cover with plastic wrap and pierce. Microwave on Power 5 for 5 minutes. Allow to stand for 5 minutes before serving. Garnish with the remaining olives.

Stewed Steak with Garlic

PREPARATION TIME: 25 minutes
MICROWAVE TIME: about 1 hour 40 minutes
SERVES: 4 people

1½lb chuck steak, cubed
1 tblsp seasoned flour
2 leeks, washed and sliced
1 medium onion, sliced
1 carrot, peeled and chopped
2 cloves garlic, crushed
2 tblsp cooking oil
2 rashers bacon, de-rinded and chopped
15oz can tomatoes, chopped
1 tblsp tomato paste
Salt and freshly ground black pepper to taste
1¼ cups well flavored beef stock
½ tsp dried parsley

Toss the meat in the seasoned flour. Put the leeks, onions, carrot and the garlic into a 2½ pint dish. Cover and microwave on Full Power for 3 minutes. Stir and set aside. Preheat the large browning dish, without the lid, for 7 minutes on Full Power. Pour the oil into the

This page: Pork with Leeks and Grapes.

Facing page: Stewed Steak with Garlic (top), Shepherd's Pie (center right) and Turkey Fricassee (bottom).

dish and quickly stir in the bacon and the meat. Press the meat against the sides of the dish. Cover and microwave on Full Power for 4 minutes. Stir, and add all the remaining ingredients. Cover. Microwave on Full Power for 4 minutes, and then on Power 4, or Simmer, for 70 minutes. Stir once after the first 30 minutes. Stir, and allow to stand for 10 minutes before serving.

Sauces and Preserves

Basic Savory White Sauce

PREPARATION TIME: 5 minutes
MICROWAVE TIME: 5 minutes
MAKES: ⅔ pint

2 tblsp butter
¼ cup flour
1¼ cups milk or chicken stock
Salt and freshly ground black pepper
 to taste

Melt the butter in a 2¼ pint jug. Microwave on Full Power for 1 minute until very hot. Stir in the flour to form a roux. Gradually stir in all the milk or stock. Season to taste with salt and pepper. Microwave on Full Power for 2 minutes. Beat well with a wire whisk. Microwave on Full Power for 2 minutes. Beat with a wire whisk and serve.

Variations on Basic White Sauce
Cheese Sauce
Beat ½ cup finely grated cheese and 1 tsp made mustard into the

Mushroom Sauce (above right), Basic Savory White Sauce (far right) and Cheese Sauce (right).

finished sauce. The heat of the sauce will melt the cheese.

Mushroom Sauce
Beat ½ cup finely chopped mushrooms into the prepared sauce. The heat of the sauce will cook the mushrooms.

Egg Sauce
Chop 1 hard-boiled egg (cooked conventionally). Beat into the prepared sauce.

Parsley Sauce
Beat 1 tblsp chopped fresh parsley into the finished sauce.

Onion Sauce
Finely chop 1 medium sized peeled onion and put it into a bowl. Cover with plastic wrap and pierce. Microwave on Full Power for 1-1½ minutes to soften. Beat the softened onion into the prepared sauce (the onion should be softened before the sauce is made).

Cranberry Sauce

PREPARATION TIME: 10 minutes

MICROWAVE TIME: 4 minutes

MAKES: about ½ pint

1 orange
8oz frozen cranberries, defrosted
½ cup granulated sugar

Finely grate the rind from the orange into a 2½ pint mixing bowl. Squeeze the juice from the orange and make up to ⅔ cup with cold water. Put the cranberries, sugar, orange juice and water into the mixing bowl. Microwave on Full Power for 4 minutes. Stir once, halfway through cooking time. Stir and serve.

Custard Sauce

PREPARATION TIME: 5 minutes

MICROWAVE TIME: 4 minutes

MAKES: 2½ cups

2 cups milk
½ cup granulated sugar
4 egg yolks
1½ tsp vanilla

Put milk into a 2¼ pint jug and microwave on Full Power for 2 minutes. Beat the egg yolks with the sugar in a 2½ pint mixing bowl until the mixture is a pale lemon colour. Very slowly pour the hot milk onto the egg mixture, stirring constantly, until blended. Pour the mixture back into the jug and microwave on Full Power for 2 minutes. Beat well with a wire whisk. Allow to cool slightly and then stir in the vanilla. Serve hot or cold.

Chocolate Sauce

PREPARATION TIME: 5 minutes

MICROWAVE TIME: 5 minutes

MAKES: about ⅔ pint

2 tblsp butter
1 tblsp cocoa powder
1¼ cups milk
1 tblsp corn syrup

Melt the butter in a 2¼ pint jug for 1 minute on Full Power. Stir in the cocoa, mixing well. Gradually add the milk, stirring. Microwave on Full Power for 2 minutes. Beat well with a wire whisk. Microwave on Full Power for 2 minutes. Beat in the corn syrup. Serve immediately.

Beefy Tomato Sauce

PREPARATION TIME: 10 minutes

COOKING TIME: 20 minutes

MAKES: 1¼ pints

¼ cup butter
2 medium sized onions, finely chopped
½ cup flour
3 cups hot beef stock
2 tblsp tomato paste
1 tblsp vinegar
1 tsp French mustard
1 tsp soft brown sugar
1 tsp Worcestershire sauce

1 tblsp tomato sauce
Salt and freshly ground black pepper to taste

Melt the butter in a really large jug or mixing bowl for 1-2 minutes on Full Power. Stir in the onion and microwave, uncovered, for 3 minutes on Full Power. Stir in the flour, mixing well. Gradually add the stock, stirring continuously. Mix the paste with the vinegar and add to the sauce together with the French mustard, sugar, Worcestershire sauce, tomato sauce and salt and pepper to taste. Microwave on Full Power for 10 minutes. Beat well twice during this time. Turn on to Power 4, or Simmer, and microwave for a further 5 minutes. Beat well. Serve with meat balls, meat loaf, etc.

St. Clement's Sauce

PREPARATION TIME: 10 minutes

MICROWAVE TIME: 3½ minutes

MAKES: about ½ pint

3 tblsp fine cut marmalade
Juice of 1 lemon
Juice of 1 orange
1 tsp arrowroot

Put the marmalade and lemon and orange juices into a 2¼ pint jug. Microwave on Full Power for 1½ minutes. Stir well. Microwave on Full Power for 1 minute. Blend the arrowroot to a smooth paste with a little cold water. Stir into the jug. Microwave on Full Power for 30 seconds. Stir. Microwave on Full Power for a further 30 seconds. Stir and serve.

Plum Jam

PREPARATION TIME: 20 minutes

MICOWAVE TIME: 1 hour

MAKES: 2½lb

Juice of 1 orange
2lb plums, halved and stoned
2lb granulated sugar

Put the juice and the plums into a large microwave container. Cover and microwave on Full Power for 10 minutes. Stir in the sugar to dissolve. Cover and microwave on Power 6 for about 40 minutes, or until setting point is reached. Test for setting. Pot and label in the usual way.

Strawberry Jam

PREPARATION TIME: 20 minutes, plus chilling overnight

COOKING TIME: 31 minutes

MAKES: about 2½lb

2lb freshly picked strawberries, hulled
2lb granulated sugar

Place the hulled strawberries in a 6¼ pint microwave dish. Add the sugar and stir. Cover and leave overnight in the refrigerator. Stir well. Cover and microwave on Full Power for 7 minutes, until boiling point is reached. Microwave on Power 5, or Simmer, for 24 minutes, until setting point is reached. Test for setting. Pot and label in the usual way.

Green Tomato Chutney

PREPARATION TIME: 40 minutes

MICROWAVE TIME: 1¾-2 hours

MAKES: about 6lbs

2 medium onions, finely chopped
1½ cups malt vinegar
1 cup wine vinegar
1 small stalk celery, chopped
½ tsp mustard seed
4lb green tomatoes, washed and chopped
2 large tart cooking apples, peeled, cored and chopped
1½ cups seedless raisins
1 clove garlic, crushed
4 peppercorns, 2 cloves and 2 chilies (tied in muslin)
2 cups soft brown sugar
Salt and freshly ground black pepper to taste

Put the onions into a 6 cup pudding basin. Microwave on Full Power for 2 minutes. Put half the vinegar, the celery, mustard seed, tomatoes, apples, raisins, garlic and onions into a very large bowl.

Parsley Sauce (top), Cranberry Sauce (center left), Onion Sauce (center right) and Egg Sauce (bottom).

Crush the muslin bag with a rolling pin and add to the bowl. Stir. Cover and microwave on Full Power for 10 minutes. Stir in the sugar to dissolve. Add the remaining vinegar and season with salt and pepper to taste. Microwave on Full Power for 20-30 minutes. Remove the lid and stir well. Microwave on Full Power, uncovered, for about 75 minutes until the mixture reduces and thickens. Stir twice during this time. Ladle into clean jam jars. Seal and label when cool. The chutney shld be kept in a cool dark place for 2 months to mature, before using.

This page: Strawberry Jam (top), Plum Jam (center right) and Green Tomato Chutney (bottom).

Facing page: Chocolate Sauce (top), St Clement's Sauce (center left), Beefy Tomato Sauce (center right) and Custard Sauce (bottom).

Sweets

Pear Upside Down Pudding

PREPARATION TIME: 25 minutes

MICROWAVE TIME: 7 minutes

SERVES: 6 people

Oil and superfine sugar
3 tblsp corn syrup
15oz can pear halves, drained
5 glace cherries, halved and rinsed
Recipe quantity Victoria Sandwich
mixture (see recipe)

Grease a 7 inch souffle dish with oil and sprinkle the base and sides lightly with superfine sugar. Spread the corn syrup over the bottom. Make an attractive pattern over the base with the pears and the glace cherries. Spoon the Victoria Sandwich mixture into the prepared dish. Smooth the top. Microwave on Full Power for 7 minutes. Allow to stand for 7 minutes in the dish before carefully turning out. Serve warm with custard or cream.

Apple and Blackcurrant Flan

PREPARATION TIME: 30 minutes

MICROWAVE TIME: 37 minutes

SERVES: 6 people

Base
1¼ cups white flour
1¼ cups whole-wheat flour
Pinch of salt
¼ cup butter
¼ cup lard
1 egg and 2 tblsp cold water, beaten
together

Filling
1lb tart cooking apples, peeled, cored
and sliced
8oz blackcurrants
¼ cup superfine sugar
¾ cup ground almonds
2 tblsp butter
2 egg yolks

Meringue
3 egg whites
¾ cup superfine sugar
Glace cherries and angelica for
decoration

To make the pastry, sieve the flours and salt into a mixing bowl. Blend the butter and lard until the mixture resembles fine breadcrumbs. Mix to a dough with the egg and cold water. Knead the dough lightly. Roll out and use to line a 10 inch fluted flan dish. Press up pastry to come ¼ inch above the rim of the dish. Prick the sides and base with a fork. Refrigerate for 15 minutes. Using a single strip of foil, about 1 inch wide, line the inside edge of the flan case. Place 2 sheets of absorbent kitchen paper in the base. Weigh down with a few baking beans. Microwave on Full Power for 6 minutes. Remove the foil, beans and absorbent paper. Microwave on Full Power for 2-3

This page: Mille Feuille (top), Apple Mousse (center right) and Pear Upside Down Pudding (bottom).

Facing page: Chocolate Rice Krispie (top), Rhubarb Sunburst (center right) and Creme Caramel (bottom).

minutes. Set aside. Put the fruits into a 2 quart mixing bowl. Cover and microwave on Full Power for about 7-8 minutes, stirring once halfway through. Stir in sugar to dissolve and beat to a puree. Cool. Beat in the ground almonds, butter and egg yolk. Put the egg whites into a large, clean bowl and whisk until stiff and dry. Beat in the sugar, a little at a time, until a thick glossy meringue results. Spread the fruit mixture into the flan case. Pipe or spread the meringue mixture on top to cover completely. Put the flan into a pre-heated moderate oven, 350°F, for 15-20 minutes, until pale golden. Serve sprinkled with tiny pieces of cherry and angelica.

Mille Feuille

PREPARATION TIME: 15-20 minutes, plus cooling time

MICROWAVE TIME: 6 minutes

SERVES: 6 people

8oz puff pastry (you can use a small packet of frozen puff pastry)
8oz fresh strawberries
1¼ cups heavy cream, whipped
2 tblsp superfine sugar
½ cup confectioner's sugar, sieved
Pink food coloring
¼ cup toasted flaked almonds

Roll the pastry out into a circle 8 inches in diameter. Place on a large dinner plate and chill for 10 minutes. Microwave, uncovered, for 5-6 minutes, on Full Power. Turn the plate once halfway through the cooking time. Brown the top under a pre-heated hot broiler for a few seconds, if required. Allow to cool completely. Hull strawberries and roughly chop them. Fold the strawberries into the cream with the superfine sugar. Split the pastry horizontally into 3 layers and place the first layer on a serving dish. Spread thickly with strawberries and cream. Top with the second pastry layer and spread with more strawberries and cream. Add the final layer of pastry, browned side uppermost. Put the confectioner's sugar into a basin. Add a few drops of pink food coloring and just enough boiling water to produce a smooth glacé frosting. Spread the frosting over the Mille Feuille using a teaspoon – see picture. Sprinkle with the cold, toasted almonds and serve immediately.

Creme Caramel

PREPARATION TIME: 15 minutes, plus chilling time

MICROWAVE TIME: 28 minutes

SERVES: 4 people

Caramel
¾ cup granulated sugar
½ cup cold water

Custard
1¾ cups milk
4 eggs, lightly beaten
¼ cup superfine sugar

To make the caramel, place the granulated sugar and water into a large jug. Microwave on Full Power for 9-11 minutes, or until a golden caramel results. Swirl the caramel evenly around the inside of a suitable, lightly-greased 2 pint dish. Leave to set. Put the milk into a large, clean jug and microwave on Full Power for 2 minutes. Add the beaten eggs and superfine sugar. Strain onto the set caramel. Cover with plastic wrap and pierce. Stand the dish in a larger container, which will act as a water bath. Pour in sufficient boiling water to come halfway up the sides of the dish containing the creme caramel. Microwave on Power 5, or Simmer, for about 15 minutes or until the custard has set. Remove from the water bath. Carefully peel away the plastic wrap and allow to cool. Chill until ready to serve. Turn out and serve very cold with whipped cream.

Apple Mousse

PREPARATION TIME: 20 minutes

MICROWAVE TIME: 7 minutes

SERVES: 6 people

1½lb tart cooking apples, peeled, cored and sliced
Juice of 1 lemon
3 cubes of lime jelly (from a packet jelly)
3 tblsp superfine sugar
1 cup heavy cream
2 egg whites
1 red-skinned eating apple

Put the prepared cooking apples into a 2 quart casserole dish with half the lemon juice and the lime jelly. Cover with a lid and microwave on Full Power for about 7 minutes until the apples are pulpy (stir once during this time). Beat with a fork, beating in the sugar until melted. Set aside and allow to cool. Blend the cooled

apple in a food processor or liquidizer until smooth. Add the half-whipped cream and process together for a few seconds. Whisk the egg whites in a clean bowl until they stand in soft peaks. Transfer the apple mixture to a large, clean bowl and fold in the beaten egg whites gently. Turn into a serving dish. Decorate with slices of eating apple, which have been brushed with the remaining lemon juice to prevent discoloration.

Rhubarb Sunburst

PREPARATION TIME: 10 minutes, plus chilling time

MICROWAVE TIME: 6 minutes

SERVES: 4 people

1lb fresh young rhubarb, cut into 1 inch pieces
Finely grated rind and juice of 1 orange
1 tblsp apricot jam
6 canned apricot halves, chopped

Place the rhubarb, orange rind and juice, and the jam into a 2 pint mixing bowl. Cover and microwave on Full Power for 6 minutes. Stir. Set aside to cool, and then chill. Stir in the chopped apricots. Serve with natural yogurt, ice cream or whipped heavy cream.

Chocolate Pudding with Cherries

PREPARATION TIME: 10 minutes

MICROWAVE TIME: 8½ minutes

SERVES: 4-6 people

6 tblsp softened butter
6 tblsp soft brown sugar
¾ cup flour
1 tsp baking powder
¼ cup cocoa powder
2 eggs
2 tblsp milk
15oz can cherry pie filling

Put all ingredients, apart from the cherry pie filling, into a mixing bowl. Beat with a wooden spoon for 1 minute. Spoon into a lightly greased 2 pint plastic pudding basin. Microwave on Full Power for 3½-4 minutes, until well risen and springy to the touch. Set aside. Empty the cherry pie filling into a bowl and microwave on Full Power for 3 minutes, stirring after 1½ minutes. Turn the sponge pudding into a dinner plate. Spoon the hot cherry sauce over the top and serve immediately.

Chocolate Rice Krispie

PREPARATION TIME: 15 minutes, plus chilling time

COOKING TIME: 5 minutes

MAKES: 16-20 wedges

A stick of butter
¼ cup superfine sugar
¼ cup cocoa powder
½ cup corn syrup
1 cup Rice Krispies

Lightly grease 2 x 8 inch sandwich tins with a little of the butter (these are not to be used in the microwave). Put the remaining butter, cut into pieces, into a 2 quart mixing bowl with the superfine sugar, cocoa powder and corn syrup. Microwave on Power 5 or Simmer for 4 minutes. Stir halfway through, and again at the end. Microwave on Full Power for a further 1 minute. Stir in the Rice Krispies, making sure that they are all coated with the chocolate mixture. Divide between the prepared tins and smooth level with a knife. Cool and then chill until set. Cut into finger wedges to serve. As an alternative, ½ cup washed, seedless raisins may be stirred in with the Rice Krispies.

Apple Ginger Crisp

PREPARATION TIME: 15 minutes

MICROWAVE TIME: 9 minutes

SERVES: 4-6 people

1lb tart cooking apples peeled, cored and sliced
¼ cup soft light brown sugar
1 tblsp orange juice
5 tblsp butter
2 cups plain ginger biscuits, crushed
½ cup flaked almonds

Place the apples, sugar and orange juice into a 3¼ pint casserole dish. Cover and microwave on Full Power for 4-5 minutes. Stir and set aside. Put the butter into a 2 quart mixing bowl. Microwave on Power 7, or Roast, for about 2 minutes, until melted. Stir the biscuits and almonds into the melted butter. Mix well. Microwave on Full Power for 2 minutes. Stir well with a fork after 1 minute. Carefully spoon the biscuit crumble over the apples. Serve immediately with whipped cream or ice cream. This pudding can also be served cold.

Chocolate Pudding with
Cherries (left), Apple Ginger
Crisp (below left) and Apple
and Blackcurrant Flan
(bottom).

Tea Time Treats

Celebration Gateau

PREPARATION TIME: 40 minutes

MICROWAVE TIME: 14 minutes

MAKES: 1 gateau

Cake
Superfine sugar and oil for preparing the dish
3 eggs
1¼ cups cake flour
¼ cup cocoa powder
1 tsp baking powder
¾ cup softened butter
¾ superfine sugar

Frosting
2 cups confectioner's sugar, sieved
6 tblsp butter
2 tsp boiling water
1 tsp liquid coffee essence
Few drops of vanilla essence

Decoration
1 packet sponge finger biscuits
6oz plain chocolate
1½ yards brown nylon ribbon, 1 inch wide

Lightly grease a deep, 7 inch diameter souffle dish with oil. Line the base with a circle of wax paper and use a little superfine sugar to dust the sides. Knock out any surplus. Put all the ingredients for the cake into a mixing bowl. Beat for 1 minute. Spoon into the prepared souffle dish and smooth the top. Microwave on Power 7, or Roast, for about 7 minutes, and then on Full Power for 2-3 minutes until the sponge has risen to the top of the souffle dish and is set. Allow to stand in the container for 10 minutes before turning out onto a clean tea towel which has been sprinkled with a little superfine sugar. Cool completely. To make the frosting: gradually beat the sieved confectioner's sugar into the butter, adding the boiling water. Take 1 tblsp buttercream out of the bowl and beat the coffee essence into it. Beat the vanilla essence into the remaining buttercream. Cut the cake in half horizontally and sandwich together with some of the vanilla buttercream. Spread the vanilla buttercream around the sides and across the top of the cake. Pipe half the cake with vanilla buttercream

and the other half with the coffee buttercream. Arrange the prepared sponge fingers, like soldiers, around the edge of the cake – see picture. Tie brown ribbon around to finish the gateau.
To prepare the sponge fingers: measure 1 sponge finger against the cooked cake. Trim all the sponge fingers to the same size. Break the chocolate into a large mixing bowl and microwave on Power 4 for 3-4 minutes. Stir. Dip the rounded end of the sponge fingers into the melted chocolate to coat the top half of each one. Arrange on a tray and leave in a cool place for 10-15 minutes to set.

Chocolate Frosting

PREPARATION TIME: 5 minutes

MICROWAVE TIME: 2½ minutes

2 tblsp softened butter
1½ tblsp cocoa powder, sieved
1¼ cups confectioner's sugar, sieved
2 tblsp milk

Put the butter and cocoa into a 2½ pint bowl. Microwave on Power 5, or Simmer, for 2½ minutes, until the butter has melted and is very hot. Stir once, halfway through. Beat in the confectioner's sugar and the milk. Beat with a wooden spoon until thick and glossy. Use to coat the top and sides of the cake.

Collettes

PREPARATION TIME: 30 minutes

MICROWAVE TIME: 7½ minutes

MAKES: 12

6oz plain chocolate
2oz milk chocolate
4 tblsp heavy cream
1 tblsp butter
2 tsp brandy or coffee essence
36 paper sweet cases, separated into twelve groups of three cases

Break the plain chocolate into pieces and put into a 2 pint bowl. Microwave on Power 3, or Defrost,

for 4-5 minutes. Stir. Using a small paint brush or teaspoon, coat the base and sides of each group of paper cases with the melted chocolate. Leave to set. Put the milk chocolate and the butter into a clean bowl. Microwave on Power 3, or Defrost, for 2-2½ minutes. Beat well for a few minutes. Beat in the brandy or coffee essence. Half whip the cream and fold into the milk chocolate mixture using a metal spoon. Chill until firm enough to pipe. Peel the paper cases away from the set chocolate and discard. Pipe rosettes of chocolate filling into the chocolate case. Serve immediately in new paper sweet cases.

Fruit and Almond Cake

PREPARATION TIME: 20 minutes

MICROWAVE TIME: 13-16 minutes

MAKES: 1 cake

Use the large spring clip ring mold, which should be lightly greased and coated with superfine sugar.
¾ cup softened butter
¾ cup soft brown sugar
½ tsp soy sauce
3 eggs, beaten
1½ cups white flour
1½ tsp baking powder
2-3 drops almond essence
¼ cup ground almonds
½ cup seedless raisins
½ cup glace cherries, washed and roughly chopped

Blend butter and sugar until light and fluffy. Beat in the soy sauce and beaten eggs, a little at a time (add 1 tblsp flour with each addition of egg to prevent curdling). Beat in the almond essence, ground almonds and milk. Fold in the remaining flour, and then the raisins and cherries. Place in the prepared ring mold and smooth the top. Microwave on Power 6, or Roast, for 12-14 minutes, and then on Full Power for 1-2 minutes until just set. Stand for 15 minutes, before turning out. When quite cold, the top may be sprinkled with a little sieved confectioner's sugar.

Cheese and Paprika Scones

PREPARATION TIME: 20 minutes

MICROWAVE TIME: 5-6 minutes

MAKES: about 10

2 cups white flour
2 tsp baking powder
Pinch salt
Pinch paprika
¼ cup firm butter
½ cup mild hard cheese, grated
1 tsp made mustard
1 egg
3 tblsp milk
1 tsp meat extract

Sieve the flour, salt and paprika into a 2 quart mixing bowl. Blend the butter and fork-in the cheese. Beat the mustard and egg together and mix with the milk. Mix into the dry ingredients, using a round bladed knife, to form a soft dough. Knead on a lightly floured board. Roll out to a thickness of ½ inch. Cut into 2½ inch rounds. Arrange the shaped scones in a ring on a non-metallic tray, leaving a gap in the centre. Mix 1 tsp meat extract with a little boiling water and brush over the surface of the scones (do not cover). Microwave immediately on Power 7, or Roast, for 5-6 minutes. Transfer to a cooling rack and allow to stand for 2-3 minutes. Serve hot with butter, or cold if preferred. As an alternative to the meat extract glaze, the cooked scones may be flashed under a pre-heated hot broiler to brown and crisp them.

Celebration Gateau (top), Collettes (center left) and Fruit and Almond Cake (bottom).

Microwave Meringues (right),
Victoria Sandwich (below) and
Porridge (bottom right).

Porridge

PREPARATION TIME: 5 minutes

MICROWAVE TIME: 9 minutes

SERVES: 3 people

2 cups milk and water, mixed
½ tsp salt
1 cup oatmeal
6 tblsp soft brown sugar
6 tblsp butter

Put the milk, water and salt into a 2 quart mixing bowl. Stir in the oatmeal. Microwave on Full Power for 3 minutes. Stir. Microwave on Full Power for 3 minutes. Stir. Microwave on Full Power for 3 minutes. Turn into individual serving dishes. Sprinkle with the brown sugar and top with the butter. Serve immediately.

Microwave Meringues

PREPARATION TIME: 20 minutes

MICROWAVE TIME: about 8 minutes

MAKES: 10 sandwiched meringues

1 egg white
12 tblsp confectioner's sugar, sieved
Pink food coloring
1½ cups chocolate buttercream
Chocolate vermicelli

Put the egg white into a 2 quart mixing bowl and beat until frothy. Gradually work in the confectioner's sugar and mix to give a really stiff frosting. Divide the frosting into two portions. Knead a few drops pink food coloring into one portion of frosting. Roll both the frostings separately into small balls, each about the size of a marble. Arrange 4 balls of frosting in a ring on a large dinner plate. Microwave on Full Power for 1½ minutes. Allow to stand for 2 minutes before removing to a cooling tray. Repeat until all the

mixture has been cooked. Fill the cooled meringue halves with the chocolate buttercream. Sprinkle with a little vermicelli and serve in paper cake cases.

Victoria Sandwich

PREPARATION TIME: 15 minutes

MICROWAVE TIME: 7 minutes

MAKES: 1 cake

Oil
Superfine sugar for dusting
3 eggs
1½ cups cake flour
1½ tsp baking powder
¾ softened butter
¾ cup superfine sugar
2 drops soy sauce
2 tblsp milk
3 tblsp strawberry jam

Lightly grease a 7 inch soufflé dish with oil, dust the sides with a little superfine sugar. Place a circle of wax paper in the base. Put the eggs, flour, butter, sugar, soy sauce and milk into a mixing bowl. Beat for 1 minute. Spoon into the prepared dish and smooth the top. Microwave on Full Power for about 7 minutes. Test by putting a wooden cocktail stick into the centre of the sponge after a 3 minute standing time. The cocktail stick should come out clean. Stand for 10 minutes. Turn out into a wire cooling rack. When quite cold, split in half horizontally. Sandwich together with the jam. Serve with a little superfine sugar sprinkled over the top.

Cream Slices

PREPARATION TIME: 15-20 minutes, plus cooling time

MICROWAVE TIME: 6-8 minutes

MAKES: about 6 slices

8oz puff pastry (small packet frozen puff pastry can be used)
Black cherry jam
3 tblsp confectioner's sugar, sieved
A few drops of pink food coloring

Roll the pastry into an oblong about 4 inches wide and 12-14 inches long. Cut in half, crossways. Dampen the surface of a suitable container. Lift one half of the pastry onto the prepared tray and microwave on Full Power for 3-4 minutes, until well puffed up (when the door is opened, the pastry should hold its shape). Allow to stand for 2-3 minutes and

and just 'set'. Remove from the microwave oven and allow to stand for 5 minutes before turning out. Allow to become quite cold. To make the buttercream, mix the cocoa with 2 tblsp boiling water to form a smooth paste. Beat with the butter and confectioner's sugar until light and creamy. Split the cooled cake in half horizontally. Sandwich together with a little of the buttercream and arrange on a cake board. Use the remaining buttercream to completely coat the 'hedgehog'. Form a 'snout' for his nose. Fork all over. Cut most of the chocolate chips in half and stud the hedgehog with these to represent the prickles. Use 1 chocolate chip for his nose and 2 raisins for his eyes. Spread some green coconut around the base for grass.

Rich Fruit Cake

PREPARATION TIME: 30 minutes

MICROWAVE TIME: 40 minutes

MAKES: 1 cake

½ cup softened butter
½ cup dark soft brown sugar
2 tblsp dark molasses
1 tsp soy sauce
3 eggs
3 tblsp milk
2 cups flour, sieved with 1 tsp mixed
    spice, a pinch of salt and ½ tsp
    baking soda
1.2lb mixed dried fruit (white raisins,
    raisins, currants and peel)
¼ cup chopped blanched almonds
½ cup glace cherries, washed and
    quartered
3 tblsp sherry or brandy

Lightly grease a deep, 9 inch diameter souffle dish. Line the base with a circle of ungreased wax paper and dust the sides with a little superfine sugar (knocking out any surplus). Beat the butter, sugar,

then remove to a cooling tray. Repeat the process with the remaining half of the pastry. Allow to cool. Using a sharp knife, divide each layer into 3 slices. Sandwich each group of three layers together with the jam. Mix the confectioner's sugar with a little boiling water to make a smooth, glossy frosting. Beat in a few drops pink food coloring. Quickly spread the frosting over the top of each layered slice. Cut each one into 3 slices.

Mr. Hedgehog Cake

PREPARATION TIME: 40 minutes

MICROWAVE TIME: 3½-7 minutes

MAKES: 1 cake

6 tblsp softened butter
6 tblsp superfine sugar
1 cup cake flour
2 eggs
1 tblsp milk
1 tblsp cocoa powder
A stick of butter
2 cups confectioner's sugar, sieved

1 packet large milk chocolate chips
2 raisins
Green colored coconut for grass

To make the sponge, put the butter, the superfine sugar, flour, eggs and milk into a mixing bowl. Beat with a wooden spoon for 1 minute. Lightly grease the base and sides of a 2 pint plastic pudding basin. Fill with the sponge mixture and smooth the top. Microwave on Full Power for 3½ minutes, or on Power 6, or Roast, for 6-7 minutes. The sponge should be well risen

This page: Mr. Hedgehog Cake (top), Cream Slice (center left) and Rich Fruit Cake (bottom).

Facing page: Pineapple Gateau (top right), Chocolate Pear Sponge (center left) and Cheese and Paprika Scones (bottom).

molasses and gravy browning in a large mixing bowl until light and fluffy. Gradually beat in the eggs and the milk. Add 1 tblsp flour with each addition of egg, to prevent it curdling. Fold in the remaining flour using a metal spoon. Fold in the fruits, nuts and glace cherries, together with the sherry or brandy. Spoon the mixture into the prepared container. Microwave on Power 4, Simmer or Defrost, for 40 minutes. Remove from the microwave oven and allow to stand in its dish for 20 minutes before turning out. When quite cold, the cake may be covered with almond paste and frosted, or finished with glace fruits, and glazed. Allow the cake to mature for at least 1 month before using.

Date and Walnut Loaf Cake (below) and Crepes Suzette (bottom).

Crepes Suzette

PREPARATION TIME: 25 minutes

MICROWAVE TIME: about 24 minutes

SERVES: 4-6 people

Pancakes
1 cup flour
Pinch salt
1 egg
⅔ cup milk
⅔ cup water
Cooking oil

Sauce
6 tblsp butter
4 tblsp superfine sugar
Grated rind of 1 orange
Grated rind and juice of ½ a lemon
4-5 tblsp brandy or Cointreau

Sieve the flour and salt into a bowl. Make a well in the centre. Add the egg and half of the milk. Beat well. Gradually beat in the remaining milk and the water. Beat in 1 tsp oil. Allow to stand for 10 minutes. Fry the pancakes in the usual way, making 12 pancakes in all. Fold the 12 cooked pancakes in half and then in half again, to form triangles. Arrange in a shallow dish. To make the sauce, put the butter into a 2¼ pint jug and microwave on Defrost for 5 minutes, or until melted and hot. Stir in the sugar to dissolve. Add the fruit rinds, lemon juice, and the brandy or Cointreau. Microwave on Full Power for 2 minutes. Stir. Pour over the pancakes. Cover with plastic wrap and microwave on Power 5, or Simmer, for 5 minutes. Turn each pancake over in the sauce before serving. Serve piping hot.

Pineapple Gateau

PREPARATION TIME: 30 minutes

MICROWAVE TIME: 7 minutes

MAKES: 1 gateau

Oil and superfine sugar
1 recipe quantity Victoria Sandwich mixture (see recipe)
8oz can pineapple slices, drained
1¼ cups heavy cream, whipped
1 cup chopped blanched almonds, toasted
Angelica for decoration

Lightly grease a 7 inch souffle dish or plastic pan with oil. Put a circle of wax paper into the base of the dish; dust the base and sides with superfine sugar (knock out any surplus). Spoon the prepared Victoria Sandwich mixture into the dish, and smooth the surface. Microwave on Full Power for about

7 minutes. Allow to stand for 10 minutes before turning out onto a wire cooling rack. Once the cake is quite cold, remove the wax paper. Split the cake in half horizontally. Chop 1 slice of pineapple and mix with 3 tblsp of the whipped cream; use to sandwich the cake layers together. Spread some of the cream round the sides of the cake and roll it in nuts to coat evenly. Arrange on a serving dish. Spread the top with the remaining cream, piping it if liked. Decorate the top with pineapple and angelica – see picture.

Chocolate Pear Sponge

PREPARATION TIME: 15 minutes

MICROWAVE TIME: 6 minutes

MAKES: 1 sponge cake

14 tblsp cake flour
1 tblsp cocoa powder
1 tsp baking powder
A stick of softened butter
1 tblsp milk
1 tsp mixed spice
4oz ripe pear, peeled, cored and chopped
Oil and superfine sugar for preparing the souffle dish

Put all the ingredients, apart from the pear, into a 2 quart mixing bowl. Mix with a wooden spoon and then beat for 1 minute. Fold in the pear, using a metal spoon. Lightly grease a 7 inch souffle dish; line the base with a circle of wax paper and coat the sides with a little superfine sugar. Turn the mixture into the prepared souffle dish and smooth the top. Microwave on Power 6, or Roast, for 4 minutes, and then on Full Power for 2 minutes. Allow to stand for 10 minutes before turning out onto a cooling rack. The cooling rack should be covered with a clean tea towel, sprinkled with a little superfine sugar. When quite cold, frost the cake with chocolate frosting.

Date and Walnut Loaf Cake

PREPARATION TIME: 15 minutes

COOKING TIME: 6 minutes

MAKES: 1 loaf

2 eggs
4 tblsp milk
1 tblsp corn syrup
1 tsp soy sauce
½ cup softened butter
1½ cups white flour
1½ tsp baking powder
¾ cup soft brown sugar
¾ cup chopped stoned dates
1 small banana, sliced
½ cup walnuts, chopped

Put the eggs, milk, corn syrup, gravy browning, butter, flour and brown sugar into a large mixing bowl. Beat with a wooden spoon. Using a metal spoon, fold in the dates, banana and walnuts. Turn into a lightly greased 2 quart microwave bread baker. Microwave on Full Power for about 6 minutes, turning the dish a half turn, halfway through cooking time. Allow to stand in the bread baker for 10 minutes before turning out. Serve sprinkled with superfine sugar.

VEGETARIAN
COOKING

**Mixed Vegetables in Yogurt (top), Noodles
and New Potato Fry (bottom).**

Contents

This page: Greenbeans with Coconut (top) and Spinach with Paneer (above). Facing page: Vegetable Stir Fry.

Introduction

It is amazing how rigid we are when it comes to the subject of food and what we eat. In all other aspects of life virtually anything goes: people walk the streets with pink hair; sail the Atlantic single-handed or jog around the houses for two hours every morning and yet if we prefer beans and lentils to beef and chicken we are considered as being rather odd.

Vegetarians are not cranks, and there is nothing weird and wonderful about a pattern of vegetarian eating; they just prefer to eat dishes which do not contain meat, poultry, game and, quite often, fish. 'Why don't they become ill?' you hear people say; 'Where do they get their energy from if they don't eat meat?'; 'How boring to live on just vegetables and those little dried peas!' As vegetarians will happily tell you, they feel perfectly healthy, have quite sufficient energy to cope with day-to-day activities and, above all, *they really enjoy their food.*

A vegetarian diet can be just as varied and interesting as one based on meat and fish. Meat is much the same the world over, which cannot be said of the wide and wonderful range of fresh fruits and vegetables. And it is variety which is very much the keynote of vegetarian eating: different pastas, rices, cheeses, nuts and pulses are just a selection of the varied ingredients of a vegetarian diet. Most important of all, vegetarian dishes are every bit as nutritious as their meat-rich counterparts. The main difference lies with the types of food which provide us with the necessary nutrients. In a typical vegetarian dish, the protein usually comes from pulses, nuts or cheese, or a combination of these ingredients. Minerals, vitamins, fats and carbohydrates come from all the other basic foods, such as those already mentioned.

Eating 'the vegetarian way' has all sorts of advantages in its favor. A meatless diet is a very healthy one since it is nutritious, low in fat and high in bulk and fiber. Vegetarians rarely need to watch their weight as a diet that is high in natural fiber and low in fat is comparatively low in calories. The traditional pattern of Western eating is relatively expensive to follow, whereas vegetarian dishes are more economical to prepare and cook. In fact, meatless meals can simply make a nice change from the traditional pattern of eating. Vegetarian cooking is fun, and eating vegetarian meals is healthy and good for you.

Vegetarian food really can be exciting and delicious and even if you are not a committed vegetarian many of the ideas in this book are well worth trying. The dishes combine unusual tastes and textures with an imaginative use of spices and fresh herbs for extra flavor. If you served many of the recipes to your family and friends they probably wouldn't even realize that their meal was meatless.

Soups

Cucumber Soup

PREPARATION TIME: 15 minutes

COOKING TIME: 8-10 minutes

SERVES: 4 people

1 large cucumber
1 cup water
2½ cups chicken stock
1¼ tblsp white wine vinegar
2½ tblsp cornstarch mixed with
2½ tblsp water
2½ tblsp soured cream
2½ tblsp natural yogurt
Salt and ground white pepper to taste
1¼ tblsp chopped chives or scallion
   tops
Chili powder

Cut ¼ of the cucumber into wafer thin rounds and keep aside for garnishing. Puree the rest of the cucumber with the water in a liquidizer. Put the chicken stock and the pureed cucumber into a saucepan and bring to the boil over a medium heat. Add the vinegar and cook for 1 minute. Add the cornstarch mixture gradually. Stir well until the soup starts to thicken. Simmer for 2-3 minutes. Remove from the heat and cool slightly. Blend in the liquidizer and add the soured cream and yogurt. Return to the saucepan and season with salt and pepper. Heat through gently to serve hot or chill to serve cold. Serve garnished with sliced cucumber and chopped chives or scallion tops. Dust with chili powder.

Daal Soup

This is a thick and hearty soup, made from lentils. The lentils most often used for making soup are red lentils, or yellow lentils which are called Toor daal. The recipe below can be made with either variety.

PREPARATION TIME: 15-20
                                      minutes

COOKING TIME: 15 minutes

SERVES: 4-6 people

3 cups red lentils (see above)
3¾ cups water
4 canned tomatoes, drained and
   crushed

1 green chili, sliced lengthways and
   seeded
2½ tblsp natural yogurt or soured
   cream
1 tblsp butter
1 medium onion, peeled and chopped
Salt and freshly ground black pepper
   to taste
1-2 sprigs fresh green coriander
   leaves, chopped

Wash the lentils in 4-5 changes of water. Drain the lentils and put them into a pan with the water. Cover the pan and bring to the boil; simmer for 10 minutes. Beat until smooth with an egg whisk. Add the crushed tomatoes and green chili and simmer gently for 2 minutes. Stir in the yogurt or soured cream. Melt the butter in a small pan and fry the onion until golden. Season the hot soup with salt and pepper and pour into a serving bowl; sprinkle with the fried onion and chopped coriander. Serve immediately with buttered brown bread, crisp rolls or croutons.

Tomato Saar

This is a thin tomato soup from the South of India. It makes a refreshing and interesting starter.

PREPARATION TIME: 15 minutes

COOKING TIME: 17-18 minutes

SERVES: 4-6 people

2½ tsp butter
1 small onion, peeled and chopped
½lb tomatoes, skinned and chopped
4 cups water
1¼ tblsp tomato paste
4-6 green Cilantro (Chinese Parsley)
   leaves
Salt and freshly ground black pepper
   to taste
3 cloves of garlic, peeled and crushed

Garnish

1-2 sprigs fresh green coriander or
   parsley leaves, chopped
1 green chili, chopped (optional)

Melt half of the butter and fry the onion for 3-4 minutes. Add the skinned and chopped tomatoes and cook for 5 minutes. Blend the

water and tomato paste and add to the onion and tomatoes. Add Cilantro (Chinese Parsley) leaves. Season with salt and pepper. Cover and simmer for 5-7 minutes. Heat the remaining butter and fry the crushed cloves of garlic until dark brown. Pour the mixture over the simmering tomato soup. Remove from the heat. Sprinkle over the chopped coriander and chili. Discard green chili before eating. Serve piping hot either with French bread or with a little plain boiled rice. Alternatively: blend the skinned tomatoes to give a smooth textured soup.

Mixed Vegetable Soup

This Indian recipe can include a wide variety of vegetables. One creates one's own dish by adding or subtracting one or more vegetables.

PREPARATION TIME: 15 minutes

COOKING TIME: about 20 minutes

SERVES: 6 people

2½ tsp butter
1 medium onion, peeled and chopped
6 cloves
1 inch piece cinnamon stick
4 small green cardamoms
1 small bayleaf
1 medium potato, peeled and
   chopped
2 carrots, peeled and chopped
1 banana, peeled and chopped
6 flowerets of cauliflower
½ cup shelled fresh or frozen peas
1 leek, washed and chopped
1 stick celery, chopped
½ cup green beans (sliced or
   chopped)
4 cups water
Salt and freshly ground black pepper
   to taste

Garnish

1-2 sprigs fresh green coriander
1-2 green chilies chopped

Melt the butter in a large saucepan and fry the onion for 3 minutes. Add the cloves, cinnamon, cardamom, bayleaf and fry for 1 minute. Add the potato, carrots, banana and cauliflower. Fry for 3 minutes. Add the remaining vegetables and cook for 2-3 minutes. Add water and salt and

pepper to taste. Cover and simmer gently for 8-13 minutes until vegetables are cooked. Adjust seasoning. Garnish with chopped coriander leaves and green chilies. Discard green chilies before eating. The vegetables should float in the clear soup; do not blend.

Carrot Soup

PREPARATION TIME: 12 minutes

COOKING TIME: 20-25 minutes

SERVES: 4 people

4-6 carrots, peeled and cut into thick
   slices
1 medium onion, peeled and
   quartered
1 medium turnip, peeled and cut into
   wedges
2 cloves garlic, peeled
3 cups water or chicken stock
¾ tsp dried thyme
Salt and ground white pepper to taste
Hot pepper sauce to taste

Garnish

1 tblsp toasted sunflower seeds,
   flaked almonds and pistachio nuts
   (mixed together)

Put the carrots, onion, turnip, garlic and water into a large saucepan. Cover and simmer for 15 minutes. Add thyme and salt and pepper to taste and simmer for a further 5 minutes. Cool slightly and blend in a liquidizer. Return to the saucepan and heat the soup through. Ladle the soup into bowls. Add hot pepper sauce to taste. Serve garnished with toasted nuts.

Facing page: Tomato Saar (top right), Daal Soup (center left) and Mixed Vegetable Soup (bottom).

Minestrone Soup

This famous vegetable and pasta soup from Italy can be made in many different ways. The recipe below is a simple, but delicious one – served with bread, it is a complete meal in itself.

PREPARATION TIME: 20 minutes
COOKING TIME: 30 minutes
SERVES: 4-6 people

4 tblsp olive oil
1 medium onion, peeled and chopped
2 cloves of garlic, peeled and crushed
2 medium potatoes, peeled and diced
3 carrots, peeled and diced
2 stalks celery, chopped
1½ cups shredded cabbage
4-5 skinned or canned tomatoes, chopped
3¾ cups water or chicken stock
1 bouquet garni
1½ cups shelled fresh, or frozen peas

Quick Tomato Soup (above right), Minestrone Soup (right) and Onion Soup (far right).

½ cup boiled and cooked red kidney
    beans
1 cup macaroni or any shaped pasta
Salt and freshly ground black pepper
    to taste
½ cup grated Parmesan cheese

Heat the olive oil in a saucepan and
fry the onion and garlic until the
onion is soft, 2-3 minutes. Stir in
the potatoes, carrots and celery
and fry for 3 minutes; add the
cabbage and tomatoes. Cook for 5-
6 minutes. Add water or stock and
bouquet garni. Add peas, kidney
beans, pasta and simmer gently,
covered, for 10-15 minutes, or until
the pasta is just tender. Season
with salt and pepper and ladle into
bowls. Sprinkle generously with
grated Parmesan cheese before
serving. Serve Minestrone soup
with crusty bread.

Quick Tomato Soup

This is quite an exotic soup and is
made within a few minutes. It is
ideal for a hot summer's day.

PREPARATION TIME: 10 minutes
plus chilling time

SERVES: 4-6 people

2½ cups chilled tomato juice
¼ cup fresh or canned tomato paste,
    chilled
¾ tsp hot red pepper sauce
¾ tsp grated lemon peel
¾ tsp grated orange peel
¼-⅓ cup dry white wine
Salt and ground white pepper to taste
Little iced water
4 tblsp natural yogurt
⅓ cup soured cream
6 balls of honeydew melon
6 balls of water melon
6 balls of ripe pear

Garnish
Mint leaves

Mix the tomato juice, tomato
paste, pepper sauce, fruit peels and
wine together. Season with salt and
pepper, cover and refrigerate for 3-
4 hours. Thin the soup with a little
iced water if necessary. Whisk the
yogurt and cream together until
smooth and light. Divide the soup
amongst 4-6 bowls. Spoon the
yogurt and cream mixture into the
centre of each portion and float the
fruit balls on top. Garnish with
mint leaves and serve.

Rice and Mushroom Soup

Ideal for a party or for summer afternoons.

PREPARATION TIME: 10 minutes	
COOKING TIME: 40-50 minutes	
SERVES: 6-8 people	

1 cup wild rice or brown rice
1 cup water
2 tblsp butter
1 medium onion, peeled and finely chopped
1 stalk celery, chopped
1 cup mushrooms, chopped
1 level tsp powdered garam masala (hot aromatic powder)
1 level tsp ground mustard seed
Salt and freshly ground black pepper to taste
4 cups water or stock
2 tblsp cornstarch blended with 2½ tblsp water
⅓ cup light cream

Garnish
1-2 sprigs fresh green coriander or parsley, chopped

Wash the rice in 3-4 changes of water; cook covered in 1 cup water for 25-30 minutes, or until rice is tender. Keep on one side. Melt the butter in a large saucepan; saute the onion until tender for 3-5 minutes. Add the celery and mushrooms. Cook for 1-2 minutes. Stir in the powdered garam masala, mustard and salt and pepper to taste. Add the water or stock. Simmer for 5 minutes. Add the cornstarch mixture and simmer for a further 3 minutes. Add the cooked rice and cream. Gently stir over a low heat for 2 minutes to heat through. Ladle the soup into bowls and garnish with coriander or parsley.

Onion Soup

Onion soup has been made famous by the French. Here is a delicious recipe based on the French style.

PREPARATION TIME: 20 minutes	
COOKING TIME: 1 hour	
SERVES: 4-6 people	

6 tblsp butter
3-4 large onions, peeled and sliced into rings
2½ tblsp flour
3¾ cups beef stock

Salt and ground white pepper to taste
6 slices of French bread (¾ inch) thick
2 cloves of garlic, peeled and bruised
6 tblsp grated Parmesan cheese

Melt the butter in a saucepan and fry the onions briskly on a very low heat. Cover and simmer the onions in their own juices for 25-30 minutes, stirring occasionally until golden brown. Remove from the heat. Stir in the flour and add the stock gradually. Season with salt and pepper and return to heat. Bring to the boil quickly; reduce the heat and simmer covered for 15-20 minutes. Rub the bread pieces each side with the bruised garlic. Float the bread rounds in the soup and sprinkle grated Parmesan cheese generously over the top. Put under the broiler and cook for 2-3 minutes or until the top is golden. Serve at once. Alternatively – fry the bread rounds or bread slices in butter prior to rubbing with garlic.

Carrot Soup (top), Rice and Mushroom Soup (center right) and Cucumber Soup (bottom left).

Snacks and Starters

Flour Pancake

This is a favorite pancake from the southern part of India and it is really worth making; good, wholesome and nutritious.

PREPARATION TIME: 10 minutes

COOKING TIME: 20 minutes

SERVES: 6 people

2½ cups whole-wheat flour
½ tsp salt
⅔ cup natural yogurt
1 egg, beaten
1 small onion, peeled and chopped
1-2 green chilies, chopped
2 sprigs fresh green coriander leaves,
*   chopped*
1¼ tblsp grated fresh coconut, or
*   desiccated coconut*
2½ tsp sugar
Olive oil

Sieve the flour and salt and add the yogurt and egg. Mix in sufficient water to make a thickish batter of pouring consistency. Beat the mixture well and add the onion, chili, coriander, coconut and sugar. Mix well. Allow to stand for 2-3 minutes. Heat 1¼ tblsp oil in a small frying pan or omelette pan. Spoon in a little of the batter to give a depth of 1¼ inches. Cover with a lid and cook over a low heat for 3-5 minutes. Turn the pancake over and pour a little oil aroundthe edge; cover and cook until the pancake is set and brown on both sides. Repeat with the remaining batter until you have several pancakes. Serve piping hot.

Dosas

Dosas can be eaten plain or with a filling. Eat them as a snack, for breakfast, or as a main meal with a filling and accompanied by chutney and daal (lentil dish).

PREPARATION TIME: overnight, plus 20 minutes

COOKING TIME: 30-45 minutes

SERVES: 6 people

1lb rice
½lb white lentils (urid daal)
½ tsp fenugreek seeds

1¼ tsp dried yeast
1¼ tsp sugar
¾ tsp salt
1¼ tblsp natural yogurt
Olive oil

Wash the rice and white lentils separately in 3-4 changes of water. Soak in fresh water for 1 hour. Grind the rice with a little water to a thick, coarse paste. Grind the white lentils with fenugreek seeds and a little water into a fine paste. (Use a food processor, food

liquidizer or food grinder). Mix the dried yeast with 1¼ tblsp tepid water and the sugar. Mix well and leave to stand for 10 minutes until frothy. Mix the ground rice and lentils with the salt, yeast and yogurt and mix well. Cover with a cloth and leave in a dark, warm place overnight. Next day mix well with sufficient water to give a smooth, thickish batter. Heat a medium non-stick frying pan and grease well with 1¼ tsp oil. Pour in 2½-3¾ tblsp of the rice batter,

Bessan Omelette (top right), Flour Pancake (center left) and Dosas (bottom).

spread it around to make a thin pancake. Cover with a lid. Cook for 3-4 minutes; spoon a little oil around the edge of the frying pan and turn the dosa over. Cook for a

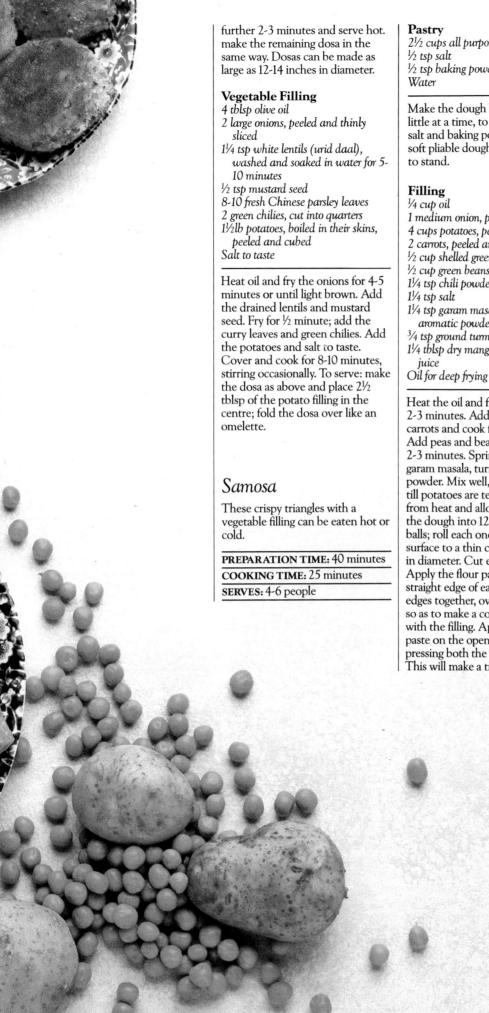

further 2-3 minutes and serve hot. make the remaining dosa in the same way. Dosas can be made as large as 12-14 inches in diameter.

Vegetable Filling

4 tblsp olive oil
2 large onions, peeled and thinly sliced
1¼ tsp white lentils (urid daal), washed and soaked in water for 5-10 minutes
½ tsp mustard seed
8-10 fresh Chinese parsley leaves
2 green chilies, cut into quarters
1½lb potatoes, boiled in their skins, peeled and cubed
Salt to taste

Heat oil and fry the onions for 4-5 minutes or until light brown. Add the drained lentils and mustard seed. Fry for ½ minute; add the curry leaves and green chilies. Add the potatoes and salt to taste. Cover and cook for 8-10 minutes, stirring occasionally. To serve: make the dosa as above and place 2½ tblsp of the potato filling in the centre; fold the dosa over like an omelette.

Samosa

These crispy triangles with a vegetable filling can be eaten hot or cold.

PREPARATION TIME:	40 minutes
COOKING TIME:	25 minutes
SERVES:	4-6 people

Pastry

2½ cups all purpose flour, sieved
½ tsp salt
½ tsp baking powder
Water

Make the dough by adding water, a little at a time, to the sieved flour, salt and baking powder. Mix to a soft pliable dough. Cover and allow to stand.

Filling

¼ cup oil
1 medium onion, peeled and chopped
4 cups potatoes, peeled and cubed
2 carrots, peeled and grated
½ cup shelled green peas
½ cup green beans, chopped
1¼ tsp chili powder
1¼ tsp salt
1¼ tsp garam masala powder (hot aromatic powder)
¾ tsp ground turmeric
1¼ tblsp dry mango powder, or lemon juice
Oil for deep frying

Heat the oil and fry the onions for 2-3 minutes. Add the potatoes and carrots and cook for 3 minutes. Add peas and beans and cook for 2-3 minutes. Sprinkle chili, salt, garam masala, turmeric and mango powder. Mix well, cover and cook till potatoes are tender. Remove from heat and allow to cool. Divide the dough into 12-14 equal sized balls; roll each one out on a floured surface to a thin circle, 2-3 inches in diameter. Cut each circle in half. Apply the flour paste on the straight edge of each half. bring the edges together, overlapping them so as to make a cone. Fill the cone with the filling. Apply a little flour paste on the open edge and seal by pressing both the edges together. This will make a triangular shape.

Make all the samosas in the same way. Heat the oil for deep frying. When the oil is hot, reduce the heat and fry the samosas, a few at a time, until golden brown on either side (about 4-5 minutes). Drain on kitchen paper and serve with chutney or tomato sauce.

Curry Puffs

Like sausage rolls, curried vegetable puffs make an ideal dish for snacks and cocktails. The size can be varied to suit the occasion.

PREPARATION TIME:	1 hour
COOKING TIME:	20 minutes
SERVES:	4-6

1lb ready-made puff pastry

Filling

¼ cup oil
1 large onion, peeled and chopped
1¼ tsp cumin seeds
4 cups potatoes, peeled and diced
2 carrots, peeled and shredded
1 cup shelled peas
1¼ tsp salt
1¼ tsp freshly ground black pepper
2-3 sprigs fresh green coriander leaves, chopped
1¼ tsp garam masala powder (hot aromatic powder)

Flour paste: mix together 2½ tsp flour with water to make a sticky paste.

Heat the oil and fry the onion for 2 minutes. Add cumin seeds and allow to crackle, then add the diced potatoes. Stir fry over a medium heat for 5-6 minutes. Add the carrots and stir fry for 2 minutes. Add the peas and season with salt, pepper and chopped coriander leaves. Stir well. Cover and cook for 5-6 minutes or until the potatoes are tender. Sprinkle with the garam masala and lemon juice. Mix well. Remove from the heat and allow to cool. Roll out the puff pastry thinly. Cut into 3 inch by 6 inch rectangles. Place 1¼ tblsp filling at one end and roll up the pastry like jelly roll. Secure the ends with the flour and water paste. Preheat the oven to 375°F.

Potato Cutlets (top), Samosa (above left) and Curry Puffs (left).

Arrange the curry puffs on greased cooky sheets and bake for 10-15 minutes or until golden. Serve hot with tomato sauce.

Potato Cutlets

PREPARATION TIME: 30 minutes

COOKING TIME: 30 minutes

SERVES: 6 people

1¼ tblsp oil
1 medium onion, peeled and chopped
1½ cups shelled peas
6 cups potatoes, boiled in their skins, peeled and mashed
1¼ tsp salt
1¼ tsp freshly ground black pepper
2½ tblsp lemon juice
2 eggs, beaten
Breadcrumbs
Oil for shallow frying

Heat 1¼ tblsp oil in a frying pan and fry the onion for 3 minutes; add the peas and fry for 2 minutes. Mix the onion and peas with the mashed potatoes. Add salt and pepper to taste and the lemon juice. Mix well. Divide mixture into 24-30 small even-sized cakes. Dip firstly into beaten egg and then coat evenly with breadcrumbs. Heat sufficient oil in a frying pan for shallow frying. Shallow fry the potato cutlets for 3-4 minutes or until golden. Serve hot or cold with chutney or tomato sauce.

Bessan Omelettes

These vegetarian omelettes are made with chickpea (baisen) flour and can be eaten as a quick snack. Easy to make and quick to prepare, they are ideal for unexpected friends or late night guests.

PREPARATION TIME: 10 minutes

COOKING TIME: 20 minutes

MAKES: 12

2½ cups sieved bessan flour (made from chick-peas)
1 small onion, peeled and finely chopped
1-2 green chilies, chopped (optional)
2 sprigs fresh green coriander, chopped
2 tomatoes, seeded and diced
½ cup shelled peas
¾ tsp salt
Pinch chili powder
Olive oil

Mix the bessan flour with the onion, chilies, coriander, tomatoes and peas. Add sufficient water to made a thick batter, about 1¾ cups. Season with salt and chili powder, Mix well and allow to stand for 5 minutes. Heat a solid based frying pan or griddle pan and brush with oil. Ladle in sufficient batter to cover the base of the pan. Cover and cook over a low heat for 4-5 minutes. Turn the omelette over and cook for 3-4 minutes. Both sides should be browned evenly. Make the rest of the omelettes in the same way. Serve hot with tomato sauce.

Stuffed Summer Squash

Summer Squash can be stuffed with a vegetable or meat filling. Here is a delectable recipe for a vegetable stuffed Summer Squash.

PREPARATION TIME: 15 minutes

COOKING TIME: 45 minutes

SERVES: 4-6 people

2 Summer Squash 6-8 inches in length

Filling
¼ cup oil
1 large onion, peeled and chopped
4 cups potatoes, peeled and diced
1¼ tsp crushed fresh root ginger
1¼ tsp crushed garlic
1¼ tsp chili powder
¾ tsp turmeric powder
1¼ tsp garam masala powder (hot aromatic powder)

1 cup shelled peas
4 tomatoes, chopped
¾ tsp salt
¾ tsp freshly ground black pepper
1 green chili, chopped
2½ tsp melted butter

Heat the oil in a wok or large frying pan and fry the onion for 2 minutes. Add the potatoes and stir-fry for 3-4 minutes. Add the ginger, garlic, chili powder, turmeric and garam masala powder. Mix well and add the peas, tomatoes, salt and pepper and the green chili; cover and cook until the potatoes are tender, about 6-8 minutes. Add the lemon juice. Remove a thin slice from each end of the summer squash. Scoop out the centre pith leaving a ¾ inch shell. Remove the skin in alternate strips to give it firmness. Fill the hollowed summer squash with the prepared potato filling. Place the stuffed summer squash on a rectangle of foil and brush with melted butter; season with salt and pepper. Wrap the foil around the summer squash; bake at 350°F for 40-45 minutes. Remove the foil from time to time and brush with the juices. Serve hot.

Vegetable Kebabs

This Turkish/Greek recipe makes an ideal side dish for barbecue parties.

PREPARATION TIME: 30 minutes

COOKING TIME: 30 minutes

SERVES: 4-6 people

1 eggplant cut into 1 inch pieces
1 large green pepper, seeded and cut into 1 inch pieces
12-14 small cherry tomatoes (or 6-8 tomatoes, halved)
12-14 small onions, peeled and blanched for 5 minutes
12-14 large mushrooms
2 medium potatoes, boiled in their skins, peeled and cut into 1 inch cubes
Olive oil
2½ tblsp lemon juice
½ tsp salt
¾ tsp freshly ground black pepper

Put all the vegetables into a large bowl and add 60ml (4 tblsp) olive oil, lemon juice and salt and pepper. Mix together and leave to stand for 10-15 minutes, turning the vegetables once or twice. Thread the vegetables alternately onto skewers. Brush with the marinade. Broil for 3-4 minutes, until evenly browned. Brush the vegetables with oil or marinade during grilling. Serve piping hot.

Stuffed Peppers

PREPARATION TIME: 30 minutes

COOKING TIME: 30-40 minutes

SERVES: 6 people

6 even sized peppers (green or red)
¼ cup oil
1 medium onion, peeled and chopped
2 cloves garlic, peeled and chopped
2 tomatoes, chopped
1 green chili, chopped
1 cup plain boiled rice
1 medium potato, peeled and diced
½ tsp salt

¾ tsp freshly ground black pepper
½ cup shelled peas
1¼ tblsp lemon juice
1¼ tblsp chopped parsley or coriander leaves
2½ tblsp beef stock or water

Cut a slice from the top of each pepper; scoop out the centre seeds. Heat the oil and fry the onion for 1-2 minutes. Add the garlic, tomatoes and green chili and stir fry for 2-3 minutes. Add the rice, potato, salt and pepper, peas and lemon juice and parsley. Cover and cook for 2-4 minutes. Arrange the peppers in an ovenproof dish and stuff the peppers with the rice mixture. Pour the stock around the peppers. Bake at 375°F for 20-30 minutes, basting occasionally with the juices. Serve hot.

Stuffed Tomatoes

Tomatoes stuffed with a vegetable filling and served with a tangy sauce make a good starter.

PREPARATION TIME: 20 minutes

COOKING TIME: 15-18 minutes

SERVES: 6 people

12 medium size firm tomatoes
2½ tblsp oil
10-12 scallions (only the white part), chopped
2½ tsp chopped parsley or coriander leaves
1 cup cooked rice
2½ tsp pine kernels, or skinned hazelnuts, chopped
2½ tsp roasted sesame seeds
¾ tsp salt
½ tsp freshly ground black pepper
½ tsp ground mixed spice
1 cup beef or vegetable stock
2½ tsp cornstarch
2½ tblsp lemon juice
1 egg, well beaten

Stuffed Summer Squash (top), Vegetable Kebabs (center right) and Stuffed Peppers (bottom).

Slice the tops off the tomatoes and scoop out the centre pulp, leaving a ¾ inch "shell". Reserve the tomato pulp. Heat the oil in the frying pan and fry the onions for 2-3 minutes. Add the parsley, cooked rice, nuts, sesame seeds, salt and pepper and allspice. Add the tomato pulp and any juice which may have formed. Cook, uncovered, for 3-4 minutes, until most of the moisture has evaporated. Stuff the hollowed tomatoes with the rice mixture and arrange in a large frying pan. Add the stock and cook for 4 minutes. Remove the tomatoes. Bring the liquid back to the boil and add the blended cornstarch and lemon juice. Remove from the heat. Add the beaten egg a little at a time. Return the mixture to the heat and cook until thickened. Add the stuffed tomatoes and cook over a low heat for 5 minutes, spooning the sauce over the tomatoes from time to time.

Fritters
(TEMPURA)

This is a Japanese dish and is very popular. The batter may be used for meats as well.

PREPARATION TIME: 10 minutes

COOKING TIME: 10-15 minutes

SERVES: 4 people

Batter
225g (8oz) all purpose flour
15ml (1 tblsp) cornstarch
¼ tsp salt
1 cup chilled water
1 egg yolk
2 egg whites, stiffly beaten

Oil for deep frying
1 cup fresh green beans, cut into 2 inch pieces
10-12 fresh asparagus spears, cut in 2 inch lengths
1 eggplant, cut into 1 inch cubes
1 large potato, peeled and sliced ¼ inch thick
10-12 fresh mushrooms, halved
6-8 cauliflower flowerets, halved

Tempura sauce: A
1 cup water
¼ cup sherry
¼ cup soya sauce
1¼ tsp sugar
½ a chicken stock cube

Mix the ingredients together and bring to the boil. Stir until dissolved.

Tempura sauce: B
1 inch fresh root ginger, peeled and grated
2½ tblsp grated turnip

2½ tblsp grated radish
¼ cup prepared mustard
¼ cup soya sauce

Mix the ingredients together and keep covered.

To make the batter: mix together the flour, cornstarch and salt. Make a well in the centre. Mix the chilled water and egg yolk together and pour into the centre of the flour. Stir in the flour and blend lightly. Fold in the whisked egg whites.

Heat oil for deep frying. Dip the vegetables into the batter and fry in hot oil for 2-3 minutes until golden. Drain on kitchen paper and serve hot with the Tempura sauces. Use the batter within a few minutes of making. Do not allow it to stand for long.

Cheese and Lentil Balls

PREPARATION TIME: 30 minutes

COOKING TIME: 1 hour

SERVES: 4 people

1½ cups red lentils
1½ cups water
1 cup grated cheese
1 medium onion, peeled and chopped
2 large eggs
½ cup fresh breadcrumbs
1½ tsp mixed dried herbs
1½ tblsp lemon juice
Salt to taste
½ tsp freshly ground black pepper
Oil for shallow frying

Wash the lentils in 3-4 changes of water. Drain the lentils and put them into a pan with the water. Cook until the lentils are tender and the water has been absorbed. Remove from heat and allow to cool. Mix the cooked lentils with the cheese, onion, egg, breadcrumbs, herbs, salt and pepper and the lemon juice. Mix well and shape into balls. Shallow fry the balls for 4-5 minutes on each side until golden brown. Drain on absorbent paper and serve immediately.

Mixed Nut Rissoles

PREPARATION TIME: 15 minutes

COOKING TIME: 20-25 minutes

SERVES: 4 people

2 tblsp hazelnuts, chopped
½ cup shelled peanuts, chopped
½ cup cashew nuts, chopped

2 tblsp pistachio nuts, chopped
1 onion, peeled and chopped
¾ cup fresh breadcrumbs
3 eggs, beaten
Salt and freshly ground black pepper to taste
¾ tsp dried, chopped marjoram
1 carrot, peeled and grated
1¼ tblsp lemon juice
Little milk
Oil for shallow frying

Mix the chopped nuts with the onion, breadcrumbs, eggs, salt and pepper, marjoram, carrot and lemon juice. Add a little milk to bind the mixture, if necessary. Shape into rissoles. Shallow fry the rissoles in oil, for 4-5 minutes on each side, until golden brown. Drain well on absorbent paper and serve immediately. Alternatively, brush the rissoles generously with oil, put them onto a cooky tray and bake in the oven at 425°F for 15 minutes. Turn the rissoles halfway through cooking and brush with extra oil.

Cashew Nut Pie

PREPARATION TIME: 20-25 minutes

COOKING TIME: 30-40 minutes

SERVES: 4 people

Filling
2 medium onions, peeled and chopped
2 tblsp oil
2 cups shredded cabbage
½ cup carrots, peeled and grated

Pie Crust
1 cup crushed cornflakes
½ cup cashew nuts, coarsely ground
1½ cup grated cheese
1 tsp mixed dried herbs
Salt and freshly ground black pepper to taste
2 large eggs
1 cup fresh breadcrumbs
1 tblsp oil
¼ cup butter

To make the filling: fry the onions in the oil for 2 minutes; add the cabbage and carrots and fry for a further 4-5 minutes. Remove from the heat and allow to cool.

To make the pie crust: mix all the ingredients together in a bowl, apart from the oil, butter and ½ cup of the grated cheese. Grease a cake pan with the oil. Press half the pie crust ingredients out to form an even base. Spread the filling mixture on top, and then press over the remaining pie crust ingredients. Sprinkle with the

remaining grated cheese and dot with butter. Bake in oven at 400°F for 25-30 minutes.

Tomato, Onion and Mushroom Flan

PREPARATION TIME: 20 minutes

COOKING TIME: 40-45 minutes

SERVES: 6 people

8oz basic pastry
2 cups grated Cheddar cheese
4 tomatoes, skinnned and chopped
1¼ tblsp chopped chives or parsley
1 cup mushrooms, sliced
2½ tsp corn oil
1 large onion, peeled and chopped
3 eggs, beaten
1⅔ cup milk
¾ tsp salt
½ tsp freshly ground black pepper

Roll out the pastry and use to line a 8-9 inch flan dish. Put ¼ cup of the grated cheese into the pastry case followed by the tomatoes, chives or parsley and the mushrooms. Heat the corn oil and fry the onion for 2-3 minutes. Mix the beaten eggs with the milk, salt and pepper and fried onion. Pour into the flan case and top with the remaining grated cheese. Bake at 400°F for 35-40 minutes, or until set. Serve hot or cold.

Mixed Nut Rissoles (left),
Cheese and Lentil Rissoles
(below) and Cashew Nut Pie
(bottom).

Pakora

This is the Indian version of vegetable fritters. Fried with or without batter, they make an interesting starter or snack.

PREPARATION TIME: 15 minutes

COOKING TIME: 15-20 minutes

SERVES: 4-6 people

1 large potato, or
2 medium potatoes, peeled and cut into ¼ inch thick slices
8-10 cauliflower flowerets, halved lengthways
6 carrots, cut into 2 inch lengths and halved
1 eggplant, cut into 2 inch cubes
6 zucchini, trimmed and cut into 2 inch pieces and then quartered
1-2 green peppers, seeded and cut into ¼ inch) thick rounds or 1 inch pieces
1¼ tsp salt
1¼ tsp red chili powder
¾ tsp turmeric powder
Oil for deep frying
6 lemon wedges

Sprinkle the vegetables with the spices and rub well in. Keep on one side. Heat the oil for deep frying. When it is beginning to smoke, reduce the heat. Fry the vegetables a few at a time, in batches. Fry for 2-3 minutes and drain on kitchen paper. Serve piping hot with wedges of lemon and a sweet and sour chutney or tomato ketchup. (These uncoated fritters are called Bhaja).

Batter

2½ cups bessan flour, sieved (made from chick-peas)
1¼ tsp salt
1¼ tsp chili powder
1¼ tsp ground cumin
1 tblsp lemon juice
1¼ cups water

Mix the sieved flour with the salt, chili powder, cumin and lemon juice. Make a well in the centre and add the water; stir in the bessan flour until all the flour has been incorporated. Beat well to give a smooth batter. Adjust seasoning. Allow the batter to stand for a few minutes. Heat the oil as above. Dip the vegetables into the batter and then fry for 2-3 minutes. Drain on kitchen paper and serve piping hot with tomato sauce. Other vegetables which may be used: onions rings, raw banana slices, green tomato slices, spinach leaves.

Stuffed Mushrooms

PREPARATION TIME: 20 minutes

COOKING TIME: 10-15 minutes

SERVES: 4-6 people

Filling

1 small onion, peeled and finely chopped
2½ tsp oil
½ inch fresh root ginger, peeled and crushed
2 cloves garlic, peeled and crushed
2 cups boiled, peeled and mashed potatoes
Salt and freshly ground black pepper to taste
1¼ tblsp lemon juice
2½ tsp chopped chives or parsley

20-24 large mushrooms
1½ cup grated Cheddar cheese
Oil for brushing

Fry the onion in the 2½ tsp oil for 2 minutes; add the ginger and garlic. Fry for 1 minute and mix with the mashed potatoes. Season to taste with salt, pepper, lemon juice and chopped parsley. Mix well. Remove the stalks from the mushrooms; stuff the hollows with the potato filling and top with a little Cheddar cheese. Brush the mushrooms with a little oil and arrange them on a baking tray. Bake the mushrooms in a moderately hot oven, 375°F, for 10 minutes until the cheese is brown.

Aloo Bonda

This is an Indian potato fritter recipe made in the shape of spicy balls. Eaten hot or cold, they are ideal for parties, snacks and picnics.

PREPARATION TIME: 25 minutes

COOKING TIME: 30 minutes

SERVES: 4-6 people

Batter

2 cups bessan flour, sieved (made from chick-peas)
½ tsp salt
½ tsp baking powder
1¼ cups water

1lb potatoes, boiled in their skins and peeled
1 large or 2 medium onions, peeled and chopped
1 inch fresh root ginger, peeled and finely chopped
2-3 green chilies, chopped
4-5 sprigs fresh green coriander leaves, chopped
¾ tsp salt
½ tsp freshly ground black pepper
1¼ tblsp lemon juice
Oil for deep frying

Mix the sieved flour with the salt and baking powder. Make a well in the centre and add the water. Beat well to give a smooth batter. Chop the boiled potatoes into tiny cubes; add the chopped onions, ginger, chilies, coriander leaves, salt and pepper to taste and lemon juice. Mix well and adjust seasoning to taste. Mould into even-sized balls with dampened hands. Heat the oil for deep frying. When hot, dip the vegetable balls into the batter and then fry for 3-4 minutes over a gentle heat until golden brown. Drain on kitchen paper and serve with tomato sauce.

This page: Aloo Bonda (top), Fritters (Tempura) (center right) and Pakora (bottom left).

Facing page: Stuffed Tomatoes (top right), Stuffed Mushrooms (center left) and Tomato, Onion and Mushroom Flan (bottom).

Salads

Onion Salad

This salad is usually served as an accompaniment to kebabs. Onion salad goes very well with a variety of main courses, as a side salad.

PREPARATION TIME: 5-7 minutes
SERVES: 4 people

2 large Spanish onions, peeled and
  thinly sliced
2-3 sprigs fresh green coriander,
  chopped
1 green chili, sliced
Juice of 1 lemon
¾ tsp salt
Pinch paprika

Combine the onion rings, coriander leaves and chili in a bowl. Add the lemon juice and salt and mix well. Put the onion salad onto a serving plate and sprinkle with paprika.

Tabbouleh

This is a Lebanese salad and it is very good for parties and picnics.

PREPARATION TIME: 2 hours 30 minutes
SERVES: 6 people

2 cups bulgar or pourgouri
  (precooked, cracked wheat)
1 cup boiling water
8-10 scallions, chopped
1 green pepper, seeded and chopped
⅔ cup parsley
2½ tblsp chopped mint leaves

Dressing
¼ cup lemon juice
¾ cup olive oil
1¼ tsp grated lemon peel
1¼ tsp ground mixed spice
¾ tsp ground cumin
1¼ tsp salt
¼ tsp freshly ground black pepper
1 small iceberg lettuce, shredded
2 large firm tomatoes, cut into wedges
10-15 pitted black olives, halved
2-3 sprigs mint
1-2 sprigs fresh green coriander

Place the pourgouri or bulgar into a bowl and add boiling water. Cover and stand for 1½-2 hours. Drain the bulgar by squeezing out the excess water. Mix the scallions, green pepper, parsley and mint with the bulgar. Combine all the dressing ingredients in a screw top jar and shake well. Pour the dressing over the bulgar mixture and mix lightly. Line a platter with shredded lettuce. Place the prepared bulgar in the centre. Garnish with tomato, olives, mint and coriander leaves.

Sweet and Sour Coleslaw

A variation on the usual theme, but a definite winner.

PREPARATION TIME: 20 minutes
SERVES: 6 people

½ small red cabbage, shredded
1 small green cabbage, shredded
1 large sweet carrot, peeled and
  shredded
3 scallions, finely chopped
6½ tblsp cider vinegar
4 tblsp brown sugar
¾ tsp salt
½ tsp freshly ground black pepper
6½ tblsp soured cream
1¼ tsp French mustard

Combine the red and green cabbage, carrots and scallions in a mixing bowl. Mix the vinegar, sugar and salt and pepper in a small saucepan and stir over the heat to dissolve the sugar. Pour the hot vinegar sauce over the cabbage mixture and mix well. Stir the soured cream and mustard together in a separate bowl; stir this mixture into the vegetables. Mix well and serve.

Mixed Bean Salad

This nutritious salad is made from a medley of beans and is very good for health conscious and athletic people. Either cook the dried beans at home or buy ready-cooked ones. Soak the beans separately overnight, and then boil them separately until tender. Drain well.

PREPARATION TIME: 15 minutes
SERVES: 4-6 people

1½ cups cooked red kidney beans
1½ cups cooked black eyed beans
  (Lobia)
1½ cups cooked chick peas
1½ cups cooked butter beans
1 cup shelled broad beans
2 cups sliced green beans, blanched

Dressing
2½ tblsp brown sugar
½ cup white wine vinegar
¾ tsp salt
½ tsp freshly ground black pepper
½ cup olive oil
¾ tsp dry mustard powder
¾ tsp dried basil leaves
1 large Spanish or red onion, peeled
  and thinly sliced into rings
2½ tblsp parsley

Mix all the beans together in a large bowl. Mix the sugar and vinegar together with salt and pepper to taste. Stir in the oil, mustard and basil. Pour this vinegar mixture over the beans. Mix thoroughly. Refrigerate until ready to serve. Before serving, mix in the onion rings and parsley.

Nutty Salad

PREPARATION TIME: 20 minutes
SERVES: 4 people

4 cups boiled potatoes, diced
1½ cups shelled green peas
1 cup cooked carrots, diced
1 medium onion, peeled and chopped
1 small green pepper, seeded and
  chopped
8-10 radishes, chopped
2 stalks celery, chopped
¼ cucumber, chopped
½ cup roasted peanuts, coarsely
  chopped
½ cup grated fresh coconut
1¼ tblsp sunflower seeds
2-3 sprigs fresh green coriander leaves
  or parsley, chopped

Dressing
2½ tblsp lemon juice
5¼ tblsp olive oil
1¼ tsp salt
¾ tsp freshly ground black pepper
1 tsp brown sugar

Mix all the vegetables together, except the nuts and sunflower seeds, in a large bowl. Mix the dressing ingredients together in a screw top jar and shake well. Add the dressing to the salad and mix throughly. Sprinkle with the nuts and sunflower seeds before serving.

Rice and Nut Salad

This salad has a very refreshing taste. The main ingredients are nuts, raisins, carrots and rice.

PREPARATION TIME: 15 minutes
SERVES: 4 people

2½ tblsp olive oil
2½ tblsp lemon juice
Salt and freshly ground black pepper
  to taste
1 cup sultanas
½ cup currants
2½ cups cooked long grain rice, well
  drained
¾ cup chopped blanched almonds
½ cup cashew nuts, chopped
½ cup shelled walnuts, chopped
15oz can peach slices, drained and
  chopped
¼ cucumber, cubed
1 cup cooked red kidney beans
1¼ tblsp chopped pitted olives

Mix the olive oil, lemon juice and salt and freshly ground black pepper in a screw top jar; shake vigorously. Soak the sultanas and currants in sufficient boiling water to cover, for 10 minutes. Drain the fruits. Mix the rice, nuts and soaked sultanas and currants. Add the chopped peaches, cucumber, red kidney beans and olives. Pour the dressing over the salad and toss lightly together. Serve on a bed of chopped lettuce.

Facing page: Onion Salad (top), Nutty Salad (center) and Tabbouleh (bottom).

Cheese Salad

This cheese salad originates from Greece and has many variations; it is popularly known as Horiatiki.

PREPARATION TIME: 10-12 minutes

SERVES: 4 people

½ a head of chicory
½ iceberg lettuce
1 cucumber, peeled and sliced
3-4 large tomatoes, cut into wedges, or
15-20 baby tomatoes, halved

8-10 pitted green or black olives, halved
1 medium Spanish or red onion, peeled and chopped
1 cup Feta cheese, cut into ½ inch pieces

Dressing
⅓ cup olive oil
2½ tblsp red wine vinegar
1½ tsp chopped fresh oregano or
½ tsp dried oregano
¾ tsp salt
½ tsp freshly ground black pepper
¾ tsp brown sugar

Wash and dry the chicory and lettuce leaves; tear into bite size pieces. Place the chicory and lettuce in a large bowl and add the cucumber, tomatoes, olives, onion and cheese. Shake the dressing ingredients together in a screw top jar. Pour the dressing over the salad. Toss lightly and serve.

Cheese Salad (bottom left), Mixed Bean Salad (below) and Rice and Nut Salad (bottom right).

Mixed Fresh Vegetable Salad

This salad can be prepared with any combination of vegetables, in any proportion. Add or subtract according to personal taste.

PREPARATION TIME: 20 minutes

SERVES: 6 people

1 large scallion, peeled and chopped
½ cucumber, diced
3 carrots, peeled and diced
6 large tomatoes, diced, or
8 baby tomatoes, halved
10 mushrooms, diced
3 stalks celery, diced
1 green pepper, seeded and diced
15-20 tiny cauliflower flowerets
15-20 radishes, quartered
1¼ tblsp chopped watercress or
    mustard and cress
2 sprigs fresh green coriander leaves
or parsley, chopped

Dressing
½ tsp salt
½ tsp freshly ground black pepper
1¼ tsp brown sugar
2½ tsp cider vinegar
1¼ tblsp lemon juice
1¼ tblsp honey
5¼ tblsp olive oil
Pinch mustard powder
8 lettuce leaves

Combine all the vegetables in a large bowl. Mix together all the dressing ingredients. Pour the dressing over the vegetables and serve on a bed of lettuce leaves.

Pasta Salad

This is a popular American salad. It can be eaten as a main dish or as a side salad – it is a wonderful combination of vegetables, pasta and kidney beans.

PREPARATION TIME: 15-20 minutes

SERVES: 6 people

4 cups cooked red kidney beans, drained
3 cups pasta shells or spirals, cooked
1 large green pepper, seeded and sliced into 1 inch long pieces
1 large red pepper, seeded and sliced into 1 inch long pieces
20-30 pitted black olives, sliced in half
1 tblsp capers
4-5 sprigs fresh parsley, chopped

Dressing
1 cup olive oil
¼ cup lemon juice
2½ tsp finely chopped fresh basil leaves
1¼ tsp salt
½ tsp freshly ground black pepper
2 cloves garlic, peeled and minced
1 small head chicory

Combine the beans, pasta, peppers, olives, capers and parsley in a large bowl. Mix all the dressing ingredients together; add to the salad ingredients and toss together. Line the serving platter or bowl with chicory leaves; place the pasta salad in the centre. Alternatively: add ½lb of thinly sliced salami or Italian sausages or can sausages in brine cut into bite size pieces.

This page: Sweet and Sour Coleslaw (top left), Mixed Fresh Vegetable Salad (top right) and Pasta Salad (bottom).

Facing page: Kedgeree (top left), Sweet Savory Rice (center right) and Vegetable Pulao Rice (bottom).

Rice and Pulses

Kedgeree

PREPARATION TIME: 15 minutes, plus soaking time

COOKING TIME: 30 minutes

SERVES: 4-6 people

2 cups long grain rice
2 cups red lentils
3 cups tepid water
A stick of butter (or an equivalent amount of olive oil)
1 medium onion, peeled and chopped
¾ tsp crushed fresh root ginger
¾ tsp crushed garlic
1 inch piece cinnamon stick
6 cloves
1 bayleaf
1¼ tsp ground coriander
½ tsp ground turmeric
¾ tsp salt
2 green chilies, sliced in half lengthwise

Wash the rice and the lentils in 4 to 5 changes of water; soak them in the 3 cups tepid water for 30 minutes. Heat the butter or oil in a large pan; add the onion and fry for 2-3 minutes. Add the ginger, garlic, cinnamon stick, cloves and bayleaf, and fry for 1 minute. Drain the water from the rice and lentils; reserve the water. Add the rice and lentils to the fried onion, together with the coriander, turmeric, salt and green chilies. Stir over the heat for 2-3 minutes, until the rice and lentils are evenly coated with fat. Add the reserved water and bring to the boil; reduce the heat and simmer covered for 8-10 minutes, without stirring, until the water has been absorbed and the rice and lentils are tender. Serve with a vegetable curry.

Vegetable Pulao Rice

PREPARATION TIME: 30 minutes

COOKING TIME: 30 minutes

SERVES: 4-6 people

4 cups long grain rice (Basmati)
3-4 cups water
1 medium onion, peeled and diced
1 inch piece cinnamon stick
1 bayleaf

6 cloves
1¼ tsp black cumin (shah-zeera)
6 small cardamoms
¾ tsp crushed fresh root ginger
¾ tsp crushed garlic
1 medium potato, peeled and diced
1 carrot, peeled and diced
1 cup shelled peas
¾ cup sliced green beans
1¼ tsp garam masala powder (hot aromatic powder)
¾ tsp chili powder
1¼ tsp ground coriander
1¼ tsp ground cumin
1¼ tsp salt
2½ tblsp lemon juice
A stick of butter (or an equivalent amount of olive oil)

Wash the rice in 4-5 changes of water and soak in the 3-4 cups water for 30 minutes. Melt the butter in a pan and fry the onion for 2-3 minutes. Add the cinnamon, bayleaf, cloves, black cumin, cardamoms, ginger and garlic. Fry for 1 minute, stirring, and add the potato, carrot, peas, green beans, garam masala, chili, coriander, cumin and salt. Mix well. Drain the soaked rice, retaining the water and add the rice to the onion and spices. Stir the mixture gently and add the reserved water. Bring to the boil and then reduce the heat; cover and simmer gently for 10-15 minutes, until the rice is tender and the water has been absorbed. Do not stir during cooking. Sprinkle with the lemon juice and serve. To colour pulao: dissolve a pinch of saffron in 1¼ tblsp warm milk; pour over the rice and allow to stand over a very low heat for 5 minutes.

Mixed Daal

This is a mixed lentil stew, using 3 or 4 varieties of daal. Add a few vegetables of your choice to turn it into a substantial meal.

PREPARATION TIME: 15 minutes
COOKING TIME: 30 minutes
SERVES: 4 people

⅔ cup split Bengal grain (Channa)
½ cup yellow lentils (Toor Daal)
1 cup red lentils (Masoor)
½ cup dehusked split mung (Moong), or any other daal
¾ tsp ground turmeric
1¾ tsp ground coriander
4 canned tomatoes, chopped
2 green chilies
3 sprigs fresh green coriander leaves

Salt to taste
A stick of butter
½ inch fresh root ginger, peeled and chopped
1 onion, chopped
1 clove garlic, chopped

As some of these pulses have different cooking times, wash each pulse separately in 3-4 changes of water. Drain. Soak separately in water for 5 minutes. Bring 2½ cups water to the boil; add the drained channa daal. Boil for 15-20 minutes or until the pulses are tender. Add the remaining pulses well drained, and simmer gently with the turmeric and ground coriander for 15-20 minutes, or until all the pulses are soft. Beat with an egg whisk. Add the tomatoes, green chilies and coriander leaves. Simmer for a further 5-6 minutes. Pour into a serving bowl and keep warm. Melt the butter in a frying pan and fry the ginger for 2 minutes. Add the onion and garlic and fry until golden brown. Pour this mixture over the mixed daal and serve immediately.

Sweet Savory Rice

PREPARATION TIME: 20 minutes
COOKING TIME: 30 minutes
SERVES: 4-6 people

4 cups rice (Basmati or long grain)
3-4 cups water
½ cup raisins
¾ cup cashew nuts, chopped
½ cup blanched almonds, split
½ cup pistachio nuts, split
A stick of butter (or an equivalent amount of olive oil)
1 inch piece cinnamon stick
6 cloves
6 small cardamoms
1 bayleaf
¾ tsp black cumin seed (shah-zeera)
1 cup sultanas
1¼ tsp salt
1¼ tsp sugar
Pinch of saffron

Wash the rice in 4-5 changes of water and soak in the 3-4 cups water for 30 minutes. Soak the raisins and nuts in a little water for 10 minutes. Drain the raisins and nuts. Melt the butter in a large pan and fry the cinnamon, cloves, small cardamoms, bayleaf and black cumin for 1-2 minutes. Add the nuts, raisins and sultanas. Drain the soaked rice retaining the water; add

the rice to the saucepan. Fry for 1 minute. Add salt, sugar and the reserved water. Bring to the boil. Reduce the heat and add a pinch of saffron. Stir once gently. Cover and simmer gently for 10-15 minutes, without stirring, until the rice is tender and the water has been absorbed. Serve with curries.

Red Kidney Bean Curry

A popular dish from the Punjab province of India. It is similar to Chilli Con-Carne and makes a hearty meal with bread or rice.

PREPARATION TIME: overnight, plus 15 minutes
COOKING TIME: 20-45 minutes
SERVES: 4 people

2 cups dried red kidney beans, washed and soaked overnight in sufficient water to cover
2 medium onions, chopped
4 tblsp oil
1 bayleaf
1 inch piece cinnamon stick
6 cloves
6 small green cardamoms
2 green chilies, quartered
3 cloves garlic, peeled and finely chopped
1 inch fresh root ginger, peeled and finely chopped
¾ tsp chili powder
¼ tsp ground turmeric
2 tsp ground coriander
1¼ tsp ground cumin
1¼ tsp garam masala powder (hot aromatic powder)
15oz can peeled tomatoes, chopped
¾ tsp salt
2-3 sprigs fresh green coriander, chopped

Either pressure cook the red kidney beans for 5-6 minutes, or cook them in their soaking water for 15-20 minutes until soft. Remove from the heat; allow to stand, covered. Fry the onions in the oil in a large saucepan over a moderate heat until tender. Add the bayleaf, cinnamon, cloves and cardamoms and fry for 1 minute. Add the chilies, garlic and ginger and fry until golden. Sprinkle with the chili powder, turmeric, ground coriander, ground cumin and garam masala. Avoid burning the mixture. Stir the mixture to blend the spices. Add the tomatoes and season with salt. Cover and

simmer for 2-3 minutes. Drain the cooked beans and collect the thick red liquid. Add the beans to the spiced tomato mixture. Stir gently and cook for 1 minute. Add the red liquid and chopped coriander; cover and simmer for 3-5 minutes. Serve with bread or boiled rice.

Red Lentil Daal

There is an abundance of natural protein in pulses and there is a great variety of pulses now available.

PREPARATION TIME: 10 minutes
COOKING TIME: 30 minutes
SERVES: 4 people

½ lb red lentils
1½ cups water
½ tsp ground turmeric
1¼ tsp ground coriander
1 green chili, cut in half
Salt to taste
4-6 canned tomatoes, chopped
2 sprigs fresh green coriander leaves, chopped
4 tblsp butter
1 small onion, peeled and finely chopped

Wash the lentils in 3-5 changes of water. Put the lentils into a pan with the 1½ cups water; cover and cook over a low heat for 10-15 minutes. Remove any froth with a spoon. Once the lentils are tender and yellow, blend until smooth with an egg whisk. Add the turmeric, ground coriander, chili, salt to taste and chopped tomatoes. Cover and simmer for 10 minutes. Add the coriander leaves and pour into a dish. Keep warm. Melt the butter in a frying pan and saute the onion until golden brown. Pour the onions and butter juices over the daal. Serve with rice or bread.

Facing page: Mixed Daal (top left), Red Kidney Bean Curry (center) and Red Lentil Daal (bottom).

Bread and Pizza

Puri

These deep-fried breads are simple to make once the art has been mastered.

PREPARATION TIME:	10-15 minutes
COOKING TIME:	20 minutes
MAKES:	30-32

4 cups whole-wheat flour
¾ tsp salt
1-1½ cups water
Oil for deep frying

Sieve the flour and salt into a mixing bowl. Mix to a soft dough with water. Knead well and leave to relax for 5 minutes, covered with a damp cloth. Divide the dough into 30-32 small even sized balls; roll out each ball into a small round about 2½-3 inches in diameter. Heat the oil for deep frying and drop in a small piece of dough. If it rises to the top instantly then the correct temperature for frying has been reached. Place one puri at a time into the hot oil, taking care not to splash the oil. Gently stir the puri and it will begin to swell. Turn over and cook on the underside until golden brown – about ½-1 minute. The flip side is always the thick side and it needs extra cooking time. Drain the puris on the side of the frying pan, and place them on kitchen paper to drain,

Puri (above), Roti (right) and Paratha (far right).

before serving. Puris are best when served piping hot. Puris can be served cold and they can also be reheated under the broiler.

Paratha

These shallow-fried breads can either be made plain, or stuffed with a favorite filling, such as cheese, potato etc.

PREPARATION TIME: 15-20 minutes	
COOKING TIME: 20-30 minutes	
MAKES: 16-18	

4 cups whole-wheat flour
¾ tsp salt
1-1½ cups water
Melted butter or oil

Sieve the flour and salt into a mixing bowl. Mix to a soft dough with water. Knead the dough well; leave to relax, covered, for 5 minutes. Divide the dough into 16-18 even-sized balls. Roll each ball into a small round about 2 inches in diameter. Brush each round of dough with oil or melted butter and fold in half. Brush the upper folded surface with oil or butter and fold in half to form a small triangle. On a well floured surface roll out these triangles thinly. Heat a solid based frying pan or a griddle. Put the paratha onto the heated frying pan and cook for ½-1 minute or until small brown specks appear. Cook the other side in the same way. Brush a little oil or butter over the paratha and turn over. Fry for 1 minute and then brush the second side with oil or butter. Fry on both sides until the

paratha is golden and crisp. Make the rest of the paratha in the same way. Keep them soft and warm, well wrapped in a clean tea towel or foil.

Roti

Roti is best made with whole-wheat flour; any variety may be used.

PREPARATION TIME: 20 minutes

COOKING TIME: 20-30 minutes

MAKES: about 24

4 cups whole-wheat flour
¾ tsp salt
1-1½ cups water

Sieve the flour and salt into a mixing bowl. Mix to a soft dough with water. Knead the dough for 2-3 minutes. Cover and allow to relax for 5-6 minutes before shaping the bread. Divide the dough into 1oz balls. Roll each ball into a thin round about 5-6 inches in diameter. Place a solid based frying pan or a griddle over a medium heat; when the pan is hot, place the shaped roti onto it. Cook for ½ minute on each side and then place under a preheated broiler to bloat (little brown specks will appear on the surface). The first 2 rotis do not usually bloat, so do not be alarmed. Make all the rotis and stack them one on top of each other. Keep them covered with a clean tea towel or foil. Serve hot with any curry or spicy savory dish.

Banana and Nut Bread

PREPARATION TIME: 30 minutes

COOKING TIME: 1 hour

MAKES: 1 loaf

A stick of butter
1 cup brown sugar
1 egg, well beaten
2 cups whole-wheat flour
½ tsp salt
¾ tsp baking powder
5 tblsp natural yogurt
2 ripe bananas, peeled and mashed
½ cup raisins
1 cup mixed nuts, chopped

Preheat the oven to 350°F. Cream the butter and sugar until light and fluffy and gradually beat in the egg. Sieve the flour, salt and baking powder together. Add half the

yogurt to the butter and sugar mixture and then mix in half the sieved dry ingredients. Beat in the remaining yogurt, flour, mashed banana, raisins and chopped nuts. Mix well. Put the mixture into a greased loaf tin. Bake at 350°F for 1 hour.

Crusty Loaf

PREPARATION TIME: 3 hours 40 minutes

COOKING TIME: 45 minutes-1 hour

MAKES: 2 loaves

1¼ cups tepid water
½oz fresh yeast or 2½ tsp dried yeast
¾ tsp salt
1 tblsp butter
1¼ tblsp sugar
3½ cups sieved all purpose flour
1¼ tblsp melted butter
1½ tblsp caraway, sesame or poppy seeds for topping (optional)

Sprinkle or crumble the yeast into the tepid water; stir to dissolve. Leave for a few minutes until frothy. Mix the salt, butter, sugar and flour together; stir in the yeast liquid and mix to a dough. Knead the dough for 10 minutes on a lightly floured surface. Place the dough in a greased bowl and brush the top lightly with melted butter; cover with a damp cloth and leave it to rise in a warm place (free from draught), until doubled in bulk (about 40-45 minutes). Punch the dough down and let it rise again until almost double its original size about (30 minutes). Punch down once again and turn out onto a floured surface, cut into two equal portions. Roll each one into an oblong about 8-10 inches in length. Beginning with the wide side, roll up each oblong tightly. Seal the edges by pinching together. Holding each end of the roll, roll it gently backwards and forwards to lengthen the loaf and shape the ends. Place the loaves on a greased baking sheet lightly sprinkled with all purpose flour. Brush the loaves either with milk, or with cornstarch glaze, and leave to rise for 1½ hours, uncovered. With a sharp knife, make ¼ inch slashes at regular intervals. Bake in a hot oven, 400°F, for 10 minutes. Brush once again with milk or cornstarch glaze and sprinkle with poppy seeds (or other seeds). Return to the oven and bake for 25-30 minutes

or until golden brown.

To make cornstarch glaze: mix 1½ tsp cornstarch with 1½ tsp cold water. Add ½ cup boiling water and cook for 1-2 minutes until smooth. Cool slightly before use.

Whole-wheat Bread

PREPARATION TIME: 2 hours 30 minutes

COOKING TIME: 50 minutes

MAKES: 1 large loaf

6 cups whole-wheat flour
¾ tsp salt
¼ cup margarine
¼ cup fresh yeast, or
1¼ tblsp dried yeast (see below)
1¼ tblsp granulated or brown sugar
1¼ cups tepid water
⅔ cup tepid milk
1¼ tblsp melted butter

Sieve the flour and salt into a warm bowl and blend the margarine. Cream the fresh yeast with the sugar and stir in the warm water and milk. (If using dried yeast, sprinkle it onto the warm water and milk, with the sugar, and leave to stand for 10 minutes until thick and frothy). Make a well in the centre of the flour and pour in the yeast liquid; gradually mix in the flour to form a dough. Knead the dough well. Cover it with a damp cloth and leave to rise until double in bulk (about 1¼ hours). Grease a loaf tin, 9 inches by 5 inches by 3 inches. Turn the risen dough onto a floured surface and knead well; place in the loaf tin. Leave in a warm place to rise for 40 minutes. Brush the loaf with melted butter and bake at 400°F for about 50 minutes.

Whole-wheat Pizza Dough

PREPARATION TIME: 50-60 minutes

1 cup tepid water
1¾ tsp dried yeast
¾ tsp salt
1¼ tsp sugar

1¼ tsp olive oil
1 cup whole-wheat flour
1¼ cups all purpose flour

Mix the dried yeast with the tepid water. Add the salt, sugar and oil. Mix in the flours a little at a time, to make a dough. Use extra water if needed. Turn the dough onto a lightly floured surface and knead until smooth (about 5-8 minutes). Cover the dough with a clean damp tea towel and leave to stand for 15-20 minutes. Knead once more for 1-2 minutes. You can make either one large pizza base or several smaller ones. Grease one 14 inch pizza pan and roll out the dough to make a round large enough to fit the pizza pan. Shape the pizza dough with the hands to fit the pan. Top with the chosen topping and bake.

Basic Pizza Dough

This is the basic recipe for pizza dough and although there are many variations, the making of the dough is very important. Pizza originated in Italy, around the Naples area, but it is now eaten and enjoyed worldwide. Once the basic dough is perfected, toppings can be adjusted to one's taste. In fact, on one single pizza, each slice can have a different taste (i.e. with a different topping). See Taco Pizza Topping and Mixed Vegetable Pizza Topping recipes.

PREPARATION TIME: about 1 hour 30 minutes

¼ tsp sugar
1¼ tblsp dried yeast
½ cup tepid water
1¼ tsp salt
2 cups all purpose flour, sieved

Mix the dried yeast with 2 tblsp of the tepid water and the sugar. Stir until dissolved. Leave to stand for 10-15 minutes until frothy. Put the flour and salt into a bowl and make

Facing page: Crusty Loaf (top), Banana and Nut Bread (center) and Whole-wheat Bread (bottom).

a well in the centre. Add the yeast liquid and the remaining tepid water; mix to form a dough. Kneed the dough on a floured surface for 8-10 minutes. Cover with a damp cloth and leave to rise in a warm place for 40-45 minutes, until double its original size. Knead once again on a lightly floured surface for 3-5 minutes until soft and elastic. You can make either one large pizza base, or several smaller ones. Grease one 14 inch pizza pan and roll out the dough. Shape the pizza dough with the hands to fit the pan. Top with the chosen topping and bake.

Taco Pizza

This idea is taken from the taco (a Mexican pancake). The pizza base is made with a mixture of cornmeal and flour and some of the topping ingredients are the same as those used in a taco filling.

PREPARATION TIME: 30-40 minutes

COOKING TIME: 30-35 minutes

SERVES: 6 people

Dough
1½ cups all purpose flour
⅔ cup fine yellow cornmeal
2½ tsp baking powder
1¼ tsp salt
½ cup margarine
½ cup milk

Sieve the flour, cornmeal, salt and baking powder into a mixing bowl. Rub in the margarine. Add the milk, gradually, to form a medium soft dough. Knead the dough on a well floured surface for 4-5 minutes, until smooth. Roll into a circle to cover a 13-14 inch pizza pan, with a 1 inch high rim. Grease the pizza pan and cover with the dough. Shape the pizza dough to fit the pan. Pinch the edges to form a deep rim. Keep on one side until the topping is ready.

Topping
2½ tblsp olive oil
1 clove garlic, peeled and crushed
1 small onion, peeled and chopped
½ green pepper, seeded and coarsely chopped
4-6 mushrooms, sliced
½lb cooked red kidney beans (or drained canned ones)
2 scallions, chopped
3 large tomatoes, chopped
6-8 pitted black olives, halved
3-4 pickled Mexican chilies, chopped
½lb Mozzarella, Cheddar or Monterey Jack cheese, cut into slivers
1 carrot, peeled and grated
⅔ cup soured cream
Bottled taco sauce

Heat the oil and fry the garlic, chopped onion, pepper and mushrooms for 2 minutes; add the kidney beans and stir fry for 1-2 minutes. Remove from the heat and stir in the scallions. Spread the above topping mixture over the pizza base. Arrange the tomatoes evenly on top. Add the olives, Mexican chilies and slivers of cheese. Bake at 400°F for 15-20 minutes until the edges turn golden brown and crusty. Serve with grated carrots, whipped soured cream and taco sauce.

Mixed Vegetable Pizza Topping

PREPARATION TIME: 30 minutes

COOKING TIME: 20 minutes

SERVES: 4-6 people

2½ tblsp olive oil
1 small onion, peeled and chopped
2 scallions, chopped
1 medium zucchini, trimmed and thinly sliced
4 mushrooms, sliced
Salt and freshly ground black pepper to taste
6-8 canned tomatoes, chopped
10ml (2 tsp) tomato paste

8 pitted black olives
2 tomatoes, thinly sliced
1 green pepper, seeded and chopped
1 green chili, chopped
1¼ tsp dried oregano
1½ cups Mozzarella cheese, Cheddar cheese or a mixture of the two, cut into thin slivers
2½ tblsp grated Parmesan cheese

Heat the olive oil in a large frying pan; add the onions and sauté for 1-2 minutes. Add the zucchini and sauté for 2 minutes. Add the mushrooms and salt and pepper to taste and stir fry for 1 minute to glaze the vegetables. Remove from the heat and cool. Mix the chopped tomato with the tomato paste and spread evenly over the pizza base. Spoon the vegetable mixture over the pizza and arrange the olives, sliced tomatoes, green pepper and green chili on top. Sprinkle with the oregano, the slivers of cheese and the grated Parmesan cheese. Bake at 450°F for 12-15 minutes, or until the edge of the pizza is golden brown and crusty.

Taco Pizza (top right) and Mixed Vegetable Pizza Topping (bottom right).

Main Meals

Okra Curry

A dry vegetable curry made with okra and potato.

PREPARATION TIME: 10-15 minutes

COOKING TIME: 30 minutes

SERVES: 4 people

3¾ tblsp oil
1 onion, peeled and chopped
2 medium sized potatoes, peeled and cut into 1 inch pieces
4 cups okra, topped and tailed, and chopped into ½ inch pieces
Salt to taste
¾ tsp ground turmeric
1¼ tsp chili powder
1¾ tsp ground coriander
2-3 sprigs fresh green coriander leaves, chopped

Heat the oil in a wok or solid based frying pan and fry the onion for 3-4 minutes. Stir in the cubed potatoes; cover and cook for 3-4 minutes. Add the okra, and stir fry for 2 minutes. Sprinkle with salt to taste, turmeric, chili and ground coriander. Mix gently; cover and cook for 8-10 minutes. Stir occasionally and continue cooking until the potatoes are tender. Sprinkle with the chopped coriander leaves. Mix well and serve.

Okra Fry

This is a dry "curry" – no spices are added; the okra supplies the hotness.

PREPARATION TIME: 15 minutes

COOKING TIME: 20-30 minutes

SERVES: 4 people

1-1½lbs okra
Oil for deep frying
1¼ tblsp oil
1 large onion, peeled and chopped
Salt and freshly ground black pepper to taste

Top and tail the okra; chop them into ¼ inch even-sized pieces. Heat the oil for deep frying; add the chopped okra, a little at a time, and deep fry until brown and crisp. Drain on absorbent paper and keep warm in a dish. Heat the 1¼ tblsp oil and fry the onion until tender about 4-5 minutes. Remove the onion and mix with the fried okra. Sprinkle with salt and pepper to taste. Serve with chapati, or as a side dish.

Eggplant Bake

PREPARATION TIME: 30 minutes

COOKING TIME: 30-40 minutes

SERVES: 6 people

3 large eggplant
2½ tsp salt
Malt vinegar
2½ tblsp oil
2 large onions, peeled and sliced
2 green chilies, chopped
15oz can peeled tomatoes, chopped
¾ tsp chili powder
1¼ tsp crushed garlic
¾ tsp ground turmeric
Oil for deep frying
⅓ cup natural yogurt
1¼ tsp freshly ground black pepper
4 tomatoes, sliced
2 cups Cheddar cheese, grated

Cut the eggplant into ¼ inch thick slices. Lay in a shallow dish. Sprinkle with 1¼ tsp salt and add sufficient malt vinegar to cover. Allow to marinate for 20-30 minutes. Drain well. Heat 2½ tblsp oil in a frying pan and fry the onions until golden brown. Add the chilies, chopped tomatoes, remaining salt, chili powder, garlic and turmeric. Mix well and simmer for 5-7 minutes. Remove from the heat. Cool and blend to a smooth sauce in the liquidizer. Keep the sauce on one side. Heat the oil for deep frying and deep fry the drained, marinated eggplant until brown on both sides (2-3 minutes each side). Drain well on kitchen paper. Grease a large deep baking tray. Arrange half the fried eggplant rounds closely together in the tray. Spoon over half the tomato sauce and beaten yogurt. Season with pepper. Add the remaining eggplant rounds and the rest of the tomato sauce and yogurt. Cover with slices of tomatoes and grated cheese. Bake at 350°F for 10-15 minutes, or until the cheese melts and turns brown. Serve hot as a side dish, or as a main course with brown bread or pitta bread.

Stuffed Zucchini

This is a delightful dish from Southern Italy.

PREPARATION TIME: 30 minutes

COOKING TIME: 30-40 minutes

SERVES: 4 people

½ cup fresh coarse breadcrumbs
5 tblsp milk
8 medium sized zucchini, trimmed
1 onion, peeled and finely chopped
2 tomatoes, chopped
6-8 mushrooms, sliced
1 clove garlic, peeled and chopped
5 tblsp olive oil
2½ tsp dried oregano
Salt and freshly ground black pepper to taste
1 egg, beaten
⅔ cup Mozzarella cheese (or Cheddar), cut into thin slivers
⅔ cup grated Parmesan cheese

Soak the breadcrumbs in the milk for 15-20 minutes. Cook the zucchini in boiling water for 5 minutes. Drain and cool. Slice them in half lengthways and scoop out the flesh, leaving a thick shell at least ¼ inch. Take care not to break or crack the zucchini. Keep the scooped flesh on one side. Squeeze out the excess milk from the breadcrumbs and put them into a bowl. Fry the scooped zucchini flesh, chopped onion, tomatoes,

This page: Eggplant Bake (top left), Okra Curry (center right) and Okra Fry (right).

Overleaf: Zucchini Bake (left), Stuffed Zucchini (center) and Spicy Corn (right).

mushrooms and chopped garlic in half the olive oil for 5 minutes. Mix with the breadcrumbs, oregano, salt and pepper to taste, the beaten egg and half the cheeses. Spoon the mixture evenly into all the zucchini shells. Arrange the stuffed zucchini on a lightly greased baking tray. Sprinkle the remaining cheese over them and brush with the rest of the oil. Bake for 18-20 minutes at 400°F or until the cheese has melted and turned golden brown. Serve at once.

Spicy Corn

This dish originates from East Africa, it makes a tasty hot snack or supper dish.

PREPARATION TIME: 15 minutes

COOKING TIME: 35-40 minutes

SERVES: 6 people

3¾ tblsp oil
1 large onion, peeled and chopped
2 medium potatoes, peeled and cubed
8 fresh Chinese parsley leaves (optional)
¾ tsp cumin seed
¾ tsp mustard seed
1¼ tsp crushed fresh root ginger
1¼ tsp crushed garlic
1½lb frozen sweetcorn kernels
1¼ tsp salt
1¼ tsp chili powder
1¼ tsp ground coriander
¾ tsp ground turmeric
15oz can peeled tomatoes, chopped
1¼ tblsp tomato paste
1-2 green chilies, chopped
2 green peppers, seeded and cut into 1 inch pieces
3 sprigs fresh green coriander, chopped
1¼ tblsp thick tamarind pulp, or
2½ tblsp lemon juice

Heat the oil and fry the onion for 3 minutes; add the potatoes and fry for 5 minutes. Add the Chinese parsley leaves, cumin and mustard seed and stir fry for 1-2 minutes. Add ginger and garlic and stir fry for 1-2 minutes. Add the sweetcorn, salt, chili powder, ground coriander and turmeric. Mix well and cook for 2-3 minutes. Add the chopped tomatoes, tomato paste, chopped chilies, green peppers and coriander leaves.

Stir in the tamarind pulp and mix well adding a little water if the mixture seems too dry. Cover and cook over a low heat until the potatoes are tender about 10-15 minutes. The spicy corn should be thick but moist. Serve hot or cold.

Spiced Peas

PREPARATION TIME: 10 minutes

COOKING TIME: 15 minutes

SERVES: 6 people

2 tblsp oil
1 large onion, peeled and chopped
2 green chilies, sliced in half lengthwise
2lb shelled peas (fresh or frozen)
Salt and freshly ground black pepper to taste
1 tblsp lemon juice
Lemon wedges

Heat the oil in a wok or solid based frying pan and fry the onion until tender. Add the chilies and fry for 1 minute. Add the peas and salt and pepper to taste; stir fry for 5-10 minutes, or until well colored and "dry". Put into a serving dish and sprinkle with lemon juice. Garnish with lemon wedges. Serve as a side dish, or as a snack.

Spinach with Paneer

Paneer is a home-made cheese; it is made by separating milk into curds and whey by means of a souring agent such as lemon juice. It is eaten extensively in northern parts of India and is a good source of protein.

PREPARATION TIME: 15 minutes, plus time for making paneer

COOKING TIME: 20-30 minutes

SERVES: 4 people

To make paneer: (This is an overnight process)
2½ pints milk
2 tblsp lemon juice

Bring the milk to the boil. Reduce the heat and sprinkle with the lemon juice. The milk will separate into pale, watery whey and thick, white paneer (or curds). Remove from the heat and allow the paneer to coagulate (if the milk has not separated properly, add a few more

drops of lemon juice. The whey should be a clear, pale, yellow liquid. Pour the paneer and liquid through a muslin-lined sieve. Discard the liquid whey and tie the muslin over the paneer. Flatten the paneer to ½ inch thick; place it on a tray and rest it in a tilted position. Place more muslin over the top and weight it down. The pressure will drag out the remaining moisture and the tilted position will channel the liquid away from the paneer. Leave to drain overnight. Next day, cut the firm paneer into 1 inch cubes.

6 tblsp butter
1 medium onion, peeled and finely chopped
1 inch piece cinnamon stick
1 bayleaf
1lb frozen spinach paste, or fresh leaf spinach, cooked and pureed
1 tsp chili powder
½ tsp salt
½ cup natural yogurt
3 sprigs fresh green coriander leaves, chopped
1 tsp garam masala powder (hot, aromatic powder)
Oil for deep frying

Heat the butter in a pan and fry the onion until golden brown. Add the cinnamon and bayleaf and fry for 1 minute. Add the spinach and stir to mix. Sprinkle with the chili powder and salt and stir in the yogurt, coriander leaves and garam masala. Cover and cook for 2-3 minutes. Simmer gently. Meanwhile, deep-fry the drained paneer cubes until golden. Add the paneer cubes to the spinach and simmer together for 4-5 minutes. Serve hot with chapati or pulao rice.

New Potato Fry

This Oriental dish is very versatile; it can be served as a side dish, as a snack, or as a main curry. It is also a wonderful way of serving potatoes with traditional roast meats.

PREPARATION TIME: 20 minutes

COOKING TIME: 10-12 minutes

SERVES: 3-4 people

3 tblsp oil
1 tsp mustard seed
1lb small, even sized new potatoes, boiled in their skins and peeled
1 tsp red chili powder

1½ tsp ground coriander
¼ tsp ground turmeric
½ tsp salt
3 sprigs fresh green coriander leaves, chopped (optional)
Lemon juice to taste

Heat the oil in a wok or solid based frying pan and add the mustard seed and the whole, peeled potatoes. Stir fry over a low heat until they are lightly browned. Sprinkle with the spices, salt and chopped coriander leaves. Stir fry over a low heat for 5-6 minutes until golden brown. Remove from heat. Put into a dish and sprinkle with the lemon juice. Serve hot or cold.

Zucchini Bake

Serve this dish as a main course with fried rice, or as a side dish.

PREPARATION TIME: 20-30 minutes

COOKING TIME: 35 minutes

SERVES: 4-6 people

2lbs zucchini trimmed and coarsely grated
1¼ tsp salt
2½ tblsp melted unsalted butter (or oil)
3-4 eggs, well beaten
1½-1¾ cups grated mild cheese (Edam, Samso, etc)
1 medium onion, peeled and finely chopped
2 cloves garlic, peeled and finely chopped
2½ tblsp chopped parsley
1¼ tsp dried basil
¾ tsp freshly ground black pepper
¼-⅓ cup grated Parmesan cheese

Put the grated zucchini into a colander and sprinkle with salt. Leave to drain for 10 minutes. Squeeze the moisture out of the zucchini until quite dry. Lightly grease a baking dish (size approx. 10

Facing page: Spiced Peas (top), Spinach with Paneer (center right) and New Potato Fry (bottom).

x 7 inches). Heat the butter in a non-stick frying pan and fry the zucchini for 3-4 minutes until tender. Mix the beaten eggs, grated cheese, chopped onion, garlic, parsley, basil and pepper. Place the sauteed zucchini in the baking dish and pour egg mixture over the top. Sprinkle with the Parmesan cheese and bake at 350°F for 25-30 minutes until set. Serve cut into squares or diamond shapes. Can be eaten hot or cold.

Vegetable Stir Fry with Tofu (Soybean Curd)

This is a Chinese stir fry dish with soybean curd which makes a filling main course.

PREPARATION TIME: 30 minutes

COOKING TIME: 10 minutes

SERVES: 4 people

2½ tsp soya sauce
2½ tsp Worcestershire sauce
1 inch fresh root ginger, peeled and thinly sliced
3 cloves garlic, peeled and crushed
½lb Soybean Curd, cut into ½inch pieces
2½ tsp cornstarch
1 cup water
3¾ tblsp oil
3 stalks celery, sliced thinly
2 carrots, peeled and cut into thin diagonal slices
2-3 zucchini, trimmed, and cut into thin diagonal slices
1 green pepper, quartered, seeded and sliced thinly
8 mushrooms, thinly sliced
1-2 tomatoes, cut into wedges
½ cup snow peas, or thinly sliced green beans

Mix the soya sauce with the Worcestershire sauce, ginger and garlic. Add the soybean curd cubes and marinate for 8 minutes. Pick out the soybean curd and keep on a plate. Stir the cornstarch into the soya sauce mixture and blend in the water. Heat the oil in a wok over a medium heat. Add the celery and carrots and stir fry for 2 minutes. Add the zucchini and green pepper and stir fry for 2 minutes. Add the tomatoes and snow peas or green beans. Stir fry for 2 minutes. Add the mushrooms and stir fry for 1 minute. Stir in the water and soya sauce mixture. Cook until thickened, stirring for

1-2 minutes. Add the soybean curd. Heat through and serve immediately.

Cheese Bourag

PREPARATION TIME: 30-40 minutes

COOKING TIME: 20-25 minutes

SERVES: 4 people

2 cups flour
Salt
4 tsp baking powder
3 tblsp unsalted butter
½-⅔ cup milk
2 cups strong Cheddar cheese, grated
3 tblsp chopped parsley
Oil for deep frying

Sieve the flour, ¼ tsp salt and baking powder into a bowl; rub in the butter. Add the milk, a little at a time, and mix to a dough with a palette knife. Cover the dough and leave in a cool place to relax. Mix the grated cheese with the chopped parsley and a little salt to taste. Roll the dough out very thinly on a floured board and cut into 2 inch squares. Brush the edges of half the squares with a dampened pastry brush. Place a little filling in the centre of each one and cover with the remaining squares. Seal the edges well by pinching with the fingers or notching with the prongs of a fork. Heat the oil for deep frying. Fry the bourags a few at a time in hot oil until golden and crisp. Drain on kitchen paper and serve hot with sweet and sour sauce.

Avial

This is a mixed vegetable dish made with coconut.

PREPARATION TIME: 30 minutes

COOKING TIME: 20 minutes

SERVES: 4 people

2 medium sized potatoes, peeled and cut into 1 inch cubes
1½ cups lobia beans, trimmed and cut into 2 inch pieces
½ cup green beans, trimmed and sliced
4 drumstick or yard long beans, strung and cut into 1 inch pieces
1½ cups squash, peeled and cut into 1 inch cubes
1 green unripe banana, peeled and cut into 1 inch pieces

1 eggplant, trimmed and cut into 1 inch chunks
1 cup shelled peas
½ fresh coconut, shelled, skin removed and thinly sliced
1½ tsp cumin seeds
2 green chilies, chopped
½ cup water
⅔ cup natural yogurt
3 tblsp coconut oil for cooking

Steam all the vegetables for 10-15 minutes until almost tender, but still slightly crisp. Grind the spices with the water in a liquidizer until smooth. Mix the spice liquid with the coconut. Heat the coconut oil in a saucepan and add the vegetables, spice mixture and yogurt. Bring to the boil and simmer with the lid on for 5 minutes. Serve with rice.

Garlic Hash Brown

This is a favorite American dish eaten with steak and burgers.

PREPARATION TIME: 20 minutes

COOKING TIME: 30 minutes

SERVES: 4 people

5 tblsp oil
4 cloves of garlic, peeled and quartered lengthwise
3 whole red chilies
Salt
1-1½lb potatoes, peeled and coarsely grated

Heat the oil in a wok or a large non-stick frying pan. Fry the garlic until lightly browned. Add the red chilies and fry for 30 seconds. Sprinkle with salt to taste and add the grated potato. Stir fry for 5 minutes. Cover and cook for a further 8-10 minutes. The potatoes should be crisp and golden brown. Cook until the potatoes are tender. Serve as a side dish or for breakfast.

Vegetable Stir Fry with Tofu (top), Avial (center left) and Cheese Bourag (bottom right).

Spiced Chick Peas

This dryish curry is a "must" on any Punjabi menu. It is usually served with milk bread or pitta bread and an onion salad.

PREPARATION TIME: overnight for soaking, plus 15 minutes

COOKING TIME: 40-50 minutes

SERVES: 4-6 people

1lb chick peas
1 tsp baking powder
4 cloves
1 tsp cumin seed
4 large black cardamoms, ground
4 small cardamoms, ground
1 large onion, peeled and chopped
3 tblsp oil
2 bayleaves
1 inch piece cinnamon stick
2 green chilies, sliced in half lengthwise
1 inch fresh root ginger, peeled and finely chopped
4 cloves garlic, peeled and crushed
1½ tsp ground coriander
1-1¼ cups canned tomatoes, chopped
½ tsp freshly ground black pepper
½ tsp salt
5-6 sprigs fresh green coriander leaves, chopped

Wash the chick peas and soak them overnight in 2½ pints water and the baking powder. The following day, cook the chick peas in their soaking liquid in a pressure cooker for 10-15 minutes. If a lot of liquid has been absorbed during soaking, add a little more. Dry roast the cloves and cumin seed in a frying pan. Grind the cloves, cumin, large and small cardamons into a fine powder. Fry the onion in the oil for 2-3 minutes. Add the bayleaves, cinnamon, chilies, ginger and garlic. Fry for 1 minute, add the ground coriander and tomatoes. Fry for 2-3 minutes. Strain the chick peas, retaining any liquid. Add the chick peas to the tomato mixture and add black pepper, salt and the dry roasted spices. Mix well and add 1 cup of the strained chick pea liquid. Sprinkle with chopped coriander; cover and cook for 8-10 minutes. Add a little extra liquid if necessary. Serve with bread or rice.

Vegetable Pancakes (far left) and Spiced Chick Peas (left).

Vegetable Pancakes

A combination of shredded vegetables makes a delicious pancake, when added to the batter before cooking.

PREPARATION TIME: 15 minutes

COOKING TIME: 15 minutes

SERVES: 4-6 people

A stick of butter
2 cups shredded or coarsely grated carrots
2 cups shredded or coarsely grated zucchini
4 cups shredded or coarsely grated potatoes
1 medium onion, thinly sliced
3 eggs, well beaten
1 cup soured cream
5 tblsp cornflour
¾ tsp salt
¾ tsp freshly ground black pepper
Oil for frying
Wedges of lemon

Melt the butter in a frying pan; add the carrots, zucchini, potatoes and onion. Saute for 3-4 minutes, stirring continuously. Beat the eggs together with the soured cream, cornstarch and salt and pepper. Mix well. Stir in the semi-cooked vegetables. Mix together gently. Heat a large non-stick frying pan and brush with 2½ tsp oil; add 1¼ tblsp batter. Cook until light brown; turn the small pancake over and cook until the other side is also brown. Make 3 or 4 at a time. The size of the pancakes can be increased by using more batter for each pancake. Serve with salads or with tomato sauce as a light meal or snack.

Green Beans with Coconut

PREPARATION TIME: 10 minutes

COOKING TIME: 20 minutes

SERVES: 3-4 people

2½ tblsp oil
2 cloves garlic, peeled and crushed
2 green or red dried chilies
1lb green beans, sliced
½ tsp salt
2½ tblsp desiccated coconut, or grated fresh coconut

Heat the oil in a wok or frying pan. Add the garlic and fry until golden brown. Add the chilies and stir fry for 30 seconds. Add the green beans and sprinkle with salt. Stir fry for 8-10 minutes until the beans are tender but still crisp. Sprinkle with the coconut and stir fry for a further 2-3 minutes. Serve as a side dish.

Mixed Vegetable Raita

Raitas are yogurt-based Indian dishes served as accompaniments to curries etc. Natural yogurt is usually mixed with fruits, vegetables, and herbs such as coriander or mint.

PREPARATION TIME: 10 minutes

SERVES: 4-6 people

1¼ cups natural yogurt
½ cucumber, chopped
1 small onion, peeled and chopped
2 tomatoes, chopped
2 stalks celery, chopped
1 small apple, cored and chopped
2 boiled potatoes, peeled and chopped
¼ tsp salt
¼ tsp freshly ground black pepper
1 sprig fresh green coriander, chopped

Beat the yogurt in a bowl. Add all the remaining ingredients, seasoning well with salt and pepper. Chill before serving.

Cannelloni with Spinach and Ricotta

PREPARATION TIME: 20 minutes

COOKING TIME: 1 hour 20 minutes

SERVES: 4 people

2½ tblsp olive oil or melted butter
1 large onion, peeled and finely chopped
2 large cloves garlic, peeled and crushed
15oz can peeled tomatoes, chopped
1¼ tblsp tomato paste
Salt and freshly ground black pepper to taste
1¾ tsp dried basil
¾ tsp dried oregano
¾lb cannelloni tubes
5 tblsp thick spinach puree
½lb Ricotta cheese
2½ tblsp grated Parmesan cheese

To make the sauce: heat the oil or butter and fry the onion and garlic for 2-3 minutes. Add the tomatoes and tomato paste and mix well. Simmer for 2 minutes. Add the salt and pepper, basil and oregano. Cover and simmer for 10-15 minutes until thick.

Bring a large pan of salted water to the boil; cook the cannelloni tubes for 10 minutes until just tender. Do not overboil. Lift out the cannelloni tubes and put them into a bowl of cold water to cool quickly. Drain well. Mix together the spinach, ricotta and salt and pepper to taste. Fill the cannelloni tubes with the spinach mixture and arrange them in a greased shallow ovenproof dish. Pour the tomato sauce over the cannelloni; sprinkle with the Parmesan cheese. Bake for 20-30 minutes at 350°F or until the top is brownd and bubbling. Serve at once.

Ginger Cauliflower

This is a very simple and extremely subtle vegetable dish spiced with ginger.

PREPARATION TIME: 15 minutes

COOKING TIME: 15 minutes

SERVES: 4 people

4 tblsp oil
1 medium onion, peeled and chopped
1 inch fresh root ginger, peeled and sliced
1-2 green chilies, cut in half lengthwise
1 medium cauliflower, cut into 1 inch flowerets, along with tender leaves and stalk
Salt to taste
2-3 sprigs fresh green coriander leaves, chopped
Juice of 1 lemon

Heat the oil in a wok or solid based saucepan; fry the onion, ginger and chilies for 2-3 minutes. Add the cauliflower and salt to taste. Stir to mix well. Cover and cook over a low heat for 5-6 minutes. Add the coriander leaves and cook for a further 2-3 minutes, or until the flowerets of cauliflower are tender. Sprinkle with lemon juice, mix well and serve immediately. Serve with pitta bread.

Noodles with Vegetables (top left), Green Beans with Coconut (center right) and Garlic Hash Brown (bottom).

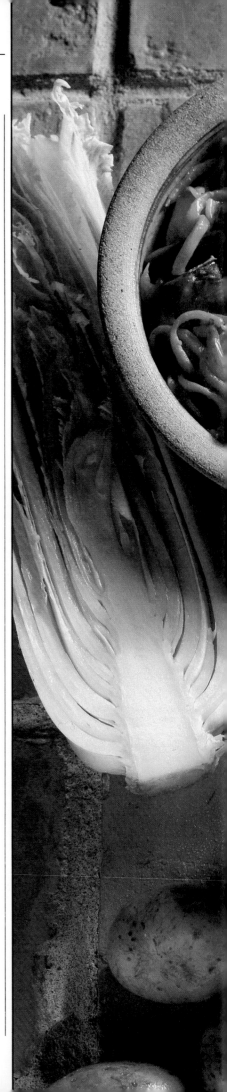

Mung Fritters

These tiny marble-sized fritters are made with mung pulse. They can be eaten as a cocktail snack or made into a curry with a well-flavored sauce.

PREPARATION TIME: 1 hour 30 minutes

COOKING TIME: 30 minutes

SERVES: 4 people

2 cups split mung pulse
1 small onion, peeled and chopped
1 tsp chili powder
1½ tsp garam masala powder (hot aromatic powder)
½ tsp cumin seed
4-5 sprigs fresh green coriander leaves, chopped
½ tsp salt
Oil for deep frying

Wash and soak the mung pulse for 1 hour in sufficient cold water to cover. Drain and then grind into a thick, coarse paste, adding ½-1 cup water as you go. It should be the consistency of peanut butter. Mix the mung paste with the onion, chili powder, garam masala, cumin seed, coriander leaves and salt. Mix well and adjust seasoning if necessary. Heat the oil for deep frying. Using a teaspoon, shape the paste into small "marbles" and fry in the hot oil until golden brown. Drain on kitchen paper and serve piping hot with chutney, a chili sauce or a dip. To turn into a curry, add the Mung Fritters to the following curry sauce.

Sauce
2 tsp oil
1 small onion, finely chopped
½ tsp chili powder
1 tsp ground coriander
1 tsp ground cumin
4-6 canned tomatoes, chopped
Salt to taste
3-4 sprigs fresh green coriander leaves, chopped

Heat the oil in a saucepan and fry the onion for 3 minutes. Stir in all the above ingredients; cover and simmer for 5-8 minutes. Add a little water to make a thickish sauce. Add ready-fried Mung Fritters and simmer for 3-5 minutes.

Noodles with Vegetables

This exotic noodle dish can be served hot or cold, as a main course, as a side dish or as a snack.

PREPARATION TIME: 20 minutes

COOKING TIME: 30 minutes

SERVES: 4 people

Salt to taste
1lb egg noodles, or broken spaghetti
3¾ tblsp oil
1 inch fresh root ginger, peeled and thinly sliced
1 large or 2 medium onions, peeled and sliced
⅔ cup green beans, sliced
⅔ cup carrots, peeled and cut into matchstick strips
1 cup white cabbage, or Chinese leaves, shredded
½ cup shelled peas
⅔ cup sprouting mung beans
1 green pepper, seeded and cut into 1 inch pieces
1-2 stalks celery, chopped
1-2 green chilies, split lengthways
¾ tsp monosodium glutamate (optional)
2½ tblsp soya sauce
1¼ tblsp lemon juice
1¼-2½ tsp Chinese red pepper sauce
5 tblsp chicken stock

Bring a large pan of water to the boil and add 1¼ tsp salt. Add the noodles or spaghetti and boil gently for 5-6 minutes. Drain the noodles. Rinse the noodles in cold water and drain once again. Heat the oil in a wok or large frying pan. Fry the ginger for 1-2 minutes. Add the onions and fry for 2-3 minutes. Add the beans and carrots and fry for 2 minutes. Add the remaining vegetables and the chilies and stir fry for 3-4 minutes. Add salt to taste and the noodles. Stir lightly with two forks. Dissolve the monosodium glutamate in the soya sauce and sprinkle over the noodle mixture; stir in the lemon juice, Chinese sauce and stock. Heat through for 2-3 minutes. Serve hot.

This page: Mung Fritters.

Facing page: Ginger Cauliflower (top left), Mixed Vegetable Raita (top right) and Cannelloni with Spinach and Ricotta (bottom).

Sauces, Dips and Chutney

Plum Chutney

Any variety of plum can be used; either singly or in a mixture of one or more varieties.

PREPARATION TIME: 10 minutes

COOKING TIME: 40 minutes

MAKES: about 6lbs

4½lb plums, pitted
1 inch fresh root ginger, peeled and finely chopped
2 tsp salt
3lb brown sugar
1 tsp cumin seed
1 tsp coriander seed
4 dried red chilies
1 tsp onion seed
2½ tblsp cider vinegar
½ cup chopped blanched almonds
½ cup chopped cashew nuts or hazelnuts
1 cup raisins
1 cup white raisins

Put the plums, ginger, salt and sugar into a saucepan, preferably a non-stick pan. Cover and cook gently until the plums are soft (about 15-20 minutes). Dry roast the cumin seed, coriander seed and red chilies in a frying pan for 1-2 minutes. Remove the red chilies and coarsely grind the cumin and coriander seeds. Add the roasted red chilies, ground spices and onion seed to the cooked plums. Add the cider vinegar, nuts, raisins and white raisins and simmer gently for 5-6 minutes. Allow to cool slightly. Pour into clean, warm glass jars and seal.

Guacamole
(AVOCADO DIP)

This is a popular Mexican dip, usually eaten with crisps, salty biscuits or sticks of raw vegetable, such as cucumber, celery etc.

PREPARATION TIME: 5 minutes

SERVES: 6-8 people

1 avocado, peeled, stoned and mashed
1 large clove garlic, peeled and crushed
1 tsp salt
¼ tsp freshly ground black pepper
1 large tomato, skinned and chopped
1 tsp olive oil
1 tblsp lemon juice
2-3 sprigs fresh green coriander leaves, finely chopped
1 small onion, peeled and grated

Blend the avocado pulp in the liquidizer with the salt, pepper, tomato, olive oil, lemon juice and coriander leaves. Put into a small bowl and mix with the onion. Serve with savory biscuits, crisps or sticks of raw vegetables.

Tamarind Dip

PREPARATION TIME: 20 minutes

MAKES: about 1½ cups

¾ cup tamarind pods
1 cup boiling water
½ tsp salt
7 tblsp brown sugar
1 green chili, chopped
¼ tsp chili powder

Soak the tamarind pods in boiling water for 5-6 minutes, or until soft. Rub the pods in the water to separate the dried pulp around the seeds. Squeeze out the seeds and skins of the pods. (Do not discard as a second extract can be obtained for future use). Add the salt and sugar to the tamarind pulp. Mix in the chili and chili powder and leave to stand for 5 minutes before using. Salt and sugar can be adjusted according to personal taste.

Savory Coconut Chutney

PREPARATION TIME: 15 minutes

MAKES: about 1¾ cups

1-2 fresh coconuts, shell removed, outer skin peeled and cut into pieces
½ inch fresh root ginger, peeled and chopped
2 green chilies, chopped
1 tsp cumin seed
1-2 bunches fresh green coriander leaves, chopped
4 tblsp thick tamarind pulp or
5 tblsp lemon juice
1 tsp sugar
½ tsp salt

Put all the ingredients into the liquidizer and blend until smooth and creamy. If the mixture is too thick, add a little water. Serve with hot snacks, such as toasted chicken sandwiches.

Mixed Fruit Chutney

This sweet-sour chutney goes particularly well with pork dishes such as spareribs.

PREPARATION TIME: 30 minutes

COOKING TIME: 40 minutes

MAKES: about 5¼lb

3 firm pears, cored and sliced
4 apples, cored and chopped
4 peaches, skinned, stoned and sliced or
15oz can peach slices, drained
1lb plums, halved and stoned
6 rings canned pineapple, cut into cubes
1 cup dates, stoned and chopped
2 cups dried prunes, soaked overnight
1 cup dried apricots, soaked overnight
2¼lb brown sugar
2 tsp salt
1 inch fresh root ginger, peeled and thinly sliced
1 cup chopped blanched almonds
1 cup cashew nuts, chopped
5 tblsp cider vinegar
8 cloves, coarsely ground
1 tsp chili powder
2 inch piece cinnamon stick
2 bananas, peeled and sliced

Put all the fruit into a saucepan (apart from the bananas) with the sugar, salt and ginger. Cover and cook for 15-20 minutes. Add the nuts, vinegar, cloves, chili powder and cinnamon stick. Stir well and cook for 6-8 minutes. Simmer gently, stirring occasionally, until most of the liquid has evaporated. The chutney should be thick and sticky. Add the sliced bananas and stir over the heat for 1 minute. Cool slightly. Pour into clean, warm glass jars and seal.

Green Tomato Relish

Use the last crop of tomatoes to make this relish. Serve with any grilled meat, barbecued chicken, etc.

PREPARATION TIME: 4 hours

COOKING TIME: about 20 minutes

MAKES: about 3lb

2lb green tomatoes, seeded and chopped
1½ cups shredded white cabbage
2 red peppers, seeded and chopped
1 onion, peeled and chopped
1¼ tblsp salt
1 cup brown sugar
1¼ cups distilled white vinegar
2 tsp mustard seed
2 tsp celery seed
1½ tblsp prepared horseradish sauce

Mix the tomatoes, cabbage, peppers and onion together. Sprinkle with the salt and mix well. Leave to stand for 2-3 hours. Drain well and then rinse under cold running water. Drain and gently squeeze out the excess moisture. Mix the sugar, vinegar, mustard seed, celery seed and horseradish sauce together in a large solid based pan. Bring to the boil over a medium heat. Add the vegetables, cover and simmer gently for another 16-18 minutes until the relish is sticky. Remove from the heat and cool slightly. Pour into clean, warm glass jars and seal. Will keep for up to 2 months.

Facing page: Plum Chutney (top right), Mixed Fruit Chutney (center) and Green Tomato Relish (bottom).

**Tamarind Dip (far left),
Savory Coconut Chutney
(center) and Guacamole
(Avocado Dip) (above).**

little olive oil or chicken stock.

Chili Sauce

This classic piquant sauce is perfect for those who love hot, spicy food.

PREPARATION TIME: 20 minutes

COOKING TIME: 2 hours
30 minutes

MAKES: about 600ml (1 pint)

*8 large ripe tomatoes, skinned and
    chopped
2-3 small green peppers, seeded and
    chopped
2 medium onions, peeled and finely
    chopped
4 stalks celery, chopped
3 tsp salt
1 cup + 2 tblsp granulated sugar
1½ cups cider vinegar
2-3 bay leaves
1 tsp coriander seeds
1 tsp freshly ground black pepper
¼ tsp ground cloves
½ tsp ground cinnamon
1 tsp ground ginger
1 tsp mustard seed*

Mix all the ingredients together in a pan and bring to the boil. Cover and simmer for about 2 hours over a low heat, until thick. Stir once to mix and simmer again for 10 minutes. Remove from the heat and cool slightly. Pour into clean, warm glass jars and seal.

Mexican Salsa

This is a beautiful fresh sauce which goes well with barbecued meats, curries and, of course, burritos and tacos.

PREPARATION TIME: 10 minutes

MAKES: about ⅔ cup

*5 tomatoes, skinned and chopped
1 small onion, chopped
1-2 pickled or canned Mexican
    chilies, chopped
2 cloves garlic, peeled and crushed
2 tsp cider vinegar
½ tsp salt
½ tsp sugar
2-3 sprigs fresh green coriander,
    chopped
1 tsp bottled chili sauce*

Mix all the ingredients together in a bowl. Chill for 2 to 3 hours before serving.

Salsa Verde

A perfect Italian sauce to serve with any pasta, or with veal.

PREPARATION TIME: 15 minutes

MAKES: about 1 cup

*6 tblsp chopped fresh parsley
2½ tblsp white wine vinegar
3 cloves garlic, peeled and sliced
2 tblsp capers, finely chopped
2 tblsp olive oil
2-3 scallions, chopped
Salt and freshly ground black pepper
    to taste*

Blend the parsley, garlic and vinegar in the liquidizer. Pour the parsley sauce into a small bowl and mix with the capers, olive oil, scallions and salt and pepper. Mix well. Cover and chill for 10-15 minutes. The sauce can be thinned to the desired consistency with a

This page: Chili Sauce (top left), Salsa Verdi (center) and Mexican Salsa (bottom).

Facing page: Rice Pudding (top), Potato Pudding (center) and Cabbage Pudding (bottom).

Sweets

Carrotella

PREPARATION TIME: 15 minutes

COOKING TIME: 35-40 minutes

SERVES: 4-6 people

2½ pints milk
1lb carrots, peeled and shredded
1 cup canned evaporated milk
½ cup granulated sugar
½ cup raisins
Seeds of 8 small cardamoms, crushed
2 drops rose-water or vanilla essence
½ cup chopped blanched almonds
½ cup pistachio nuts, chopped

Put the milk into a pan and simmer over a low heat until reduced to 2 pints. Add the carrots; cover and cook over a medium heat for 15 minutes. Add the evaporated milk, sugar and raisins. Cover and simmer gently for another 5 minutes. Remove from the heat. Stir in the crushed cardamom seeds and essence and pour into a serving dish. Allow to cool slightly. Sprinkle nuts on the top and serve. On hot summer days, the Carrotella is best chilled.

Carrot Cake

PREPARATION TIME: 30 minutes

COOKING TIME: 45-50 minutes

MAKES: 10 inch loaf

¾ cup butter
¾ cup brown sugar
½ cup granulated sugar
2 eggs, well beaten
2 cups flour
1½ tsp bicarbonate of soda
½ tsp baking powder
¼ tsp ground cinnamon
½ tsp salt
2 cups peeled carrots, shredded
¾ cup raisins
½ cup chopped walnuts
¼ tsp small cardamom seeds, crushed
Confectioner's sugar for dredging

Cream the butter and sugars together. Add the eggs, a little at a time, beating well after each addition. Sieve the flour, bicarbonate of soda, baking powder, cinnamon and salt

together. Fold the dry ingredients into the egg mixture. Add the carrots, raisins, nuts and crushed cardamom. Mix well and pour the mixture into a well buttered 10 inch loaf tin. Bake at 350°F for 45-50 minutes, or until a fine metal skewer comes out clean when inserted into the centre of the cake. Cool in the tin for 10-15 minutes, before turning out. Dredge with Confectioner's sugar before serving.

Rice Pudding

There are many ways of making a rice pudding, but this is definitely one of the best. It is suitable for serving on any occasion, from everyday meals to smart dinner parties.

PREPARATION TIME: 10 minutes

COOKING TIME: 1 hour 30 minutes

SERVES: 6 people

¼ cup unsalted butter
1 bayleaf, crumbled
1 inch piece cinnamon stick, crushed
1½ cups pudding rice, washed and drained
2½ pints milk
1½ cups canned evaporated milk
¾ cup granulated sugar
½ cup raisins
½ cup chopped blanched almonds
½ cup pistachio nuts, chopped or cut into slivers
Seeds of 8 small cardamoms, crushed

Melt the butter in a saucepan and fry the bayleaf and cinnamon for 1 minute. Add the rice and stir well. Add the milk and bring to the boil. Reduce the heat and simmer for 40-50 minutes, stirring occasionally to prevent the rice from sticking to the pan. Add the sugar and evaporated milk, and simmer for a further 20-30 minutes, stirring frequently. Thin layers of light brown skin form on the base of the pan, this is what gives the pudding its rich reddish tinge and flavor. Add the raisins and half the chopped almonds. Mix well and simmer for a further 5-10 minutes,

or until the pudding is really thick. Mix in the crushed cardamom seeds and pour into a serving dish. Decorate with the remaining chopped almonds and pistachio nuts. Serve hot or cold.

Carrot Halva

A delightful sweet from the mysterious East. Serve it hot or cold, with or without cream.

PREPARATION TIME: 20 minutes

COOKING TIME: 50 minutes

SERVES: 8-10 people

4lb large sweet carrots, peeled and shredded
2 pints canned evaporated milk
3 cups granulated sugar
¾ cup unsalted butter
¾ cup raisins
Seeds of 10 small cardamoms, crushed
1 cup chopped mixed nuts (blanched and chopped almonds, cashews, pistachios etc.)
Light cream

Put the carrots, evaporated milk and sugar into a large, solid based pan and bring to the boil. Reduce the heat and cook the carrots gently for 30-40 minutes, or until the milk has evaporated. Add the butter and raisins and stir over a gentle heat for 8-10 minutes, until the Halva is dark and leaves the sides of the pan clean. Add the cardamom seeds and mix well. Pour into a flat shallow dish about 1 inch deep. Flatten the Halva evenly with a spatula. Sprinkle with the chopped nuts. Serve hot or cold, cut into squares, with light cream.

Potato Pudding

This old-fashioned Oriental pudding has a rich and lovely flavor. It keeps for weeks and can be frozen.

PREPARATION TIME: 15 minutes

COOKING TIME: 1 hour 15 minutes

SERVES: 6 people

2lb potatoes, peeled and shredded
1 cup unsalted butter
1½ pints canned evaporated milk
1½ cups granulated sugar
1 cup ground almonds
¼ tsp saffron
½ cup chopped almonds and pistachios

Wash the potatoes thoroughly and drain them well. Squeeze the potatoes to remove all excess moisture. Put the potatoes, butter and evaporated milk into a large solid based saucepan and cook slowly until mushy. The potatoes will disintegrate into a mashed state as they cook. Add the sugar and stir to dissolve. The mixture will bubble and splatter like bubbling mud from hot springs. Wrap a damp tea towel around your hand and stir the mixture for 20-30 minutes over a gentle heat. Add the ground almonds and saffron. Continue stirring over the heat until the pudding becomes thick, sticky and oily on the surface. Pour the pudding into a shallow dish and decorate with the chopped nuts.

Cabbage Pudding

PREPARATION TIME: 10 minutes

COOKING TIME: 40 minutes

SERVES: 4-6 people

1½ cups finely shredded white cabbage
2 tblsp pudding rice
2½ pints milk
1 cup canned evaporated milk
1 inch piece cinnamon stick
1 bayleaf
½-¾ cups granulated sugar
½ cup raisins

Facing page: Carrot Cake (top), Carrot Halva (center) and Carrotella (bottom).

½ cup chopped blanched almonds
½ cup pistachio nuts, chopped
Seeds of 6 small cardamoms, crushed

Put the cabbage, rice, both milks, cinnamon and bayleaf into a pan. Bring to the boil and simmer gently for 15-20 minutes, stirring occasionally to prevent the mixture from sticking to the pan. Add the sugar and simmer gently until the mixture is thick. Add the raisins and nuts. Remove from the heat when the rice is tender and the milk has been reduced to approx. 1¼ pints. Pour into a serving dish and sprinkle with the crushed cardamom seeds. Mix well and serve.

Frozen Lemon Yogurt Souffle

PREPARATION TIME: 20 minutes

SERVES: 4-6 people

2 pints natural yogurt
1 cup superfine sugar
Juice and finely grated rind of 2 lemons
1 tsp vanilla essence
2 egg whites
¼ tsp salt
¼ tsp cream of tartar
½ cup heavy cream, whipped
Few thin lemon slices for decoration

Mix the yogurt, sugar, lemon juice, lemon rind and vanilla essence together. Whisk the egg whites, salt and cream of tartar until stiff but not dry. Fold the egg whites gently into the yogurt mixture, and then fold in the whipped cream. Pour the mixture into a souffle dish and freeze overnight. Garnish with lemon slices before serving. Serve either frozen or partially thawed.

Mango Fool

This delicious sweet can be made with fresh or canned mangoes; crushed cardamom seeds give it a characteristic flavor.

PREPARATION TIME: 10 minutes

SERVES: 4-6 people

1lb canned mango slices or the

equivalent amount of fresh mango, stoned and peeled
1 cup canned evaporated milk
Seeds of 6 cardamoms, crushed
Sugar to taste
Whipped cream

Put the mango, evaporated milk and cardamoms into a liquidizer and blend until smooth. Add a little sugar if necessary. Pour into a serving bowl and chill for 20 minutes before serving. Serve with whipped cream.

Tropical Fruit Dessert

An exotic sweet dish to finish any special meal. A delightful dessert from nature's fruit garden.

PREPARATION TIME: 30 minutes

SERVES: 8-10 people

4 bananas, cut into ¼ inch thick slices
5 rings pineapple, cut into chunks (fresh or canned)
2 semi-ripe pears, peeled, cored and cut into chunks
2 medium red-skinned apples, cored and cut into chunks
8 peach slices, chopped
2 cups red cherries, pitted
4 tblsp grated fresh coconut
1 honeydew melon, peeled and cut into chunks
1lb marshmallows
6-8 slices mango, cut into chunks (fresh or canned)
2 kiwi fruit, peeled and cut into chunks
20-25 strawberries, halved
Few seedless white and black grapes, halved
1½ tblsp icing sugar
1 cup cottage cheese
Few drops vanilla essence

Mix all the ingredients together in a large bowl. Cover and chill for 1 hour.

Tropical Fruit Salad

This medley of fruits is very colorful and it offers a variety of tastes and textures.

PREPARATION TIME: 40 minutes

2 bananas, sliced
4 kiwi fruit, peeled and sliced
10 dates, stoned and sliced in half

2 guavas, halved and then sliced into wedges
1 pawpaw, cut into thin crescent shapes
1lb canned lychees, drained
8oz canned pineapple chunks, drained (or pieces of fresh pineapple)
2 fresh mangoes, peeled and sliced
Few seedless grapes, white and black, halved
1 small melon, cut into chunks
¼ water-melon, cut into chunks
4 fresh figs, halved

Dressing
2 tblsp lemon juice
Pinch salt
½ cup chopped toasted walnut or pine kernels

Prepare the fruits as suggested and arrange in a large glass bowl, in layers. Spoon over the lemon juice and sprinkle with salt. Sprinkle over the chopped nuts.

Semolina and Coconut Slices

PREPARATION TIME: 10 minutes

COOKING TIME: 30 minutes

SERVES: 6 people

¾ cup unsalted butter
1½ cups coarse semolina
2 cups shredded coconut
1½ cups granulated sugar
1 cup canned evaporated milk
1 cup water
1 cup chopped mixed nuts: blanched almonds, cashews, walnuts, hazelnuts and pistachios
¾ cup raisins
Seeds of 6 cardamoms, crushed

Melt the butter in a frying pan and add the semolina. Dry roast the semolina by stirring it until it turns lightly golden. Spoon onto a plate. Dry roast the coconut in the same pan until lightly golden. Add the

Tropical Fruit Dessert (top right), Frozen Lemon Yogurt Souffle (top left) and Tropical Fruit Salad (bottom).

semolina, sugar, milk and water to the coconut. Stir the mixture over the heat for 5-8 minutes. Add the chopped nuts, raisins and crushed cardamom seeds. Mix well and stir over a gentle heat for 5-6 minutes, until the mixture is thick and the oil begins to separate. Pour into a shallow dish, smooth with a spatula and allow to cool. Cut into diamond shapes or squares.

Mint Barley Sherbet

PREPARATION TIME: 10 minutes

COOKING TIME: 20 minutes

SERVES: 4-6 people

1 cup whole barley
2 pints water
¼ cup mint leaves, minced
Pinch salt

6 tblsp granulated sugar
Juice of 3 lemons
1-2 drops green food coloring
Grated rind of 1 lemon
Few mint leaves and lemon slices to decorate

Wash the barley in 2-3 changes of water. Soak the barley in the measured water for a few minutes; add the minced mint leaves and

This page: Yogurt, Almond and Saffron Sherbet (top center), Mango Sherbet (left), Maori Shake (center) and Tropical Blizzard (right).

Facing page: Mint Barley Sherbet (top left), Spiced Tea (top right) and Rich Coffee (bottom).

bring to the boil. Simmer gently for 10-15 minutes. Remove from the heat and strain; discard the barley grains. Dissolve the salt and sugar in the barley liquid; add the lemon juice, colouring and lemon rind. Mix well and make up to 2 pints with water. Pour into glasses and add crushed ice. To make clear sherbet; allow the barley water to stand for 10 minutes, so that the starch settles. Pour off the clear liquid and serve with a twist of lemon and mint leaves floating on the top.

Yogurt Dessert

This yogurt dessert is a light, delicious way of ending a rich meal; it is also simple and easy to make.

PREPARATION TIME: 15 minutes, plus setting time

COOKING TIME: 15 minutes

SERVES: 4-6 people

3 quarts milk
8-10 tblsp granulated sugar or to taste
½ cup finely chopped blanched almonds
½ cup raisins
Seeds of 8 small cardamoms, crushed
2-3 drops rose water or vanilla essence
2½ tblsp natural yogurt
¼ cup pistachio nuts, chopped

Simmer the milk in a large pan until it is reduced by half. Add the sugar to the milk and stir until dissolved. Add half the almonds, the raisins and cardamom seeds. Allow to cool until the milk is just tepid. Add the essence and beaten yogurt to the milk and stir well. Pour into a large, shallow serving dish. Cover and leave in a warm place, such as an airing cupboard, until the yogurt has set (about 5-6 hours). Sprinkle with the chopped pistachio nuts and remaining chopped almonds. Chill for 1 hour before serving. Will keep for up to 15 days in the refrigerator.

Tropical Blizzard

PREPARATION TIME: 3-4 minutes

SERVES: 4 people

1 cup pineapple juice or orange juice
1¼ cups natural yogurt
6 slices mango (canned or fresh)
1 tblsp sugar
Soda water
Ice cubes

Put the fruit juice, yogurt, mango and sugar into the liquidizer; blend for ½ minute. Pour into 4 glasses and dilute with soda water. Serve with ice cubes.

Maori Shake

A new taste experience; kiwi fruit blended with lemon yogurt.

PREPARATION TIME: 5 minutes

SERVES: 4-6 people

1 cup pineapple juice
2 kiwi fruits, peeled and chopped
1¼ cups lemon yogurt
Ice cubes
Lemonade
1 kiwi fruit, peeled and thinly sliced for decoration

Put the pineapple juice, chopped kiwi fruit and lemon yogurt into the liquidizer; blend for 30 seconds-1 minute, until smooth. Pour into 4-6 tall glasses; add ice cubes and top up with lemonade. Stir to mix. Serve with slices of kiwi fruit on top.

Mango Sherbet

This is a pretty green mango sherbet made from unripe mangoes. Windfallen mangoes are usually used for making this refreshing drink in India.

PREPARATION TIME: 20 minutes

COOKING TIME: 5-6 minutes

SERVES: 6 people

2 medium size unripe mangoes
⅓ tsp salt
2¼ pints water
Sugar to taste
Crushed ice

Boil the mangoes in sufficient water to cover for 5-6 minutes. Remove and allow to cool under cold running water. Peel off the skins. Put the water and salt into a punch bowl. Scrape all the mango flesh away from the stones and add to the punch bowl. Discard the stones. Whisk the sherbet until well blended. Pour into tall glasses; add sugar to taste and crushed ice.

Yogurt, Almond and Saffron Sherbet

A good healthy drink, which can be given a sweet or salty flavor.

PREPARATION TIME: 5 minutes

SERVES: 5-6 people

2¼ pints water
1 pint natural yogurt
2 tsp lemon juice
12 blanched almonds
¼ tsp saffron
2 drops vanilla essence or rose water
Salt or sugar to taste